iSeries & AS/400 VisualAge for Java

```
gettfAnnualInterestRate().setText("0");
gettfNumberOfPayments().setText("360");
gettfLoanAmount().setText("100");
gettfMonthlyPayment().setText("");
return;
```

A Step-by-Step Guide to Building Java Graphical Business Applications

JERRY ROPELATO

A Division of
Penton Technology Media

221 E. 29th Street • Loveland, CO 80538 USA
(800) 650-1804 • (970) 663-4700 • www.29thStreetPress.com

Library of Congress Cataloging-in-Publication Data on file.

29th Street Press® is a division of
Penton Technology Media
Loveland, Colorado USA

© 2002 by Jerry Ropelato

This book was printed and bound in Canada.

ISBN 1-58304-090-0

2004 2003 2002 WL 10 9 8 7 6 5 4 3 2 1

This book is dedicated to my family,
my pride and joy,
for encouraging me to complete the book.

I appreciate your patience for all the times I said
"Just a minute, I need to finish this thought."

Thanks to my wife Darinda;
to my children David, Jeff, Marc, and Stacey;
and to my new family members
Natalie and Nate.

Acknowledgments

Special thanks need to be given to those who helped create this book.

John Dietz, a good friend and colleague, for sharing his feedback in the initial stages of the book

Sharon Hoffman, senior technical editor for *iSeries NEWS* magazine, for her technical review of the manuscript

Katie Tipton, 29th Street Press, for her great work and sharp eyes in editing the book

Martha Nichols, 29th Street Press, for putting that special crisp look on the final version of the book

Matt Wiebe, 29th Street Press, for creating the book cover

Wayne Madden, Penton Technology Media, for inspiring me with the idea for the book

Table of Contents at a Glance

Table of Contents

Unit 1: Getting Started with VisualAge for Java

Unit 2: Accessing AS/400 Objects from Java

Chapter 8 Executing AS/400 Commands from Java 137

Chapter 9 Accessing AS/400 Object Lists from Java 155

Unit 3: Working with AS/400 Databases from Java

Unit 4: Building AS/400 Graphical Applications

Unit 5: ET/400, Work, and Execution Environments

Unit 6: Appendixes

Introduction

Over the years, I've had the fortunate opportunity to be involved with many software development projects on several different platforms and languages. Even with all the new Internet development occurring, I'm proud to say my favorite platform has always been the IBM midrange. I started out on the System/38 and moved to the AS/400, which is now known as the iSeries. (You'll notice I still use the "AS/400" moniker throughout this book.) Very little time in my career has been spent in a maintenance mode. Most of it has been spent cranking out large amounts of new code.

As I moved into the Java programming environment, I found myself coding very slowly and being very unproductive, even though I had coded in other PC-based programming languages. Coming from an AS/400 background, I had lots of questions about where to start and what to focus on. I remember feeling very frustrated. I'd always felt confident about my ability to quickly build applications. As I began to work in the VisualAge for Java development environment, I found myself being able to accomplish coding tasks much more quickly and cleanly.

One of my other frustrations as I began working in Java was the lack of resource materials available to help an AS/400 developer learn VisualAge for Java and the connectivity to the AS/400. I believe I read every book, article, Redbook, white paper, and piece of Internet research I could get my hands on. I spent a lot of time in trial and error learning.

A year and a half ago, I was teaching a VisualAge for Java course to a group of AS/400 developers. One student asked, "Where can I get more detailed information to help me learn VisualAge for Java and the AS/400?" My response was short, explaining the small handful of options that were available to her. She responded, "If there's not much out there, why don't you write a book?" I took the suggestion, and here is the book.

Most of the AS/400 community grew up through the "green-screen" era, so design and development for building graphical business applications has been foreign to us. VisualAge for Java isn't an easy development environment to learn. Most of the materials available for learning it aren't written with the AS/400 developer in mind. My goal was to write a how-to guide to help AS/400 developers take the first step into an exciting AS/400 graphical development environment. I truly believe that AS/400 RPG and Cobol are going to be around for a long time, but I also believe it's time for all AS/400 developers to start adding to their arsenal of development tools. VisualAge for Java is a great place to begin.

Throughout this book, I have purposefully chosen to relate back to AS/400 concepts and terminology with which you may already be familiar. My goal is to help you learn how to use VisualAge for Java in harmony with the AS/400. Many of the chapters are titled with Java-equivalent AS/400 topics instead of true Java topics. I'm sure many Java purists would disagree with my approach in the book. My rebuttal is that I have the advantage of understanding the mindset of AS/400 developers and where they are coming from.

I hope you have as much fun reading the book and working through the chapter projects as I've had in writing the book. This is really fun stuff!

Conventions Used in This Book

Much of this book is composed of step-by-step instructions for completing the project identified in each chapter. Several conventions are used to make these instructions as clear as possible:

➢	This symbol is used to identify the actual steps you should perform.
Bold	Bold type is used to identify field names, components, classes, screen elements, and options.
<u>Bold and underlined</u>	Bold and underlining is used to identify something you need to type. The book uses the terms "type" and "enter" interchangeably.

Tips and Tricks

Tips and Tricks are used to point out very important topics. Make sure you don't skip over these.

Source code:
Changes or additions to be made to source code are identified in boxes similar to this one. You'll sometimes see both a "Before" and "After" image of the code. When creating new code for the first time, you may not see a Before image box.

The book contains many screen captures to help you visualize the projects as you proceed through the chapters. If you're working through the chapter projects, which I strongly recommend you do, you'll be using your mouse quite a bit. Some further definitions related to your mouse are as follows:

Click	Perform a single left-click on the mouse.
Double-click	Perform a double left-click on the mouse.
Right-click	Perform a single right-click on the mouse.
Select	Sometimes used interchangeably with a click command, "select" can also mean to point with the mouse and wait for a submenu to appear.

As the book proceeds, you'll see that less text is written about detailed steps and explanations that I assume you learned in the early chapters. Later chapters build on earlier chapters! There's no doubt in my mind that some AS/400 developers will jump right to the chapters discussing the AS/400. Keep in mind, however, that there's an immense amount of information covered in the first few chapters that you'll need as a foundation to be able to complete the projects in the AS/400-focused chapters.

Terms Used in This Book

As you may or may not be aware, the Java language includes some terms that, at times, may be used interchangeably. For example, you may see terms such as "Java classes" and "JavaBeans" used in different, but similar, contexts. You may see the terms "applet," "application," "servlet," and "program" used to describe the development of a particular Java program.

In addition, for purposes of this book, the terms "AS/400" and "iSeries" refer to the same computer system. I primarily use "AS/400" because, as of this writing, the actual toolkit name is still Enterprise Toolkit for AS/400. You may also notice "AS400" (no slash) used in some of the descriptions. That is part of the toolkit and Java naming conventions.

Who Should Read This Book?

This book is targeted at AS/400 professionals who have had an introduction to Java. The text walks you through each of the chapter projects, so it's possible to do the projects with no understanding of Java. However, if you've had no exposure at all to Java, it's a good idea to gain a beginning familiarity with Java and Java terminology. A general understanding of graphical user interfaces will also be very helpful to you.

This book can also help the Java expert who is trying to understand AS/400 topics and how they relate to VisualAge for Java. Anyone trying to learn the basics of VisualAge for Java and how it relates to the AS/400 will find this book a great help.

Unit 1

Getting Started

with

VisualAge

for Java

Chapter 1

What Is VisualAge for Java?

 **Chapter Objectives**

- ❏ Gain an overview of VisualAge for Java
- ❏ Learn what it's like to work in VisualAge for Java
- ❏ Learn about the various parts of the integrated development environment

IBM's VisualAge for Java is a full integrated development environment (IDE) for building Java applications. VisualAge for Java generates 100 percent pure Java–compatible applications, applets, and JavaBeans. In addition to being a powerful code generator for Java, VisualAge for Java incorporates all necessary software development functions: design, coding, integration, testing, debugging, documentation, and distribution. The tight integration of these functions lets you, the developer, create top-of-the-line Java software in a controlled team development environment.

The underlying architecture of VisualAge for Java uses a code repository system to manage the various objects. The repository is where the depositing and retrieving of Java objects occur, in contrast to most file-based systems. From an AS/400 perspective, this means no files are used. Your source code is managed by a repository system that keeps track of the different versions and editions of the code.

VisualAge for Java is currently part of IBM's WebSphere Development Tools for iSeries offering. Over the past few years, IBM has received 37 different awards and positive third-party reviews for the capabilities, power, and productivity benefits of the product.

VisualAge for Java 4.0, the most current version as of the writing of this book, has seen numerous changes since the first version. From a client development perspective, Versions 3.5 and 4.0 are virtually identical. There are four editions of VisualAge for Java 3.5 and 4.0:

- Professional Edition — a full working copy of VisualAge for Java
- Enterprise Edition — a complete edition of VisualAge for Java, including various support toolkits, including the Enterprise Toolkit for AS/400
- Entry Professional Edition — a free copy of the Professional Edition, limited to 750 classes
- Entry Enterprise Edition — a free copy of the Enterprise Edition, limited to 750 classes

Anyone serious about developing Java systems that work with the AS/400 should strongly consider using the Enterprise Edition because it provides the full set of tools for productivity in this environment.

The Real World of VisualAge for Java

If you've done any programming in the AS/400 Integrated Language Environment (ILE), you're probably familiar with the process of developing programs in a source file–based environment. You write your code in source files, compile the source files, and then bind all the related dependencies together to create executable objects. As you build your systems, managing all the various programs, modules, procedures, and related dependencies can become quite cumbersome. VisualAge for Java performs the tasks of managing and compiling code for you. Browsers let you view and edit classes and methods individually. When saving, VisualAge for Java automatically generates and compiles the Java source code.

VisualAge for Java is a great tool for developing enterprise applications. It incorporates many development tools to speed up development. Java code generation is only a byproduct of the features available in VisualAge for Java. When your Java development project reaches the stage of moving from development into a production environment, you can take advantage of tools in VisualAge for Java that make this an easy task. Tracking and implementing changes and software version levels are functions also built into this rich IDE. In addition, you can import and export Java code using VisualAge for Java.

Does VisualAge for Java have any drawbacks? Yes, it does, but with a little planning, these can be overcome. One major drawback is that VisualAge for Java is a resource-intensive application. That fact will make sense once you understand how the product works. Unlike most applications you've probably dealt with in the past, VisualAge for Java requires a lot of memory and processor speed. When buying and installing this product, pay close attention to the hardware and software requirements. I've experienced much frustration when working with the minimum and even with the suggested requirements for hardware. Exceed these, and your life will be much happier and more productive — the investment is well worth the money. Keep in mind that your finished applications will typically run much faster in the production environment.

A second drawback that occurs from time to time is the locking up of VisualAge for Java. If this happens to you, just restart the program; most likely, you won't have lost anything. For those who don't have the latest release of the product, patches are available from IBM's Internet site (*http://www-3.ibm.com/software/ad/vajava*).

The third drawback for developers is VisualAge for Java's learning curve (which happens to be a great opportunity for trainers and book publishers). With all the development features involved with VisualAge for Java, becoming proficient at coding Java applications in this IDE can be a fairly time-consuming activity. Once you get past the learning curve, though, you'll find you can quickly develop professional, high-quality Java applications.

The VisualAge for Java Interface

The Java Development Kit (JDK) that is supplied free of charge from Sun Microsystems includes all the necessary tools to be able to write, compile, and execute Java code. But working with the JDK poses some problems:

- Managing development projects of any substantial size is cumbersome.
- The biggest surprise for first-time Java developers is working with the DOS command line.
- Setup problems are encountered frequently when attaching to access AS/400 objects.
- No syntax-checking text editor is provided.
- Working with applets requires extra steps in writing Hypertext Markup Language (HTML) code and using a browser or the AppletViewer.

Even though the JDK is free and widely available, it lacks many of the management controls needed to be able to accomplish rapid application development. VisualAge for Java is at the opposite extreme. It is a rich, Windows-based (2000, 98, or NT) development environment. It runs on your PC workstation and generates code that can be run on many different platforms. It has a wealth of import, export, and SmartGuide (wizard) functions, as well as many development tools to facilitate access to external systems and databases. Connectivity to the AS/400 and use of the Enterprise Toolkit for AS/400 (which provides tools for deploying Java programs on the AS/400) is almost transparent to the developer.

Integrated Development Environment

IBM designed the VisualAge for Java IDE to support a full team development effort. The product includes full version control based on a shared code repository. You can compare source code versions side by side on your screen to view changes from one version to the next. Developers can also work on different in-house release levels of your Java applications at once.

Once source code is modified, you save it, and VisualAge for Java automatically compiles the code. You never see any of the .java or .class files that you normally see during development using the JDK. VisualAge for Java manages the source code and its corresponding compiled bytecodes for you.

Source code is compiled incrementally in VisualAge for Java. Only the source code that has been changed and any dependencies are recompiled — an approach that significantly reduces overall compilation time.

Many tools make up the components of the VisualAge for Java IDE. A brief explanation of each follows.

Workbench

You use VisualAge for Java's workbench to view, using various browsers, all objects and their relationships with each other. The workbench also lets you navigate between windows and provides access to the various development tools. Figure 1.1 shows an example of the workbench. Tools such as the Scrapbook, Repository Explorer, Input and Output Console, Log, and Development options are all available from here. Editors provide Java syntax checking and speed-up keys.

Figure 1.1
VisualAge for Java Workbench

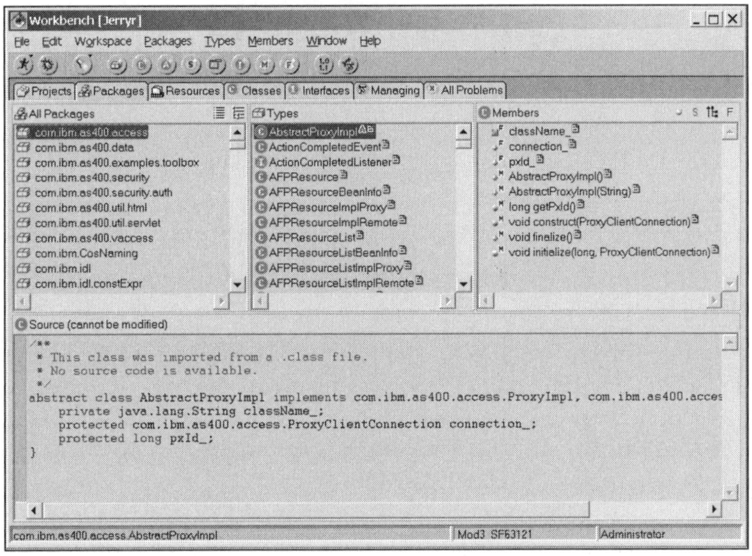

Visual Composition Editor

You use VisualAge for Java's Visual Composition Editor (VCE) to create graphical user interfaces (GUIs) from a collection of predefined JavaBeans, or visual components. Once all the visual development work is completed and saved, VisualAge for Java automatically generates all the associated Java source code as well as the compiled byte-codes. With the Enterprise Edition of VisualAge for Java, you have access to various categories of JavaBeans, including the AS/400 prebuilt JavaBeans.

Another main function of the VCE is to build connection relationships. You define these relationships to link visual and nonvisual (or logic) beans together. Figure 1.2 shows an example of the VCE.

Figure 1.2
Visual Composition Editor

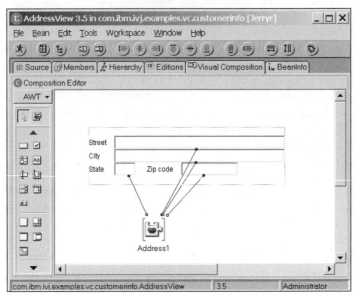

Java Server Pages Development Environment

VisualAge for Java's Java Server Pages environment enables you to develop, run, and test Java Server Pages (JSPs) and servlets. A Java Server Pages Execution Monitor is also included, as well as a test environment for WebSphere Application Server.

SmartGuides

VisualAge for Java provides numerous SmartGuides — commonly known as wizards — for step-by-step creation of projects, packages, classes, applets, applications, servlets, and many other tasks.

Enterprise Toolkits

Enterprise toolkits let you work in the VisualAge for Java IDE and then export your development work to other development environments, such as the AS/400 and OS/390 systems. With the AS/400 interface, there are SmartGuides to help you convert Data Description Specifications (DDS), build call interfaces to AS/400 applications, and compile Java code optimized for the AS/400. The AS/400 Toolbox for Java, which can be purchased with an AS/400, is part of the VisualAge for Java Enterprise Toolkit for AS/400.

Debugging

VisualAge for Java provides two types of debugging environments. The integrated debugger lets you debug applets and applications running inside the IDE. Once in debug mode, you can access a wealth of powerful features to

- trace the flow of execution
- inspect and change variables
- change source code and recompile without leaving program execution
- watch for certain conditions
- manage breakpoints
- evaluate expressions

The distributed debugger lets you detect and diagnose errors in your programs. You can debug programs that were developed inside or outside the IDE and programs that execute on different platforms, such as the AS/400 and AIX, NT, OS/390, and Solaris systems.

Integration Toolkits

Numerous toolkits provide integration between VisualAge for Java and other environments, such as the C++Access Builder, Enterprise JavaBean Development, Persistence Builder for relational database mapping, Rational Rose Modeling, WebSphere, and Extensible Markup Language (XML) Generator and Parser.

Enterprise Access Builders

VisualAge for Java also includes access to various databases that support Open Database Connectivity (ODBC) and Java Database Connectivity (JDBC) drivers. In addition, access builders to Customer Information Control System (CICS), C++ servers, Domino, Interface Definition Language (IDL), MQSeries, Remote Method Invocation (RMI), and SAP R/3 business objects are provided.

Summary

In this chapter, you

- gained a general overview of VisualAge for Java
- were introduced to the various components of the IDE
- learned about working with VisualAge for Java in real-world scenarios
- compared the working environment of VisualAge for Java with the standard JDK

Now, let's leave behind the hype of what VisualAge for Java can do and go on a visual tour of the product.

Chapter 2

A Visual Tour of VisualAge for Java

 ## Chapter Objectives

- ❑ Learn to navigate through VisualAge for Java's windows
- ❑ Become familiar with the workbench
- ❑ Use the Quick Start option to load projects
- ❑ Use the help function
- ❑ Understand browsers and views in the IDE
- ❑ Modify your first Java application
- ❑ Compare different versions of source code
- ❑ Learn how to exit VisualAge for Java

 ## Chapter Project

- ❑ An IBM Java example — a clock — will be loaded into the workspace.
- ❑ While the clock is running, you will change the color of the hands of the clock.
- ❑ Figure 2.1 shows what the clock looks like.

Figure 2.1
Chapter Project

Developing a Java application is a big job, and VisualAge for Java is a big program. Both can be overwhelming when you first approach them. If you're new to VisualAge for Java, you've probably at least started trying to use it. If you're like most people, you probably didn't get too far. I've found that working on a small project right out of the gate seems to help people get more comfortable with the product.

This chapter presents a visual tour of many aspects of VisualAge for Java. We'll focus on learning how to maneuver around in the product. Don't become too ingrained in thinking that what follows is the only way to use this product. As with any world-class software development program, there are many ways to use VisualAge for Java.

My experience has taught me that most AS/400 professionals like to start out with a sample Java program and build from there. VisualAge for Java just doesn't work that way. Taking the time to learn how to find your way around the product is well worth the effort.

This chapter assumes that your VisualAge for Java is installed and ready to use; if that's not the case, see Appendix B for installation instructions. This book will be referring to the Enterprise Edition of VisualAge for Java 4.0/3.5. There are very few differences between the 4.0 and the 3.5 versions. Most of what is presented here applies to older versions as well. If you want to complete the AS/400 chapter projects, you'll need the Enterprise Edition of VisualAge for Java.

Getting Started

➤   On the Windows taskbar, click **Start**. Point to **Programs**, and then click **IBM VisualAge for Java**.

Tips and Tricks

If you've used the Java Development Kit to begin your Java journey, you've experienced many tools with different command-line commands to start them. In VisualAge for Java, once you start the program, all the related tools are loaded. Be patient; it can take some time before the first window appears.

The first screen that's displayed is the VisualAge for Java splash screen (Figure 2.2). Figure 2.3 shows the screen that appears next: the "What would you like to do?" dialog box.

➤   Click **Close**. Later, you can turn off the "What would you like to do?" dialog box so that it doesn't appear during the start-up process.

Figure 2.2
VisualAge for Java Splash Screen

Figure 2.3
What Would You Like to Do?

Workbench

After a small amount of time, the VisualAge for Java workbench appears on your screen as shown in Figure 2.4. The workbench's function is somewhat like that of a main menu on the AS/400. It's where you begin navigating to get to other window views (or browsers) of Java objects or window views of other Java tools. The **Projects** tab is the default view displayed when you first enter the workbench. Different views of Java-related objects are available via the tabs across the upper portion of the workbench window.

Figure 2.4
Workbench

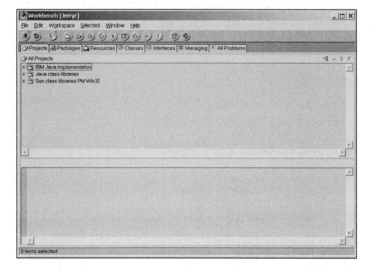

VisualAge for Java is structured as a hierarchy of different objects, layered as follows:

> Workbench
> > Project
> > > Package
> > > > Class or interface
> > > > > Method or constructor
> > > > > > Variable or field

The package, class, and method levels are built on existing Java definitions. If you've been doing anything with Java, you're already familiar with these terms. (For some brief definitions, see "Common Java Terms," below). The concept of a project is something new. It is used only in the context of VisualAge for Java as a way to organize various collections of packages. The workbench is also used to manage multiple software development environments at once. You use the workbench window to view, create, change, and manage various program elements that are currently loaded in the workspace.

Workspace

The VisualAge for Java *workspace* contains all the Java programs with which you're currently working. There are two general categories of Java projects with which you might work:

- Standard Java projects — These are all the packages, classes, methods, and interfaces found in the standard Java class libraries and other libraries your classes may need. You should have the following standard projects loaded into your workspace:
  - IBM Java Implementation
  - Java class libraries
  - Sun class libraries PM Win 32
- User projects — These are the Java programs you're currently developing.

Common Java Terms

Class — A class is a template for an object. It is similar in concept to an AS/400 Integrated Language Environment (ILE) module. While a class is a collection of methods and variables, an ILE module is a collection of procedures or subroutines. Classes and modules are designed to support a particular function. In a common-sense view, classes are a way to assemble a set of data and then define all the methods needed to access, use, and change that data.

Constructor — A constructor is a special method inside a class that has the same name as the class. A constructor is called to set up a new instance of a class. It can also be used to initialize variables and perform setup tasks for the class.

Field — A field is a data object in a class. This can also be referred to as a variable.

Interface — An interface enables a class to have several superclasses, letting you build on other objects. You use interfaces when you want to define a certain functionality to be used in several classes.

Method — A method is the executable code that takes place in any applet or application. A method is similar in concept to an RPG procedure or function. You can pass a set of parameters to a method, which, in turn, performs a specific task.

Package — A grouping of related classes and interfaces is called a package. An AS/400 ILE service program is similar in concept to a package. While a package contains one or more classes, an ILE service program contains one or more modules.

Project — In VisualAge for Java, a project is defined as a unit of organization used to group packages.

You can think of the workspace and its projects as somewhat analogous to the concept of an AS/400 library list. In this analogy, the standard Java projects are equivalent to the system library list, the user projects are equivalent to the user library list, and the entire workspace is equivalent to the full library list.

Tips and Tricks

It's easy to let the workspace grow. For performance reasons, your workspace should contain only the program elements you're currently working on.

Adding a Project to the Workspace

You are now going to add an IBM project to the workspace. This new project is a collection of various packages showing sample Java applications and applets.

➢   On the menu bar, click **File** to display the **File** menu.
➢   Click **Quick Start**.
➢   On the left side of the resulting dialog box, shown in Figure 2.5, click **Features**.
➢   On the right side, click **Add Feature**.
➢   Click **OK**.

Figure 2.5
Quick Start Features

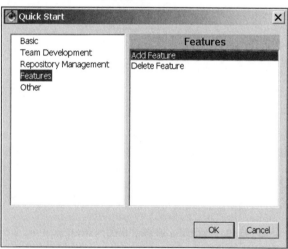

➢   Select a project by scrolling down until you see **IBM Java Examples 3.5**. Select the project as shown in Figure 2.6. (If you're using VisualAge for Java 4.0, select **IBM Java Examples 4.0**.)
➢   Click **OK**.

Figure 2.6
Select a Project

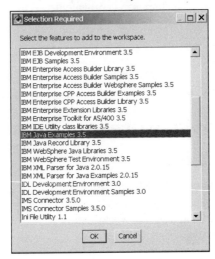

Loading this project into the workbench may take a minute. You may notice some occasional error messages, which is normal. There may be some missing methods or some deprecated methods (older versions of code). Any error messages will be reported in the **All Problems** window of the workbench, which we'll discuss later.

When the loading is completed, your workbench should look similar to Figure 2.7.

Figure 2.7
Workbench with IBM Java Examples

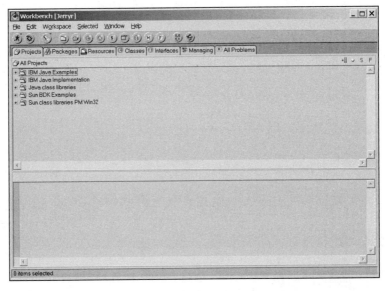

At this point, you may have a couple of questions. What actually occurred? Where did the project come from, and where did it go? Now is a good time to discuss the repository.

Repository

In the VisualAge for Java IDE, the *repository* is a centralized collection, or store, of all Java program elements. The repository also includes a change control system that allows for the tracking of changes to each program element. When started, VisualAge for Java automatically connects to the repository. As you create and/or modify program elements in the IDE workspace, VisualAge for Java automatically stores the changes in the repository. You can undo changes by retrieving previous *editions* from the repository.

One helpful feature of the repository is that it contains all editions of all program elements. When you delete program elements from the workspace, they remain in the repository. As you can guess, the repository grows over time. Repositories can be local to each developer's workstation or can be set up in a team environment through a shared repository. Chapter 23 covers the repository and team development in more detail.

 Tips and Tricks

You should periodically purge (permanently remove) and compact all your program elements in the repository. This task is similar to doing some occasional housecleaning of unused objects. We'll cover this two-step process in Chapter 23.

Repository vs. Workspace

Some differences between the repository and the workspace are:

- Multiple editions of any program are allowed in the repository. In other words, every program you ever worked on and every edition of every program are contained within the repository. Only one edition of any program element is allowed in the workspace at any given time.
- Program elements must be added to the workspace before they can be modified. Program elements in the repository can be viewed only.
- Changes to the workspace are not saved until you select **Save Workspace** from the **File** menu or until you exit the IDE. Changes to the source repository are saved immediately every time you save changes to a class, interface, or method.

IBM Enterprise Toolkit for AS/400

In later chapters of this book, you'll be using the IBM Enterprise Toolkit for AS/400 for all the work associated with the AS/400. Let's add this toolkit to your workspace now.

➤ On the menu bar, click **File**.
➤ Click **Quick Start**.
➤ On the left side of the resulting window, click **Features**.
➤ On the right side, click **Add Feature**.
➤ Click **OK**.
➤ Select a project by scrolling down until you see **IBM Enterprise Toolkit for AS400 3.5**. Select this project. (If you're using VisualAge for Java 4.0, select **IBM Enterprise Toolkit for AS400 4.0**.)
➤ Click **OK**.

When the loading is completed, your workbench should look similar to Figure 2.8.

Figure 2.8

Workbench with IBM Enterprise Toolkit for AS400

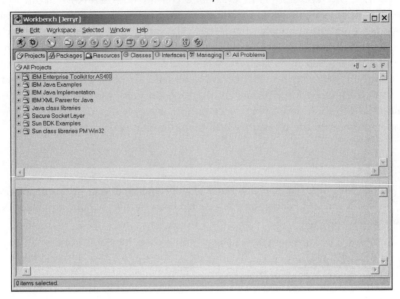

Help for VisualAge for Java

The help system for VisualAge for Java can be installed on your hard drive or can be completely accessible online through the Internet, depending on how you installed VisualAge for Java.

➢ On the menu bar, click **Help**.

➢ Click **Help Home Page**.

You should see the Help home page, shown in Figure 2.9.

Figure 2.9

Help Home Page

The help system has a lot of information in it. As with any online help system, changes occur frequently. At the time of the printing of this book, the following features were among those available:

- Search — You can use the search facility to find general information or details about a particular class or method. Be as specific as possible in your searches, or you may end up waiting for a long list of useless topics.
- Tasks — The tasks option provides procedural information that answers the question "How do I... ?"
- Reference — You can use the reference option to search for detailed keywords or application programming interface (API) information. Select the J2SDK API to see a list of all the Java APIs. The reference option is also where you'll find information about the Enterprise Toolkit for AS/400.
- Samples — This option lists different types of coding examples.
- PDF documents — The help page links to numerous Portable Document Format (PDF) documents available for reading and printing. You need Adobe's Acrobat PDF reader loaded to access these documents. If you don't have the reader, you can download it for free at *http://www.adobe.com.*

Take a few minutes to familiarize yourself with the help system. There will come a day when you'll need it. It's nice to know ahead of time what's available.

➢ Try a few of the features in the help system.
➢ Then close the help browser and return to the main workbench.

Tips and Tricks

By pressing F1 anywhere in VisualAge for Java, you can get context-sensitive help — that is, help related to whatever task you're trying to accomplish. To get reference help for Java keywords, classes, and methods, click the word or name in the *Source* pane (which we'll look at later), and then select *View Reference Help* from the pop-up menu.

Navigating the Workbench

The workbench lets you view all the Java program elements with which you're working. VisualAge for Java offers many ways to view the same information with a large degree of flexibility. With flexibility comes complexity. You can easily get lost among all the available options for looking at the same object.

From the workbench, you can open other views (windows) and browsers. *Views* are nothing more than the result of selecting a tab on the workbench. Views show you the contents of *all* objects based on the view you selected. You can view Projects, Packages, Resources, Classes, Interfaces, Managing, and All Problems.

Browsers are specialized windows in the workspace that help you with various programming tasks. A browser gives you a focused view of an individual program element and, typically, all the program elements contained within it. You have browsers for projects, packages, classes, interfaces, and methods.

Panes are smaller windows that further divide both views and browsers. Each pane has a pane name displayed in the upper-left corner of the pane.

You're probably a little confused about the real differences between views and browsers. Before we walk through some examples, these general rules can help with navigation:

- Double-clicks open a new browser (window).
- Single-clicks let you drill down into, or expand through, the contents of a selected object.

As you've seen, the **Projects** view is the default view displayed when you first start VisualAge for Java. Let's take a look at the other views available to you in the workbench.

Packages View

The **Packages** view contains all the packages in the workspace. Figure 2.10 shows a sample **Packages** view.

Figure 2.10
Packages View

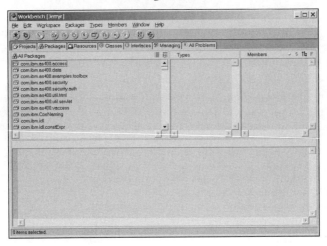

➤   From the workbench, click the **Packages** tab.
➤   Click the package **com.ibm.as400.access**.

Notice, as Figure 2.11 shows, that the **Packages** view now lists the contents of the package **com.ibm.as400.access** in the **Types** window pane. Each of the items in this pane is identified (by the symbol immediately to its left) as either a class 🅲 or an interface 🅸.

Figure 2.11
Packages View with Types Pane

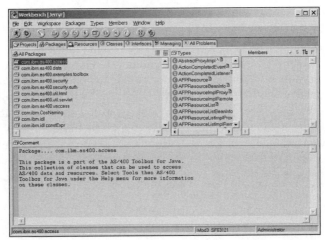

➤   Click the class named **AbstractProxyImpl**.

The **Packages** view displays the contents of class **AbstractProxyImpl** in the **Members** pane, as shown in Figure 2.12. Each item is identified as either a field 🄵 or a method 🄼. In addition, if you look in the lower pane of the figure, you'll see source code associated with class **AbstractProxyImpl** displayed in the **Source** pane.

Figure 2.12
Packages View with Types, Members, and Source Panes

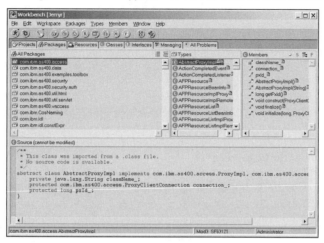

You are now going to change the *orientation* of the **Packages** view.

➢   On the menu bar, click **Window** to display the **Window** menu.
➢   Click **Flip Orientation**.

As shown in Figure 2.13, the view "flips" from a horizontal view to a vertical one.

Figure 2.13
Packages in Vertical View

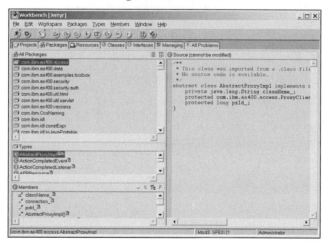

Go ahead and return to the horizontal view.

➢   On the menu bar, click **Window**.
➢   Click **Flip Orientation**.

Resources View

At certain times during development, you may use files that aren't Java source files — for example, you might have some HTML or image files. You create these resource files outside the VisualAge for Java IDE and store them in the project resources directory. The **Resources** view shows these files. VisualAge for Java looks for resource files in the particular project directory when you run applications.

➢   From the workbench, click the **Resources** tab.

Classes View

The **Classes** view contains all the classes in the workspace. This can be a large number of classes.

➢   From the workbench, click the **Classes** tab.

Interfaces View

The **Interfaces** view shows all the interfaces in the workspace.

➢   From the workbench, click the **Interfaces** tab.

Managing View

You use the **Managing** view to drill down within projects, packages, and types. This view also lets you identify and change owners of the objects.

➢   From the workbench, click the **Managing** tab.

All Problems View

The **All Problems** view identifies all existing problems. Whenever a problem exists, it is logged in this view, letting you come back later to determine whether you want to fix the problem.

➢   From the workbench, click the **All Problems** tab.

As you can see in the **All Problems** view shown in Figure 2.14, some problems were identified earlier when you loaded the **IBM Java Examples** project into the workspace. Don't worry about trying to fix any of these problems.

Figure 2.14
All Problems View

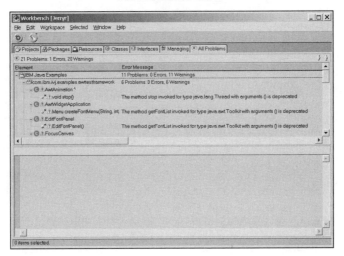

The Project Tree View

It's often convenient to start at the **Projects** view of the workbench and then drill down to other objects by way of a tree view. The tree view gives you a handy way to quickly see the hierarchy of any object. I find myself using this feature quite a bit.

➢   Click the **Projects** tab.

Notice the plus signs (+) to the left of all the projects. You use the + to expand the tree view.

➢   Next to the project named **Secure Socket Layer**, click the +. Notice that the view expands to show the package named **com.ibm.sslight**, as shown in Figure 2.15.

Figure 2.15
Project Drill-Down View

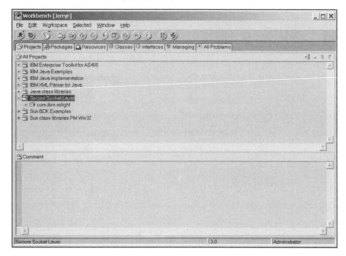

➢   Next to package **com.ibm.sslight**, click the +. The view expands again, this time to show all the classes contained within this package.
➢   Next to the class named **Debug**, click the +. The view expands to show all the fields and methods associated with this class.
➢   Next to class **Debug**, click the minus sign (–). Doing so closes the tree, or drill-down, view.
➢   Close the package and the project the same way.

Package Browser

The *package browser* is a separate window that lets you focus on the contents of a particular package.

➢   From the workbench, click the **Packages** tab.
➢   Double-click the package **com.ibm.as400.access**.

As Figure 2.16 shows, a new window is created that focuses on the contents of package **com.ibm.as400.access**. This is the package browser.

Figure 2.16
Package Browser

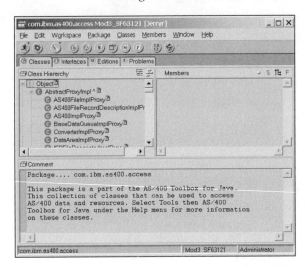

You've now seen two ways to look at the contents of packages: the **Packages** view and the package browser. You'll quickly observe that it's easy to get lost when you open many different browsers.

➢   Close the package browser by clicking the Windows **Close** button.

Classes Browser

The *classes browser* is a separate window that lets you focus on the contents of a particular class. You'll probably find yourself using this browser more than all the other browsers put together. We'll cover the classes browser in great detail starting in Chapter 4.

➢   Click the **Projects** tab.
➢   Next to the project named **IBM Java Examples**, click the +.
➢   Next to the package named **com.ibm.ivj.examples.vc.customerinfo**, click the +.
➢   Double-click the class named **AddressView**.

As Figure 2.17 shows, a new window is created that focuses on the contents of class **com.ibm.ivj.examples.vc .customerinfo**. This is the classes browser. Looking at the figure, the first thing that grabs your attention is the Visual Composition Editor. This is where you build the graphical representation of the class. You'll spend much of your time in this editor. The VCE is similar in function to Screen Design Aid (SDA) on the AS/400.

Figure 2.17
Classes Browser with Visual Composition View

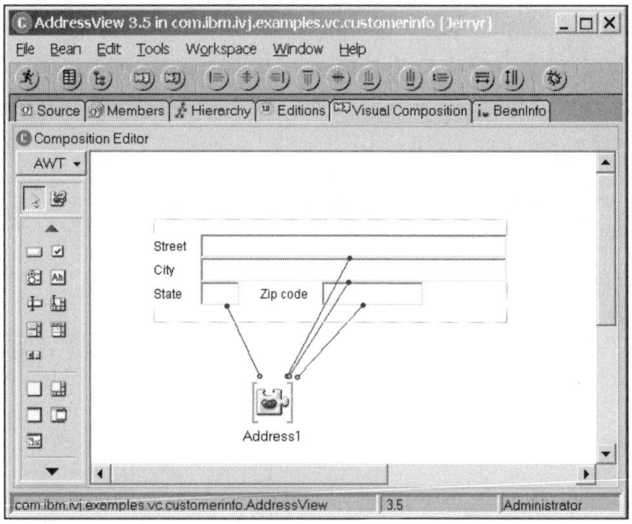

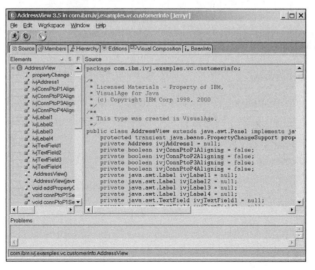

Notice the tabs across the upper portion of the classes browser screen. As in the workbench, different views are available here.

➤ Click the **Source** tab.

As Figure 2.18 shows, the **Source** view lets you view the entire class's source code. This view shows all the methods in the class, one after another. The other views available from the classes browser are **Members**, **Hierarchy**, **Editions**, and **BeanInfo**; we'll discuss these views later in the book.

➤ Close the classes browser.

Figure 2.18
Classes Browser with Source View

Modifying a Java Application

It's easy to change Java source code. Let's step through an example of how to change source code and compile, while the application is running.

➤ From the workbench, double-click the project **IBM Java Examples** to open up the **Packages** view.

➤ You may want to enlarge the **Packages** pane so that you can read all the packages. To do so, move your mouse pointer to the side of the pane. When the pointer changes to an expand pointer, click and drag to widen the pane.

➤ In the **Packages** pane, click package **com.ibm.ivj.examples.awttests**.

➤ In the **Types** pane, click class **AwtClock**.

➤ In the **Members** pane, click method **Color getClockColor()**.

Your screen should look like Figure 2.19.

Figure 2.19
Source Code for getClockColor() Method

Notice the Java source code displayed in the **Source** pane. This is the source code you're going to change. Before doing so, you're going to run the application.

Run the clock application, **AwtClock**:

➤ In the **Types** pane, move your pointer to the class **AwtClock**. Right-click to display the shortcut menu.

➤ Find and select the **Run** menu item. A second menu automatically appears.

➤ Click **Run Main**.

The application starts, and you see a clock like the one shown in Figure 2.20. Congratulations, you've just run your first Java application!

Figure 2.20
Application AwtClock

> Now, resize the **Packages** view so that you can see the clock and the entire **Packages** view at the same time, as shown in Figure 2.21.

Figure 2.21
Packages View and AwtClock Displayed Together

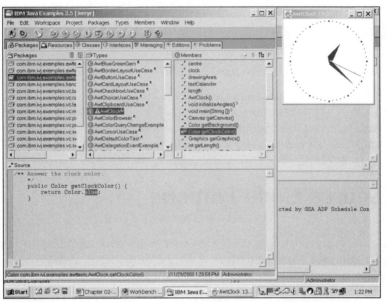

To change the source code:

> Move the pointer down to the **Source** pane, double-click to select **blue**, and then type **green** to change the color. Figure 2.22 shows the before and after images of the code changes. Be careful to type **green** using all lowercase letters.

Figure 2.22
Source Code for Method getClockColor()

```
Before:
public Color getClockColor() {
    return Color.blue;
}
```

```
After:
public Color getClockColor() {
    return Color.green;
}
```

Save the source code:

➤   With the pointer in the **Source** pane, right-click to display the shortcut menu.

➤   Click **Save**. This option actually saves and compiles the Java code at the same time.

Watch the color of the clock. It changes from blue to green when the compile is completed. Pretty neat!

➤   Close the clock.

Again, congratulations are in order. You have just modified, saved, and recompiled your first Java application. What actually occurred when you performed the **Save** function?

- The changes to the method **getClockColor()** were saved in the repository.
- A new edition of method **getClockColor()** was created.
- The source code was compiled incrementally. This means that changes to source methods were compiled right after the change and save. Any errors would have been identified at that time.
- When method **getClockColor()** was called again, the new edition of the method was called.

Comparing Source Code Editions

Now, you're going to compare the old and new editions of the source code.

➤   In the **Types** pane, move the pointer to class **AwtClock**. Right-click to display the shortcut menu.

➤   Find and select the **Compare With** menu item. A second menu automatically appears. Click **Another Edition**. When the next window appears, double-click the edition named **3.5**. (This is the original edition name of the source code that was supplied with VisualAge for Java.)

➤   Click method **getClockColor()**, as shown in Figure 2.23.

Figure 2.23
Comparing Two Editions of Source Code

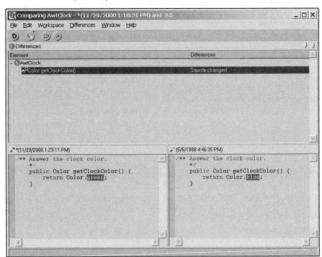

The screen changes to show, side by side, the Java source code of the current and previous edition. Recall from earlier in the chapter that multiple editions of the same program can be stored in the repository. This means that every change you make gets stored as an edition. It also means that you can go back to earlier editions of your code.

Replacing an Edition

At times, you may want to return to an earlier edition of your Java source code. Let's do that now, replacing the source code changes you just made with the original edition of the source code.

➢   Close the compare window.
➢   Move your pointer to class **AwtClock**. Right-click to display the shortcut menu.
➢   Find and select the **Replace With** menu item. A second menu automatically appears.
➢   Click **Another Edition**. When the next window appears, double-click the edition named **3.5**.

Look at the source code in the **Source** pane. It has now returned to the original edition. If you run the application again, you'll notice everything is back to the way it originally was.

Printing

Printing a particular program element in VisualAge for Java is simple. The general rule is that when you print an element, all the elements it contains are also printed. You can print from projects, packages, classes, and methods. To print:

• Select the particular object or program element you want to print.
• Right-click to display the shortcut menu.
• Click **Document**, and then click **Print**.

When you're in the **Source** pane, you can print the Java source code by doing the following:

• Right-click to display the shortcut menu.
• Click **Print Text**.

Exiting VisualAge for Java

Exiting VisualAge for Java is easy when you understand one general rule: The next time you re-enter VisualAge for Java, everything starts back up as it was when you exited the previous session. If you have five browsers open when you exit, you'll have the same five browsers open the next time you start VisualAge for Java (assuming you save your workspace).

To exit, you can select the **File** menu and then click **Exit VisualAge**. Another way to exit is to close each of the browsers and the workbench using the Windows **Close** button. When you exit the workspace, you're prompted to save it. Normally, you will always save your workspace.

Summary

In this chapter, you participated in a very high-level overview of some of the functions in VisualAge for Java. There are many more aspects of VisualAge for Java that we'll cover later in the book. You should now

- have a general understanding of how to navigate the numerous windows from the workbench
- feel comfortable looking for help information
- understand the differences between browsers, views, and panes
- be able to load projects from the repository
- have a general overview of how to save, compile, and execute an applet
- be able to compare different versions of source code and replace them

There's much more to learn. In the next chapter, we'll focus on setting up your preferences.

Chapter 3

Setting Your Preferences

Chapter Objectives

- ☐ Set workbench options
- ☐ Customize your working environment
- ☐ Learn how to set bookmarks

Chapter Project

- ☐ Customize your workbench by changing one of the default settings in the **Code generation** options.
- ☐ Figure 3.1 shows the **Code generation** options window.

Figure 3.1
Chapter Project

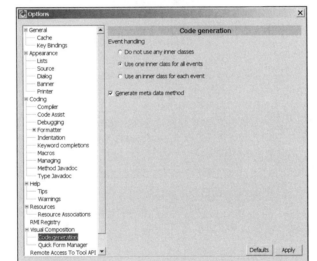

Everyone is different. We each have our own preferences when working with software products. This chapter focuses on learning how to set your own preferences in VisualAge for Java. These small preferential changes can help you better enjoy your work and be more productive at the same time.

You may have exited VisualAge for Java. If so, go ahead and restart it now. Remember, whatever your workbench looked like when you exited is exactly what it will look like when it starts up again. To speed the starting of VisualAge for Java, make sure you close all your browsers (windows) before exiting VisualAge for Java.

The assignment for this chapter assumes you'll be changing one of the **Code generation** options. *If you skip this chapter, make sure you at least consider changing the **Visual Composition Code generation** options as described here.*

Window Options

The **Window** menu, shown in Figure 3.2, provides four menu items that work like toggle switches to turn several preferential settings on or off:

- **Lock Window** — When you lock a window, you cannot close it without receiving a warning message that prompts you to confirm your intent to close the window. At times, you may want to leave a particular window open.
- **Maximize/Restore Pane** — The maximize/restore switch either fully opens the pane or restores it to normal size.
- **Flip Orientation** — You used the flip option in Chapter 2 to change from a horizontal view to a vertical view.
- **Show Edition Names** — This switch displays all objects with the version number of the particular object.

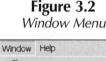

Figure 3.2
Window Menu

➢   On the workbench menu bar, click **Window** to display the **Window** menu.
➢   Click **Show Edition Names**. Look at the object names.
➢   Click **Show Edition Names** again.

You should have noticed that each of your objects had an edition number appended to it.

Workbench Options

There are many options you can change to customize your VisualAge for Java work environment. As a beginner, you probably won't make too many changes, but it's nice to know the options are available for the future. We'll look at the options you most normally would change. For information about other options not covered here, you can press the F1 key to get additional help.

General Options

➤ On the workbench menu bar, click **Window** to display the **Window** menu.

➤ Click **Options**.

The window of **General** options appears as shown in Figure 3.3.

Figure 3.3
General Options

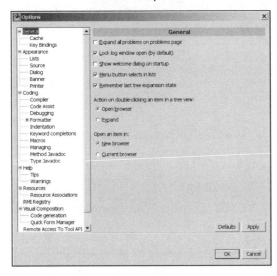

You may want to set your **General** options as shown in the figure. The **General** options function as follows:

- **Expand all problems on problems page** — When selected, this option causes the list of problems to be fully expanded when you first go to the **All Problems** view. There can be quite a few errors, so retaining the unexpanded tree view is beneficial because it is easier to view. To show the unexpanded view, clear this option.

- **Lock log window open** — When selected, this option causes the log window to remain open. You'll receive many messages in this log area, so it's best to keep this window open but minimized.

- **Show welcome dialog on startup** — When selected, this option causes the start-up "What would you like to do?" dialog box to list some common tasks for easy access. You saw this dialog box in Chapter 2 (Figure 2.3). You'll probably want to clear this option. Once you become familiar with VisualAge for Java, you will navigate directly to where you want to go.

- **Menu button selects in lists** — When selected, this option causes a right-click to first select the list item over which the pointer is positioned and then pop up the menu for that item. When this option is not selected, a right-click pops up the menu for the previously selected list item, regardless of where the pointer is when you click. The default, selecting this option, is probably the right way to go on this one.

- **Remember last tree expansion state** — When selected, this option causes the IDE to "remember" the level to which a drill-down or tree view was last expanded. When you collapse the tree and expand it again, it returns you to the expansion state you left.

To apply any changes you make to the **General** options, you click **Apply**.

Cache Options

You can improve the performance of the IDE by changing the **Cache** settings, which are a subset of the **General** options.

➢   In the **Options** window, click **Cache** as shown in Figure 3.4.

Figure 3.4
Cache Options

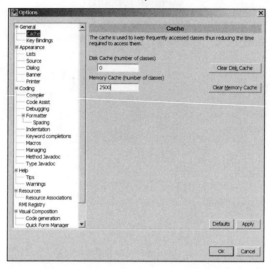

Two options are worth noting here:

- **Disk Cache** — The disk cache option creates a separate file for each cached class to improve performance. These files can impact disk fragmentation. The default disk cache setting may not improve performance; you may want to change the value to 200. To achieve optimal performance, you may have to adjust this setting numerous times.
- **Memory Cache** — VisualAge for Java uses a substantial amount of memory. If you have 128 MB of memory or more, you should probably increase the memory cache value to approximately 2000. You can experiment with this value to get your best results. Note that the memory cache is different from the system memory cache.

Key Bindings Options

Another subgroup of the **General** options, **Key Bindings**, lets you map editor commands to your choice of shortcut keys. This is more of an advanced function. You probably shouldn't change anything here until you become more familiar with VisualAge for Java.

➢   In the **Options** window, click **Key Bindings**.

Appearance Options

You use the **Appearance** options to change the visual aspects of your development environment.

➢   In the **Options** window, click **Appearance** as shown in Figure 3.5.

Figure 3.5
Appearance Options

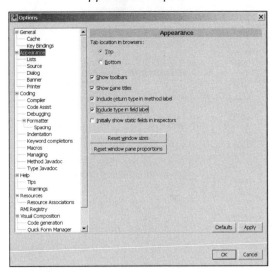

Two **Appearance** options are worth noting:

- **Include return type in method label** — When this option is selected, the return type will be shown for all methods displayed in the workbench. For example, a method called **getPrice()** that returns an integer will be listed as **int getPrice()** as opposed to **getPrice()**.
- **Include type in field label** — When this option is selected, the type of all fields is shown. For example, an integer field called **calculate** will be listed as **int calculate** as opposed to **calculate**.

It's a good idea to select both of these options.

Lists Options and Source Options

Two subgroups of the **Appearance** options may be useful to you. You can use the **Lists** options to change the color, font, and size of the lists of objects that appear in the workbench.

➢   In the **Options** window, click **Lists**.

Similarly, the **Source** options let you change the appearance of your source code. Figure 3.6 shows the panel where you can change the color, font, and size of the source code as it appears in the source editors. For example, you can use different colors for source code, comments, literals, and keywords.

➢   In the Options window, click **Source**.

Figure 3.6
Source Options

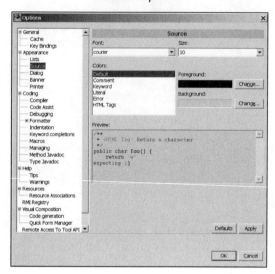

Coding Formatter Options

The coding formatter lets you set some options for formatting your Java code. For example, most IBM and Sun developers like to use a wraparound-style brace in their Java source code:

```
public class HelloWorld {
    . . .
    }
```

AS/400 developers often prefer the opposite approach, an inline brace:

```
public class HelloWorld
    {
    . . .
    }
```

As Figure 3.7 shows, the **Opening braces begin new line** check box lets you choose your preferred brace style. There is no right or wrong style here. It's just that: style.

➢   In the **Options** window, click **Formatter**.
➢   Select the **Opening braces begin new line** check box to see which style you like.

Figure 3.7

Formatter Options

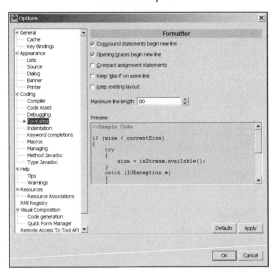

Help Tips and Warnings Options

The **Help** options section lets you specify which tips to show and which warnings to display when you're doing certain tasks. These aids can be great for beginning VisualAge for Java developers, but they can become annoying for more experienced developers. You may want to accept the defaults until you become more experienced with VisualAge for Java.

➢   Click **Tips** in the **Options** window.
➢   Click **Warnings** in the **Options** window.

Visual Composition Code Generation Options

VisualAge for Java Version 3 came out with new code-generation options, shown in Figure 3.8, for handling events. Here is a summary of the event-handling generation options.

- **Do not use any inner classes** — If selected, this option generates an event handler method for each visual connection.
- **Use one inner class for all events** — If selected, this option generates one inner class containing methods defined to handle all events used in the outer class. This is the default setting, and it is the one used in this book's examples.
- **Use an inner class for each event** — If selected, this option generates an anonymous inner class for each event set used in the outer class. This option generates more code and performs more slowly than the other two options, but it ensures that the events are handled properly by the runtime Java Virtual Machine.

Figure 3.8
Code Generation Options

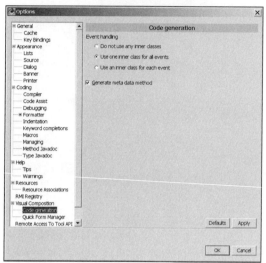

Figure 3.8 lists another code-generation option, **Generate meta data method**, that is probably the most important option to consider changing from the default. There is certain visual information that cannot be expressed in Java source code. If the **Generate meta data method** option is cleared, be aware of the following:

> *If you use the Visual Composition Editor and you export the Java source code from VisualAge for Java and then later import the same Java source code, you will have lost certain information required to display the visual aspects of your JavaBeans.*

In contrast, if you select the **Generate meta data method** option, a method called **getBuilderData()** is generated automatically. Figure 3.9 shows an example of what this method looks like. There is no meaningful code in this method. The method contains binary data inside a Java comment representing the meta data required by the Visual Composition Editor. This special binary data is used only by VisualAge for Java.

Figure 3.9
Source Code for getBuilderData() Method

```
/* WARNING: THIS METHOD WILL BE REGENERATED. */
private static void getBuilderData() {
/*V1.1
**start of data**
 D0CB838494G88G88GAE0DFCA9GGGGGGGGGGGGGG
8CGGGE2F5E9ECE4E5F2A0E4E1F4E135BA8BD4D4D
712492E49F1CF5CDDF3C2A64E0C59B5B34E9C126
3CCCCA40699FFA4CA4408C6A346CFBCA34EC8626
C1A041DB567E4E7BC1BCB73111F50580D10C1149
8CCB04186848DA2029FA46020F28415EC1C238F7
A81AD2F7BF5DE3F961C985D2AFB5FFD7D3A69EE2
2A7C3D25EF72B6E272AEED55D2A771AD877CCC9C
FB1D989C9C9A75A5F67A904C4D69372508B9FEF6
038442713B208616FC3008272
```

Change the default for the **Generate meta data method** option:

➤ In the **Options** window, click **Code generation**.
➤ Select the **Generate meta data method** option as shown in Figure 3.8.
➤ Click **Apply**.
➤ Click **OK**.

Bookmarks

A handy feature of the workbench is the option to set up bookmarks. Bookmarks make it quick and easy to go to your frequently used program elements. You can set a total of nine bookmarks. The bookmark button 📑 is located in the upper-right corner of the workbench view, as shown in Figure 3.10.

Figure 3.10
Bookmark Button

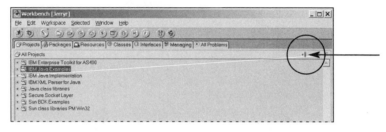

Setting Bookmarks

Bookmarking a program element is as simple as locating the program element and then clicking the bookmark button. Here's an example.

➤ From the workbench, expand the project **IBM Java Examples** by clicking the + sign beside it.
➤ Click package **com.ibm.ivj.examples.awttests** to select it.
➤ Move the pointer to the upper-right corner of the **All Projects** pane. As you place the pointer over the bookmark button, the *hover help* appears, as shown in Figure 3.11.

Figure 3.11
Expanded IBM Java Examples

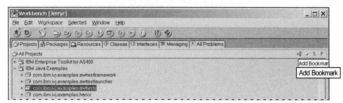

➤ Click the bookmark button. Notice that a **1** appears in the pane border to the left of the bookmark button, as shown in Figure 3.12. This number signifies a bookmark.
➤ Move the pointer to the **1**. Notice how the hover help appears (Figure 3.13), identifying the item to which the bookmark is set.

Figure 3.12
Bookmark Being Set

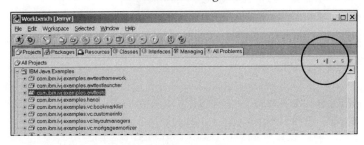

Figure 3.13
Bookmark Hover Text

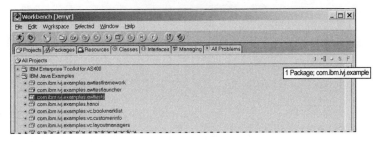

Set another bookmark:

➢ From the workbench, click package **com.ibm.ivj.examples.vc.customerinfo** to select it.

➢ Again, set a bookmark by clicking the bookmark button. As Figure 3.14 shows, the pane now shows a **2**, or a second bookmark, for this package.

Figure 3.14
Second Bookmark

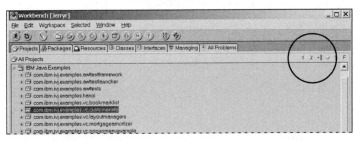

Moving to Bookmarks

To move to a bookmarked program element, you simply click the appropriate bookmark number in the pane border. Here is an example.

➢ Collapse, or close, the drill-down of project **IBM Java Examples** as shown in Figure 3.15.

Figure 3.15
Fully Collapsed Workbench

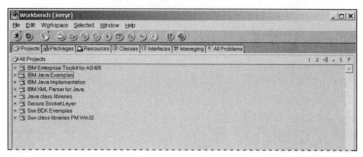

➢ Click bookmark **1**. You're taken to the expanded package **com.ibm.ivj.examples.awttests**, as Figure 3.16 shows.

➢ Click bookmark **2**. You're taken you to the expanded package **com.ibm.ivj.examples.vc.customerinfo**, as Figure 3.17 shows.

As you can see, bookmarks give you an easy way to maneuver to frequently used program elements.

Figure 3.16
Bookmark 1: com.ibm.ivj.examples.awttests

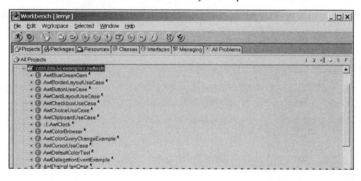

Figure 3.17
Bookmark 2: com.ibm.ivj.examples.vc.customerinfo

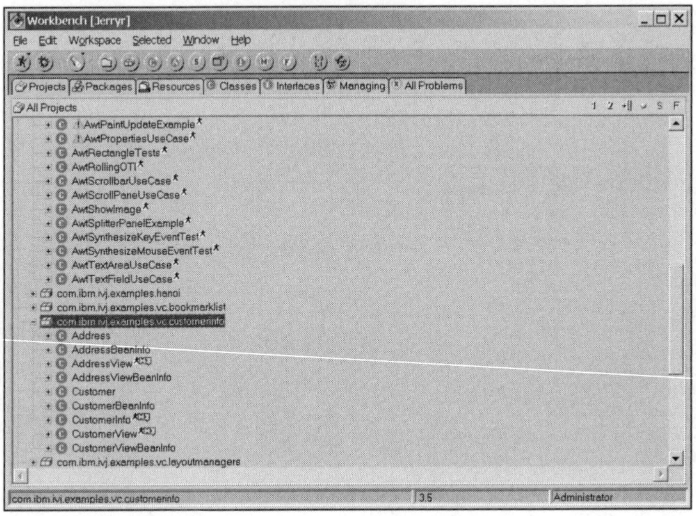

Removing Bookmarks

To remove a bookmark from a program element, you simply right-click any bookmark number or the bookmark button. Then choose **Remove Bookmark** from the shortcut menu, and select the bookmark you want to remove.

Remove the two bookmarks you previously set.

➤   Right-click the bookmark button. On the shortcut menu, click **Remove Bookmark**. Then click **1 Package com.ibm.ivj.examples.awttests**.

➤   Right-click the bookmark button. On the shortcut menu, click **Remove Bookmark**. Then click **2 Package com.ibm.ivj.examples.vc.customerinfo**.

Other Options

You've seen only a few of the options available for customizing your VisualAge for Java work environment. There are many more. As you become more experienced, you'll want to explore some of these other options.

To save your options, you must either exit VisualAge for Java and save your workspace or directly save your workspace as follows:

➤   From the menu bar, click **File** to display the **File** menu.
➤   Click **Save Workspace**.

Summary

In this chapter, you learned how to customize your work environment. You now know how to

- change and use window options
- change VisualAge for Java systemwide workbench options
- set, use, and remove bookmarks

Now, the fun really begins. In the next chapter, you'll write your first applet and become familiar with VisualAge for Java's Visual Composition Editor.

Chapter 4

Building Your First Applet

 ## Chapter Objectives

- ❏ Create a project, package, and class
- ❏ Build the first applet
- ❏ Become familiar with the Visual Composition Editor
- ❏ Learn how to use Abstract Window Toolkit beans
- ❏ Save, compile, and run programs
- ❏ Review generated Java source code

 ## Chapter Project

- ❏ A simple applet will be created.
- ❏ The applet will accept input into a text input field and then will redisplay the text on the screen.
- ❏ The redisplay will occur when the **Duplicate** button is clicked.
- ❏ Figure 4.1 shows what the sample applet will look like.

Figure 4.1
Chapter Project

```
Applet Viewer: firstapplets.WorkWithBeans.class  _ □ X
 Applet

    Input Text:              Mary had a little lamb


    Duplicated Text:         Mary had a little lamb



                        Duplicate


 Applet started.
```

If you're an AS/400 development programmer, you probably think of Java as a programming language similar to RPG or Cobol. Yes, there are some similarities, but Java is much more powerful. Not only does Java function on multiple platforms, but it also works closely as a browser language. In addition, it is a language that's used in all types of nontypical computer hardware, such as appliances. You can use Java to build a huge variety of applications.

Some of the general types of applications you can create in Java are

- client graphical applications
- client command-line applications
- applets (mini-applications)
- servlets (server-side applications)
- embedded applications (applications inside nontypical computer hardware)

Applets

In the next couple of chapters, you'll become familiar with creating applets. The rest of the book will focus on client graphical applications. To get started with applets, you need to understand a little about what they are.

An *applet* is a small application that runs inside a Java-enabled Web browser, such as Microsoft Internet Explorer or Netscape Navigator. You can also run an applet inside the JDK AppletViewer or the Applet Viewer contained within VisualAge for Java. You'll use the VisualAge for Java Applet Viewer later in this chapter.

Web browsers were developed primarily to display HTML documents. HTML is a tag-based language. If you've ever used the User Interface Manager (UIM) to create help pages on the AS/400, you're probably familiar with the concept of tags.

To use an applet within a browser, you must embed a small section of code inside the HTML. This can be done with an <APPLET> tag. Figure 4.2 shows some sample HTML code along with the <APPLET> tag. In this example, the Java class **Airplane** will be executed.

Figure 4.2
Sample HTML Source Code

```
<HTML>
<TITLE>My First Applet</TITLE>
<BODY>
<APPLET CODE="Airplane.class" HEIGHT=200 WIDTH=350></APPLET>
</BODY>
</HTML>
```

When you use an applet, certain methods are called throughout the applet's existence, which is also known as the applet life cycle. The applet life cycle consists of calls to four specific Java methods:

- **init()** — This method is called the first time an applet is loaded into the browser. This is where all initialization steps occur.
- **start()** — This method is called after the **init()** method. It is also called every time the browser returns to a page that contains the applet.
- **stop()** — This method is called any time the browser leaves a page that contains the applet.
- **destroy()** — This method is called before the browser closes or shuts down.

You can use these methods to perform certain activities during each step in the applet life cycle.

Tips and Tricks

When using applets, remember that applets have a security restriction. They cannot access or update files or directories on the local workstation. Nor can applets change any local properties. You can modify this security restriction by using digital signatures supplied with the JDK JAVAKEY tool.

Creating Projects

You're going to create a new project named **My Introduction Projects**. The work you accomplish in the next few chapters will be stored in this newly created project.

➢   On the workbench menu bar, click **Selected** to display the **Selected** menu. On the submenu, point to the **Add** option, and then click **Project**. Figure 4.3 shows this choice. As an alternative, you can simply right-click in the upper pane of the workbench to display the shortcut menu, select **Add**, and then select **Project**. A third approach is to double-click the **New Project** button ⬚ on the workbench toolbar. Any of these methods starts the **Add Project** SmartGuide, shown in Figure 4.4.

Figure 4.3
Selected Menu

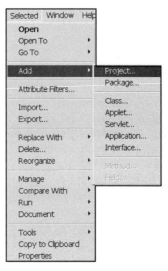

Figure 4.4
Add Project SmartGuide

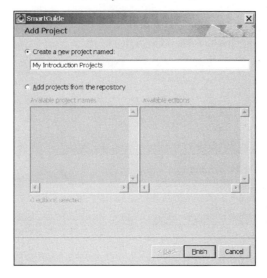

The **Add Project** SmartGuide, or wizard, simply prompts you for the information required to create a new project. Project names must begin with an uppercase letter and can contain blank spaces. Each project must have a unique name in the workspace.

Tips and Tricks

Java is extremely case sensitive. It's important to make sure you do all your typing in the correct case. There will be times when everything must be all upper case, all lower case, or mixed case. Getting the case wrong is one of the most common errors programmers make when first converting to Java programming.

Create the project **My Introduction Projects**:

➢   In the **Add Project** SmartGuide, make sure the **Create a new project named** option is selected, as shown in the figure.

➢   Type **My Introduction Projects** into the space provided.

➢   Click **Finish** to complete the creation of the project.

Tips and Tricks

In Chapter 2, you used the *QuickStart / Features / Add Feature* option to retrieve two IBM projects from the repository. The screen in Figure 4.4 provides an option called *Add projects from the repository* that has not been selected. This option provides another way to accomplish the same task as the QuickStart function you performed earlier. One advantage of using this method to retrieve projects from the repository is that you can also retrieve your own personal projects that may have been deleted from your workspace.

Once the project is created, you'll see it listed in the workbench **All Projects** pane as shown in Figure 4.5.

Figure 4.5
My Introduction Projects Project

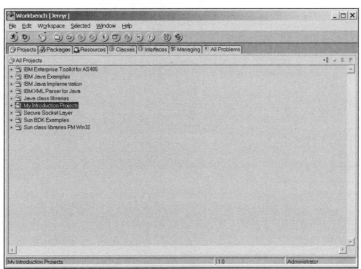

Creating Packages

As you saw with the creation of projects, there are three ways to create a package. If you use the right-click approach to create a package, you'll find you can save keystrokes by not having to type the project name.

➤ In the **All Projects** pane, select the project **My Introduction Projects** with a click. Right-click to display the shortcut menu, select **Add**, and then select **Package**. Another approach is to double-click the **New Package** button 🖳 on the workbench toolbar.

Figure 4.6 shows the **Add Package** SmartGuide.

Figure 4.6

Add Package SmartGuide

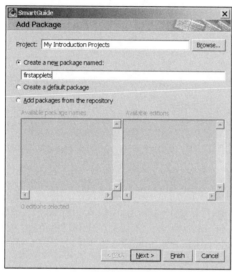

Packages are the logical grouping of related classes. A package is similar to the concept of an AS/400 Integrated Language Environment (ILE) service program. Packages are normally exported from the VisualAge for Java environment for the deployment of your application.

Package names should comply with standard Java naming conventions. They are written using all lowercase letters and no blank spaces. Typically, a high-level part of your company's unique domain name is included as part of the package name. For example, an engineering department at Sun might use **com.sun.eng** as a valid package name. If you don't enter a package name that meets standard Java naming conventions, you'll receive a warning message.

➤ In the **Add Package** SmartGuide, make sure the **Project** name is **My Introduction Projects**, as shown in the figure.
➤ Make sure the **Create a new package named** option is selected.
➤ Type **firstapplets** into the space provided.
➤ Click **Finish** to complete the creation of the package.

Once the package is created, you'll see it listed in the workbench **All Projects** pane under **My Introduction Projects**. Figure 4.7 shows this new package.

Figure 4.7
firstapplets Package

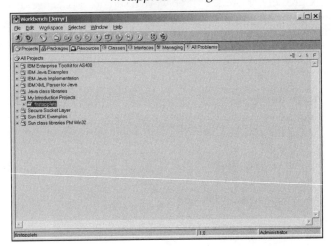

Creating Applets

Next, you're going to build a simple applet. An applet is a special type of class.

➢   Select the package **firstapplets** with a click. Right-click to display the shortcut menu, select **Add**, and then select **Applet**. Or, double-click the **New Applet** button [icon] on the workbench toolbar.

Java naming conventions call for applet and class names to appear in mixed case, with the first letter and each internal word capitalized. No blank spaces are allowed. When naming applets and classes, use whole words. Avoid acronyms and abbreviations (unless the abbreviation is much more widely used than the long form, as with "HTML" or "URL").

Tips and Tricks

The AS/400 name is very commonly used in AS/400 Java applications. Be alert when using AS/400 Toolbox packages, classes, and method names. You'll often be using the lowercase "as400". Out of habit, you may type the uppercase "AS400", which can cause problems later on.

Figure 4.8 shows the first window of the **Create Applet** SmartGuide. You're going to create an applet named **WorkWithBeans**.

Figure 4.8
Create Applet SmartGuide

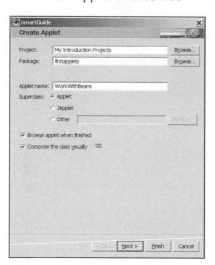

Create the **WorkWithBeans** applet:

➢ Make sure the **Project** name is **My Introduction Projects**, as shown in the figure.
➢ Make sure the **Package** name is **firstapplets**.
➢ Type **WorkWithBeans** into the **Applet name** field.
➢ Make sure the superclass **Applet** is selected.
➢ Select the **Browse applet when finished** check box.
➢ Select the **Compose the class visually** check box.
➢ Click **Next**.

You can also use the **Create Applet** SmartGuide to create JApplets (which you'll learn about in Chapter 5) and other types of applets. You use the SmartGuide's **Superclass** option to identify which type of class you'll be extending. In this case, you'll be extending the **java.applet.Applet** class. Using a superclass of **Applet** automatically defines and causes your applet to inherit certain properties and attributes from this class.

Tips and Tricks

The *Browse applet when finished* and *Compose the class visually* options are used only as follow-on navigation tools. When the *Create Applet* SmartGuide is finished, you will automatically be placed inside the Visual Composition Editor. The VCE is where you will visually design the applet.

Next, the **Applet Properties** window of the **Create Applet** SmartGuide (Figure 4.9) appears. The upper portion of this window specifies whether to create a **main()** method. When a **main()** method exists, the applet can be run as an application as well as an applet. In the lower portion of the window, you can specify threads for use in animation.

➢ Accept the defaults for this window.
➢ Click **Next**.

Figure 4.9
Applet Properties

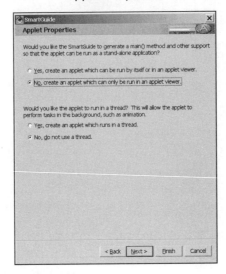

The **Events** window of the **Create Applet** SmartGuide (Figure 4.10) appears next. Here, you can register certain events (e.g., keyboard events, mouse events) for which the applet should "listen." For the applet you're creating, you won't need any of these events.

➤ Click **Next**.

Figure 4.10
Events

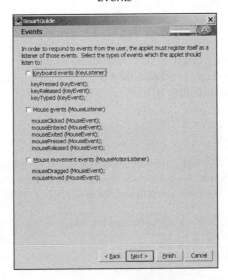

The **Code Writer** window of the **Create Applet** SmartGuide (Figure 4.11) appears next. This window lets you create additional methods, which you won't be using for this applet.

➤ Click **Next**.

Figure 4.11
Code Writer

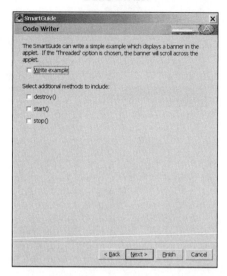

The **Parameters** window of the **Create Applet** SmartGuide (Figure 4.12) appears next. This window lets you pass parameters directly to the applet. You won't be using this window.

➢   Click **Next**.

Figure 4.12
Parameters

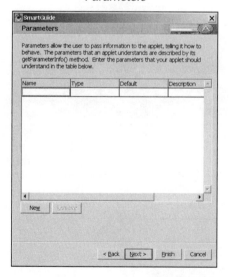

The last window of the **Create Applet** SmartGuide, the **Applet Info** window (Figure 4.13), appears next. Here, you can input information about the applet, primarily for documentation purposes.

➢   Click **Finish**.

Figure 4.13
Applet Info

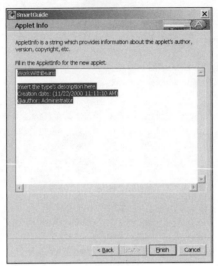

Visual Composition Editor

At this point, the Visual Composition Editor appears. Figure 4.14 shows the VCE. You will probably spend more time here than in any other function associated with the VisualAge for Java IDE. The VCE is where you create the visual aspects of your applet or application, better known as your JavaBeans. The entire graphical user interface is designed inside the VCE. The VCE is also where you identify the connections (or relationships) between one bean and another.

Figure 4.14
Visual Composition Editor

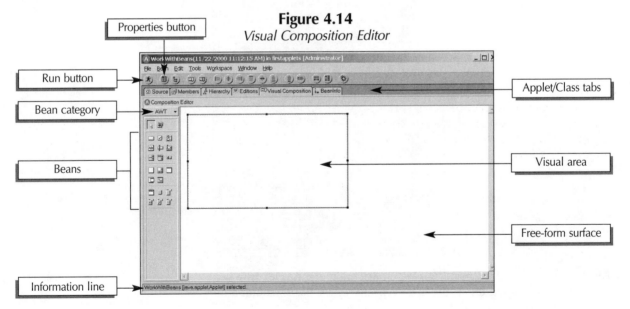

The figure identifies some of the major functions in the VCE. On the left side of the screen, you'll find all the bean categories and their individual beans (more about these in a moment). The *visual area* is the portion of the screen where you design the visual elements of your applet or application. It is considered part of the *free-form surface*, the larger area in which the entire GUI is defined. Beans placed outside the visual area are defined as nonvisual beans, or logic beans. All connections (relationships) between beans are defined in the free-form surface. The GUI definitions can become very large. To increase the size of your free-form surface, use the scroll bars.

The *information line*, shown at the bottom of the screen, displays a selected bean's name and any connections that exist for it. The VCE's *applet/class tabs* let you maneuver among the various functions associated with an applet or class.

Two important toolbar buttons are noted in the figure. The **Run** button automatically runs the applet or application. The **Properties** button displays the **Properties** sheet for a selected bean. Table 4.1 lists the full complement of VCE toolbar buttons and their meanings. As you become more comfortable within the VCE, you'll begin using these buttons more often.

Table 4.1
VCE Toolbar Buttons

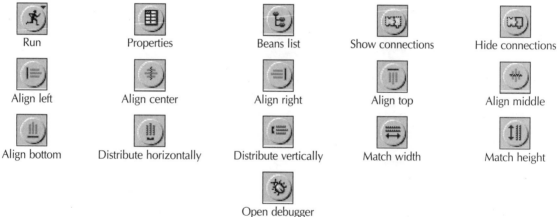

Run	Properties	Beans list	Show connections	Hide connections
Align left	Align center	Align right	Align top	Align middle
Align bottom	Distribute horizontally	Distribute vertically	Match width	Match height
		Open debugger		

VCE Bean Categories

The VCE contains three major bean categories — Abstract Window Toolkit (AWT), Swing, and the AS/400 Toolbox — plus some special bean categories. In the VCE as shown in Figure 4.14, the AWT bean category is currently selected. To change from one bean category to another, you simply click the drop-down arrow on the bean category box and make your selection, as shown in Figure 4.15.

Figure 4.15
Bean Categories

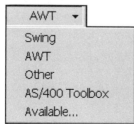

Tips and Tricks

When switching from one bean category to another, you'll notice a considerable wait time. You may think your computer has locked up, but be patient. When you switch to the AS/400 Toolbox beans — the largest category — you may wait as long as a few minutes before you receive control. After the first switch takes place, subsequent switches occur much more quickly.

The following paragraphs provide details about the three major bean categories. You may want to mark these pages to help you easily identify the beans until you become more familiar with them.

Abstract Window Toolkit JavaBeans

The Abstract Window Toolkit is a standard Java package by the name of **java.awt**, more commonly known as AWT. It is made up of various beans, or controls, used to develop attractive graphical interfaces for applets and applications. Table 4.2 shows all the available AWT JavaBeans. AWT is an older technology, implemented using platform-specific versions of the controls, but it is easy to use. Swing, which we discuss next, is becoming the standard for graphical interfaces. In this book, you'll use AWT in your first programming example. The remainder of the book will focus on Swing.

Table 4.2
AWT JavaBeans

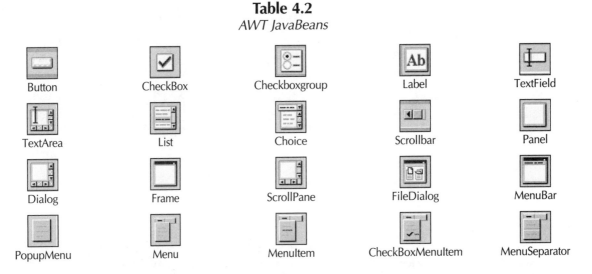

Swing JavaBeans

Sun created the Java Foundation Classes (JFC) to help alleviate some of the limitations encountered with the AWT controls. The JFC includes a set of GUI components called the Swing component set that extends and replaces AWT. The Swing components are completely written in Java but don't rely on platform-specific libraries, as AWT does. With the JFC, you can choose to write programs that have the same look-and-feel on Unix workstations as on PC workstations, or you can change the look-and-feel to match the platform on which the program is running. Table 4.3 lists the Swing JavaBeans.

Table 4.3
Swing JavaBeans

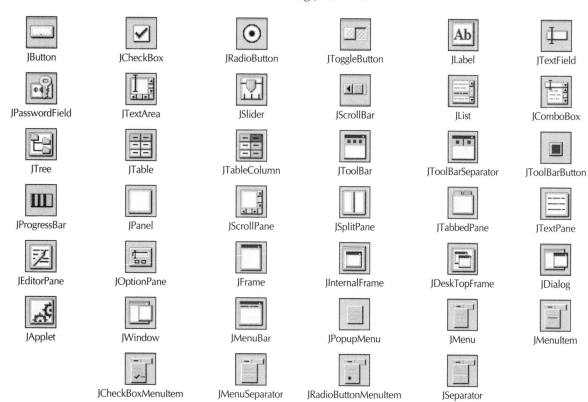

JButton	JCheckBox	JRadioButton	JToggleButton	JLabel	JTextField
JPasswordField	JTextArea	JSlider	JScrollBar	JList	JComboBox
JTree	JTable	JTableColumn	JToolBar	JToolBarSeparator	JToolBarButton
JProgressBar	JPanel	JScrollPane	JSplitPane	JTabbedPane	JTextPane
JEditorPane	JOptionPane	JFrame	JInternalFrame	JDeskTopFrame	JDialog
JApplet	JWindow	JMenuBar	JPopupMenu	JMenu	JMenuItem
	JCheckBoxMenuItem	JMenuSeparator	JRadioButtonMenuItem	JSeparator	

 Tips and Tricks

Don't mix and match AWT beans with Swing beans. (These beans can also be called *components* in pure Javanese.) The AWT controls use the native controls in the operating system. The Swing or Java Foundation Classes (JFC) manage their own rendering. Using both AWT and Swing components together can cause unpredictable runtime results.

Enterprise Toolkit for AS/400 JavaBeans

As most AS/400 developers transition into Java and VisualAge for Java, one of the first questions asked is: "What can be done to access the AS/400 and various objects?" As of this writing, there are 140 AS/400 JavaBeans included in the Enterprise Toolkit for AS/400 for this purpose. The Enterprise Toolkit for AS/400 beans are specific to VisualAge for Java; Table 4.4 lists them. You won't be using these beans until Chapter 5.

Table 4.4
Enterprise Toolkit for AS/400 JavaBeans

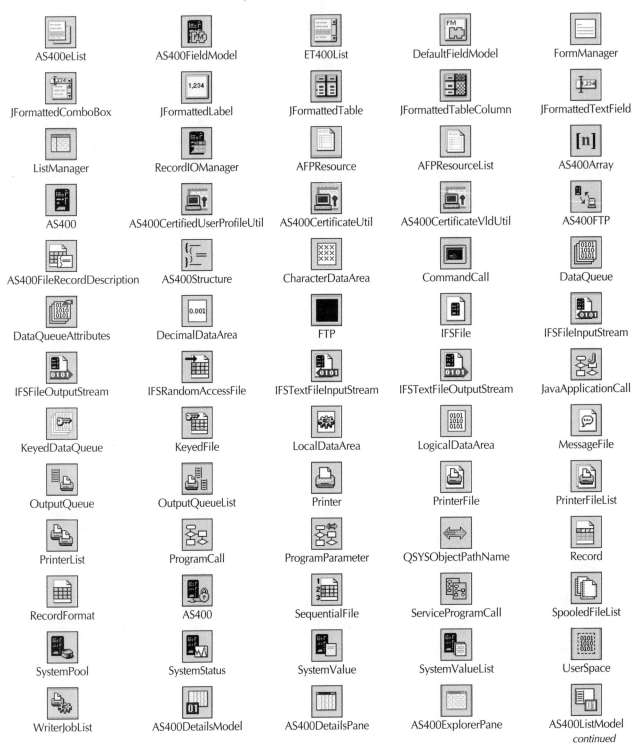

AS400eList	AS400FieldModel	ET400List	DefaultFieldModel	FormManager
JFormattedComboBox	JFormattedLabel	JFormattedTable	JFormattedTableColumn	JFormattedTextField
ListManager	RecordIOManager	AFPResource	AFPResourceList	AS400Array
AS400	AS400CertifiedUserProfileUtil	AS400CertificateUtil	AS400CertificateVldUtil	AS400FTP
AS400FileRecordDescription	AS400Structure	CharacterDataArea	CommandCall	DataQueue
DataQueueAttributes	DecimalDataArea	FTP	IFSFile	IFSFileInputStream
IFSFileOutputStream	IFSRandomAccessFile	IFSTextFileInputStream	IFSTextFileOutputStream	JavaApplicationCall
KeyedDataQueue	KeyedFile	LocalDataArea	LogicalDataArea	MessageFile
OutputQueue	OutputQueueList	Printer	PrinterFile	PrinterFileList
PrinterList	ProgramCall	ProgramParameter	QSYSObjectPathName	Record
RecordFormat	AS400	SequentialFile	ServiceProgramCall	SpooledFileList
SystemPool	SystemStatus	SystemValue	SystemValueList	UserSpace
WriterJobList	AS400DetailsModel	AS400DetailsPane	AS400ExplorerPane	AS400ListModel

continued

Table 4.4 *Continued*

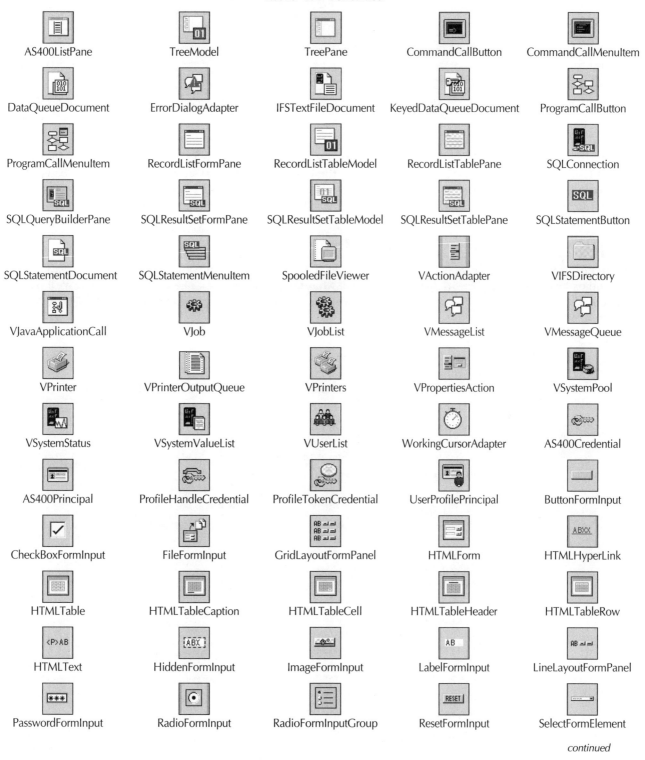

AS400ListPane	TreeModel	TreePane	CommandCallButton	CommandCallMenuItem
DataQueueDocument	ErrorDialogAdapter	IFSTextFileDocument	KeyedDataQueueDocument	ProgramCallButton
ProgramCallMenuItem	RecordListFormPane	RecordListTableModel	RecordListTablePane	SQLConnection
SQLQueryBuilderPane	SQLResultSetFormPane	SQLResultSetTableModel	SQLResultSetTablePane	SQLStatementButton
SQLStatementDocument	SQLStatementMenuItem	SpooledFileViewer	VActionAdapter	VIFSDirectory
VJavaApplicationCall	VJob	VJobList	VMessageList	VMessageQueue
VPrinter	VPrinterOutputQueue	VPrinters	VPropertiesAction	VSystemPool
VSystemStatus	VSystemValueList	VUserList	WorkingCursorAdapter	AS400Credential
AS400Principal	ProfileHandleCredential	ProfileTokenCredential	UserProfilePrincipal	ButtonFormInput
CheckBoxFormInput	FileFormInput	GridLayoutFormPanel	HTMLForm	HTMLHyperLink
HTMLTable	HTMLTableCaption	HTMLTableCell	HTMLTableHeader	HTMLTableRow
HTMLText	HiddenFormInput	ImageFormInput	LabelFormInput	LineLayoutFormPanel
PasswordFormInput	RadioFormInput	RadioFormInputGroup	ResetFormInput	SelectFormElement

continued

Table 4.4 *Continued*

SelectOption   SubmitFormInput   TextAreaFormElement   TextFormInput   ListMetaData

ListRowData   RecordFormatMetaData   RecordListRowData   SQLResultSetMetaData   SQLResultSetRowData

As you'll see later, these 140 AS/400 JavaBeans are also identified in VisualAge for Java as the AS/400 Toolbox. This convention can be confusing because the 140 AS/400 Toolbox beans are *not* the same as the 427 AS/400 Toolbox Java classes that come standard with the OS/400 operating system. In this book, we focus on the VisualAge for Java Enterprise Toolkit for AS/400 JavaBeans and not the 427 AS/400 Toolbox Java classes. If you want to access some of the 427 standard AS/400 Toolbox Java classes, you can do so through the bean categories in VisualAge for Java. For more information about these additional classes, see Appendix A.

Building Your Applet Visually

You are now going to build the visual aspects and connections associated with your applet. You might want to take a quick look back at Figure 4.1 (page 39) to recall what the applet will look like when completed. We'll be using the AWT bean category. If you've changed to Swing or AS/400 Toolbox, switch back to the AWT bean category now.

First, add a button bean to the free-form surface:

➤   Move the pointer over to the bean palette on the left side of the VCE.
➤   Click the **Button** bean ▭ to select it.
➤   When the pointer changes to a crosshair pointer, move it over to the visual area of the free-form surface, and drop the button in the lower portion of the screen with a click. Figure 4.16 shows this placement.

Figure 4.16
Adding a Button

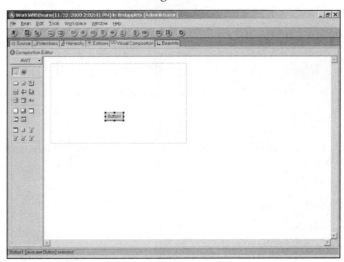

You will now change some of the properties associated with the new button. There are four ways to reach the bean's **Properties** sheet:

- Double-click the new button bean (i.e., the button in the visual area).
- Right-click the button bean, and click **Properties**.
- After selecting the button with a click, click **Tools** on the menu bar, and then click **Properties**.
- After selecting the button with a click, click the **Properties** button 🔲 on the VCE toolbar.

Try all four methods. You'll be using the **Properties** sheet a lot, so find a method you like. This book will use the first method described above, double-clicking the button bean.

➢   Using your preferred method, select the **Properties** sheet for the button bean.

Figure 4.17 shows the **Properties** sheet. The first column identifies each of the bean's properties. You'll make your changes in the second column. Notice the scroll bar. Most of the bean properties have more information available than what you can see in the window; use the scroll bar to maneuver up and down.

Figure 4.17
Button Properties Sheet

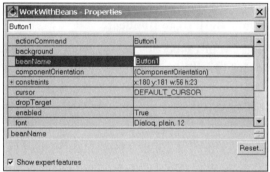

Make the following changes on the button bean's **Properties** sheet.

➢   We'll be using this button to trigger the duplication of the input text in your applet. To give the button a meaningful name, change the value of the **beanName** property from the default, **Button1**, to **btDuplicate**. The **bt** prefix means "button."

➢   Change the **background** color. To do so, click in the background box (right column). When the **Details** button 🔲 appears, click it to choose the color. In the resulting window, select **green** as shown in Figure 4.18. Then click **OK** to return to the **Properties** sheet.

Figure 4.18
Background Color Window

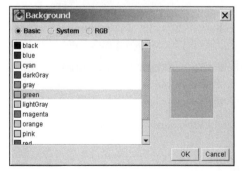

➤   Change the **font**. Click in the font box. When the **Details** button appears, click it to change the font. Select **Serif**, **bold**, and **14** for the font attributes, as shown in Figure 4.19. Click **OK** to return to the **Properties** sheet.

Figure 4.19
Font Window

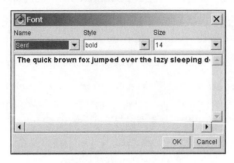

➤   Scroll down to the **label** property. This property specifies the text, or label, that will appear on the face of the button. Change its value from **Button1** to **Duplicate**.

Once you've made all your changes, your **Properties** sheet should look like Figure 4.20. If you were looking at a color version of this window, you'd see that the background box is now green, reflecting your new background color selection.

➤   Close the **Properties** sheet. Doing so will save the changes you've made to the bean's properties.

Figure 4.20
btDuplicate Button Properties Sheet

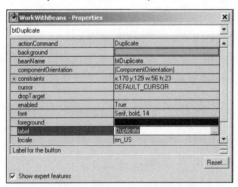

When you return to the VCE screen, you may notice that the color of your button either did or did not change. Certain versions of VisualAge for Java change the color immediately; others do not. If the color didn't change, that's okay. When your applet is executed, you'll see the color change take effect.

➤   Enlarge the size of your button so that you can see the entire button label text ("Duplicate"). Do this by moving the pointer to one of the button's black corners, clicking and holding down the left mouse button, and dragging the corner to enlarge the button.

At this point, the free-form surface should look similar to Figure 4.21.

Figure 4.21
Visual Area with Enlarged Button

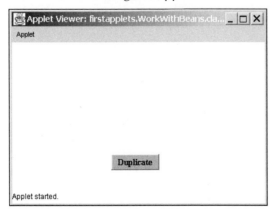

Next, you'll perform a three-part process:

1. Generate and save the Java source code. This code is generated from the work you've done in the VCE.
2. Compile the Java source code into bytecode.
3. Run your applet.

➤ On the menu bar, click **Bean**, and then click **Save Bean**. This option generates and saves your Java source code. It also compiles the Java source code into bytecode.

➤ Click the **Source** tab. This view shows all the Java source code that has been generated so far.

➤ Click the **Visual Composition** tab.

➤ You have two choices for running the applet. Either click the **Run** button 🛠 on the VCE toolbar or click **Bean** on the menu bar, click **Run**, and then click **In Applet Viewer**. Either approach will run your applet in the Applet Viewer as shown in Figure 4.22.

Figure 4.22
Running the Applet

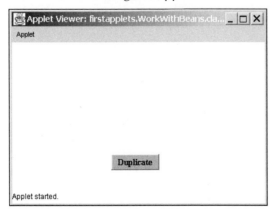

At this point, the applet is not very useful. Nevertheless, pat yourself on the back. You have now created, compiled, and run your first fully working applet. Congratulations!

Now, let's make some changes to the applet.

➤   Close the applet.

You're going to add an input-capable text field and three labels. Figure 4.23 shows the desired alignment of these visual components. Later in the book, you'll learn about some easy ways to align graphical components such as these in the VCE.

First, add an input-capable text field to the visual area of the free-form surface:

➤   Move the pointer to the bean palette on the left side of the screen.
➤   Select the **textField** bean 🖽 with a click.
➤   When the cursor changes to a crosshair pointer, move it over to the free-form area, and click to drop the **textField** bean in the upper-right portion of the visual area.
➤   Lengthen the textField. See Figure 4.23 for the approximate size.
➤   Go to the **Properties** sheet by double-clicking the textField. Change the **beanName** to **tfTextIn**. (The prefix "tf" indicates a text field.)
➤   Close the **Properties** sheet.

Figure 4.23
Alignment of Visual Components

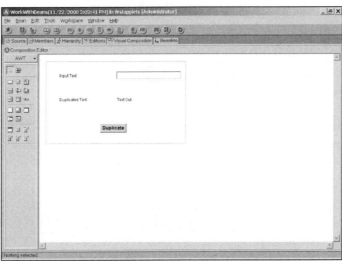

Next, you're going to add a label that will be used to display the output text. At run time, the output text will be overwritten onto the label. Add label 1:

➤   Move the pointer to the bean palette on the left side of the screen.
➤   Select the **label** bean 🔠 with a click.
➤   When the pointer changes to a crosshair pointer, move it to the free-form area, and click to drop the label bean in the middle-right portion of the visual area.
➤   Lengthen the label to match the size of the textField **tfTextIn** (see Figure 4.23).
➤   Double-click the label to display the **Properties** sheet. Change the **beanName** to **lbTextOut**, and change the **text** to **Text Out**.
➤   Close the **Properties** sheet.

Add labels 2 and 3:

➢ Move the pointer to the bean palette on the left side of the screen.

➢ Select the **label** bean with a click.

➢ Drop the label in the upper-left portion of the visual area with a click. Align it horizontally with textField **tfTextIn**.

➢ Go to the **Properties** sheet by double-clicking this label. Change the **text** to **Input Text:**.

➢ In the visual area, lengthen the label so that you can see the entire label text.

➢ Close the **Properties** sheet.

➢ Select another **label** bean, and drop it in the middle-left portion of the visual area. Align this label horizontally with label **lbTextOut**.

➢ Go to the **Properties** sheet by double-clicking this label. Change the **text** to **Duplicated Text:**.

➢ Lengthen the label so you can see the entire label text.

➢ Close the **Properties** sheet.

Run the applet:

➢ On the menu bar, click **Bean**. Click **Run**, and then click **In Applet Viewer**. This choice saves your code, compiles it, and runs it.

➢ Try entering some data into the text field. Then click the **Duplicate** button. Don't expect the button to do anything.

➢ Close the applet.

When you clicked the **Duplicate** button, nothing changed. That's because at this point no instructions exist yet to tell your applet what to do when the button is clicked.

Reviewing Generated Java Source Code

Up to this point, VisualAge for Java has generated a substantial amount of Java source code. Several Java fields and Java methods have been created for you. If you're not familiar with Java methods, a quick review might be helpful.

To review the generated Java source code:

➢ Click the **Source** tab to see all the Java code that has been generated. You'll see a screen similar to the one shown Figure 4.24.

Figure 4.24

Elements and Source of Applet WorkWithBeans

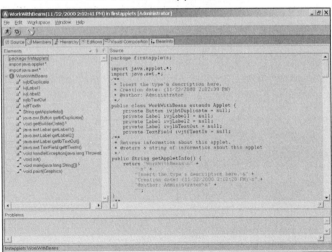

You're looking at two panes of information. The left pane has the title **Elements** in its upper-left corner. This pane lists the elements — the fields and methods — of your applet, **WorkWithBeans**. The right pane, titled **Source**, shows all the Java code that has been generated.

➢ Move the cursor to the **Elements** title bar. Double-click the word **Elements**. The view changes to a single pane.

➢ Double-click **Elements** again. The screen returns to two panes. As you can see, the **Elements** title acts as a toggle switch.

➢ Do the same exercise for the **Source** pane.

Let's view the source code associated with a particular method.

➢ In the **Elements** pane, click the method named **getAppletInfo()**. (Notice that the display lists the method's return type, **String**, along with the method name.) You can tell this is a method because of the uppercase **M** beside it. When you select the method, all the code associated with it appears on the right in the **Source** pane.

Review each of the following methods to look at the code that was generated. The following table briefly summarizes what each method is doing.

Method	Description
getAppletInfo()	Stores documentation about the applet.
getbtDuplicate()	Defines the **Duplicate** button, which you named **btDuplicate**.
getBuilderData()	Created to save off the meta data — the ASCII representation of everything done in the VCE. If you want to retain all the VCE components when importing and exporting with VisualAge for Java, don't edit or delete this method.
getLabel1()	Defines the **Input Text** label. Because you didn't give this label a name, the next available default name was used (**Label1**).
getLabel2()	Defines the **Duplicated Text** label. Because you didn't give this label a name, the next available default name was used (**Label2**).
getlbTextOut()	Defines the **Text Out** label, which you named **lbTextOut**.
gettfTextIn()	Defines the textField that you named **tfTextIn**.
handleException()	Defined to handle exception errors.
init()	Called the first time an applet is loaded.
main()	Begins all Java applications. You may wonder why we have a **main()** method in our applet when we selected No for the applet wizard's option to generate one. VisualAge for Java automatically generates this method for all visual components so that you can test your components in a standalone environment.
paint()	Called each time the applet needs to be displayed.

VisualAge for Java uses some general rules to generate source code. You may have noticed some of these as you reviewed the methods above:

- The prefix "ivj" is appended to variables (fields) used to represent VCE components or beans.
- "Getters" and "setters" are created for VCE components.
- Java **try** and **catch** exception blocks are created.
- Fully qualified names are used for standard Java classes.
- User code areas are created automatically by the insertion of the comment lines **// User code begin** and **// User code end** throughout the code. You'll use these areas later in the book to insert your own Java source code. You should make source code changes only in between these two comment lines, or your code will be lost the next time it is regenerated.

You'll learn other rules as you advance through this book.

Visually Connecting Beans Together

You are now going to add the connections, or relationships, that will take the input data and display it when the **Duplicate** button is clicked. This process will identify the event — the clicking of the button — and the "source" and "target" properties of the connection. This discussion will introduce you to making visual connections, but there's a lot more to learn. Don't worry if the details of what you're doing here aren't perfectly clear. We'll delve deeper into connections in Chapter 5 and throughout the rest of the book.

Identify the event:

➢   Click the **Visual Composition** tab to display the VCE.

➢   Select the **Duplicate** button (**btDuplicate**) with a click.

➢   Right-click to display the shortcut menu. Point to **Connect**, and then click **actionPerformed**. Figure 4.25 shows this option.

Figure 4.25

Defining the Event Connection (Step 1 of 2)

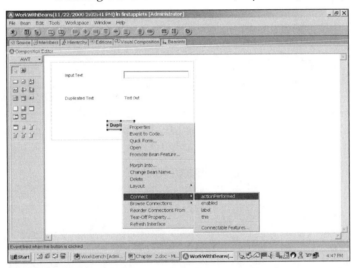

The pointer is transformed into what looks like a spider attached by its web. You'll use this spider pointer to make the connection between the **Duplicate** button and the output field.

➢   Take the spider end of the line, and drop it on top of the label field **Text Out** (named **lbTextOut**) with a click.

You may have noticed something. As you moved the spider over the component objects in the VCE, they received *focus*, indicating a component about to be selected. When you selected the component, a new menu, shown in Figure 4.26, automatically appeared.

Figure 4.26
Defining the Event Connection (Step 2 of 2)

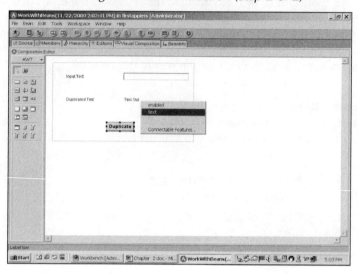

➢   Select the **text** option.

A dashed green line will appear, connecting the **Duplicate** button to the **Text Out** field, as shown in Figure 4.27. The dashed line signifies that the connection is *not* complete. To complete the connection, you will pass a value, or parameter, into it.

Figure 4.27
Incomplete Connection

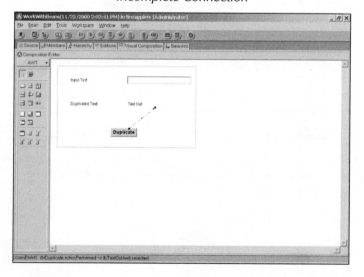

First, identify the source property:

➢   Move the pointer so that its tip is directly over the dashed line. Right-click to display the shortcut menu. Select **Connect**, and then select **value**.

Next, identify the target property:

➢   Take the spider end of the line and drop it on top of the textField named **tfTextIn** (the text input field). From the menu that automatically appears, select **text** to complete the connection.

When the connection is completed, it should appear as shown in Figure 4.28. Look at the information line in the lower-left corner of the screen in the figure. The connection number and its source and target information are now displayed here. It reads

```
connPfromP1: (connEtoM1: (btDuplicate,actionPerformed → lbTextOut,text),value → tfTextIn,text)
```

Figure 4.28
Connection Completed

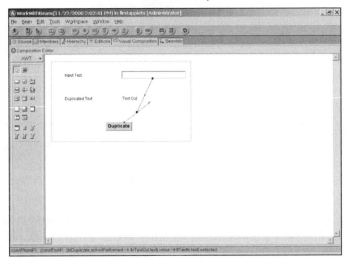

Now, run the applet:

➢   On the menu bar, click **Bean**. Click **Run**, and then click **In Applet Viewer** to save, compile, and run your code.
➢   Try entering some data into the text field. Then click the **Duplicate** button. It should work now. Whatever data you enter into the text input field will be duplicated onto the lower label when you click the button, as Figure 4.29 shows.
➢   Close the applet.

Figure 4.29
WorkWithBeans Applet

You have now completed your first Java applet. Not bad, considering you didn't write a single line of code to do this. That will change as you get into more complex applications.

Review the Java source code generated by your latest modifications:

➤ Click the **Source** tab to see all the Java code that has been generated.

You now have one additional class and three additional methods. Here's a brief summary of each:

Class or method	Description
IvjEventHandler	This class is an inner class generated to handle all the applet's events. It contains one method called **actionPerformed**(). In the method, only one event is identified: the clicking of the **Duplicate** button. When this event occurs, the **connEtoM1**() method is executed.
actionPerformed()	This method identifies the clicking of the **Duplicate** button. When this event occurs, the **connEtoM1**() method is executed.
initConnections()	This method registers the event.
connEtoM1()	This method gets the text from the input field and sets the text in the output field.

By now, I hope you've seen some of the advantages of naming your various beans. This practice makes it much easier to follow the generated Java source code.

Review VCE Connections

Let's review the details of the connections you've just created. First, look at the details of the first connection, the event definition:

➤ Click the **Visual Composition** tab.
➤ Move the pointer so its tip is on the green line representing the event connection. Double-click this connection.

As Figure 4.30 shows, you're looking at the details of an *event-to-method* connection. This connection is defined as an **actionPerformed** event that calls a **text** method. In other words, when the **Duplicate** button is clicked (the event), a call to method **connEtoM1** is executed.

Figure 4.30
Event-to-Method Connection

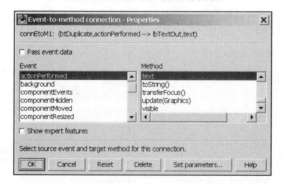

Look at the details for the second connection, the source and target properties definition:

➤ Click **Cancel**.
➤ Move the pointer so its tip is on the purple line representing the source/target connection. Double-click the connection.

As Figure 4.31 shows, you're looking at the details of a *parameter-from-property* connection. The source property **value** and the target property **text** are both defined. In other words, calls to standard Java methods **getText()** and **setText()** are executed.

Figure 4.31
Parameter-from-Property Connection

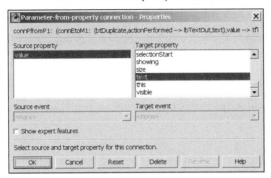

Close the Visual Composition Editor, and return to the workbench.

➢   Click **Cancel**.
➢   Close the VCE.

Your workbench should now look similar to Figure 4.32. Your newly created applet, **WorkWithBeans**, appears under project **My Introduction Projects**, package **firstapplets** in the tree view.

Figure 4.32
Workbench

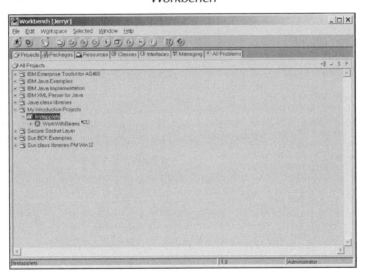

Summary

At this point, you probably have mixed emotions. You feel good that you've been able to create an applet, but there are so many questions and topics you're unsure about. The whole connections topic is probably a little fuzzy. Relax, that's normal. We've only scratched the surface. In this chapter you

- learned how to create a project, a package, and an applet
- became familiar with some of the basics of the Visual Composition Editor
- used various visual components, or JavaBeans
- changed bean properties
- made some visual connections
- Saved, compiled, and executed an applet

Now that you have your feet wet, you're ready to start learning more about VisualAge for Java.

Chapter 5

Building a "View" Bean:
Loan Payment

 ## Chapter Objectives

- ☐ Understand the Model-View-Controller design
- ☐ Become familiar with Java Swing GUI beans
- ☐ Understand connections and connection types
- ☐ Be introduced to the Enterprise Toolkit for AS/400
- ☐ Learn to morph to AS/400 JavaBeans
- ☐ Learn to set edit checks for input data
- ☐ Understand layout managers
- ☐ Use panels

 ## Chapter Project

- ☐ A JApplet will be created to build the "View" portion of a loan payment calculation application.
- ☐ JFormattedTextFields with edits will allow the entry of loan information.
- ☐ A **Clear** button will execute logic to clear/initialize all the JTextFields.
- ☐ Figure 5.1 shows what the sample JApplet will look like.

Figure 5.1
Chapter Project

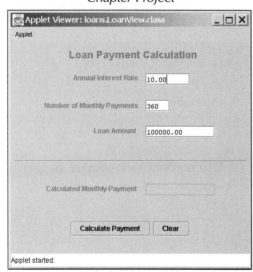

In 1970, a group of Smalltalk developers introduced a new concept called the Model-View-Controller (MVC) design paradigm. The underlying intent of this new concept was to separate the presentation of data from the data model itself. Three distinct design parts accomplished this separation:

- Model — the data associated with the application shared with the business logic that defines access and manipulation of the data
- View — the presentation of the model's data. This is how you see the component on the screen.
- Controller — the ability to gather user input from the View and then update the Model or notify the View about changes to the Model. This is how your component reacts to events such as mouse clicks, keyboard events, and so on.

You may be thinking, isn't this the same concept the AS/400 is built on? In the most simplistic terms, you could answer this question with a yes. From a very simplistic view, you could think of an AS/400 display file as the View, the RPG program and the AS/400 database as the Model, and the F6 (Update) key on the display file as the Controller. However, in a truly object-oriented design environment, you'd have to answer no.

A better example of the MVC would be an application that displays a table of database information on the screen (View). The table has a scroll bar attached to it to control the loading of the table (Controller), which comes from the application or logic that is accessing the database (Model). Sometimes the View and the Controller are combined together to make implementation of the application easier. A combined View and Controller is known as a *delegate* (Sun uses this term to describe the Swing GUI components). In our example, it makes sense to combine the View (table) with the Controller (scroll bar).

Some of the benefits of AS/400 externally described display files also apply to the Model-View-Controller design. The MVC design and VisualAge for Java let you separate the GUI from the business logic of your application, making it easy to change one without impacting the other. You can also have specialist programmers working on the business logic portion of the application and other graphical programmers working on the graphical-interface portion of the application.

This chapter and the next one will help you understand some basics associated with the Model-View-Controller design. In this chapter, you'll implement a view bean. Chapter 6 will introduce you to a logic bean, which can be one part of the Model.

LoanView Bean Setup

Chapters 5 and 6 work together to produce a program that calculates a loan payment. In this chapter, you'll get your first exposure to some JavaBeans from the AS/400 Toolbox. You won't actually log on to the AS/400 until Chapter 8.

Create a Package

To begin, you're going to create a new package named **loans**. Your work in Chapters 5 and 6 will be stored in this newly created package.

➢ If the workbench is not started, start it now.
➢ From the workbench, select the project **My Introduction Projects** with a click. Right-click to display the shortcut menu, select **Add**, and then select **Package**.
➢ Make sure the **Project** name is **My Introduction Projects**.
➢ Make sure the **Create a new package named** option is selected. Then type **loans** into the space provided.
➢ Click **Finish** to complete the creation of the package.

Once the package is created, you'll see it listed in the workbench **All Projects** pane below **My Introduction Projects**, as shown in Figure 5.2.

Figure 5.2
Workbench Setup for Chapter 5

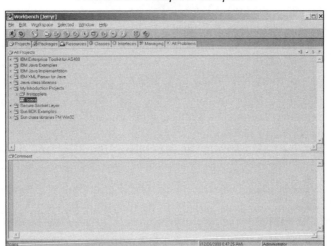

Create a JApplet

In Chapter 4, you created an applet. As you may recall, an applet is a special type of a class that is designed to run inside a browser. When you create an applet, you can specify the superclass you're using. When you created the applet in Chapter 4, you specified a superclass of **Applet**, which by default uses the Abstract Window Toolkit (AWT) bean category. In this chapter, you're going to define your applet with a superclass of **JApplet**, which by default uses the Swing GUI component set. You'll learn more about superclasses in Chapter 8.

➢   From the workbench, select the **loans** package with a click. Right-click to display the shortcut menu, select **Add**, and then select **Applet**. Figure 5.3 shows the **Create Applet** SmartGuide.

Figure 5.3
Create Applet LoanView

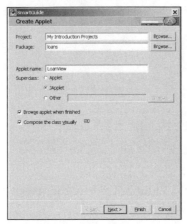

➢   Make sure the **Project** name is **My Introduction Projects**.
➢   Make sure the **Package** name is **loans**.
➢   For **Applet name**, type **LoanView**.

➤ Select the superclass **JApplet**.
➤ Select the **Browse applet when finished** check box.
➤ Select the **Compose the class visually** check box.
➤ Click **Finish** to complete the creation of the applet.

Field Creation

You should now be in the Visual Composition Editor of applet **LoanView**. Notice which bean category appears on the left side of the VCE. It is the Swing bean category. As you design your applet, you may notice that the Swing graphical components look a bit different from the AWT components you used in Chapter 4. They are very different! They also have a different look.

First, you're going to expand the visual area in the free-form surface. Figure 5.4 shows what the resized visual area should look like.

➤ On the menu bar, click **Tools**. Then click the **Beans List** menu item. The **Beans List**, shown on the right in the figure, is displayed.
➤ In the **Beans List**, click **LoanView** to select the entire visual area of the **LoanView** applet.
➤ Drag the bottom-center point of the visual area down so that the visual area expands to look like the figure.
➤ Close the **Beans List**.
➤ Click in the *nonvisual* free-form surface to release the selection.

Figure 5.4
Resized Visual Area

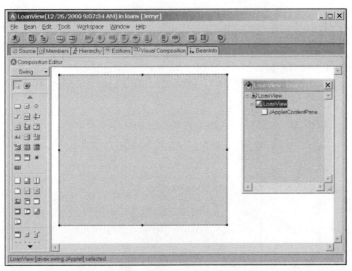

You're now going to create four text fields (JTextFields) for the applet. Figure 5.5 shows what the fields will look like when you're finished.

➤ Move the pointer to the bean palette on the left side of the screen.
➤ Select a **JTextField** bean ⊞ with a click.
➤ When the pointer changes to a crosshair pointer, move it to the free-form area and drop the **JTextField** bean in the upper-right portion of the visual area. Drop it with a click.
➤ Select and place three more **JTextField** beans.
➤ Expand each JTextField to the approximate size shown in the figure.

Figure 5.5
Four Aligned JTextFields

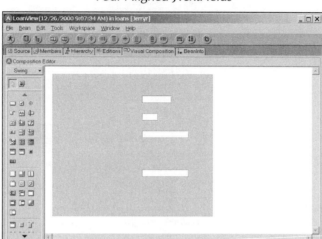

Tips and Tricks

There's an easy way to copy a component in the VCE: In the visual area, simply click the component you want to copy, and then hold down the Ctrl key and drag the component where you want it. Doing so makes a duplicate of the component. You can also use the normal Windows Clipboard copy/paste features to copy a component as well as to copy JavaBeans from one VCE window to another.

Next, left-align the four JTextFields. There's an easy way to do this:

➢   Click the top JTextField.
➢   Hold the Shift key, and click the next JTextField.
➢   Continue holding the Shift key, and click the remaining two JTextFields.
➢   With your pointer on one of the selected JTextFields, right-click to display the shortcut menu. Select **Layout**, then select **Align**, and then click **Left**.

Notice that the **Align** option provides six different reference points: left, right, center, top, middle, and bottom. You may also notice the **Match Size** option and its three choices: width, height, and both. As you can see, the **Layout** option is a powerful aid for lining up components on the screen. Table 5.1 (repeated from Chapter 4) shows that most of the VCE toolbar functions are associated with the **Layout** option.

Tips and Tricks

When using the *Layout* option, your base component is determined by the component on which the pointer is positioned when you right-click. For example, if you're trying to match the size of a group of components, make sure the pointer is on the component to which all the other components will be matched when you right-click.

Table 5.1
VCE Toolbar Buttons

Run   Properties   Beanslist   Showconnections   Hideconnections

Alignleft   Aligncenter   Alignright   Aligntop   Alignmiddle

Alignbottom   Distributehorizontally   Distributevertically   Matchwidth   Matchheight

Opendebugger

Now, set the properties of the JTextFields:

➤   Double-click the first JTextField to display its **Properties** sheet.

➤   Change the **beanName** to **tfAnnualInterestRate**, as shown in Figure 5.6.

➤   Close the **Properties** sheet.

➤   In top-down order, change the **beanName** on each of the other JTextFields to **tfNumberOfPayments**, **tfLoanAmount**, and **tfMonthlyPayment**, respectively.

➤   On the last JTextField, **tfMonthlyPayment**, also change the **editable** property to **False**, as shown in Figure 5.7. You don't need to allow editing of this field because you'll be calculating the loan monthly payment.

➤   Close the **Properties** sheet.

Figure 5.6
Changing the beanName Property

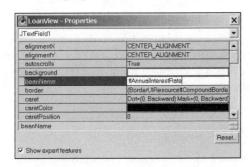

Figure 5.7
Changing the editable Property

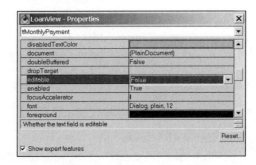

When you return to the VCE, you should notice that the loan monthly payment JTextField now appears as uneditable (i.e., unavailable for user input). You've accomplished the equivalent of using the AS/400 DDS protect keyword DSPATR(PR).

Tips and Tricks

Often, you'll need to change the same property on multiple beans. You can do so easily by *not* closing the *Properties* sheet and instead just clicking the next component. The *Properties* sheet will be refreshed with that component's properties. Then, change the property. You can also change properties for more than one component at once. To do so, select the components, go to the *Properties* sheet, and then change all the common properties. Uncommon properties, such as the bean name, are protected from being changed.

Next, add five labels to the screen as shown in Figure 5.8.

➢ Click the **JLabel** bean ![Ab], and drop it on the visual area of the free-form surface.
➢ Select and place four more **JLabel** beans.
➢ In top-down order, change the **text** property on each JLabel to **Loan Payment Calculation**, **Annual Interest Rate**, **Number of Monthly Payments**, **Loan Amount**, and **Calculated Monthly Payment**, respectively.
➢ Expand each JLabel so that all the label text appears.
➢ On the title label — **Loan Payment Calculation** — change the **font** property to **18** and **bold**.

Figure 5.8
JLabels Added

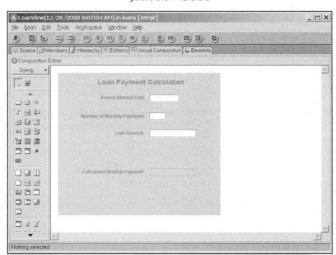

Align each of the four JLabels, as shown in the figure.

➢ Click one of the JLabels. Drag it near its associated JTextField.
➢ Hold the Shift key, and click the other three JLabels.
➢ Place your pointer on the already-aligned JLabel, and right-click to display the shortcut menu. Select **Layout**, then select **Align**, and then click **Right**.

Next, add a separator bar to distinguish the input fields from the output field.

➢ Click the **JSeparator** bean ![], and drop it on the visual area of the free-form surface. The **JSeparator** bean is the very last bean in the Swing category.
➢ Figure 5.9 shows the JSeparator on the screen. When you first drop the **JSeparator** bean, it appears as a box. You're only concerned about the top of the box. Widen the box, and move its top edge to the position where you want the separator bar to appear.
➢ Click in the nonvisual free-form surface to make the JSeparator box disappear, leaving only the separator.

Figure 5.9

JSeparator

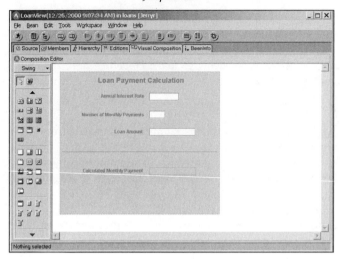

Save and run your Java applet:

➤ On the VCE menu bar, click **Bean** to display the **Bean** menu.
➤ Click **Run**, and then click **In Applet Viewer**.

Tips and Tricks

What happens if you don't see your applet when you run it? If you expanded the size of the applet in the VCE (as you did in this chapter), you may have to change a *Code generation* option before running the applet. To do so:

➤ On the VCE menu bar, click *Bean*.
➤ Click *Code Generation Options*.
➤ Click the *Applet* tab.
➤ Change the width or height attribute to match the layout of the visual area more closely. You may need to add 200 units, or pixels, to both the width and height attributes until the applet appears.
➤ Click *OK*.

At this point, the applet isn't very functional. You'll add more functionality to it over the next few sections of this chapter.

Connections

In Chapter 4, you created your first few connections. In this section, you'll learn more about the various connection types that are specific to VisualAge for Java. Don't breeze through this section too quickly — connections can be one of the hardest concepts to understand and implement in the VCE. You won't be a connections expert after reading this section. This discussion is simply meant to give you an overview of the various types of connections and what they do. As you proceed through the book, you'll be exposed to many different examples.

Each type of connection has a source (starting point) and a target (ending point). The way you draw the connection determines the source and the target. If you're using an event connection, the event is always the source. The primary connection types are

- *Property-to-property* — A property-to-property connection links two property values together. A property is basically a class variable (we discuss properties further in Chapter 6). You have already used properties in the **Properties** sheets. In a property-to-property connection, a change in either property can signal an event to the other property. Be careful using this type of connection because it can signal an event in either direction. You can also use property-to-property connections to initialize a JavaBean's property to the value of another property in the same or another bean. In the VCE, this type of connection is identified as a blue line and has the default name **connPtoP1**.

- *Event-to-method* — When an event occurs, the associated method is called. In Chapter 4, you used an event-to-method connection to duplicate the entered text into another text field. You identified the **Duplicate** button as the event source. In the next section, you'll create an event-to-method connection to accomplish the same thing as the DDS Position Cursor function. In the VCE, an event-to-method connection is identified as a green line and has the default name **connEtoM1**.

- *Event-to-property* — When an event occurs, the associated set method of the property is called. If the property doesn't have a public set method, you can't make the connection. In the VCE, this connection type is identified as a green line and has the default name **connEtoP1**.

- *Event-to-code* — When an event occurs, the associated method is called. The called method is a class method that contains additional Java code to be executed. This connection type provides a good way to gain access to needed references at the class level. For example, say you designed a menu system and had a common **About** menu item. You might use an event-to-code connection to display the **About** screen. The event would be the **actionPerformed** of the **About** menu item being selected. The code would be the call to a method called **showAboutBox()**. You'll set up an event-to-code connection later in this chapter. In the VCE, this connection type is identified as a green line and has the default name **connEtoC1**.

To complete a connection, you often need to make two connections. You saw an example of this in Chapter 4. In the VCE, a dashed line indicates that a secondary connection is required. This situation occurs when a connection needs an input value to be passed to the target. You can pass either a value from a property or a return value from a method. The original or primary connection is always the source of the connection. In Chapter 4, you set up a secondary connection to pass the text value from the source property to the target method. This secondary connection was a *parameter-from-property* connection named **connPFromP1**. In the VCE, a secondary connection is identified as a violet line.

Tips and Tricks

VisualAge for Java helps protect you from making an incorrect type of connection. It doesn't make the connection for you, but once you start down a connection path, it permits you to make only valid connection types.

Showing Focus: Java's DDS Position Cursor

When you executed your first applet, did you notice that there was no pointer in any of the input fields? To begin typing a number, you had to either use the Tab key or click in the input field. In AS/400 display file DDS, you can use the position cursor keyword DSPATR(PC) to determine the field in which data entry begins. You're now going to accomplish the same function in Java using the **requestFocus()** method.

When an applet is first loaded into a browser, the **init()** method is executed and then sends an **init()** event. You are going to add a visual connection to identify which input field receives this initial focus from the **init()** event.

Tips and Tricks

Throughout the rest of the book, each connection discussion will identify the connection specifications. For example:

`connEtoM1: (LoanView,init() → tfAnnualInterestRate,requestFocus())`

You can view these specifications on the information line at the bottom of the VCE and also at the top of the connection's *Properties* window. This ability comes in handy when you're trying to determine how a connection is set up.

Event-to-Method Connection: requestFocus()

`connEtoM1: (LoanView,init() → tfAnnualInterestRate,requestFocus())`

Identify the event:

➢ In the VCE, right-click in the *nonvisual area* of the free-form surface.
➢ Click **Connect**.
➢ Click **Connectible Features**. The **Start Connection from** window (Figure 5.10) appears.
➢ As shown in the figure, double-click the **init()** method. The pointer changes to a spider-end pointer.

Figure 5.10
Selection of init() Event

Tips and Tricks

You may be trying to find a JavaBean feature that you know exists but which you can't find. The JavaBean features are often considered expert features. You'll see the expert features only when the *Show expert features* check box, available on many of the VisualAge for Java windows, is selected. You can see this option in Figure 5.10.

Identify the method:

➢ Click the spider-end pointer on the **tfAnnualInterestRate** JTextField.
➢ Click **Connectible Features**. The **End Connection to** window (Figure 5.11) appears.
➢ As shown in the figure, double-click the **requestFocus()** method.

➢   In the VCE, double-click the connection to verify that it is correct, as shown in Figure 5.12.

➢   Close the connection's **Properties** window.

Figure 5.11

Selection of requestfocus() Method

Figure 5.12

Connection connEtoM1

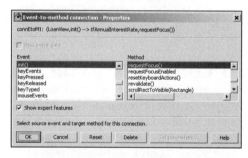

When the connection is completed, it should appear as shown in Figure 5.13. The visual connection shows that focus (Position Cursor) occurs in the **tfAnnualInterestRate** field when the applet is first loaded. You could have accomplished the same task by directly adding the Java statement

```
gettfAnnualInterestRate().requestFocus();
```

to the applet's **init()** method. However, making the connection visually, as opposed to adding a line of code, makes it much easier to identify where the focus begins, and it also makes the connection much easier to change.

Figure 5.13
Initial Focus Established

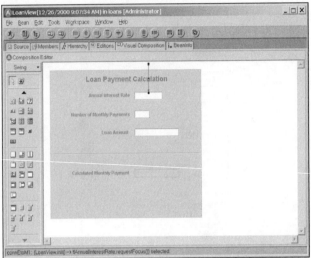

Save and run your applet:

➢   On the menu bar, click **Bean**.
➢   Click **Run**, and then click **In Applet Viewer**.

Notice that when the applet first appears, the pointer is positioned in the first input-capable field.

➢   Close the applet.

Morphing to AS/400 Edit Codes/Edit Words

You may have noticed that it's perfectly acceptable to enter alphanumeric characters into a JTextField. The JTextField, as its name implies, is based on strings, or text input. Java provides different approaches for limiting and editing input-capable fields. Contained within the Enterprise Toolkit for AS/400 are certain JavaBeans used to emulate many of the everyday AS/400 editing functions with which you're already familiar. You can incorporate AS/400 display attributes, keying options, validity checks, and editing keyword functions into your Java programs by using the Enterprise Toolkit for AS/400 JavaBeans. Accessing AS/400 JavaBeans is as easy as switching to the AS/400 Toolbox bean category in the VCE and using its beans as you would any other JavaBean. One of those AS/400 Toolbox beans is the **JFormattedTextField** bean. You'll be using this bean to emulate many AS/400 editing functions.

Within the VCE, an operation exists to let you change the class, or type, of component without having to significantly rework your connection settings. This operation is known as *bean morphing*. Bean morphing lets you preserve common property settings between two beans and also use the new property settings with the morphed bean.

You're going to replace each of your applet's Swing JTextFields with an AS/400 Toolbox JFormattedTextField by way of a morphing function. Doing so is easy. What you gain by making this change is the ability to retain all the JTextField properties while picking up all the additional properties associated with the **JFormattedTextField** bean.

➢   In the VCE, right-click JTextField **tfAnnualInterestRate**.
➢   On the shortcut menu, click **Morph Into**.

➤ The **Morph Into** window (Figure 5.14) appears. To choose a class name, click **Browse**.

Figure 5.14
Morph Into Window

➤ The **Choose a valid class** window (Figure 5.15) appears. In the **Pattern** field, begin typing **JFormattedTextField**. As you type, different matching combinations of classes will appear in the **Class Names** list. Continue typing until you see "JFormattedTextField" as shown in Figure 5.16.
➤ Click **JFormattedTextField**.
➤ Click **OK**.
➤ The updated Morph Into window reappears, showing the newly selected JFormattedTextField entered in the **Class name** field (Figure 5.17). Click **OK**.

<table>
<tr>
<td align="center">

Figure 5.15
Choose a Valid Class Window

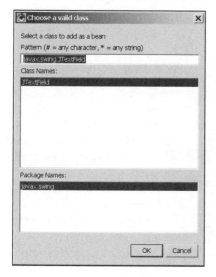

</td>
<td align="center">

Figure 5.16
Selected JFormattedTextField

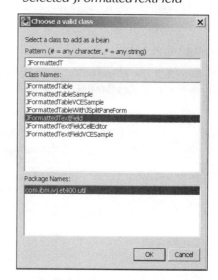

</td>
</tr>
</table>

Figure 5.17

Morph Into Window with Newly Selected JFormattedTextField

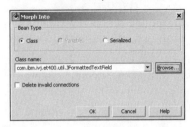

➢   Use the same procedure to morph **tfNumberOfPayments**, **tfLoanAmount**, and **tfMonthlyPayment** from JTextFields to JFormattedTextFields.

➢   Then, on the menu bar, click **Bean** to display the **Bean** menu.

➢   Click **Save Bean**.

You probably noticed that nothing looks different in the VCE. But if you examine the **Properties** sheet on any of the fields you just changed, you'll see a few more properties present. One is the **fieldModel** property. You're now going to use this property to add various edit and keying options for the different fields.

Edit and Keying Options: tfAnnualInterestRate

First, you're going to change the **tfAnnualInterestRate** JFormattedTextField to incorporate the following:

- a numeric field with a length of 6 and four decimal places
- a range of 0.00 to 24.00 percent interest
- a field initialized to 10.00 percent
- error messages displayed in reverse-image red with a beep

To implement these changes:

➢   Double-click the **tfAnnualInterestRate** JFormattedTextField to display the **Properties** sheet. Figure 5.18 shows the new **fieldModel** property.

Figure 5.18

JFormattedTextField Properties Sheet

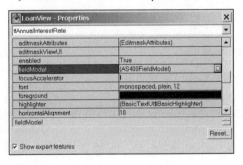

Set the data attributes:

➤ Click the property value **(AS400FieldModel)**. The **Details** button 🔲 appears. Click the button. The **FieldModel Implementor** window (Figure 5.19) appears.

➤ In the Property column, click **dataAttributes**. Click the **Details** button. The **Attributes Implementor** window (Figure 5.20) appears.

➤ Change **dataLength** to **6**, **dataType** to **Numeric**, and **decimalPlaces** to **4**. Figure 5.21 shows these changes. For future reference, notice that **errorBeep** is **True** and **reverseImageColor** is **Red** in this window.

➤ Click **OK**.

Figure 5.19
FieldModel Implementor

Figure 5.20
Attributes Implementor

Figure 5.21
Attribute Changes

Set the valid range of values:

➤ In the **FieldModel Implementor** window, click **validator**. The **Details** button appears. Click the button. The **Validator Implementor** window (Figure 5.22) appears.

➤ Change **maximumRange** to **24.00**, **minimumRange** to **0.00**, and **validityCheckType** to **Range**. Figure 5.23 shows these changes.

➤ Click **OK**.

➤ Click **OK**.

Figure 5.22
Validator Implementor

Figure 5.23
Validator Changes

Tips and Tricks

When changing *dataAttributes*, *validator*, and *formatter* (used later in this chapter) properties, make sure you click *OK* on every window you exit. If you make changes to any of these values and don't click *OK* on the *FieldModel Implementor* window, you'll lose the changes you made in any of the subordinate windows.

Initialize the field:

➢   On the **Properties** sheet for **tfAnnualInterestRate**, change the **text** property to **10.00**, as shown in Figure 5.24, to initialize the JFormattedTextField when it appears on the screen.
➢   Close the **Properties** sheet.
➢   On the menu bar, click **Bean**.
➢   Click **Save Bean**.

Figure 5.24
Initialization of text Property on Properties Sheet

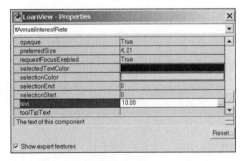

Edit and Keying Options: tfNumberOfPayments

Next, you're going to change the **tfNumberOfPayments** JFormattedTextField to incorporate the following:

- a numeric field with a length of 3 and zero decimal places
- a range of 1 to 480 months
- a field initialized to 360 months
- error messages displayed in reverse-image red with a beep

To implement these changes:

➤ Double-click the **tfNumberOfPayments** JFormattedTextField to display the **Properties** sheet.
➤ Click **(AS400FieldModel)**. The **Details** button appears. Click the button.
➤ Click **dataAttributes**. Click the **Details** button. The **Attributes Implementor** window appears.
➤ Change **dataLength** to **3**, **dataType** to **Numeric**, and **decimalPlaces** to **0**.
➤ Click **OK**.
➤ Click **validator**. The **Details** button appears. Click the button. The **Validator Implementor** window appears.
➤ Change **maximumRange** to **480**, **minimumRange** to **1**, and **validityCheckType** to **Range**.
➤ Click **OK**.
➤ Click **OK**.
➤ On the **Properties** sheet, change the **text** property to **360**.
➤ Close the **Properties** sheet.
➤ On the menu bar, click **Bean**.
➤ Click **Save Bean**.

Edit and Keying Options: tfLoanAmount

Next, you're going to change the **tfLoanAmount** JFormattedTextField to incorporate the following:

- a numeric field with a length of 9 and two decimal places
- a range of 0.00 to 9,999,999.00 dollars
- a field initialized to 100,000.00 dollars
- error messages displayed in reverse-image red with a beep

To implement these changes:

➤ Double-click the **tfLoanAmount** JFormattedTextField to display the **Properties** sheet.
➤ Click **(AS400FieldModel)**. The **Details** button appears. Click the button.
➤ Click **dataAttributes**. Click the **Details** button. The **Attributes Implementor** window appears.
➤ Change **dataLength** to **9**, **dataType** to **Numeric**, and **decimalPlaces** to **2**.
➤ Click **OK**.
➤ Click **validator**. The **Details** button appears. Click the button. The **Validator Implementor** window appears.
➤ Change **maximumRange** to **9999999.00**, **minimumRange** to **0.00**, and **validityCheckType** to **Range**.
➤ Click **OK**.
➤ Click **OK**.
➤ On the **Properties** sheet, change the **text** property to **100000.00**.
➤ Close the **Properties** sheet.
➤ On the menu bar, click **Bean**.
➤ Click **Save Bean**.

Edit and Keying Options: tfMonthlyPayment

Next, you're going to change the **tfMonthlyPayment** JFormattedTextField to incorporate the following:

- a numeric field with a length of 9 and two decimal places
- a 1 edit code associated with the input field to print a dollar sign, a comma, and a decimal point. Yes, this is the same as an AS/400 EDTCDE(1).

To implement these changes:

➤ Double-click the **tfMonthlyPayment** JFormattedTextField to display the **Properties** sheet.

➤ Click **(AS400FieldModel)**. The **Details** button appears. Click the button. The **FieldModel Implementor** window appears.

➤ Click **dataAttributes**. The **Details** button appears. Click the button. The **Attributes Implementor** window appears.

➤ Change **dataLength** to **9**, **dataType** to **Numeric**, and **decimalPlaces** to **2**.

➤ Click **OK**.

➤ Click **formatter**. The **Details** button appears. Click the button. The **Formatter Implementor** window (Figure 5.25) appears.

➤ Click **editCode**. The **Details** button appears. Click the button. The **EditCode** window (Figure 5.26) appears.

➤ In the **Edit Code** list, select **1**, as shown in Figure 5.27.

➤ Click **OK**.

Figure 5.25
Formatter Implementor

Figure 5.26
EditCode

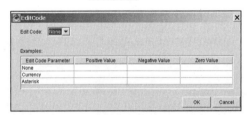

Figure 5.27
EditCode 1 Selected

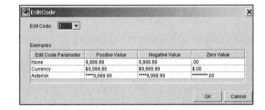

➤ Back in the **Formatter Implementor** window, click **editCodeParmType**. The **Details** button appears. Click the button.

➤ In the **editCodeParmType** list, select the **Currency** option.

➤ Click **OK**.

➤ Click **OK**.

➤ Close the **Properties** sheet.

➤ On the menu bar, click **Bean**.

➤ Click **Save Bean**.

At this point, your VCE should look similar to Figure 5.28.

Figure 5.28
Completed Edits

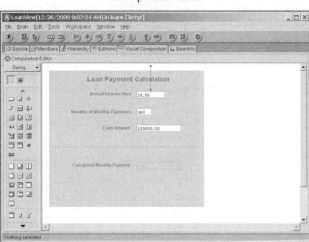

Go ahead and run your applet now.

➢   On the menu bar, click **Bean**.
➢   Click **Run**, and then click **In Applet Viewer**.

Test some of the input fields with the different edit checks you just set up.

➢   Try typing **25.00** in the **tfAnnualInterestRate** JFormattedTextField.
➢   Try typing more than three digits in the **tfNumberOfMonthlyPayments** JFormattedTextField.

Your next task is to add some JButtons to be able to calculate the monthly payment and to clear the input fields. Before you add the JButtons, you're going to gain some exposure to some different *Layout Managers*. You'll use a new Layout Manager to add the JButtons.

Layout Managers

In Chapter 4 when you built your first applet, and then again in this chapter when you built your JApplet, you didn't define a Layout Manager. In actuality, both of these examples used a *null* Layout Manager by default. Layout Managers are part of the Java language and are supported by VisualAge for Java.

Using a null Layout Manager is probably the easiest way to go. This type of Layout Manager uses fixed pixel coordinates to position each of the components, whether in an applet or in an application. Depending on the many different browsers and screen resolutions, your Java program may appear differently when it runs.

What looks appealing in screen design on the developer's machine may be quite different and unattractive on an end-user's machine. When the window container is defined as a null Layout Manager and you expand your window with the mouse, you may notice that the fields don't expand in relationship to the window; everything uses fixed coordinates. When you expand, all you get is extra blank space around the entire group of components. Other Layout Managers can allow for expansion and retraction based on certain behavioral properties.

You've used some of the alignment tools in this chapter to help with the visual positioning of your components — Align Left, for example. When you use any Layout Manager other than the null Layout Manager, the alignment tools are disabled. You'll often find it advantageous to begin your development with a null Layout Manager and then switch to another Layout Manager when you're further along in the development process.

Layout Managers are easy to set in each of the container types (e.g., applets, frames, panels). When you change a single property in a container, all components within the container are affected. This can sometimes be a great little feature, but at other times you may become a little frustrated trying to get the Layout Manager to do exactly what you intend. Understanding each of the Layout Managers can alleviate the frustration you may experience when first starting out in VisualAge for Java.

There are many Layout Managers to choose from, and they each have their own behavioral differences. You can also create custom Layout Managers for use with your bean components. Custom Layout Managers must inherit from the **Object** class and implement a **LayoutManager** interface.

The Layout Managers provide visual assistance when you're placing components onto the VCE's visual area of the free-form surface. Temporary lines are automatically drawn to help you with the visual placement of the bean component. Once a bean component is dropped onto the free-form surface, the temporary lines disappear. Figure 5.29 shows what these temporary lines look like in one Layout Manager, GridBagLayout. *Don't change to a GridBagLayout; this example is for illustration purposes only.*

Figure 5.29
Temporary Lines on a GridBagLayout Layout Manager

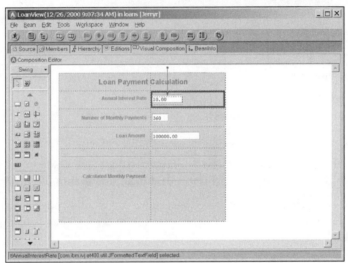

Each Layout Manager has a different visual assistance drawing. The following descriptions summarize the major Layout Managers supported by VisualAge for Java.

BorderLayout

The *BorderLayout* Layout Manager arranges components along each edge of the container and in one area in the center, as shown in Figure 5.30. This means that all components will fit into one of five areas in the container. These areas are called North, South, East, West, and Center. Components placed in a BorderLayout manager will assume the shape and size necessary to conform to the new layout. You can specify spacing between adjacent components.

Figure 5.30
BorderLayout Manager

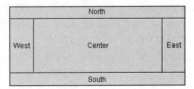

BoxLayout

The *BoxLayout* Layout Manager arranges components vertically or horizontally without wrapping. If you use vertical alignment, the BoxLayout manager tries to make all components the same width. If you use horizontal alignment, the BoxLayout manager tries to match the component height.

CardLayout

The *CardLayout* Layout Manager arranges components in a linear sequence similar to a deck of cards. Developers use this layout to achieve a tabbed pane or notebook look. Each component is called a card. You use the shortcut menu's **Switch To** option to navigate through the various cards. On the **Properties** sheet, you can specify the size of the frame around each component.

FlowLayout

The *FlowLayout* Layout Manager arranges components in horizontal wrapping lines as shown in Figure 5.31. On the **Properties** sheet, you specify spacing and the starting alignment of the components from the center, left, or right. You'll use the FlowLayout manager later in this chapter to place multiple button components together.

Figure 5.31
FlowLayout Manager

GridLayout and GridBagLayout

The *GridLayout* Layout Manager arranges components in a table with all cells having the same size. On the **Properties** sheet, you can specify the number of rows and columns and the spacing between components.

You saw an example of the *GridBagLayout* Layout Manager in Figure 5.29. This Layout Manager arranges components in a highly complex grid. As you add components, the free space is shuffled so that the components are centered while retaining your visual arrangement. Grid cells don't have to be identical in size, and components can span multiple cells. You can customize grid sizing down to each individual component. If you place components in any other layout and then change to the GridBagLayout manager, the components are set to maintain the look created in the original layout.

Create a New JPanel with Two JButtons

You're going to use the FlowLayout Layout Manager to create a JPanel to contain the two JButtons for your applet. Later in the book, you'll explore some of the other Layout Managers.

Add a new panel to contain the JButtons:

➢   In the bean palette, click the **JPanel** bean ☐, and drop it *below* the visual area on the nonvisual area of the free-form surface.

➢   Click the JPanel. Expand it to the size shown in Figure 5.32. You'll need to use the scroll bar to view the entire JPanel.

➢   Double-click the JPanel to display the **Properties** sheet. Change the **layout** property to **FlowLayout** as shown in Figure 5.33. By doing so, you switch to the FlowLayout Layout Manager.

➢   Close the **Properties** sheet.

Figure 5.32
JPanel

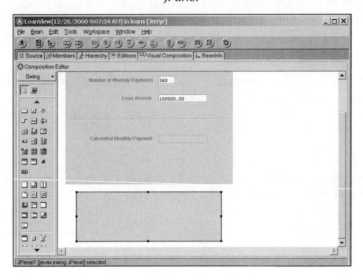

Figure 5.33
JPanel Properties Sheet

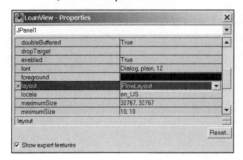

> ➤ In the bean palette, click the **JButton** bean 🔲, and drop it on the new JPanel. It doesn't matter where because the FlowLayout manager will position it automatically.
>
> ➤ Double-click the JButton to display the **Properties** sheet. Change the **beanName** to **btCalculate**. Change the **text** to **Calculate Payment**.
>
> ➤ In the bean palette, click the **JButton** bean again, and drop it on the new JPanel.
>
> ➤ Double-click the JButton to display the **Properties** sheet. Change the **beanName** to **btClear**. Change the **text** to **Clear**.
>
> ➤ Click the JPanel, and resize it so that it fits snugly around the two new JButtons, as shown in Figure 5.34.
>
> ➤ Click and hold on the JPanel. Drag the JPanel onto the JApplet, positioning it as shown in Figure 5.35. If you can't grab hold of the JPanel, go to the menu bar, click **Tools**, and select **Beans List**. From there, you can select the **JPanel**.
>
> ➤ On the menu bar, click **Bean**.
>
> ➤ Click **Save Bean**.

Figure 5.34
JPanel with JButtons

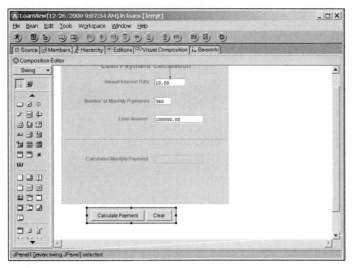

Figure 5.35
JPanel Placed on JApplet

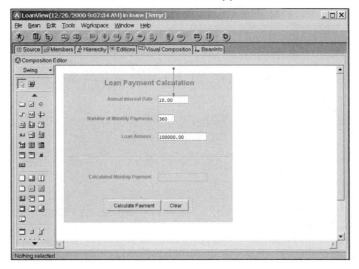

Clearing Screen Fields

You've just added a **Clear** JButton, named **btClear**, to your screen. There are many ways to clear (and reinitialize) the input text fields on a screen. Here are a few options:

A. Use connections from the **Clear** JButton to each of the input fields, and set the **text** property on each of them.
B. Use the logic bean that you'll create in the next chapter to create a method to set the **text** properties.
C. Create a class method in the JApplet that will set the **text** properties of the input fields.
D. Write a generic method that will clear all screen fields.

Option A works, but it requires one visual connection per input field. You can easily clutter up your screen with all the connections for this approach. Option B works fine, but it takes part of the GUI behavior from the View and places it in the Logic model. Option C is a good choice. It requires one line of code for each input field, but it can also be used to reinitialize fields to specific values. Option D can be the best choice if you don't need to initialize the input fields to different values. If they are generic values, this method works the best.

You're now going to implement option C. Later in the book, we'll go through an example using option D.

Event-to-Code Connection: btClear

```
connEtoC1: (btClear,actionPerformed → LoanView void,
            btClear_ActionPerformed(java.awt.event.ActionEvent))
```

You're going to create a class method and add a few lines of Java code to it. In this event-to-code connection, you will use some different numbers. This will show you how a component's property initialization and an event-to-code initialization can be set with different values.

➤   In the VCE, right-click the **btClear** JButton.
➤   Click **Connect**.
➤   Click **actionPerformed**.
➤   Click the spider-end pointer anywhere on the nonvisual free-form surface.
➤   Click **Event to Code**. You should see the **Event-to-Code Connection** window displayed as shown in Figure 5.36.

Figure 5.36
Event-to-Code Connection Window

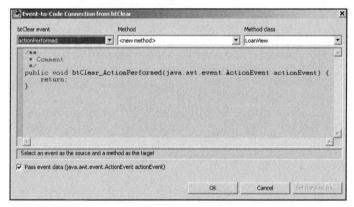

   Tips and Tricks

Whenever typing Java code, you have a code-assist function available to you: the Ctrl-Space key combination. For example, you can start typing one of the set*xxx* methods and press Ctrl-Space. A pop-up menu will appear, positioned at the set methods. You can also press Ctrl-Space after a period (.) to display all the methods.

To change the Java source code:

➤   Take the pointer down to the pane where the source code is displayed, and insert the four lines of code highlighted in Figure 5.37.

Figure 5.37
Source Code for Event-to-Code Connection

```
Before:
public void btClear_ActionPerformed(java.awt.event.ActionEvent actionEvent)  {
    return;
}

After:
public void btClear_ActionPerformed(java.awt.event.ActionEvent actionEvent)  {
    gettfAnnualInterestRate().setText("0");
    gettfNumberOfPayments().setText("360");
    gettfLoanAmount().setText("100");
    gettfMonthlyPayment().setText("");
    return;
}
```

When you've completed the changes, the screen should look like Figure 5.38. Each line of code sets the **text** property for one of the four fields. A 0, 360, 100, and blanks are placed in each respective field.

Figure 5.38
Event-to-Code Java Source Code Changes

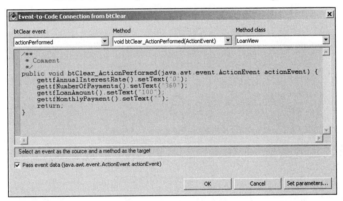

Save the source code:

➢   When you're finished typing, click **OK**.

If you made any typographical errors, you'll receive an error message immediately. If that happens, go ahead and fix the errors. If the code you entered matches that in Figure 5.37 but you still receive errors, it probably means one of your JFormattedTextFields has a different name. If so, change the code accordingly.

Your free-form surface should look similar to Figure 5.39.

Figure 5.39
Completed "View"

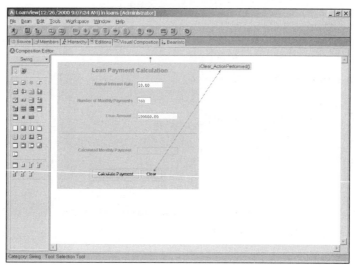

Run the applet:

➤   On the menu bar, click **Bean**.

➤   Click **Run**, and then click **In Applet Viewer**.

➤   While the applet is running, click the **Clear** JButton. Doing so should reset the fields to the new initialized values.

You're probably wondering when you will add the logic for the **Calculate Payment** JButton. That will occur in Chapter 6.

Review Generated Java Source Code

In Chapter 4, after creating your applet, you reviewed numerous Java methods that were automatically created for you. Most of those same methods were created again in this chapter. There is one slight difference you may not have noticed. The components each begin with the letter J. This J signifies that you're using Swing components. For example, you used a Swing **JLabel** as opposed to an AWT **label**. There are also a few new methods worth reviewing here.

To review the generated Java source code:

➤   Click the **Source** tab. This shows all the Java code that has been generated.

To view the source code associated with a particular method:

➤   In the **Elements** pane, click the method name. (You may have to expand the pane to be able to see the entire name.) All the code associated with the method will be displayed in the **Source** pane.

Review each of the following methods to look at the code that was generated. Here is a brief summary of what each method is doing.

```
getLocalFieldModel1ComparisonRangeValidator()
```
Defines the range comparisons used on the text fields. The minimums and maximums are set in this method.

`getLocalFieldModel1DataAttributes()`
Defines the data attributes used on the text fields. The data length, decimal places, data type, decimal type, and error-handling specifics are set in this method.

`getLocalFieldModel3EditcodeEditwordFormatter()`
Defines the edit code or edit word used on the text fields. In this case, you set up a 1 edit code.

`connEtoC1()`
Calls the **btClear_ActionPerformed()** method to clear each of the text fields.

`btClear_ActionPerformed()`
Contains the four lines of code you added to setText (clear) on each of the text fields.

As you may have noticed, the method names that are derived from the Enterprise Toolkit for AS/400 are long and can be a bit cumbersome to read. That's something you'll have to get used to.

Summary
We covered a lot of material in this chapter. Your first exposure to the AS/400 Toolbox was probably a welcome sight if you have an AS/400 background. In this chapter, you

- learned about the Model-View-Controller design
- learned how to show focus
- morphed Swing JavaBeans into AS/400 JavaBeans
- used edit properties with the AS/400 JavaBeans
- learned more about the various connection types
- became exposed to Layout Managers and used a FlowLayout Manager
- wrote some Java code in an event-to-code connection
- learned how to clear screen fields

Many of the topics in this chapter will be covered in more detail in later chapters. Right now, you need to finish the "logic" of the loan payment calculation. The next chapter will finish up the loan payment calculation project.

Chapter 6

Building a "Logic" Bean: Loan Payment

 ## Chapter Objectives

- ❏ Create a logic bean
- ❏ Use the **BeanInfo** page of the workbench
- ❏ Learn to use properties, features, and methods through BeanInfo
- ❏ Add a logic bean in the Visual Composition Editor
- ❏ Create connections to logic beans

 ## Chapter Project

- ❏ Create a nonvisual class, or logic bean, called **LoanLogic**.
- ❏ Create properties to build the interface between the **LoanView** and **LoanLogic** beans.
- ❏ Write a method to calculate the monthly loan payment.
- ❏ Figure 6.1 shows what the sample applet will look like.

Figure 6.1
Chapter Project

Applet Viewer: loans.LoanView.class	_ □ ×

Applet

Loan Payment Calculation

Annual Interest Rate	8.25
Number of Monthly Payments	360
Loan Amount	116250.00

| Calculated Monthly Payment | $873.00 |

[Calculate Payment]   [Clear]

Applet started.

In this chapter, you'll complete the rest of the Model-View-Controller design. Here, you will build the logic piece to calculate the loan monthly payment. In terms of AS/400 development, you might look at this chapter as equivalent to writing an AS/400 procedure to calculate the payment. You would pass the procedure three parameters: annual interest rate, number of monthly payments, and loan amount. You would receive a return parameter of the loan monthly payment.

LoanLogic Bean Setup

You're going to create a nonvisual Java class, or what is known as a *logic bean*. This logic bean will hold all the business logic for the **LoanView** JApplet you created in Chapter 5.

Create a Nonvisual Class

You'll be working out of the same **loans** package you created in Chapter 5.

> ➤ If the workbench isn't started, start it now.
> ➤ From the workbench, select the project **My Introduction Projects** with a click.
> ➤ With another click, expand **My Introduction Projects** to see the **loans** package.
> ➤ Right-click the **loans** package to display the shortcut menu. Select **Add**, and then select **Class** to display the **Create Class** SmartGuide (Figure 6.2).

Figure 6.2
Create Class SmartGuide

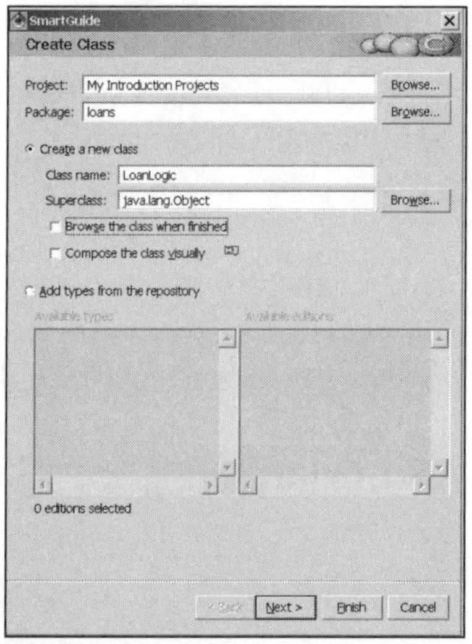

> ➤ Make sure the **Project** name is **My Introduction Projects**.
> ➤ Make sure the **Package** name is **loans**.
> ➤ In the **Class name** field, type **LoanLogic**.
> ➤ Leave the **Superclass** entry as **java.lang.Object**. (You'll learn more about superclasses in Chapter 8.)
> ➤ Clear the **Browse the class when finished** check box.
> ➤ Clear the **Compose the class visually** check box. There won't be any graphical components to this class.
> ➤ Click **Finish** to complete the creation of the class.

Once the **LoanLogic** class is created, you'll see it listed in the workbench **All Projects** pane below the **loans** package, as shown in Figure 6.3.

Figure 6.3
Workbench View of loans Package

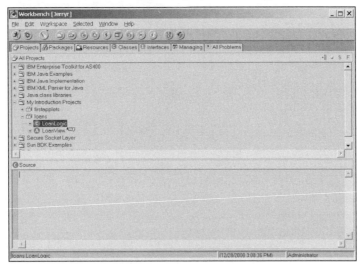

The BeanInfo Page

In this section, you'll be using the **BeanInfo** page to create some *property features* and *method features*. The **BeanInfo** page is used to work with bean interface features. These features — consisting of properties, events, and methods — represent the characteristics and behavioral aspects of your class. If you were creating a procedure on the AS/400, you would define a procedure prototype that defines the call interface or parameters to the outside world. This is sometimes known as the "black box" approach: Tell me what the procedure does and what its parameters are, and that's all I need to know. The same is true with the **BeanInfo** page. Here, you define to the outside world what the external view of the bean is.

➤   From the workbench, double-click the **LoanLogic** class.
➤   Click the **BeanInfo** tab.

You should be looking at the **BeanInfo** page as shown in Figure 6.4.

Figure 6.4
BeanInfo Page

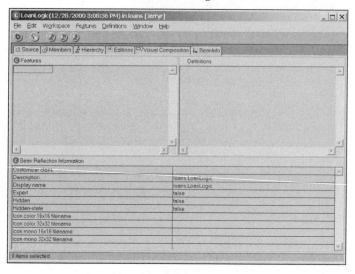

At this point, no features are defined yet. That's what you'll do next. Before you do so, you need to understand the features you'll be creating.

Property Features

Properties are basically class variables. They have a defined interface to be able to store data. When you create a property feature, methods are automatically created to be able to *set* and *get* the property or field. These setter and getter (accessor and mutator) methods are created based on whether you specify the property or field as writeable (set) or readable (get). In this chapter, you're going to create the properties **annualInterestRate**, **numberOfMonths**, **loanAmount**, and **monthlyPayment**. For each of these property features, VisualAge for Java will create a set and a get method. For example, you'll see a get method called **getAnnualInterestRate()** and a set method called **setAnnualInterestRate()**. This is how the property or field is accessed.

You can define properties with any Java data types, including primitive data types such as int, double, short, and float, or as arrays of int[], short[], double[], float[], and so on. The type must be the same for each of the following: the definition of the property, the get method, the set method, and the property.

Method Features

You're already familiar with methods. The most important thing to remember about method features is that they are *public* class methods contained within the BeanInfo. You define the method name, the return type, the parameter count, and the parameters themselves. Later in this chapter, you'll create a method feature called **calculateMonthlyPayment()** to perform the calculation of the loan monthly payment.

Event Features

Many events can occur within the Java language. Events represent all the activity that occurs between a program, the system, and a user. Events can be caused by clicking a button, typing text, clicking the mouse, or closing a window. They can also be caused by the system or by other logic beans.

Events have a source, such as a button being clicked. Events also have a *listener* that receives the event notification and determines how to handle the event. Just as there are many event sources, there are also many different event listeners. If a user clicks a button, the user expects the command associated with that particular button to be executed. If an event isn't registered with a listener, nothing happens.

Tips and Tricks

When you create a feature, pay close attention to the prompts on the screen. You can change a feature's information once the feature is created, but doing so is difficult and time-consuming. If you realize you've created a feature incorrectly, it's usually easier to delete the feature and re-create it. If you've added Java code to a method feature, make sure you copy the code to the Clipboard before you delete the feature, so you can paste the code after you re-create the method feature.

Feature SmartGuides

VisualAge for Java provides separate SmartGuides to guide you through the process of creating the various types of features. To use the feature SmartGuides, simply right-click in the **Features** pane of the **BeanInfo** page (upper-left corner) and use the shortcut menu to select the type of feature you want to create.

Table 6.1 shows the icons displayed in the **BeanInfo** page panes to indicate the various types of features and information associated with each type of feature.

Table 6.1
BeanInfo Icons

Property	Bound	Hidden	Writeable	Event

Constrained	Indexed	Method	Expert	Readable

New Property Feature

You are going to create a property feature using the **New Property Feature** SmartGuide.

➢ In the **Features** pane of the **BeanInfo** page, right-click to display the shortcut menu.
➢ Click **New Property Feature** to display the **New Property Feature** SmartGuide (Figure 6.5).
➢ As shown in the figure, type **annualInterestRate** in the **Property name** field. Be sure to type the first letter in lower case; otherwise, you'll receive a warning message.
➢ Click to display the **Property type** drop-down list, and select **double**, as shown in Figure 6.6.

Tips and Tricks

When selecting the property type, be careful to choose the correct type. It's easy to make a mistake. For example, if you want a double floating property type, make sure you select *double* and not *double[]* — double[] is an array of double floats.

Figure 6.5
New Property Feature SmartGuide

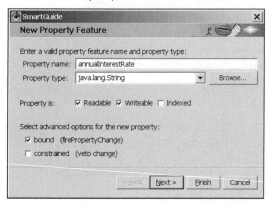

Figure 6.6
Property Type double Selected

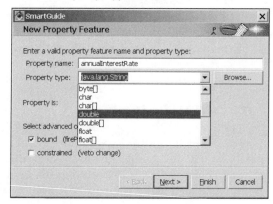

> Make sure the **Readable**, **Writeable**, and **bound** check boxes are all selected, as shown in Figure 6.7.

A check mark next to **Readable** indicates that you want to create a **getAnnualInterestRate()** method. A check mark next to **Writeable** indicates that you want to create a **setAnnualInterestRate()** method. The **bound** check mark indicates that the property will fire a **propertyChange()** method whenever the property changes.

Figure 6.7
New Property Feature SmartGuide Completed

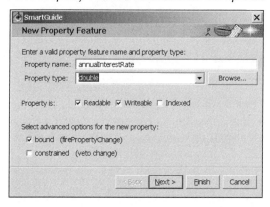

> Click **Next**.

The SmartGuide's **Bean Information** window (Figure 6.8) appears next. This window's **Display name** field is used in the Visual Composition Editor's connections shortcut menu. If you define no display name, the value defaults to the bean name. You can leave both the **Display name** field and the **Short description** field blank on this window.

Figure 6.8 also shows three options at the bottom of the window. The **expert**, **hidden**, and **preferred** check boxes are used to set the information in a class named **PropertyDescriptor**. Expert features are those identified as rarely used or advanced features. Hidden features are those that should not be used by a Java tool. Preferred features are those that will automatically appear in the VCE connections shortcut menu. You do not need to select any of these options.

Figure 6.8
Bean Information Window

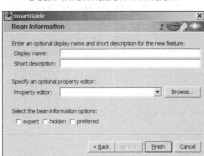

➢   Click **Finish**.

You'll notice some heavy activity occurring at this point. The **New Property Feature** SmartGuide is creating a property named **annualInterestRate**, a method named **getAnnualInterestRate()**, a method named **setAnnual InterestRate()**, and a variable named **FieldAnnualInterestRate**.

Figure 6.9 shows the property and the two methods created. Notice the case style that the SmartGuide used in naming them. It converted the bean name "annualInterestRate" to the appropriate case when naming the other objects. It also added **Field** as a prefix to the variable it created.

Figure 6.9
A Property and Two Methods

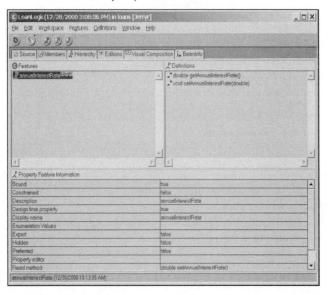

In the lower half of the **BeanInfo** page, you see the property feature information. You can change this information by clicking any of the fields in the right-hand column.

➢   Click the **Members** tab.

Figure 6.10 shows the **Members** page. Everything you see here was just created. Notice the nine different methods that were created to deal with the property change functions: registering listeners and firing property changes. Yes, the SmartGuide has created quite a bit of code.

Figure 6.10
Members Created

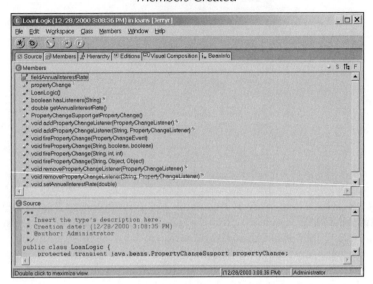

> Click the **BeanInfo** tab.

Create the next property feature, **numberOfPayments**:

> In the **Features** pane, right-click to display the shortcut menu.
> Click **New Property Feature**.
> In the **Property name** field, type **numberOfPayments**.
> In the **Property type** list, select **short**.
> Make sure the **Readable**, **Writeable**, and **bound** check boxes are all selected.
> Click **Finish**.

Create the next property feature, **loanAmount**:

> In the **Features** pane, right-click to display the shortcut menu.
> Click **New Property Feature**.
> In the **Property Name** field, type **loanAmount**.
> In the **Property Type** list, select **double**.
> Make sure the **Readable**, **Writeable**, and **bound** check boxes are all selected.
> Click **Finish**.

Create the next property feature, **monthlyPayment**:

> In the **Features** pane, right-click to display the shortcut menu.
> Click **New Property Feature**.
> In the **Property name** field, type **monthlyPayment**.
> In the **Property type** list, select **double**.
> Make sure the **Readable**, **Writeable**, and **bound** check boxes are all selected.
> Click **Finish**.

At this point, your **BeanInfo** page should look similar to Figure 6.11.

Figure 6.11
BeanInfo Page

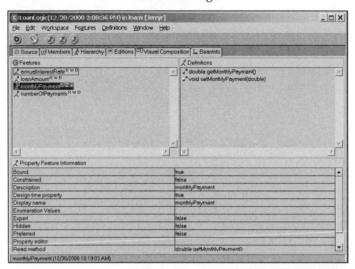

Earlier in the chapter, you learned about the automatic creation of the get and set methods. Look at a get and a set method now:

➢   In the **Definitions** pane (upper-right corner of the **BeanInfo** page), click method **getMonthlyPayment()**.

As Figure 6.12 shows, the lower part of the **BeanInfo** page changes to display, in the **Source** pane, the method code that was created to perform the get function. The get method returns an object of type double.

Figure 6.12
Method getMonthlyPayment()

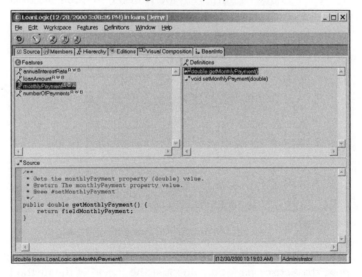

➢   In the **Definitions** pane, click method **setMonthlyPayment()**.

Figure 6.13 shows the method that was created to perform the set function. The set method is passed an object of type double.

Figure 6.13
Method setMonthlyPayment()

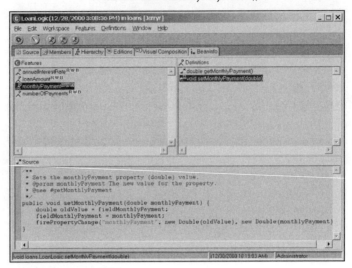

New Method Feature

Next, you're going to use the **New Method Feature** SmartGuide to create a method feature. This method is the one that will actually do the complex calculation to derive the loan monthly payment.

Create the method feature **calculateMonthlyPayment**:

➤   In the **Features** pane, right-click to display the shortcut menu.
➤   Click **New Method Feature** to display the **New Method Feature** SmartGuide (Figure 6.14).
➤   As shown in the figure, type **calculateMonthlyPayment** in the **Method name** field.
➤   Leave the **Return type** value as **void** and **Parameter count** as **0**.
➤   Click **Finish**.

Figure 6.14
New Method Feature SmartGuide

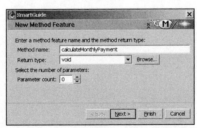

➤   In the **Definitions** pane, click the **calculateMonthlyPayment()** method.

As Figure 6.15 shows, **calculateMonthlyPayment()** is the method that will contain the Java code to do the complex calculation. Right now, the **Source** pane contains just the "shell" of the method; you will add the code to it to perform the calculation. Before you write the code, though, you're going to jump over to the **LoanView** bean and connect the **LoanView** and **LoanLogic** beans together.

Figure 6.15
Method calculateMonthlyPayment()

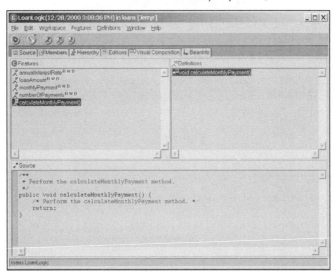

Connecting the Logic and View Beans

➢ Click the workbench window. Or, if you've closed the workbench window, open it by clicking **Window** on the menu bar and then clicking the **Workbench** menu item.

As the **All Projects** tree view in Figure 6.16 shows, you now have a class called **LoanLogic** and another class called **LoanLogicBeanInfo**. The **LoanLogicBeanInfo** class was created automatically when you created the logic bean. This class is where the various descriptor methods are kept. You won't be working with this class. You'll be jumping back and forth between the **LoanView** JApplet and the **LoanLogic** class.

Figure 6.16
Workbench

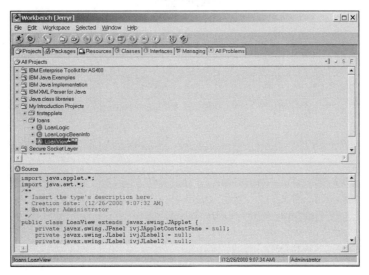

Jump to the **LoanView** JApplet:

➢   In the **All Projects** pane, double-click the **LoanView** JApplet.

Now, you're now going to bring the **LoanLogic** bean into the **LoanView** VCE and connect the two beans together. This function is used often, so you'll want to get very familiar with this task. You'll be using the VCE's **Choose Bean** button to choose the logic bean and then drop it on the nonvisual free-form surface.

➢   If you're not in the VCE, select the **LoanView** VCE by clicking the **Visual Composition** tab.
➢   In the upper-left corner of the VCE (above the Swing category beans), click the **Choose Bean** button. You can see the hover text for this button in Figure 6.17. The **Choose Bean** window (Figure 6.18) appears.

Figure 6.17
VCE Choose Bean

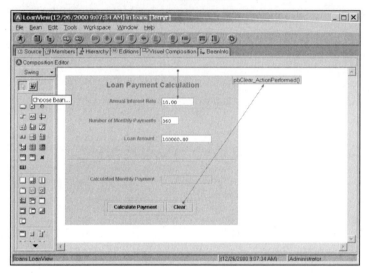

Figure 6.18
Choose Bean Window

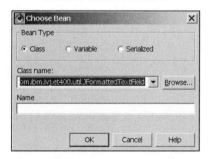

➢   In the **Choose Bean** window, click **Browse** to choose a class name. The **Choose a Valid Class** window (Figure 6.19) is displayed.
➢   In the **Pattern** field, type **loan**, as shown in the figure.

➢   When the matching names appear in the **Class Names** list, select **LoanLogic**.
➢   Click **OK**.
➢   Back in the **Choose Bean** window, type **MyLoanLogicBean** in the **Name** field (Figure 6.20).
➢   Click **OK**.

Figure 6.19
Choose a Valid Class Window

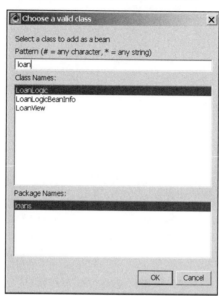

Figure 6.20
MyLoanLogicBean

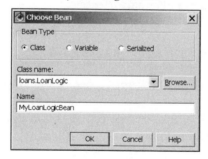

➢   Move the cross-hair pointer to the nonvisual free-form surface, and click to drop the **MyLoanLogic** bean there, as shown in Figure 6.21.

Figure 6.21
MyLoanLogicBean on Nonvisual Free-Form Surface

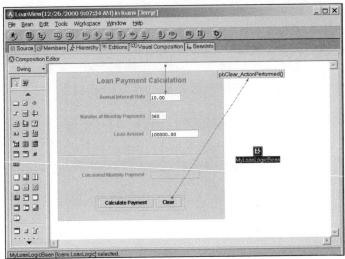

Now, you'll connect each of the properties (fields) in the visual area to the **LoanLogic** bean named **MyLoanLogicBean**. As you proceed through the connections, you might notice that you're connecting source and target properties of different types: string and double. That's okay because the VCE will generate the proper conversions to accommodate the incompatibilities. This is a very powerful feature of the VCE.

Property-to-Property Connection: annualInterestRate

```
connPtoP1: (tfAnnualInterestRate,text ↔ MyLoanLogicBean,annualInterestRate)
```

First, connect the **tfAnnualInterestRate** JFormattedTextField with the **MyLoanLogicBean** bean.

➢ Right-click the **tfAnnualInterestRate** JFormattedTextField.
➢ Select **Connect**.
➢ Click **text**.
➢ Click the spider-end pointer on the **MyLoanLogicBean** bean.
➢ Click **Connectible Features**.
➢ In the **End Connection to** window (Figure 6.22), click property **annualInterestRate**.
➢ Click **OK**.
➢ Double-click the connection to verify that it is correct, as shown in Figure 6.23.
➢ Close the connection's **Properties** window.

The new connection in the VCE should appear as shown in Figure 6.24.

Figure 6.22
End Connection to annualInterestRate

Figure 6.23
Connection connPtoP1

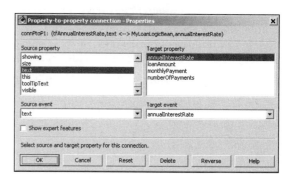

Figure 6.24
connPtoP1 Connection: tfAnnualInterestRate

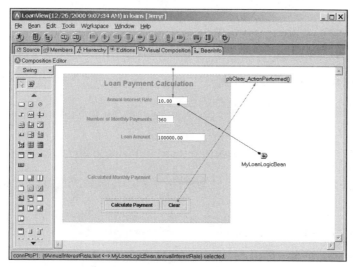

Property-to-Property Connection: numberOfPayments

```
connPtoP2: (tfNumberOfPayments,text ←→ MyLoanLogicBean,numberOfPayments)
```

Connect the **tfNumberOfPayments** JFormattedTextField with the **MyLoanLogicBean** bean.

➢ Right-click the **tfNumberOfPayments** JFormattedTextField.
➢ Select **Connect**.
➢ Click **text**.

➤ Click the spider-end pointer on the **MyLoanLogicBean** bean.
➤ Click **Connectible Features**.
➤ Click property **numberOfPayments**.
➤ Click **OK**.

Property-to-Property Connection: loanAmount

`connPtoP3: (tfLoanAmount,text ↔ MyLoanLogicBean,loanAmount)`

Connect the **tfLoanAmount** JFormattedTextField with the **MyLoanLogicBean** bean.

➤ Right-click the **tfLoanAmount** JFormattedTextField.
➤ Select **Connect**.
➤ Click **text**.
➤ Click the spider-end pointer on the **MyLoanLogicBean** bean.
➤ Click **Connectible Features**.
➤ Click property **loanAmount**.
➤ Click **OK**.

Event-to-Method Connection: calculateMonthlyPayment()

`connEtoM2: (btCalculate,actionPerformed → MyLoanLogicBean,calculateMonthlyPayment())`

Connect the **Calculate Loan** JButton with the **calculateMonthlyPayment()** method.

➤ Right-click the **Calculate Loan** JButton (named **btCalculate**).
➤ Select **Connect**.
➤ Click **actionPerformed**.
➤ Click the spider-end pointer on the **MyLoanLogicBean** bean.
➤ Click **Connectible Features**.
➤ Click method **calculateMonthlyPayment()**.
➤ Click **OK**.
➤ Double-click the connection to verify that it is correct, as shown in Figure 6.25.
➤ Close the connection's **Properties** window.

The connections in the VCE should now look similar to those in Figure 6.26.

Figure 6.25
Connection connEtoM2

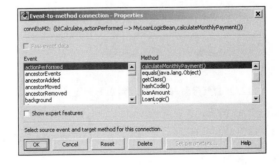

Figure 6.26

connEtoM2 Connection: btCalculate

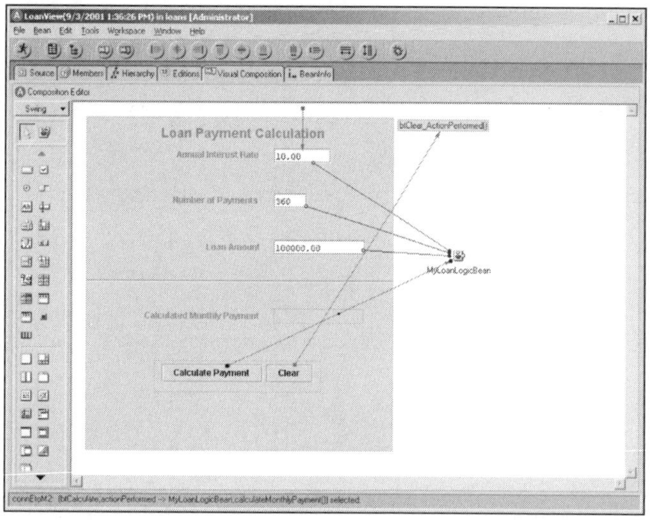

Property-to-Property Connection: monthlyPayment

`connPtoP4: (MyLoanLogicBean,monthlyPayment ↔ tfMonthlyPayment,text)`

Connect the **MyLoanLogicBean** bean with the **tfMonthlyPayment** JFormattedTextField.

➢ Right-click the **MyLoanLogicBean** bean.
➢ Select **Connect**.
➢ Click **Connectible Features**.
➢ In the **End Connection to** window, select the **Property** option to change from a list of events to a list of properties.
➢ Click **monthlyPayment**.
➢ Click **OK**.
➢ Click the spider-end pointer on the **tfMonthlyPayment** JFormattedTextField.
➢ Click **text**.

The connections in the VCE should now look similar to those in Figure 6.27.

Figure 6.27
Connection connPtoP4: MyLoanLogicBean

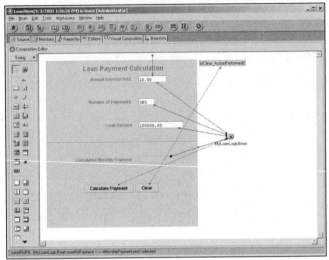

Running the Applet

Run the applet:

➤ On the menu bar, click **Bean**.
➤ Click **Run**, and then click **In AppletViewer**.

It may take a while to save, compile, and run the applet. Be patient.

➤ Click the **Calculate Payment** button.

As you can see in Figure 6.28, all you see is "$.00" for the calculation result. That's okay. You still need to do a couple of things to finish up:

• You need to pass the events to the **MyLoanLogicBean** bean when the numbers are typed during execution.
• You need to add the complex calculation to the **calculateMonthlyPayment()** method.

Figure 6.28
JApplet Executing

➤ Close the applet.

Passing Events to the Logic Bean

When a property changes, an event is passed. A JFormattedTextField has several different events that can be passed at execution time. If you were using the TextField in Abstract Window Toolkit, you would probably use the **textValueChanged** event to pass the property change event to the logic bean. In Swing, you use the **KeyReleased** event to accomplish the same function.

To pass the event from **tfAnnualInterestRate** to the **MyLoanLogicBean** bean:

➢   Double-click the **connPtoP1** connection from **tfAnnualInterestRate** to **MyLoanLogicBean** to display the connection properties.

➢   In the **Source event** list (lower-left part of the resulting window), select the **KeyReleased** event, as shown in Figure 6.29.

➢   Click **OK**.

Figure 6.29
KeyReleased Source Event

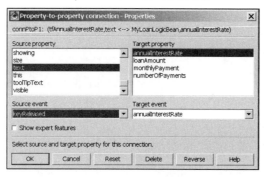

Now, pass the event from **tfNumberOfPayments** to the **MyLoanLogicBean** bean:

➢   Double-click the **connPtoP2** connection from **tfNumberOfPayments** to **MyLoanLogicBean**.

➢   In the **Source event** list, select **KeyReleased**.

➢   Click **OK**.

Pass the event from **tfLoanAmount** to the **MyLoanLogicBean** bean:

➢   Double-click the **connPtoP3** connection from **tfLoanAmount** to **MyLoanLogicBean**.

➢   In the **Source event** list, select **KeyReleased**.

➢   Click **OK**.

Loan Payment Calculation

You're now going to return to the **LoanLogic BeanInfo** page to make the source code changes to the **calculateMonthlyPayment()** method.

➢   Select the **LoanLogic** BeanInfo.

➢   In the **Features** pane, click the **calculateMonthlyPayment()** method.

➢   In the **Definitions** pane, click the **calculateMonthlyPayment()** method.

➢   In the **Source** pane, type the Java code shown in Figure 6.30, inserting the highlighted lines of code where shown.

Figure 6.30
calculateMonthlyPayment() Method

Before:
```
public void calculateMonthlyPayment() {
    /* Perform the calculateMonthlyPayment method. */
    return;
}
```

After:
```
public void calculateMonthlyPayment() {
    /* Perform the calculateMonthlyPayment method. */
    double  monthlyInterestRate = getAnnualInterestRate() / 1200;
    double  factor = Math.pow(1 + monthlyInterestRate, getNumberOfPayments());
    setMonthlyPayment(Math.rint((getLoanAmount() * monthlyInterestRate * factor) / (factor -1)));
    return;
}
```

The source code contained in the figure represents the calculation for the monthly payment. In general terms, the formula is

$$Monthly\ Payment = Loan\ Amount * (I * (1 + I)^N) / ((1 + I)^N - 1)$$

where *I* represents monthly interest rate and *N* represents the number of months for the loan. In the source code shown in the figure, the 1200 represents the adjustment of two decimal places from the interest rate multiplied by 12 months. In other words 9.75 percent interest is calculated monthly as 0.008125 percent (9.75/1200).

When you've completed the source code changes, your screen should look similar to Figure 6.31.

Figure 6.31
calculateMonthlyPayment() Java Source Code

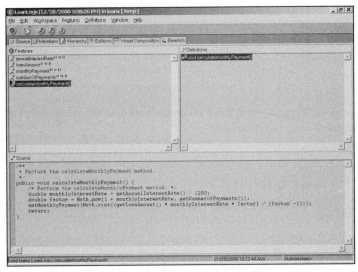

Save your changes:

➢ Right-click in the **Source** pane to display the shortcut menu.
➢ Click **Save**.

Now, return to **LoanView** to run your JApplet:

➢ Select the **LoanView** VCE.
➢ On the menu bar, click **Bean**.
➢ Click **Run**, and then click **In Applet Viewer**.
➢ Click the **Calculate Payment** JButton.

The resulting calculation should come up with $878.00 as shown in Figure 6.32. Why do the decimal positions contain zeros? In your calculation, you added the **Math.rint()** method to round the answer; otherwise, you'd end up with a very long resulting calculation because of the double float type. Converting numbers to a two-decimal result isn't as easy in Java as it is on the AS/400.

Figure 6.32
LoanView Execution

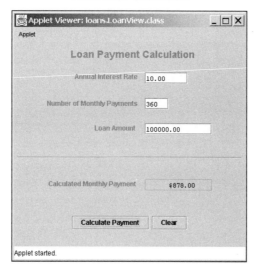

➢ Close the applet.

Congratulations! You have now completed the creation of a small Model-View-Controller program.

Summary

This chapter required quite a bit of work to be able to calculate the monthly loan payment. Keep in mind that this was a simple example of how to build a logic bean. You'd normally have much more code and functionality in a typical production-type logic bean. You learned about JavaBean features and how to use the SmartGuides to create and define your own logic beans. In this chapter you

- created a logic bean
- defined properties from the **BeanInfo** page
- defined methods from the **BeanInfo** page
- connected your new logic bean to the view bean in the VCE
- added logic to your new method

In the next chapter, you'll learn how to use the debugging feature in VisualAge for Java.

Chapter 7

Using Debug

 **Chapter Objectives**

- ☐ Learn to use the Interactive Debugger
- ☐ Use the Console
- ☐ Learn how to manage breakpoints
- ☐ Use the evaluation area
- ☐ Use the Scrapbook
- ☐ Use the Inspector

 Chapter Project

- ☐ Use the Chapter 4 applet to demonstrate each of the debug topics.
- ☐ Figure 7.1 shows what the sample applet will look like.

Figure 7.1
Chapter Project

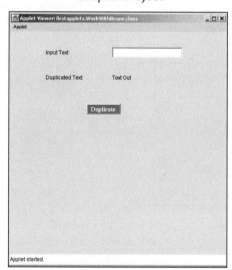

In this chapter, you'll learn about many tools that can help in the testing and debugging of your Java programs. You'll probably use some of these tools quite often. If you've used the standard AS/400 Debug or the AS/400 Interactive Debugger, you're probably very familiar with debugging concepts. Many of the tools used in this chapter have no functional equivalent to anything you're used to on the AS/400.

General Debugging

Many times when debugging, you just want a simple piece of information to be displayed at a certain time during the execution of your program. The easiest way to accomplish this in Java is to use the standard **System.out.println()** method defined in the **java.io.PrintStream** class. This method is very powerful because it supports most of the major types of objects. For example, if you wanted to print the results of an integer, you would simply specify the following line of code:

```
System.out.println("Integer Results = " + integer);
```

Introduction to the Console

In VisualAge for Java, when you use the **System.out.println()** method, the multi-pane **Console** window, shown in Figure 7.2, is used to display the results. You can also use the Console as a way to pass standard input to a Java program through its **main()** method. The Console window appears automatically whenever messages are sent to the console. These messages can originate from a System.out method or from some type of exception processing (System.err). The Console will stay open until you manually close it. You can also open the Console from any VisualAge for Java **Window** menu.

The following line of Java code produces the Console results shown in Figure 7.3.

```
System.out.println("This is where you might display something");
```

Figure 7.2
Console

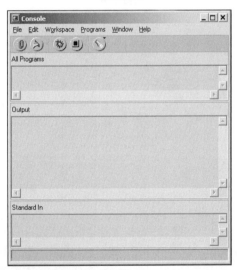

Figure 7.3
Console with Output Displayed

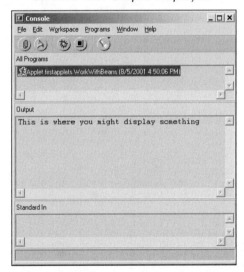

Although **System.out.println()** can be a useful tool, the problem with using it for debugging is that you need to know exactly where to place the particular line of code. This technique works great for small debugging sessions, but it can become very cumbersome for large, complex situations.

The Integrated Debugger

The Integrated Debugger in VisualAge for Java lets you easily (no exaggeration) set breakpoints, remove breakpoints, inspect and change variables, and add additional Java code during execution. The Integrated Debugger is started automatically when a breakpoint is reached. The debugger is also started if an uncaught exception occurs. If you want to start the Integrated Debugger manually, you can select it on the **Window** menu.

In this chapter, you'll learn how to use some of the features of the Integrated Debugger by stepping through a debugging session. You'll be using the applet you created in Chapter 4.

Managing Breakpoints

Adding a breakpoint in VisualAge for Java is as simple as finding the desired line of code and right-clicking the mouse. Removing a breakpoint is the same.

➢   If the workbench isn't started, start it now.
➢   Expand the project **My Introduction Projects** with a click.
➢   Select the package **firstapplets** with a click.
➢   Double-click the **WorkWithBeans** class.

You should be inside the Visual Composition Editor. You are now going to add some breakpoints.

➢   Click the **Members** tab.
➢   In the **Members** pane, click the **init()** method. Doing so will display the method's source code in the **Source** pane at the bottom of the screen.

Notice the narrow gray column at the left edge of the **Source** pane. This column is where breakpoints are identified. If a blue dot is present, a breakpoint is set on the corresponding line. If no blue dot is present, no breakpoint exists. It's as simple as that.

➢   In the **Source** pane, find the line of code that reads

```
setName("WorkWithBeans");
```

➢   Double-click in the gray column area next to this statement.

You should now see a blue dot in the gray area, as shown in Figure 7.4. The blue dot signifies that a breakpoint has been set on this line of code. You can set breakpoints on any executable line of Java code. To remove a breakpoint, you just double-click the blue dot.

Figure 7.4
Breakpoint Set

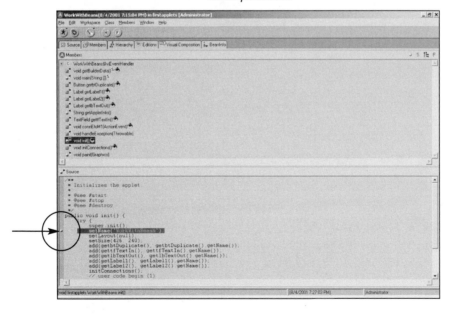

You can also use a shortcut menu to add or remove breakpoints.

➤   Take your pointer and hold it over the blue dot. Right-click to display the shortcut menu, which is shown in Figure 7.5.

You can use this menu to add or remove (clear) breakpoints.

Figure 7.5
Breakpoint Shortcut Menu

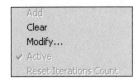

Set another breakpoint the same way you did above:

➤   In the **Members** pane, click the **getbtDuplicate()** method. The source code will be displayed.
➤   In the **Source** pane, find a line of code similar to the following (the numbers probably won't match exactly; look for the **setBounds()** method):

```
ivjbtDuplicate.setBounds(175, 162, 79, 23);
```

➤   Double-click in the gray column area beside this line to set a breakpoint as shown in Figure 7.6.

Figure 7.6
Another Breakpoint Set

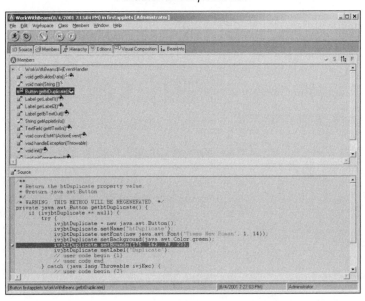

Tips and Tricks

You can configure an *iteration breakpoint* to stop execution on a prespecified iteration. For example, if you prespecify 6 as the integer iteration, your code execution will stop after the sixth time of passing that breakpoint. To accomplish this, you would take these steps:

1. Right-click on an existing breakpoint dot to display the shortcut menu.
2. Select *Modify.*
3. Select *On Iteration.*
4. Type <u>6</u>.
5. Click *OK.*

Return to the VCE now, and run your applet.

➤   Click the **Visual Composition** tab.

➤   On the menu bar, click **Bean**. Click **Run**, and then click **In Applet Viewer**.

After a few seconds, the applet appears and then the debugger window opens automatically, as shown in Figure 7.7. The debugger window opens because the Java program encountered a breakpoint. There are three separate tabs in the debugger: Debug, Breakpoints, and Exceptions.

Figure 7.7
Debug Page

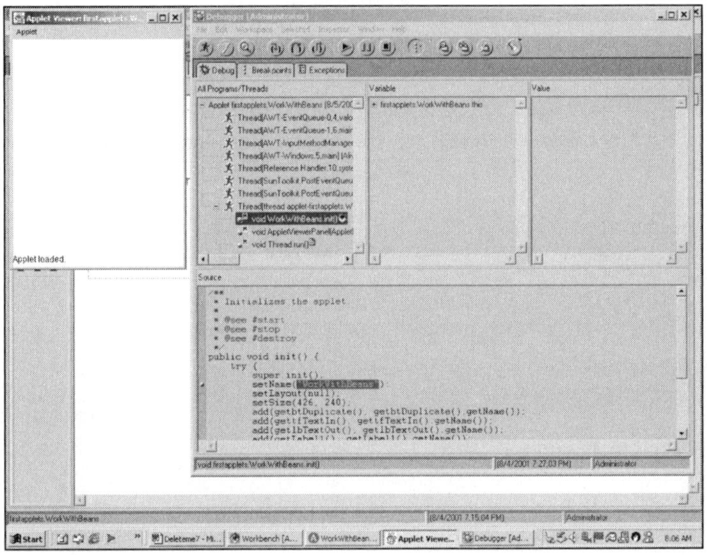

![Screenshot of the Debug Page showing the Applet Viewer window and the Debugger window with Debug, Breakpoints, and Exceptions tabs, thread list, variable and value panes, and source code.]

Debug Page

The **Debug** tab page is the one that appears when the debugger first opens. This page shows all currently running threads, grouped by active programs, and the source code associated with the selected program. The current breakpoint is highlighted, indicating that the program is in the process of executing that piece of Java code. At this point, you can either begin stepping through the program or resume execution. You'll learn more about these two functions in the next few sections.

Breakpoints Page

The **Breakpoints** tab page lists all the methods in the workspace that have breakpoints set.

➢   Click the **Breakpoints** tab.

As Figure 7.8 shows, the two breakpoints you set earlier are listed in the **Methods** pane.

Figure 7.8
Breakpoints Page

From the **Breakpoints** page, you can clear one or all of the breakpoints. To clear breakpoints, you right-click to display the shortcut menu and select either **Clear** or **Clear All**. Notice that you also have a **Source** pane available to you on the **Breakpoints** page. You can click any breakpoint to view the source code associated with each method.

Exceptions Page

On the **Exceptions** page, you can specify exceptions for which you want to stop execution when the first "throw" occurs. (This differs from when the exception is caught in a catch block.)

➢   Click the **Exceptions** tab.

Figure 7.9 shows the list of exceptions from which you can choose. You can sort the exceptions by class, package, or hierarchy. To sort, click one of the three sort icons shown in the upper-right corner of the tab page. The hover text will appear when you move your mouse over one of the sort icons. If you know the name of the exception you're looking for, you can just begin typing it on your keyboard (you won't see anything typed), and you'll be positioned to the exception that matches what you're typing.

Figure 7.9
Exceptions Page

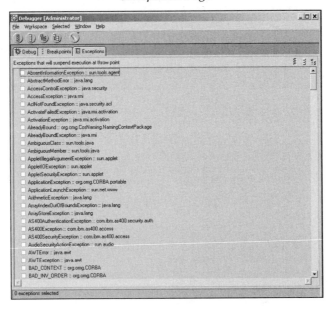

Debug Buttons

➤   Click the **Debug** tab.

The Integrated Debugger's **Debug** page provides many toolbar buttons you can click to perform desired debug functions. Table 7.1 identifies each of these buttons. You'll be using most of these buttons throughout the rest of the chapter as you continue your debugging session.

Table 7.1
Debug Buttons

Step Over

The **Step Over** button executes a method without debugging through the method. When you click this button, the highlighter moves to the next method.

➤   Click the **Step Over** button. Click the button again. In the **Source** pane, observe how the Java source code is highlighted.

Step Into

The **Step Into** 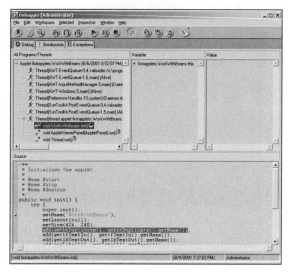 button actually steps into a method as it is executed. When you click this button, you'll be stepping through methods with which you may not be familiar.

➤   Click the **Step Into** button. Click the button three or four times until you get the hang of it.

➤   Click the **Step Over** button until you return to the **setSize()** statement in the **init()** method.

➤   Click the **Step Over** button once more so that you're positioned to the line of code highlighted in Figure 7.10. (If you go past this line by a few statements, that's okay.) The statement reads

```
add(getbtDuplicate(), getbtDuplicate().getName());
```

Figure 7.10
Step Over

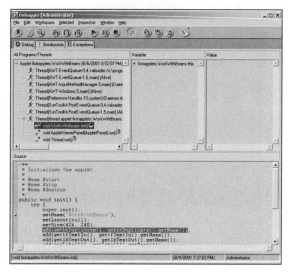

Run to Return

To reach the end of each method, you can click the **Run to Return** button, which continues execution until a **return** statement is encountered.

Evaluation Area

The evaluation area is a very useful area of the debugger. Here, you can enter small snippets of Java code, highlight the code, and then execute it. The code is executed as part of the existing method even though it is not part of the method. This ability can come in handy when you need to test a few lines of code in a particular area of a Java program.

Even though the size and background color of your applet are already set, change them now so that you can see how easy it is to execute lines of Java code that aren't part of the program.

➤   Click the **Evaluation Area** button. The **Evaluation** window is displayed.

➤   In the **Evaluation** window, enter **setSize(500,500);** and **setBackground(Color.yellow)**, as shown in Figure 7.11.

➤   As shown in Figure 7.12, highlight the Java code you just entered.

➤   Right-click to display the shortcut menu, and select **Run**.

Figure 7.11
Evaluation Area

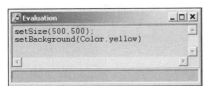

Figure 7.12
Highlighted Evaluation Area

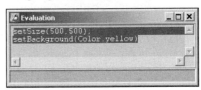

What did you notice? The applet should have increased in size immediately. Why didn't the background color change? That's because the **show()** method hasn't been executed yet.

➢   Close the **Evaluation** window.

Resume

The **Resume** toolbar button resumes execution until either the program ends or the next breakpoint is reached.

➢   Click the **Resume** button.

Program execution should have continued until the next breakpoint. Execution should have stopped in the **getbtDuplicate()** method, as shown in Figure 7.13. Notice, in the **Source** pane, that execution stopped right after the line of code that sets the background color of the **Duplicate** button (i.e., at the second breakpoint you set).

Figure 7.13
Breakpoint

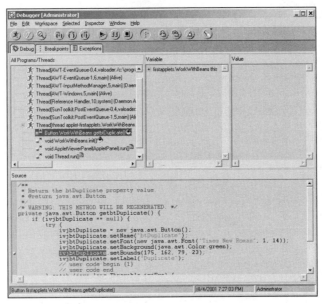

Visible Variables

You can use the Integrated Debugger to view the contents of any variable. There are several ways to do this. You can click the **Visible Variables** toolbar button, which will display a separate window of variables. You can also select the **Window** menu's **Visible Variables** option, or you can look at the **Variable** pane in the **Debug** page.

When you view variables, you can continue expanding down to the lowest component variable. You can also choose to display only variables in a particular format. If you click **Inspector** on the menu bar, you can use the **Inspector** menu to specify whether to show **Field Names Only** or **Public Fields Only** and to **Hide Static Fields**. The menu in Figure 7.14 shows the default Inspector settings.

Figure 7.14
Inspector Options

Specify to show **Field Names Only**, and then examine a variable:

➤   On the menu bar, click **Inspector** to display the **Inspector** menu.
➤   Click **Field Names Only**.
➤   In the **Variable** pane, expand variable **this**.

Your **Variable** pane should look similar to Figure 7.15.

Figure 7.15
Variable Pane

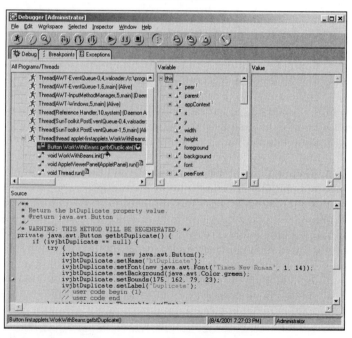

➤   In the **Variable** pane, scroll down until you see the **ivjbtDuplicate** variable. It is located almost at the bottom of the scroll pane. This is the variable associated with the applet's **Duplicate** button.
➤   Expand the **ivjbtDuplicate** variable.
➤   Within the **ivjbtDuplicate** variable, click the **foreground** field, as shown in Figure 7.16.

Notice that the value of the **foreground** field, **null**, is now displayed in the **Value** pane.

Figure 7.16
Selected Variable

Changing Variables

Changing the contents of a variable during execution is easy. You simply type over the current value in the **Value** pane of the **Debug** page.

You're going to change your applet's **Duplicate** button to use a white foreground on a red background.

➤   In the **Value** pane, replace the **ivjbtDuplicate** variable value **null** with **Color.white**. Be sure to use this exact case.

➤   Save the variable change by right-clicking to display the shortcut menu and clicking **Save**.

Notice what happened. As you can see in Figure 7.17, the **Color.white** entry that you typed in the **Value** pane was changed to the equivalent of white:

```
java.awt.Color[r=255,g=255,b=255]
```

Figure 7.17
Changed Value

Now, change the background color.

➢   In the **Variable** pane, click **background**.
➢   In the **Value** pane, type **Color.red**. Be sure to use this exact case.
➢   Right-click to display the shortcut menu, and click **Save**.
➢   Click the **Resume** button.

Your applet should be displayed using the new applet colors.

What just happened? The **show()** method was executed, so the applet background is now yellow, reflecting the color change you made earlier. In addition, the **Duplicate** button now uses a white foreground on a red background. That's because you just changed the foreground and background colors of the **ivjbtDuplicate** variable.

Notice that no source code appears now in the **Source** pane of the **Debug** page. That's because the debugger is waiting for user input to occur in the applet; control has now passed to the applet.

At this point, if you were to exit and save your workspace, your breakpoints would still exist the next time you entered this class. To clear them:

➢   Close the applet.
➢   In the debugger, click the **Breakpoints** tab.
➢   Right-click in the **Methods** pane to display the shortcut menu.
➢   Click **Clear All**.

You've just gone through a step-by-step debugging session. This session was fairly simple, but you learned most of the common functions needed to successfully debug a Java program. VisualAge for Java offers other tools that can help in a testing and debugging environment. You'll learn about these other tools next.

Scrapbook

You can use VisualAge for Java's Scrapbook to test and execute small pieces of Java code. You don't have to write a method or a class to execute these lines of code.

You typically would use the Scrapbook to test-drive some new Java code you've never used. You also might want to verify the syntax of a method or prove a concept. You can also use the Scrapbook as a place to store notes about the development project on which you're working. As you can see, there are many ways to take advantage of the Scrapbook.

You're going to open a Scrapbook window.

➢   On the menu bar, click **Window**.

➢   Click **Scrapbook**.

As shown in Figure 7.18, your **Scrapbook** window should be open. Notice that Page 1 is already defined for you. A Scrapbook page is nothing more than an area in which to write your code. You can have multiple pages open in the Scrapbook. You can save Scrapbook pages and can retrieve them later if necessary. You use the normal **File** menu to do this. Note that the Scrapbook doesn't save your pages to the repository; it uses the normal file system to save scrapbook files.

Figure 7.18
Scrapbook

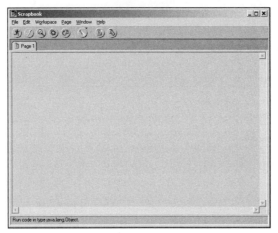

You're going to add some Java code to your new Scrapbook page.

➢   Type the following lines of code on Page 1, as shown in Figure 7.19:

```
int arr[] = {0, 4+28, 5-2, 17};
return arr;
```

Figure 7.19
Newly Entered Java Code

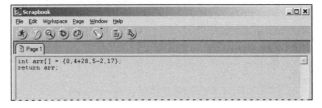

Inspector

To view or inspect the values of your newly created Java code, you can use the Inspector. To compile and execute your code, take these steps:

➤ With your pointer, highlight the two lines of code you just entered.
➤ Right-click to display the shortcut menu.
➤ Click **Inspect**.
➤ In the **Fields** pane, click **1**.

You should be looking at an **Inspector** window similar to Figure 7.20. In the **Value** pane, you see the value of element 1 in the arr[] array. Notice that the value is 32. Where did 32 come from? Recall that you specified the expression **4+28** as the value of element 1. Pretty cool, huh?

Figure 7.20
Inspector

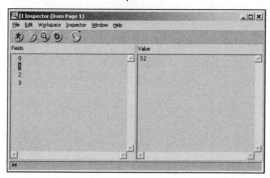

➤ Close the **Inspector** window.

Add a new page to the Scrapbook:

➤ On the Scrapbook menu bar, click **Page**.
➤ Click **New Page**.

Notice that the code you just created still appears on Page 1. Now, add some additional code to the Scrapbook as shown in Figure 7.21.

➤ Enter the following code into Page 2 of your Scrapbook:

```
Frame frame = new Frame("Title is here");
return frame;
```

➤ With your pointer, highlight both lines of code.
➤ Right-click to display the shortcut menu.
➤ Click **Inspect**.

You should have received the error shown in Figure 7.22: "The type named Frame is not defined."

Figure 7.21
Scrapbook Page 2

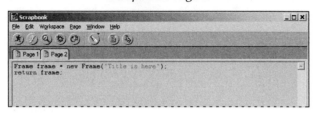

Figure 7.22
Scrapbook Error

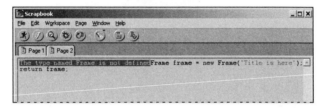

Context

Why did you receive the error? The Scrapbook uses what is known as *context* to execute lines of code. In this case, it didn't understand what Frame was because Frame was out-of-context. The execution context in the Scrapbook needs to be set to any class contained in the VisualAge for Java workspace. The default context is set to the **Object** class. Code in the Scrapbook is treated as a method in the class of the designated context and has access to other methods and fields in the specified context class. How do you get the correct context? That's what you'll do next.

➤   Delete the error message by pressing the Delete key.
➤   On the menu bar, click **Page**.
➤   Click **Run In**.
➤   In the **Run** window's **Pattern** field, type **Frame**.
➤   In the **Type Names** list, click the **Frame** class, as shown in Figure 7.23.
➤   Click **OK**.
➤   With your pointer, highlight both lines of code again on Page 2.
➤   Right-click to display the shortcut menu.
➤   Click **Inspect**.

You should be looking at an **Inspector** window like the one shown in Figure 7.24.

Figure 7.23
Run In

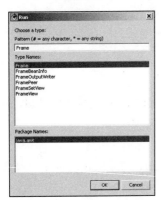

Figure 7.24
Inspector Window

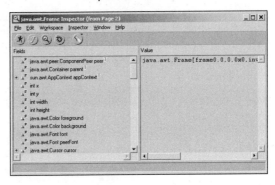

The **Inspector** window has a neat little feature for executing methods:

➤   As shown in Figure 7.25, type **show();** in the **Value** pane.
➤   With your pointer, highlight the **show();** method.
➤   Right-click to display the shortcut menu.
➤   Click **Run**.

Figure 7.25
Run Show()

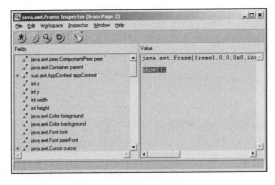

Look closely at the upper-left corner of the screen. You should notice a very small Frame, or title bar, like the one shown in Figure 7.26. You may have to look closely for the Frame before you find it.

Figure 7.26
Frame

➢   Try closing the Frame.

It won't close, because there is no method available to do that. Let's fix that.

➢   In the Inspector's **Value** pane under **show()**, type **dispose();**.
➢   With your pointer, highlight the **dispose();** method.
➢   Right-click to display the shortcut menu.
➢   Click **Run**.

The Frame disappears. That's because the **dispose()** method has been executed. Pretty neat stuff to be able to test small snippets of code!

AS400 Context

Next, you're going to use the **AS400** class to display a simple AS/400 sign-on prompt. You'll learn much more about the AS/400 prompt in later chapters.

➢   Close the **Inspector** window.
➢   Click **OK**.
➢   On the menu bar, click **Page**.
➢   Click **New Page**.
➢   Enter the following lines of code into Page 3 of your Scrapbook, as shown in Figure 7.27:

```
AS400 system = new AS400();
system.connectService(AS400.RECORDACCESS);
```

Figure 7.27
Page 3

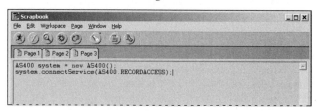

➢   On the menu bar, click **Page**.
➢   Click **Run In**.
➢   In the **Pattern** field, type **AS400**. Make sure you use no slash character (/).
➢   Click the **AS400** class.
➢   Click **OK**.
➢   With your pointer, highlight your lines of code.
➢   Right-click to display the shortcut menu.
➢   Click **Run**.

You should be looking at an AS/400 sign-on prompt identical to the one shown in Figure 7.28.

Figure 7.28
AS/400 Prompt

Don't bother entering your sign-on information; it won't do anything. Why not? That's because you executed only the **connectService()** method. In later chapters, you'll learn what to do after you reach the AS/400 prompt.

➢ Close the AS/400 prompt.
➢ Close the Scrapbook.
➢ When you're prompted to save the contents of the Scrapbook page, click **No**.
➢ Click **No**.
➢ Click **No**.

Other Debug Features

Some additional VisualAge for Java debug features you may want to check out include conditional breakpoints, external class breakpoints, and watches.

Conditional Breakpoints

You can set conditional breakpoints that will cause the interruption of an executing program when a true condition is encountered. To do this, you perform these steps:

1. Set the breakpoint as usual.
2. On the blue-dot breakpoint, change the breakpoint by right-clicking to display the shortcut menu.
3. In the **Configuring Breakpoint** window, select the **On expression** check box.
4. Type the expression that will control the conditional breakpoint.

You can also specify a conditional breakpoint to occur on a certain iteration within a loop.

External Class Breakpoints

You can add breakpoints to external Java classes. To do so, you go to the debugger. On the **Methods** menu, select the **External .class file breakpoints** menu item. Select or browse for the class you're seeking. Then, specify the method to set the breakpoints.

Watches

You can watch the values of certain expressions or variables throughout the debug process by using the **Watches** window. To do so, you go to the debugger. On the **Window** menu, select the **Watches** menu item. Figure 7.29 shows a sample **Watches** window. In this example, two variables are being watched: **getLabel1()** and **getTextField1()**. When the debugger stops or a step is executed, the window displays each variable's value in the Value column.

Figure 7.29
Watches Window

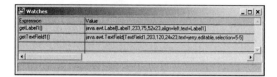

Additional VisualAge for Java Debuggers

This chapter has focused on the standard Integrated Debugger that is part of VisualAge for Java. The Enterprise Edition of VisualAge for Java also includes a Distributed Debugger that lets you debug Java applications that are developed outside the VisualAge for Java environment. You can use the Distributed Debugger to debug on AIX, OS/400, OS/2, OS/390, Solaris, and Windows platforms. The Distributed Debugger is beyond the scope of this book. For more information about distributed debugging, see the VisualAge for Java help system.

Summary

The VisualAge for Java Interactive Debugger can be very helpful when you're trying to figure out why something isn't working the way you expected it to. It's also a great tool for experimenting with a particular method and how it works.

In this chapter you learned

- how to use the Interactive Debugger
- how to use the Console
- how to manage breakpoints
- how to use the evaluation area
- how to use the Scrapbook and to execute snippets of code
- how to inspect and change variables

In the next chapter, you'll begin learning how to use AS/400-specific JavaBeans.

Unit 2

Accessing AS/400 Objects from Java

Chapter 8

Executing AS/400 Commands from Java

Chapter Objectives

- ❑ Become familiar with AS/400 Toolbox JavaBeans
- ❑ Connect to the AS/400
- ❑ Execute AS/400 commands from the client workstation
- ❑ Create a class with a superclass

Chapter Project

- ❑ A simple class will be created to run AS/400 commands.
- ❑ This class will execute runtime commands when the **Execute AS/400 Command** button is clicked.
- ❑ A hard-coded compile-time command will be executed when the **Clear My OUTQ** button is clicked.
- ❑ Figure 8.1 shows what the sample application will look like.

Figure 8.1
Chapter Project

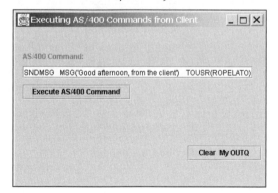

As a curious AS/400 programmer, you may have skipped over the first seven chapters of this book to look at this one, which is the first chapter that really demonstrates the use of AS/400 objects. If that's the case, get your curiosity out of the way, and then go back and start at the beginning of the book. If you've been diligent in studying each of the chapters up to this point, pat yourself on the back. You are now ready to continue on.

Unit Two Setup

In Unit 2, which begins with this chapter, you'll become familiar with how to access various AS/400 objects. Each chapter in this unit will focus on accessing a particular AS/400 object using step-by-step examples. In this chapter, you'll learn how to connect to the AS/400 and how to execute AS/400 commands. The rest of the Unit 2 chapters focus on the following:

Chapter 9   Accessing AS/400 Object Lists from Java
Chapter 10   Retrieving OS/400 System Values from Java
Chapter 11   Accessing the IFS from Java
Chapter 12   Accessing a Local Data Area from Java

To begin, you're going to create a new project named **My AS400 Access Projects**. The work accomplished in all the Unit 2 chapters will be stored in this newly created project.

➤   If the workbench isn't started, start it now.
➤   From the workbench **All Projects** pane, right-click to display the shortcut menu, select **Add**, and then select **Project**.
➤   Make sure the **Create a new project named** option is selected. Type **My AS400 Access Projects** into the space provided.
➤   Click **Finish** to complete the creation of the project.

Once the project is created, you'll see it listed in the upper pane of the workbench.

You are now going to create a package called **accessingas400objects**.

➤   Select the project **My AS400 Access Projects** with a click. Right-click to display the shortcut menu, select **Add**, and then select **Package**.
➤   Make sure the **Project** name is **My AS400 Access Projects**.
➤   Make sure the **Create a new package named** option is selected. Type **accessingas400objects** into the space provided.
➤   Click **Finish** to complete the creation of the package.

Once the package and project are created, you'll see them listed in the workbench **All Projects** pane, as shown in Figure 8.2.

Figure 8.2
Workbench Setup for Unit 2

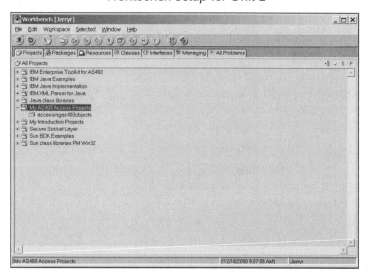

Creating an Application Class

In Chapters 4 and 5, you created applets. As you may recall, an applet is a special type of class designed to run inside a browser. A Java program or class is typically called either an applet or an application, depending on the environment in which it runs. Applets call an **init()** method when they are loaded. Applications call a **main()** method to start execution. A Java class can actually be both an applet and an application if it has both methods defined.

In this chapter, you're going to create a class that is designed to run from a command line. It will be created as an application-type class. Outside the VisualAge for Java workbench, you execute a class by specifying the Java interpreter and the name of the Java class. For example, by typing

```
java CommandCallExample
```

at a command line, you would execute the class **CommandCallExample** (which just happens to be the name of the class you'll create in this chapter). The command line could be an AS/400 command line, or it could be a DOS command line on a PC workstation.

Using a JFrame Superclass

Many times when we create a class, we refer to a *superclass*. A class can inherit properties from another class, which is called the superclass or parent. In this chapter, you'll use a superclass of **JFrame**, which is part of the Java Foundation Classes (JVC) and the Swing GUI component set. You can use the **JFrame** class as a container, or window, to generate events when things happen to the window — such as the window being closed, opened, or activated. These events can be sent to a **WindowListener** if one is registered with the JFrame.

You are now going to create a class called **CommandCallExample**, which inherits properties from superclass **JFrame**.

➤ Select the package **accessingas400objects** with a click. Right-click to display the shortcut menu, select **Add**, and then select **Class**. The **Create Class** SmartGuide will be displayed.

➤ Make sure the **Project** name is **My AS400 Access Projects**.

➤ Make sure the **Package** name is **accessingas400objects**.

➢   In the **Class name** field, type **CommandCallExample**.

➢   Click **Browse** to select a superclass.

➢   When the **Superclass** window appears, type **JFrame** into the **Pattern** field.

➢   In the **Type Names** list, double-click **JFrame**. When you return to the **Create Class** SmartGuide window, you should see **javax.swing.JFrame** entered in the **Superclass** field, as shown in Figure 8.3.

➢   Select the **Browse the class when finished** check box.

➢   Select the **Compose the class visually** check box.

➢   Click **Finish** to complete the creation of the class.

Figure 8.3
Class CommandCallExample

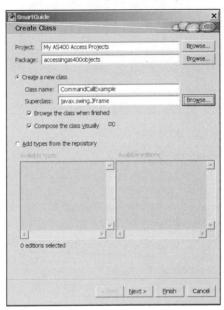

You should be inside the Visual Composition Editor. Notice that you now have a JFrame that contains standard Windows buttons to minimize, maximize, and close. This JFrame will have the default name **CommandCallExample**, the same name as your class. Contained within the JFrame is a JPanel that will be used to hold your visual components. The JPanel was created automatically when you created the class **CommandCallExample** and specified a superclass of JFrame. The JPanel will have the default name **JFrameContentPane**. This can be a little confusing. In the next section, you'll learn how to use the beans list to be able to distinguish between the JFrame and the JPanel. Remember, the JPanel is contained within the JFrame.

You are now going to change the title of the JFrame.

➢   On the menu bar, click **Tools**.

➢   Click **Beans List**.

➢   In the **Beans List** window, shown in Figure 8.4, double-click the **CommandCallExample** JFrame to display the **Properties** sheet.

➢   For the **title** property, type **Executing AS/400 Commands from Client**.

➢   Close the **Properties** sheet.

➢   Close the **Beans List**.

Figure 8.4
JFrame CommandCallExample

You are going to add a button as shown in Figure 8.5. On the left side of the VCE, you should see the Swing bean category open. Swing, not Abstract Window Toolkit, is the open bean category because you specified a **JFrame** superclass, which is part of the Swing component set.

➢ Click the **JButton** bean ▭, and drop it in the lower-right corner of the free-form surface visual area, or the **JFrameContentPane** JPanel.
➢ Double-click the JButton. Change the **beanName** from **JButton1** to **btClearOUTQ**.
➢ Change the **text** property to **Clear My OUTQ**.
➢ Close the **Properties** sheet.
➢ Expand the button so that you can see all the text.

Figure 8.5
Clear My OUTQ JButton

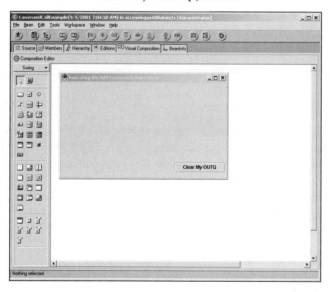

AS/400 Beans

In Chapter 4, you were given a list of all the AS/400 JavaBeans available in the Enterprise Toolkit for AS/400. You're going to use a couple of these beans now to connect to the AS/400 and to execute AS/400 commands. The first step is to identify the AS/400 to which you're going to connect when the Java application is executed. You'll use the **AS400** bean to do this. This bean lets you specify the name of the AS/400, whether to use a user profile name, and whether to use password caching.

➤ On the left side of the VCE, click the bean category drop-down arrow to display the bean category list, and then click to select the **AS/400 Toolbox** bean category. You may have to wait a minute for the new category to appear. Switching bean categories can take some time. Once you've switched once, though, it goes much faster the next time.

Look at Figure 8.6. A new bean category, the AS/400 Toolbox category, is now selected. Notice that the entire palette of JavaBeans has changed. All the AS/400 JavaBeans are now available to you. You can hover your pointer over the various AS/400 beans to get an idea of what they do. For the detailed list of all the AS/400 JavaBeans, see Chapter 4.

Figure 8.6
AS/400 Toolbox

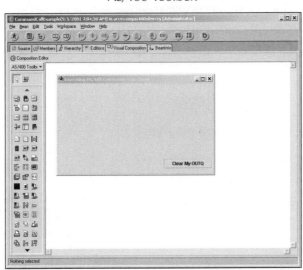

Now, add the bean that will enable AS/400 access:

➤ In the bean palette, click the **AS400** bean ▣, and drop it on the free-form surface as shown in Figure 8.7. When you insert the **AS400** bean, the bean is automatically named **AS4001**. If you were to add another **AS400** bean, it would be named **AS4002**, and so on.
➤ Double-click the new bean to display its **Properties** sheet (Figure 8.8).
➤ Change the **systemName** property to the name of the AS/400 you're going to access.
➤ Change the **userID** property to your AS/400 user profile name.
➤ Close the **Properties** sheet.

> **Note:** *Your AS/400 systemName and userID values will differ from the examples of S1021CCM and ROPELATO shown in Figure 8.8.*

Figure 8.7

AS/400-Related Beans

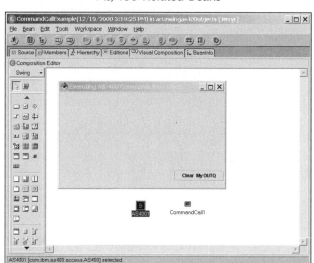

Figure 8.8

AS400 Bean Properties

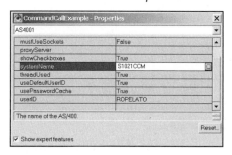

Next, you'll add a **CommandCall** bean. This bean lets you specify the actual AS/400 command you want to execute on the AS/400. You'll use a hard-coded approach for this example.

➢ In the bean palette, click the **CommandCall** bean ▣, and drop it on the free-form surface beside your **AS4001** bean. The new bean will automatically be given the default name **CommandCall1**.

➢ Double-click the **CommandCall1** bean. Change the **command** property to **CLROUTQ OUTQ(*xxxxxx*)**, where **xxxxxx** is the name of an output queue on your AS/400 that can be cleared without causing any harm. (If you don't feel comfortable clearing any of your existing output queues, you can create a temporary output queue.) Figure 8.9 shows a sample **command** value. Notice that this will be a hard-coded command. At run time, you won't be able to change it.

➢ Close the **Properties** sheet.

> ***Note:*** *Your AS/400 command property value will differ from the example shown in Figure 8.9,*
>   *CLROUTQ OUTQ(ROPELATO).*

Figure 8.9
CommandCall Bean Properties

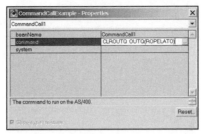

Connecting AS/400 Beans

In Chapter 6, you learned about different types of event, property, and method connections. You're now going to set up a property-to-property connection between the two AS/400 beans you just created.

Property-to-Property Connection: system

`connPtoP1: (AS4001,this ←→ CommandCall1,system)`

The property-to-property connection lets you associate the properties of the **AS400** JavaBean (**systemName** and **userID**) with the properties of the **CommandCall** JavaBean. If you didn't specify this connection, you would have to specify which AS/400 you wanted to connect to any time you used any of the AS/400 JavaBeans.

Connect the **AS4001** bean with the **CommandCall1** bean:

➢ Right-click the **AS4001** bean.
➢ Click **Connect**.
➢ Click **this**. The **this** property is a special variable that lets you represent the value of the variable itself. There is no associated **setThis()** or **getThis()** method. You can use the **this** property as the source of a connection, which means that the variable has been assigned. In this example, you are connecting the **AS4001** bean directly to the **CommandCall1** bean.
➢ Click the spider-end pointer on the **CommandCall1** bean.
➢ Click **Connectible Features**.
➢ Double-click the **system** property.
➢ Double-click the connection to verify that it is correct as shown in Figure 8.10.
➢ Close the connection's **Properties** window.

Figure 8.10
connPtoP1

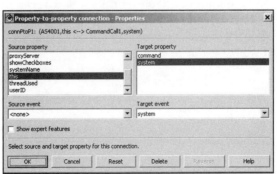

Event-to-Method Connection: run()

`connEtoM1: (btClearOUTQ,actionPerformed → CommandCall1,run())`

Next, you'll create an event-to-method connection, with the **Clear My OUTQ** button triggering the event and the method defined as a **run()** command method. At run time, when a user clicks the button, your application will execute the hard-coded CLROUTQ (Clear Output Queue) command. To accomplish this, you'll use a Java **run()** method that passes no parameters. You don't need any parameters because you've hard-coded the command.

Connect the **Clear My OUTQ** JButton with a **run()** method:

➢ Right-click the **btClearOUTQ** JButton.
➢ Click **Connect**.
➢ Click **actionPerformed**.
➢ Click the spider-end pointer on the **CommandCall1** bean.
➢ Click **Connectible Features**.
➢ Double-click the **run()** method.
➢ Double-click the connection to verify that it is correct as shown in Figure 8.11.
➢ Close the **Properties** window.

Figure 8.11
connEtoM1

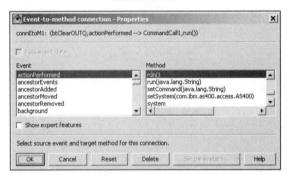

The two beans, **AS4001** and **CommandCall1**, work together. When a user clicks the **Clear My OUTQ** JButton, the **run()** method executes the AS/400 command defined in the **CommandCall1** bean, which in turn, triggers an event for the **AS4001** bean to make the connection to the AS/400. To be able to run this Java program, you need to successfully connect to the AS/400. Doing so requires you to have some kind of available connection to your AS/400. This could be a TCP/IP Internet connection or some physical connection to the system.

Save and run your Java program:

➢ On the menu bar, click **Bean**.
➢ Click **Run**, and then click **Run Main**.

You'll see the window shown in Figure 8.12 appear. Note that at this point you are *not* signed on to the AS/400.

Figure 8.12
Clear My OUTQ JButton

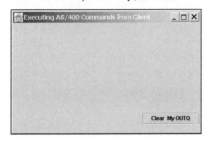

➤   Click the **Clear My OUTQ** JButton.

AS/400 Sign-on Screen

By clicking the **Clear My OUTQ** JButton, you initiate the bean to communicate with the AS/400. You may have noticed that the color of the JButton changed when you clicked the button. This is normal. The color change indicates that communication with the AS/400 is occurring.

The next screen you see is the AS/400 graphical sign-on screen, shown in Figure 8.13.

Figure 8.13
AS/400 Sign-on Prompt Screen

What's nice about this standard AS/400 sign-on screen is that all the logic associated with signing on to the AS/400 is self-contained. You don't have to worry about writing logic to handle an invalid password or to limit the number of sign-on attempts. This is the same process normally used when signing on to the familiar green screen.

Your AS/400 prompt should appear with the AS/400 name and user profile that you entered into the **AS4001** bean **Properties** sheet. (You should have set these up to be *your* AS/400 and user profile.)

➤   Enter your AS/400 password, and click **OK**.

How can you tell whether clicking the **Clear My OUTQ** JButton actually worked?

➤   Sign on to the AS/400 from your normal Client Access sign-on screen. Look at the output queue that you specified on the **AS4001** bean **Properties** sheet. If everything worked, the output queue should be empty.

➤   Close your **CommandCallExample** application.

Way to go! You just completed your first Java program that made an AS/400 connection and executed an AS/400 command. You may be surprised at how easy this was to accomplish. The problem with the example you just completed is that it is basically a hard-coded command. Next, you're going to take your **CommandCallExample** class and make it a little more flexible.

Runtime Execution of AS/400 Commands

In the previous section, you executed a hard-coded AS/400 command. In this section, you're going to add components to the VCE so that you can change the AS/400 command at run time. Look at Figure 8.14. You will add some components to make your application look like the screen shown in this figure.

Figure 8.14
New Components for CommandCallExample

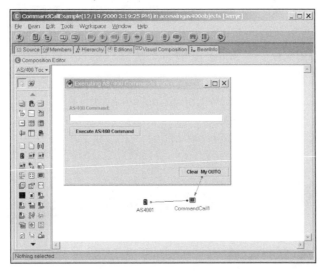

First, you're going to add a button. The **AS/400 Toolbox** bean category should still be open in the VCE. You need to change back to the **Swing** bean category.

➢ Click the bean category drop-down arrow to display the bean category list, and then click to select the **Swing** bean category. You may have to wait a minute for the change to take effect.
➢ Click the **JButton** bean, and drop it on the left side of the **JFrameContentPane**.
➢ Double-click the JButton. Change the **beanName** from **JButton1** to **btExecuteCommand**.
➢ Change the **text** property to **Execute AS/400 Command**.
➢ Close the **Properties** sheet. Expand the JButton so that you can see all the text.

Now, add the command-entry field and its text label:

➢ Click the **JTextField** bean ⊞, and drop it on the left side of the **JFrameContentPane**. Expand the JTextField to cover the entire width of the pane.
➢ Double-click the JTextField. Change the **beanName** from **JTextField1** to **tfCommand**.
➢ Close the **Properties** sheet.
➢ Click the **JLabel** bean ⊡, and drop it on the left side of the **JFrameContentPane**.
➢ Double-click the JLabel. Change the **beanName** from **JLabel1** to **lbCommand**.
➢ Change the **text** property to **AS/400 Command:**.
➢ Close the **Properties** sheet. Expand the JLabel so that you can see all the text.

Now, align the JButton, the JTextField, and the JLabel you just created:

➢ Click the JButton **btExecuteCommand**.
➢ Holding down the Shift key, click the JTextField **tfCommand**.
➢ Still holding the Shift key, click the JLabel **lbCommand**.

➤   Right-click to display the shortcut menu.

➤   Select **Layout**, then select **Align**, and then click **Left**.

Your three beans should now be aligned as shown in the figure.

Now, you need to add another **CommandCall** bean. On this **CommandCall** bean, you're not going to specify any AS/400 command. Later, you'll add a connection to be able to execute the command.

Recall that **CommandCall** is an AS/400 Toolbox bean. You'll need to switch bean categories again.

➤   Click to display the bean category drop-down list. Click the **AS/400 Toolbox** bean category. You may have to wait a minute.

➤   Click the **CommandCall** bean, and drop it on the free-form surface as shown in Figure 8.15. This bean will be **CommandCall2**.

Figure 8.15
New CommandCall Bean

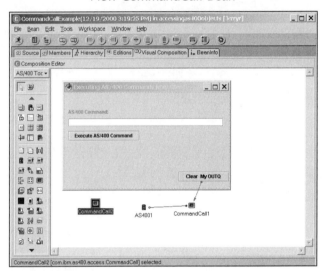

Property-to-Property Connection: system

```
connPtoP2: (AS4001,this ←→ CommandCall2,system)
```

Once again, you're going to associate the properties of the **AS4001** JavaBean with a **CommandCall** JavaBean. You'll set up this **CommandCall** bean to use a variable command, as opposed to the hard-coded command you used earlier.

Connect the **AS4001** bean with the **CommandCall2** bean.

➤   Right-click the **AS4001** bean.

➤   Click **Connect**.

➤   Click **this**.

➤   Click the spider-end pointer on the **CommandCall2** bean.

➤   Click **Connectible Features**.

➤   Double-click the **system** property.

➤   Double-click the connection to verify that it is correct as shown in Figure 8.16.

➤   Close the **Properties** window.

Figure 8.16
connPtoP2

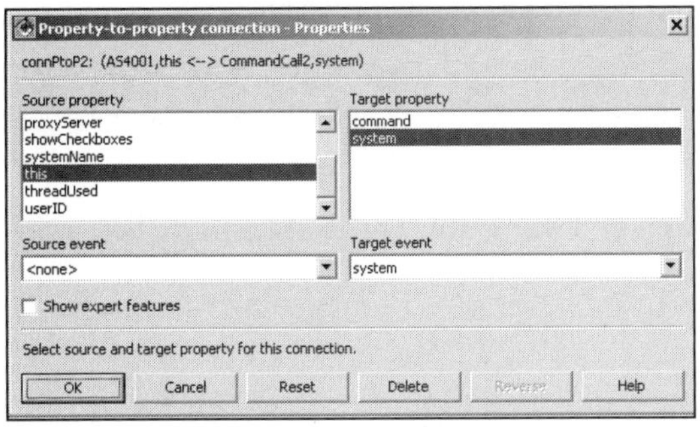

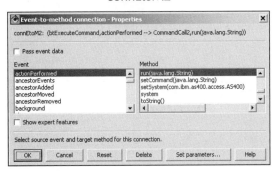

Event-to-Method Connection: run(java.lang.String)

```
connEtoM2: (btExecuteCommand,actionPerformed → CommandCall2,run(java.lang.String))
```

To give the user the flexibility of entering any AS/400 command at run time, you need to set up two connections. The first connection (event-to-method) defines which method is executed when the user clicks the execute button. The second connection (parameter-from-property) passes the AS/400 command that the user enters at run time.

With the event-to-method connection, you want the user to be able to enter any AS/400 command at run time. To accomplish this, you will use a **run(java.lang.String)** method that passes a variable of a **String** data type. The contents of the String will be defined at run time by the user.

Connect the **Execute AS/400 Command** button with a **run(java.lang.String)** method:

➢ Right-click the **btExecuteCommand** JButton.
➢ Click **Connect**.
➢ Click **actionPerformed**.
➢ Click the spider-end pointer on the **CommandCall2** bean.
➢ Click **Connectible Features**.
➢ Double-click the **run(java.lang.String)** method.
➢ Double-click the connection to verify that it is correct as shown in Figure 8.17.
➢ Close the **Properties** window.

Notice that the connection is not complete, as denoted by the dashed line in the VCE.

Figure 8.17
connEtoM2

Parameter-from-Property Connection

```
connPfromP1: (connEtoM2: (btExecuteCommand,actionPerformed →
              CommandCall2,run(java.lang.String)),arg1 → tfCommand,text)
```

You will now complete the connection by passing a value, or parameter, into the primary connection. The connection is expecting a **String** data type.

Identify the source property:

➢   Move the pointer so that its tip is directly over the dashed line. Right-click to display the shortcut menu. Select **Connect**, and then select **arg1**.

Identify the target property:

➢   Take the spider-end of the line, and drop it on top of the JTextField named **tfCommand**. A new menu will automatically appear. Select the **text** option.
➢   Double-click the connection to verify that it is correct as shown in Figure 8.18.
➢   Close the **Properties** window.

Figure 8.18
connPfromP1

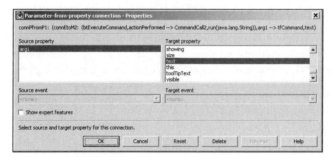

When the connection is completed, it should look as shown in Figure 8.19. Notice the information line at the bottom edge of the screen. The connection number and its source and target information are displayed here.

Save your class. Before you run it, you'll need to sign on to the AS/400 so that you can easily see your results.

➢   On the menu bar, click **Bean**.
➢   Click **Save Bean**.

Figure 8.19
Connection Completed

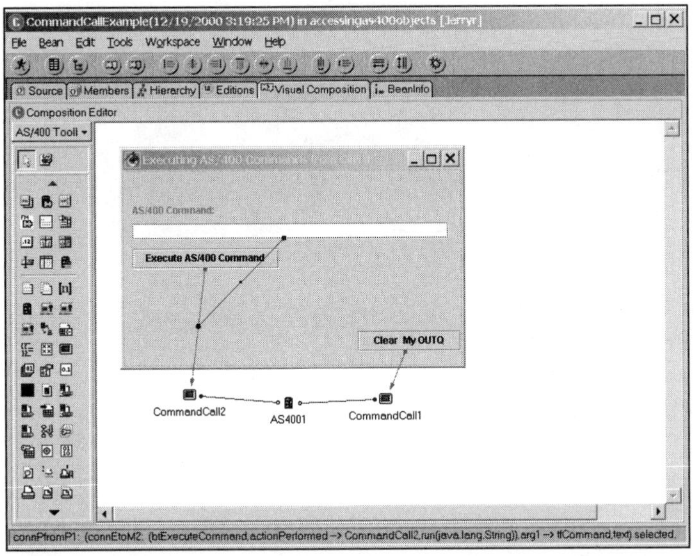

> If you're not signed on to the AS/400, go ahead and sign on from your normal Client Access sign-on screen. Make sure your workstation is in *BREAK mode.

> On the menu bar, click **Run**, and then click **Run Main**.

> In your Java application's entry field, type a valid AS/400 command, such as the following SNDMSG (Send Message) command (where *yourmsgq* is the name of your own message queue):

```
SNDMSG  MSG('Good afternoon, from the client') TOUSR(yourmsgq)
```

> Click the **Execute AS/400 Command** button.

Within a few seconds you should see a user message appear, as shown in Figure 8.20. Feel free to try some other AS/400 commands.

Tips and Tricks

What happens when you enter an AS/400 command designed to give user feedback, such as WRKACTJOB (Work with Active Jobs)? The *CommandCall* class is not designed to handle this type of command. A WRKACTJOB command will not work.

Figure 8.20

AS/400 Message with Java Program

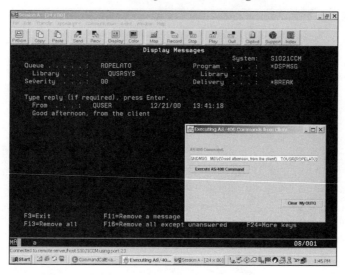

Review AS/400 Classes and Methods

A few methods in the source code of your Java application are worth looking at even though they are very straightforward. These methods use classes defined in the IBM AS/400 Java Toolbox. To review the generated Java source code, do the following:

➢   Close the **Executing AS/400 Commands from Client** application.
➢   Click the **Source** tab to display all the Java code that has been generated.
➢   In the **Elements** pane, click the method name **getAS4001()**.

As shown in Figure 8.21, the **getAS4001()** method uses the **AS400** class. It uses a couple of set methods — **setSystemName()** and **setUserId()** — to set the system name and user profile.

Figure 8.21

Source Code for getAS4001() Method

```
Source code: getAS4001()
private com.ibm.as400.access.AS400 getAS4001() {
     if (ivjAS4001 == null) {
          try {
               ivjAS4001 = new com.ibm.as400.access.AS400();
               ivjAS4001.setSystemName("S1021CCM");
               ivjAS4001.setUserId("ROPELATO");
```

➢   In the **Elements** pane, click the method name **getCommandCall1()**.

Figure 8.22 shows the use of the **CommandCall** class with a **setCommand()** method to invoke the hard-coded AS/400 CLROUTQ command.

Figure 8.22

Source Code for getCommandCall1() Method

```
Source code: getCommandCall1()
private com.ibm.as400.access.CommandCall getCommandCall1() {
    if (ivjCommandCall1 == null) {
        try {
            ivjCommandCall1 = new com.ibm.as400.access.CommandCall();
            ivjCommandCall1.setCommand("CLROUTQ  OUTQ(ROPELATO)");
```

➢   In the **Elements** pane, click the method name **connEtoM1()**. Review method **connEtoM1()**.

➢   Click the method name **connEtoM2()**.

Figure 8.23 shows the difference between the hard-coded command (**connEtoM1**) and the runtime command (**connEtoM2**). Method **connEtoM1()** uses a **run()** method with no parameters. Method **connEtoM2()** uses a parameter retrieved from the input text field, **tfCommand**.

Figure 8.23

Source Code for connEtoM1() and connEtoM2() Methods

```
Source code: connEtoM1
private boolean connEtoM1(java.awt.event.ActionEvent arg1) {
    boolean connEtoM1Result = false;
        try {
            connEtoM1Result = getCommandCall1().run();

Source code: connEtoM2
private boolean connEtoM2(java.awt.event.ActionEvent arg1) {
    boolean connEtoM2Result = false;
        try {
            connEtoM2Result =  getCommandCall2().run(gettfCommand().getText());
```

Summary

You have now written your first Java-to-AS/400 connection program. In this chapter you also

- used the AS/400 Toolbox beans **AS400** and **CommandCall**
- connected to your AS/400 through Java
- executed AS/400 commands through Java, both runtime and compile-time
- used the **JFrame** superclass
- created an application class

You are now ready to move on to the next chapter, where you'll learn about accessing AS/400 object lists from Java. You'll use some additional AS/400 JavaBeans to access and display object lists on the screen.

Chapter 9

Accessing AS/400 Object Lists from Java

Chapter Objectives

- ❑ Become familiar with AS/400 Toolbox Object List JavaBeans
- ❑ Connect to the AS/400 without using the **AS400** bean
- ❑ Retrieve AS/400 objects
- ❑ Display AS/400 objects in a list box

Chapter Project

- ❑ A class will be created to display AS/400 objects.
- ❑ This class will retrieve AS/400 objects when the Retrieve List button is clicked.
- ❑ Selection of AS/400 objects will be based on criteria entered by the user.
- ❑ Criteria will consist of an object name, library name, and object type.
- ❑ Figure 9.1 shows what the sample application will look like.

Figure 9.1
Chapter Project

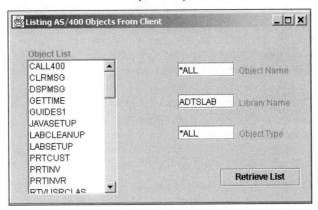

In this chapter, you're going to learn how to access AS/400 objects in a list format. In very simple terms, this operation is equivalent to using the AS/400 DSPOBJD (Display Object Description) command. This chapter builds on some of the concepts you learned in Chapter 8. You will also learn more about connecting to the AS/400 with other classes.

AS/400 Object List Beans

There are two AS/400 beans that accomplish the function of retrieving specified types of AS/400 objects: the **ET400List** bean and the **AS400eList** bean. The **ET400List** bean displays the names of the AS/400 objects in a list box. The **AS400eList** bean is a nonvisual cousin of the **ET400List** bean. It has more retrieving capabilities, but it must be used with other beans, such as **JList**, **JTable**, **JTree**, or **Java Server Page**. This chapter focuses on the **ET400List** bean. This bean calls the AS/400 QUSLOBJ (List Objects) API. If you've ever called API QUSLOBJ from a CL or RPG program, you're probably familiar with its parameters.

You are now going to create a class called **ObjectListExample** that inherits properties from superclass **JFrame**. You'll store your new class in the project **My AS/400 Access Projects** and in the package **accessingas400objects**, shown in Figure 9.2.

Figure 9.2
accessingas400objects Package

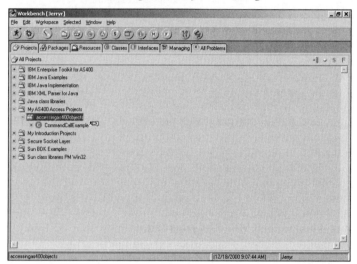

> ➤   If the workbench isn't started, start it now.
> ➤   Expand the project **My AS/400 Access Projects** with a click.
> ➤   Select the package **accessingas400objects** with a click. Right-click to display the shortcut menu, select **Add**, and then select **Class** to display the **Create Class** SmartGuide.
> ➤   Make sure the **Project** name is **My AS400 Access Projects**.
> ➤   Make sure the **Package** name is **accessingas400objects**.
> ➤   For **Class name**, type **ObjectListExample**.
> ➤   Click **Browse** to select a superclass.
> ➤   When the **Superclass** window appears, type **JFrame** in the **Pattern** field.
> ➤   In the **Type names** list, double-click **JFrame**. When you return to the SmartGuide, you should see **javax.swing.JFrame** entered in the **Superclass** field, as shown in Figure 9.3.
> ➤   Select the **Browse the class when finished** check box.
> ➤   Select the **Compose the class visually** check box.
> ➤   Click **Finish** to complete the creation of the class.

Figure 9.3
Class ObjectListExample

You should be inside the Visual Composition Editor. As in Chapter 8, you have a JFrame with standard Windows buttons. Contained within the JFrame is the JPanel (default name **JFrameContentPane**) that will hold your visual components. Your first task here is to change the title of the **ObjectListExample** JFrame.

➢   On the menu bar, click **Tools**.
➢   Click **Beans List**.
➢   As shown in Figure 9.4, double-click the **ObjectListExample** JFrame to display the **Properties** sheet.
➢   For the **title** property, type **Listing AS/400 Objects from Client**. Close the **Properties** sheet.
➢   Close the **Beans List**.

Figure 9.4
JFrame ObjectListExample

Next, you're going to add a button as shown in Figure 9.5. Because you specified a **JFrame** superclass, you should see the **Swing** bean category open on the left side of the VCE.

➢   Click the **JButton** bean , and drop it in the lower-right corner of the free-from surface visual area, or the **JFrameContentPane**.
➢   Double-click the JButton. Change the **beanName** from **JButton1** to **btRetrieveList**.

➤   Change the **text** property to **Retrieve List**.
➤   Close the **Properties** sheet.
➤   Expand the button so that you can see all the text.

Figure 9.5
JButton and JTextField Layout

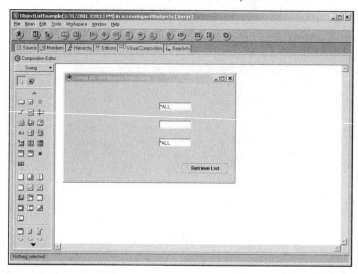

Now, add the three text fields shown in the figure.

➤   Click the **JTextField** bean 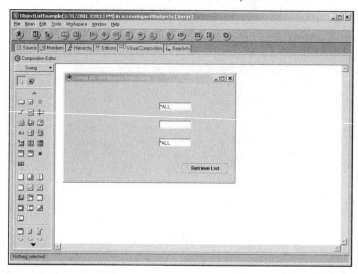, and drop it on the upper-right side of the JFrameContentPane.
➤   Double-click the new JTextField. Change the **beanName** from **JTextField1** to **tfObjectName**.
➤   Change the **text** to ***ALL**.
➤   Close the **Properties** sheet.
➤   Expand the JTextField to the size shown in the figure.
➤   Click the JTextField bean again, and drop it on the center-right side of the visual area, below the first JTextField.
➤   Double-click the JTextField. Change the **beanName** from **JTextField1** to **tfLibraryName**.
➤   Close the **Properties** sheet.
➤   Click the **JTextField** bean one more time, and drop it on the lower-right side of the visual area, below the second JTextField.
➤   Double-click the JTextField. Change the **beanName** from **JTextField1** to **tfObjectType**.
➤   Change the **text** to ***ALL**.
➤   Close the **Properties** sheet.

Now, align the three JTextFields you just created.

➤   Click the JTextField **tfObjectName**.
➤   Holding down the Shift key, click the JTextField **tfLibraryName**.
➤   Still holding the Shift key, click the JTextField **tfObjectType**.
➤   Still holding the Shift key, move the pointer up to the first JTextField. You'll use this field as the base field.
➤   Right-click to display the shortcut menu.
➤   Select **Layout**, then select **Align**, and then click **Left**.

Your three JTextFields should be aligned as shown in the figure. To get all the widths the same size, you may need to select the **Layout|Match Size|Width** option.

Next, add three labels as shown in Figure 9.6.

> Click the **JLabel** bean 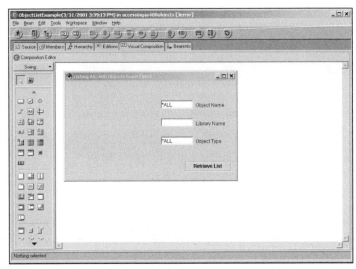, and drop it on the right side of the JTextField **tfObjectName**.
> Double-click the JLabel. Change the **beanName** from **JLabel1** to **lbObjectName**.
> Change the **text** property to **Object Name**.
> Close the **Properties** sheet. Expand the JLabel so that you can see all the text.
> Add two more **JLabels** as shown in the figure.
> Change the **beanName** property of these two JLabels to **lbLibraryName** and **lbObjectType**, respectively.
> Change the **text** property to **Library Name** and **Object Type**, respectively.
> Expand both JLabels so that you can see all the text.
> Align all three JLabels as shown in the figure.

Figure 9.6
JLabel Layout

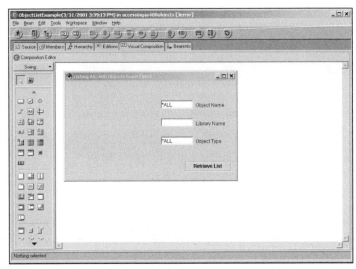

Now, you're going to add an object list bean as shown in Figure 9.7. This bean, **ET400List**, is the third bean listed in the AS/400 Toolbox bean category.

> Click to display the bean category drop-down list, and select the **AS/400 Toolbox** bean category. You may have to wait a minute.
> Click the **ET400List** bean 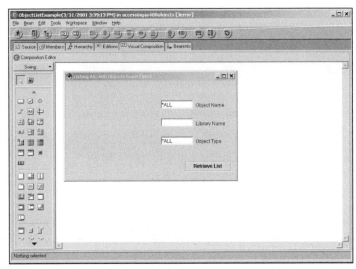, and drop it on the left side of the visual area.
> Double-click the ET400List. Change the **beanName** from **ET400List1** to **lsObjectList**.
> Close the **Properties** sheet.
> Expand the ET400List so that it extends to the bottom of the pane, as shown in the figure.

Figure 9.7
ET400List Layout

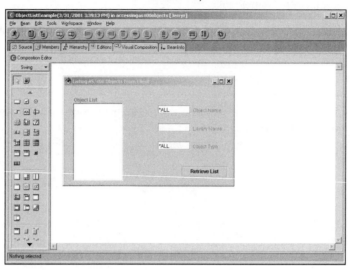

Look at the properties of the ET400List bean.

➢   Double-click the **lsObjectList** bean you just created to display its properties.

➢   Scroll down until you see the **libraryName** property (Figure 9.8).

Figure 9.8
ET400List Bean Properties

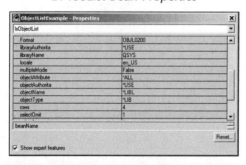

You may notice that you can hard-code a library name, object name, and object type in the properties. In this program, you're going to connect the JTextFields to the **lsObjectList** bean so you can change the object-list criteria at run time. This is similar to what you did in Chapter 8 to enable the runtime execution of a command.

In Chapter 8, you also created an **AS400** bean to be able to connect to your AS/400. In this example, you won't use a separate **AS400** bean. You'll use the **ET400List** bean to enable this connection for you.

➢   Scroll down further until you see the **serverName** property in the **lsObjectList** bean.

➢   Change the **serverName** to the name of the AS/400 you're going to access. Figure 9.9 shows an example.

➢   Close the **Properties** sheet.

*Note: Your AS/400 **serverName** will differ from the example of S104WHBM shown in Figure 9.9.*

Figure 9.9
ET400List Bean serverName Property

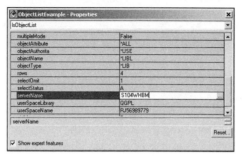

Tips and Tricks

Using a *serverName* or *systemName* property in an AS/400 bean lets you quickly set up an AS/400 connection. With this approach, you don't have to use a separate *AS400* bean and the associated visual connection. Most of the AS/400 beans that allow connection to the AS/400 don't give you the option to specify user ID, password, or caching defaults. When you use the *AS400* bean, you do have these options.

Tips and Tricks

Figure 9.9 shows the *serverName* property being defined with the value S104WHBM. If you leave the *serverName* blank, you'll be prompted with an AS/400 sign-on screen every time you try to retrieve an object list. To avoid this nuisance, either enter a value for the *serverName* property or create a separate connection to place a value into the *serverName*.

Add a label above the object list box.

➢ Click to display the bean category drop-down list. Select the **Swing** bean category.
➢ Click the **JLabel** bean 🔲, and drop it just above the **lsOjectList** bean, as shown back in Figure 9.7.
➢ Double-click the JLabel. Change the **beanName** from **JLabel1** to **lbObjectList**.
➢ Change the **text** property to **Object List**.
➢ Change the **font** property to **Bold (dialog,bold,12)**.
➢ Close the **Properties** sheet.
➢ Expand the JLabel so that you can see all the text.
➢ On the menu bar, click **Bean**.
➢ Click **Save Bean**.

Connecting to the ET400List Bean

You are now going to set up five event-to-method connections. At run time, when a user presses the **Retrieve List** button, you'll want to set the value of the object name, library name, and object type. To accomplish this, you'll use three event-to-method connections in conjunction with three parameter-from-property connections to be able to pass the three parameters. The parameters will pass all the data collected from the input fields into the **ET400List** bean.

You will also create a fourth event-to-method connection to retrieve the object list. The fifth event-to-method connection will be created to perform a "show focus."

Event-to-Method Connection: setObjectName()

`connEtoM1: (btRetrieveList,actionPerformed → lsObjectList,setObjectName(java.lang.String))`

Connect the **Retrieve List** JButton with a **setObjectName(java.lang.String)** method.

➢ Right-click the **btRetrieveList** JButton.
➢ Click **Connect**.
➢ Click **actionPerformed**.
➢ Click the spider-end pointer on the **lsObjectList** bean.
➢ Click **Connectible Features**.
➢ Double-click the **setObjectName(java.lang.String)** method.
➢ Double-click the connection to verify that it is correct as shown in Figure 9.10.
➢ Close the **Properties** window.

Figure 9.10
Connection connEtoM1

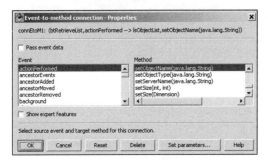

Parameter-from-Property Connection

`connPfromP1: (connEtoM1: (btRetrieveList,actionPerformed →`
`            lsObjectList,setObjectName(java.lang.String)),arg1 → tfObjectName,text)`

Complete the connection by passing a value or parameter into the primary connection. The connection is expecting a **String** data type. In this case, whatever the user enters into the **Object Name** input field is passed. If nothing is entered, ***ALL** is passed.

Identify the source property:

➢ Right-click the dashed line.
➢ Click **Connect**.
➢ Click **objectName**.

Identify the target property:

➢ Click the spider-end pointer on the **tfObjectName** JTextField bean.
➢ Click **text**.
➢ Double-click the connection to verify that it is correct as shown in Figure 9.11.
➢ Close the **Properties** window.

Figure 9.12 shows what the connection should look like.

Figure 9.11
Connection connPfromP1

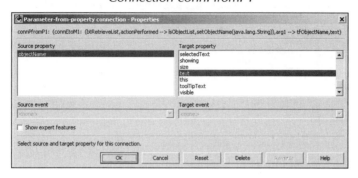

Figure 9.12
Connection Completed

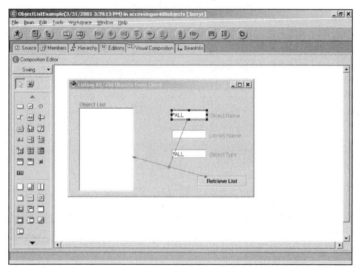

Event-to-Method Connection: setLibraryName()

connEtoM2: (btRetrieveList,actionPerformed → lsObjectList,setLibraryName(java.lang.String))

Connect the **Retrieve List** JButton with a **setLibraryName(java.lang.String)** method.

➢   Right-click the **btRetrieveList** JButton.

➢   Click **Connect**.

➢   Click **actionPerformed**.

➢   Click the spider-end pointer on the **lsObjectList** bean.

➢   Click **Connectible Features**.

➢   Double-click the **setLibraryName(java.lang.String)** method.

➢   Double-click the connection to verify that it is correct as shown in Figure 9.13.

➢   Close the **Properties** window.

Figure 9.13
Connection connEtoM2

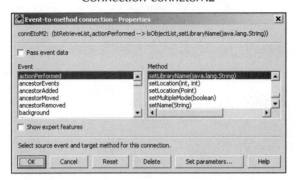

Parameter-from-Property Connection

```
connPfromP2: (connEtoM2: (btRetrieveList,actionPerformed →
             lsObjectList,setLibraryName(java.lang.String)),arg1 → tfLibraryName,text)
```

Identify the source property:

➢ Right-click the dashed line.
➢ Click **Connect**.
➢ Click **libraryName**.

Identify the target property:

➢ Click the spider-end pointer on the **tfLibraryName** JTextField bean.
➢ Click **text**.

Event-to-Method Connection: setObjectType()

```
connEtoM3: (btRetrieveList,actionPerformed → lsObjectList,setObjectType(java.lang.String))
```

Connect the **Retrieve List** JButton with a **setObjectType(java.lang.String)** method.

➢ Right-click the **btRetrieveList** JButton.
➢ Click **Connect**.
➢ Click **actionPerformed**.
➢ Click the spider-end pointer on the **lsObjectList** bean.
➢ Click **Connectible Features**.
➢ Double-click the **setObjectType(java.lang.String)** method.

Parameter-from-Property Connection

```
connPfromP3: (connEtoM3: (btRetrieveList,actionPerformed →
             lsObjectList,setObjectType(java.lang.String)),arg1 → tfObjectType,text)
```

Identify the source property:

➢ Right-click the dashed line.
➢ Click **Connect**.
➢ Click **objectType**.

Identify the target property:

➢   Click the spider-end pointer on the **tfObjectType** JTextField bean.
➢   Click **text**.

Event-to-Method Connection: getObjectList()

connEtoM4: (btRetrieveList,actionPerformed → lsObjectList,getObjectList())

Connect the **Retrieve List** JButton with a **getObjectList()** method. This method retrieves the object list, based on the parameter information from the previous connections.

➢   Right-click the **btRetrieveList** JButton.
➢   Click **Connect**.
➢   Click **actionPerformed**.
➢   Click the spider-end pointer on the **lsObjectList** bean.
➢   Click **Connectible Features**.
➢   Double-click the **getObjectList()** method.
➢   Double-click the connection to verify that it is correct as shown in Figure 9.14.
➢   Close the **Properties** window.

Figure 9.14
Connection connEtoM4

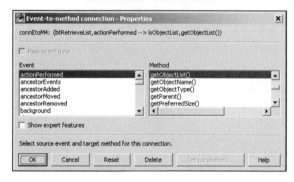

Show Focus

You have one last step to do before you run your application. In Chapter 5, you learned how to "show focus" — that is, position the cursor into a particular input field. You're going to do that now for the **ObjectListExample** application.

Event-to-Method Connection: requestFocus()

connEtoM5: (ObjectListExample,initialize() → tfObjectName,requestFocus())

➢   Right-click the nonvisual area of the free-form surface.
➢   Click **Connect**.
➢   Click **Connectible Features**.
➢   Click the **Event** button.
➢   Double-click the **initialize()** method.
➢   Click the spider-end pointer on the **tfObjectName** JTextField.
➢   Click **Connectible Features**.
➢   Double-click the **requestFocus()** method.

Your connections should look similar to Figure 9.15. Save your bean.

➤   On the menu bar, click **Bean**.
➤   Click **Save Bean**.

Figure 9.15
Completed Connections

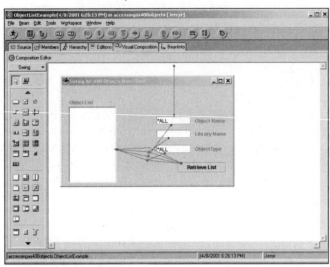

To run this Java program, you need to successfully connect to the AS/400. Run the Java program.

➤   On the menu bar, click **Bean**.
➤   Click **Run**, and then click **Run Main**.

Most AS/400 systems have an IBM-supplied library named ADTSLAB. You'll be using this library in many of the examples in future chapters.

➤   Type **ADTSLAB** in the **Library Name** input field. You can also use any other valid AS/400 library name.
➤   Click the **Retrieve List** button.

Your AS/400 sign-on prompt should appear, displaying the AS/400 name that you specified in the **ET400List** bean **Properties** sheet.

➤   Enter your AS/400 user profile ID and password, and then click **OK**.

After a few seconds, you'll see a screen like the one shown in Figure 9.16 appear.

Figure 9.16
Objects from Library ADTSLAB

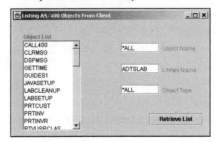

➤   Try some different combinations of object name, object type, and library name.

You may have noticed that the **ET400List** bean automatically builds a scroll bar when the list contains more objects than will fit on one page of the bean. For a short object list, the scroll bar is absent.

➢   Close your **ObjectListExample** application.

Congratulations! You've finished another application — one that calls an AS/400 API from Java. Calling this same API (QUSLOBJ) from RPG or Cobol would have been much more difficult.

If you look at the **Properties** sheet for the **ET400List** bean, you'll notice, under **objectType**, that you can specify different types of objects. These object types are the same as the object types you can specify in a regular DSPOBJD command on the AS/400 (*ALL, *JRN, *LIB, *MSGF, *PGM, and so on).

Order of Connections

When you have multiple connections originating from the same JavaBean (e.g., a JButton), the order of the connections becomes an issue. For example, what if in this chapter assignment you had tried to retrieve the object list before you had set the object name, library name, or object type? The application wouldn't have retrieved anything. Programmers who are just beginning to learn Java sometimes get caught up in the object-oriented programming environment and forget about the timing of the execution of different methods.

You are now going to look at the order of the connections you created earlier in the chapter.

➢   Right-click the **btRetrieveList** JButton.
➢   Click the **Reorder Connections From** menu item.

Figure 9.17 shows the **Reorder connections** window. Notice that it lists your four connections that originate from the **btRetrieveList** JButton. The connections appear in the same order in which you created them. Look at the last entry. It is the **getObjectList()** method. What if you wanted to change the order in which the **getObjectList()** method is executed? Doing so would be simple. In this window, you'd just select this connection with a click and then hold and drag it into the proper order.

Figure 9.17
Reorder Connections

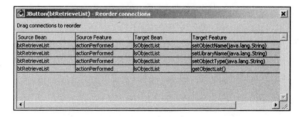

Summary

You can now access different types of objects from the AS/400. In this chapter you also

- used the **ET400List** (list objects) bean
- connected to your AS/400 without using an **AS400** bean
- became familiar with parameters used to call the QUSLOBJ API
- used the **JFrame** superclass
- created an application class
- learned how to order connections

Chapter 9 was a short chapter. Chapters 10, 11, and 12 will also be short chapters that focus on using certain AS/400 JavaBeans. In the next chapter, you'll learn how to retrieve system values from the AS/400 using Java.

Chapter 10

Retrieving OS/400 System Values from Java

Chapter Objectives

- ❏ Become familiar with AS/400 Toolbox System Value JavaBeans
- ❏ Retrieve AS/400 system values
- ❏ Understand AS/400 panes

Chapter Project

- ❏ A class will be created to display AS/400 system values.
- ❏ This class will retrieve AS/400 system values as part of the program initialization.
- ❏ Figures 10.1A, 10.1B, and 10.1C show what the sample application will look like.

Figure 10.1A
Chapter Project (Screen 1 of 3)

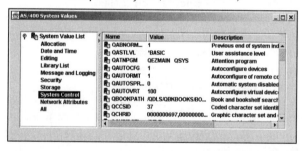

Figure 10.1B
Chapter Project (Screen 2 of 3)

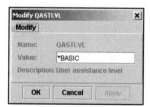

Figure 10.1C
Chapter Project (Screen 3 of 3)

In this chapter, you're going to learn how to access the AS/400 system values through an AS400ExplorerPane. This function is similar to using the AS/400 WRKSYSVAL (Work with System Values) command. You'll see from this chapter project that with the use of existing JavaBeans, you can build a powerful program will very little coding. That's what we all like: fast results with little effort.

AS/400 System Value Beans

The AS/400 system values are a collection of small pieces of information that control the operating environment throughout the AS/400. Hundreds of system values are used to define various system functions, such as the system date and time. There are different categories of system values:

- allocation
- date and time
- editing
- library lists
- messages and logging
- security
- storage
- system control
- network attributes

To change system values in this chapter project, you'll need to have *USE authority to the CHGSYSVAL (Change System Value) command.

To access a single system value, you use the **SystemValue** bean from the Enterprise Toolkit for AS/400. To access a group of system values, you use the **VSystemValueList** bean. This chapter focuses on using the **VSystemValueList** bean together with an **AS400ExplorerPane** bean.

You are going to create a class called **SystemValueExample** that inherits properties from superclass **JFrame**. You'll store the class in the project **My AS/400 Access Projects** and in the package **accessingas400objects**.

➤ If the workbench isn't started, start it now.
➤ Expand the project **My AS/400 Access Projects** with a click.
➤ Select the package **accessingas400objects** with a click. Right-click to display the shortcut menu, select **Add**, and then select **Class.**
➤ Make sure the **Project** name is **My AS400 Access Projects**.
➤ Make sure the **Package** name is **accessingas400objects.**
➤ In the **Class name** field, type **SystemValueExample**.
➤ Click **Browse** to select a superclass.
➤ When the **Superclass** window appears, type **JFrame** in the **Pattern** field.
➤ In the **Type names** list, double-click **JFrame**. When you return to the SmartGuide, you should see **javax.swing.JFrame** entered in the **Superclass** field, as shown in Figure 10.2.
➤ Select the **Browse the class when finished** check box.
➤ Select the **Compose the class visually** check box.
➤ Click **Finish** to complete the creation of the class.

You should be inside the Visual Composition Editor. You are now going to change the title of the JFrame.

➤ On the menu bar, click **Tools**.
➤ Click **Beans List**.
➤ As shown in Figure 10.3, double-click the **SystemValueExample** JFrame to display the **Properties** sheet.
➤ For the **title** property, type **AS/400 System Values**.
➤ Close the **Properties** sheet.
➤ Close the **Beans List**.
➤ Expand the width of your free-form surface by dragging a corner of the free-form surface over to the right.

Figure 10.2
Class SystemValueExample

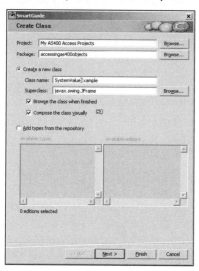

Figure 10.3
JFrame SystemValueExample

AS/400 Panes

AS/400 panes are powerful JavaBeans used to display certain AS/400 resources. An AS/400 resource can be a system value; a resource can also be an Integrated File System (IFS) directory, an AS/400 job, a message list or queue, a list of printers or output queues, or a list of users. This chapter focuses on the use of system value AS/400 resources.

The AS/400 panes use a graphical interface to display AS/400 resources. You may already be familiar with using a "tree" graphical representation through Microsoft Windows Explorer. All AS/400 panes extend the Java **Component** class, which means they can be used in frames, windows, and containers. The following table lists the AS/400 panes.

AS/400 pane	Description
AS400DetailsPane	This pane shows, in a table-type format (fields or columns), the details associated with each AS/400 resource. One or more AS/400 resources can be selected.
AS400ListPane	This pane displays AS/400 resources in a list format. One or more AS/400 resources can be selected.
AS400TreePane	This pane uses a tree hierarchy to display AS/400 resources. Drilling down to the various levels of the hierarchy is available. One or more AS/400 resources can be selected.
AS400ExplorerPane	This pane is a combination of the AS400DetailsPane and the AS400TreePane. If an AS/400 resource is selected in the tree pane, the details of that resource are displayed in the details pane.

As shown in Figure 10.1A (page 169), you're going to use the AS400ExplorerPane to show the general system value categories in the tree pane and the details of each system value in the details pane.

Using the AS/400 Explorer Pane

First, you're going to add an **AS400ExplorerPane** bean. This bean is located about halfway through the list of beans in the AS/400 Toolbox bean category.

➢   Click to display the bean category drop-down list, and select the **AS/400 Toolbox** category. You may have to wait a minute.

➢   Click the **AS400ExplorerPane** bean ▢, and drop it in the center of the free-form surface visual area.

➢   Reduce the size of the **AS400ExplorerPane** to the size shown in the upper portion of Figure 10.4.

Figure 10.4
AS400ExplorerPane Bean

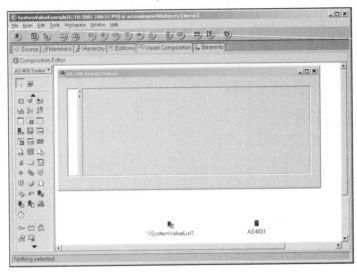

Next, you'll add an **AS400** bean. This is the same bean you used in Chapter 8 to connect to the AS/400.

➢   Click the **AS400** bean ▢, and drop it on the free-form nonvisual surface as shown in Figure 10.4. You won't change any properties of this bean.

Next, you'll add a **VSystemValueList** bean to provide access to the AS/400 system values. This bean is located toward the end of the AS/400 Toolbox beans.

➢   Click the **VSystemValueList** bean ▢, and drop it on the free-form nonvisual surface as shown in Figure 10.4. You won't change any properties of this bean.

Connecting the AS/400 Beans

Next, you're going to set up three event-to-method connections and two parameter-from-property connections.

Event-to-Method Connection: setSystem()

```
connEtoM1: (SystemValueExample,initialize() →
           VSystemValueList1,setSystem(com.ibm.as400.access.AS400))
```

In previous chapters, you learned how to initiate a connection to the AS/400. The user clicked a button, and then the AS/400 sign-on prompt appeared. In this example, you're going to make the AS/400 sign-on prompt appear *before* the application does. You'll do this by connecting to the **initialize()** event of the JFrame.

Connect the **SystemValueExample** JFrame with a **setSystem(com.ibm.as400.access.AS400)** method.

➤ Select the **SystemValueExample** JFrame by clicking the outside edge of the visual area as shown in Figure 10.5. *Caution: Make sure it is the outside edge of the JFrame.*
➤ Right-click the **SystemValueExample** JFrame.
➤ Click **Connect**.
➤ Click **Connectible Features**.
➤ Double-click the **initialize()** event, as shown in Figure 10.6.

Figure 10.5
Selected JFrame

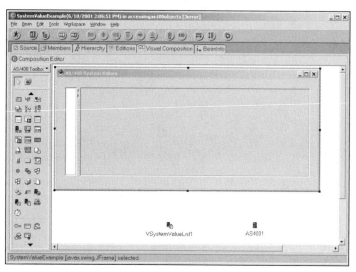

Figure 10.6
Selection of initialize() Event

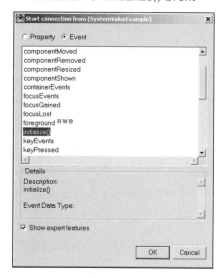

➢   Click the spider-end pointer on the **VSystemValueList1** bean.
➢   Click **Connectible Features**.
➢   Click the **setSystem(com.ibm.as400.access.AS400)** method, as shown in Figure 10.7.
➢   Click **OK**.

Figure 10.7
Selection of setSystem(com.ibm.as400.access.AS400) Method

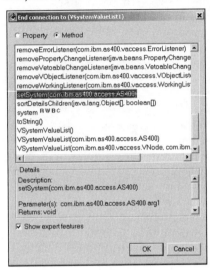

Parameter-from-Property Connection

```
connPfromP1: (connEtoM1: (SystemValueExample,initialize() →
            VSystemValueList1,setSystem(com.ibm.as400.access.AS400)),arg1 → AS4001,this)
```

Complete the connection by passing a value, or parameter, into the primary connection. The connection is expect-ing an **AS400** data type.

Identify the source property:

➢   Right-click the dashed line.
➢   Click **Connect**.
➢   Click **arg1**.

Identify the target property:

➢   Click the spider-end pointer on the **AS4001** bean.
➢   Click **this**.

Figure 10.8 shows what the connection should look like.

Figure 10.8

setSystem() Connections: connPfromP1 and connEtoM1

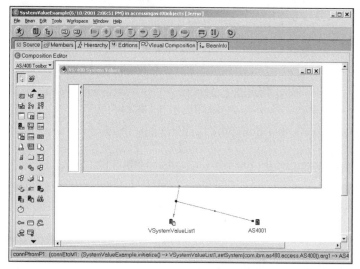

> Double-click each connection to verify that it is correct as shown in Figures 10.9 and 10.10.
> Close each **Properties** window.

Figure 10.9

Connection connEtoM1

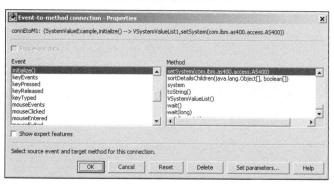

Figure 10.10

Connection connPfromP1

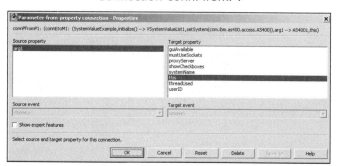

Event-to-Method Connection: load()

`connEtoM2: (SystemValueExample,initialize() → VSystemValueList1,load())`

To load the contents of the AS400ExplorerPane, the **load()** method must be called. There are a couple of timing strategies to accomplish this:

A. Load the system values *before* adding the pane to the frame. The frame will not appear until all the system values are loaded.
B. Load the system values *after* adding the pane to a frame. The frame will appear more quickly, with a waiting cursor. The system values will begin appearing as the pane is loaded.

You're going to accomplish strategy A by loading the system values before the frame is displayed, during initialization.

Connect the **SystemValueExample** JFrame with a **load()** method.

➢ Select the **SystemValueExample** JFrame by clicking the outside edge of the visual area, as you did earlier.
➢ Right-click the **SystemValueExample** JFrame.
➢ Click **Connect**.
➢ Click **Connectible Features**.
➢ Double-click the **initialize()** event.
➢ Click the spider-end pointer on the **VSystemValueList1** bean.
➢ Click **Connectible Features**.
➢ Click the **load()** method, as shown in Figure 10.11.
➢ Click **OK**.

Figure 10.11
Selection of load() Method

➢ As shown in Figure 10.12, drag the connection over to the left to make it easier to see.
➢ Double-click the connection to verify that it is correct as shown in Figure 10.13.
➢ Click **OK**.

Figure 10.12
load() Connection

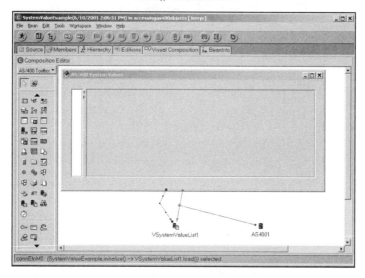

Figure 10.13
Connection connEtoM2

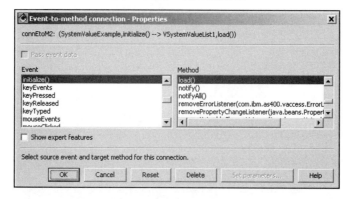

Event-to-Method Connection: setRoot()

```
connEtoM3: (SystemValueExample,initialize() →
        AS400ExplorerPane1,setRoot(com.ibm.as400.vaccess.VNode))
```

When using an AS/400 pane, you need to identify the AS/400 resource type. You accomplish this by setting the root, or by use of the **setRoot()** method. The root allows the specification of the top-level AS/400 resource. In this project, you'll be specifying a system value type of resource by using a **setRoot(VNode)** method and connecting it to the VSystemValueList. The **VNode** parameter identifies the visual node — in other words, the visual resource type to be displayed.

Connect the **SystemValueExample** JFrame with a **setRoot(VNode)** method.

➤ Select the **SystemValueExample** JFrame by clicking the outside edge of the visual area.
➤ Right-click the **SystemValueExample** JFrame.
➤ Click **Connect**.

> ➤ Click **Connectible Features**.
> ➤ Double-click the **initialize()** event.
> ➤ Click the spider-end pointer on the **AS400ExplorerPane1** bean, which is located in the middle of the visual area.
> ➤ Click **Connectible Features**.
> ➤ Click the **setRoot(com.ibm.as400.vaccess.VNode)** method as shown in Figure 10.14.
> ➤ Click **OK**.

Figure 10.15 shows what the connection should look like.

Figure 10.14

Selection of setRoot(VNode) Method

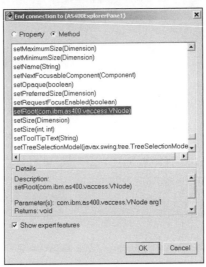

Figure 10.15

setRoot() Connection

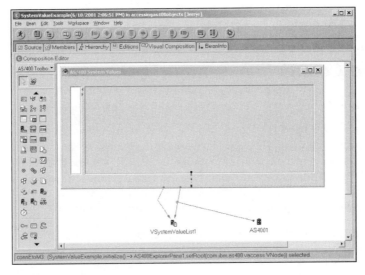

> ➤ Double-click the connection to verify that it is correct as shown in Figure 10.16.
> ➤ Click **OK**.

Figure 10.16
Connection connEtoM3

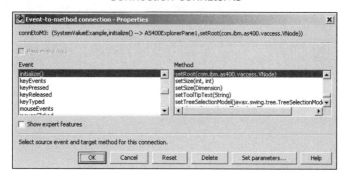

Parameter-from-Property Connection

```
connPfromP2: (connEtoM3: (SystemValueExample,initialize() →
            AS400ExplorerPane1,setRoot(com.ibm.as400.vaccss.VNode)),arg1 →
            VSystemValueList1,this)
```

Complete the connection by passing a parameter into the primary connection. The connection is expecting a **VNode** data type.

Identify the source property:

> ➤ Right-click the dashed line.
> ➤ Click **Connect**.
> ➤ Click **arg1**.

Identify the target property:

> ➤ Click the spider-end pointer on the **VSystemValueList1** bean.
> ➤ Click **this**.

Figure 10.17 shows what the connection should look like.

> ➤ Double-click the connection to verify that it is correct as shown in Figure 10.18.
> ➤ Click **OK**.

Figure 10.17
setRoot() Connection: connPfromP2 and connEtoM3

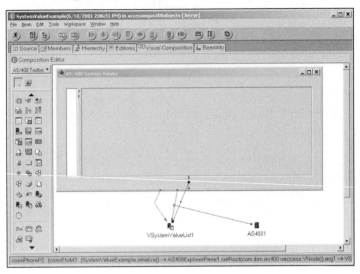

Figure 10.18
Connection connPfromP2

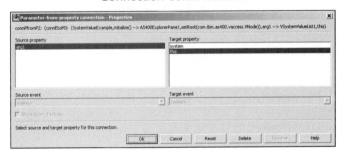

Retrieving AS/400 System Values

Save your Java program.

➢   On the menu bar, click **Bean**.
➢   Click **Save Bean**.

To run this Java program, you need to successfully connect to the AS/400. Run your Java program.

➢   On the menu bar, click **Bean**.
➢   Click **Run**, and then click **Run Main**.

Did you notice that the AS/400 sign-on prompt appeared without the rest of the application? That's because you specified to load the system values before loading the JFrame.

➢   Sign on to the AS/400.

After you enter your sign-on information, a few seconds may pass before the application appears. It takes a while to retrieve all the system values from the AS/400.

➢ When the application appears, as shown in Figure 10.19, double-click **System Control** in the system value list.

You should see a window similar to Figure 10.20.

Figure 10.19
AS/400 System Value Categories

Figure 10.20
AS/400 System Control Details

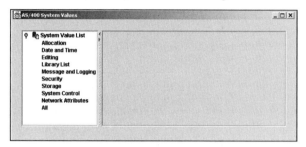
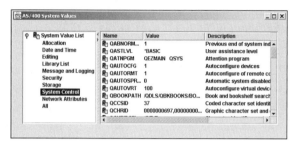

➢ On the right side of the window, right-click the **QASTLVL** system value name. QASTLVL is the User Assistance Level system value. A shortcut menu appears, as shown in Figure 10.21.

Figure 10.21
QASTLVL Prompt

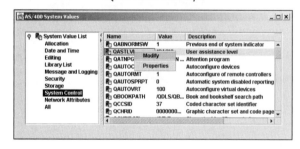

➢ Click **Modify**. Figure 10.22 shows the window where you could change the system value to *BASIC, *INTERMEDIATE, or *ADVANCED.
➢ Click **Cancel**.
➢ Double-click the system value category **Library List**.
➢ Right-click the **QSYSLIBL** system value name. QSYSLIBL is the system library list system value.
➢ Click **Modify**.

Look at Figure 10.23. Compare it with to Figure 10.21. Notice the difference between the two modify functions. The **VSystemValueList** bean automatically adjusts for multiple entries within a system value.

Figure 10.22
Modify QASTLVL

Figure 10.23
QSYSLIBL Modify

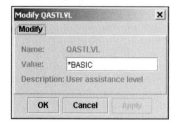

Feel free to play around with different aspects of this AS400ExplorerPane. Try clicking some of the small directional components, the tree components, and the slide bars.

➢   Close your **SystemValueExample** application.

Congratulations! You just completed another Java application. Would you agree there is much power in this application for the small amount of programming you had to do?

Review AS/400 Methods

There is one method worth reviewing in this application. To review the generated Java source code, do the following:

➢   Click the **Source** tab.
➢   In the **Elements** pane, click the method name **connEtoM3()**.

How does your application pane know how to retrieve system values as opposed to an output queue? Figure 10.24 shows method **connEtoM3()**. The code in this connection is how it's all tied together — one line of Java code.

You may want to look at the **initialize()** method to view the code that was created for you.

Figure 10.24
Source Code for Method connEtoM3()

```
private void connEtoM3() {
    try {
            // user code begin {1}
            // user code end
            getAS400ExplorerPane1().setRoot(getVSystemValueList1());
```

Summary

In this chapter you learned

- about the different types of AS/400 panes
- how to use an AS400ExplorerPane
- how to set the root of a pane
- how to retrieve system values
- how to display a sign-on screen before the application is displayed

Are you finding that using VisualAge for Java is getting a little easier? You may be noticing that you're not needing the step-by-step instructions as much as you did in the first few chapters. If so, that's great — you're learning. If you still need the detailed steps, relax; that's normal. The detailed, step-by-step instructions will remain throughout the rest of the book.

You are now ready to move on to the next chapter and to work within the AS/400 Integrated File System.

Chapter 11

Accessing the IFS from Java

 ## Chapter Objectives

- [ ] Understand the AS/400 Integrated File System (IFS) structure
- [ ] Become familiar with the AS/400 Toolbox IFS Directory JavaBean
- [ ] Learn how to access directories and files in the IFS
- [ ] Understand how to implement editing of IFS text files
- [ ] Learn about AS400 detail panes

 ## Chapter Project

- [ ] A class will be created to display IFS directories.
- [ ] The class will retrieve IFS directories as part of program initialization.
- [ ] The class will also allow editing of text files.
- [ ] Figure 11.1 shows what the sample application will look like.

Figure 11.1
Chapter Project

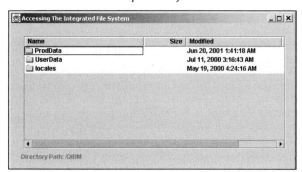

In this chapter, you're going to learn how to access the Integrated File System (IFS) on the AS/400. You'll learn how to position yourself in the file structure and how to retrieve files.

The Integrated File System

If you haven't been involved with Java on the AS/400, you may never have worked with the Integrated File System. Since V3R1, the IFS has been part of the base OS/400 operating system. With all the file systems supported by the AS/400, the IFS provides a common interface layer between the users and these multiple file systems.

Figure 11.2 shows a graphical representation of the IFS through Client Access. The "root" has characteristics similar to DOS or OS/2, meaning stream-file support and hierarchical directories. If you look at the root, you'll notice a directory, or folder, called /QIBM. This directory is where much of the AS/400 Java-related information is stored. You'll be using the /QIBM directory in this chapter project.

Figure 11.2
Integrated File Structure (IFS)

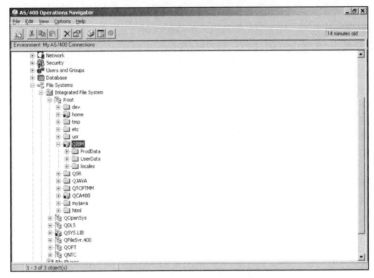

If you look closely at Figure 11.2, you'll notice /QSYS.LIB. If you've done anything at all on the AS/400, you'll be very familiar with this directory. It is the standard AS/400 library structure, in which all the database files and your RPG, Cobol, and CL programs are stored. A discussion of the other file systems within the IFS is reserved for another book.

AS/400 IFS Beans

You can access the IFS and certain directories using OS/400 commands such as CRTDIR (Create Directory), RMVDIR (Remove Directory), DSPCURDIR (Display Current Directory), CPYTOSTMF (Copy To Stream File), and many others. In the AS/400 Toolbox, many JavaBeans and classes are available to you to accomplish many of these same functions. These beans include **IFSFile**, **IFSFileDialog**, **IFSFileInputStream**, **IFSFileOutputStream**, **IFSRandomAccessFile**, **IFSTextFileDocument**, **IFSTextFileInputStream**, **IFSTextFileOutputStream**, **VIFSDirectory**, and others. This chapter focuses on working with the **VIFSDirectory** bean and indirectly with the **IFSTextFileDocument** bean. The **VIFSDirectory** bean lets you represent directories in the IFS through the use of AS/400 panes. The **IFSTextFileDocument** bean lets you create, edit, or delete any text document in the IFS.

There are a few important requirements concerning the use of these beans. You need to set both the system and the path properties. This is done with the **setSystem()** and **setPath()** methods. When setting a path, it's a wise idea not to use /QSYS.LIB. This directory is usually quite large, and accessing all its objects takes a long time. You also need to specifically make a call to the **load()** method to begin the loading the contents of the directory.

You can use any of the AS/400 panes with the **VIFSDirectory** bean. In the last chapter, you learned about the AS400ExplorerPane. To expose you to a different type of AS/400 pane, this chapter's project uses the AS400DetailsPane.

As in previous chapters, you're going to create a class that inherits properties from superclass **JFrame**. You'll store this class, called **IFSExample**, in the project **My AS/400 Access Projects** and in the package **accessingas400objects**.

➢ If the workbench isn't started, start it now.

➢ Expand the project **My AS/400 Access Projects** with a click.

➢ Select the package **accessingas400objects** with a click. Right-click to display the shortcut menu, select **Add**, and then select **Class**.

➢ Make sure the **Project** name is **My AS400 Access Projects**.

➢ Make sure the **Package** name is **accessingas400objects**.

➢ In the **Class name** field, type **IFSExample**.

➢ Click **Browse** to select a superclass.

➢ When the **Superclass** window appears, type **JFrame** in the **Pattern** field.

➢ In the **Type names** list, double-click **JFrame**. When you return to the SmartGuide, the **Superclass** field should contain **javax.swing.JFrame**, as shown in Figure 11.3.

➢ Select the **Browse the class when finished** check box.

➢ Select the **Compose the class visually** check box.

➢ Click **Finish** to complete the creation of the class.

Figure 11.3
Class IFSExample

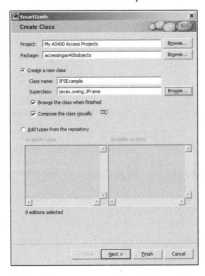

You should be inside the Visual Composition Editor. Change the title of the JFrame.

➢ On the menu bar, click **Tools**.

➢ Click **Beans List**.

➢ Double-click the **IFSExample** JFrame to display the **Properties** sheet.

➢ For the **title** property, type **Accessing The Integrated File System**.

➢ Close the **Properties** sheet.

➢ Close the **Beans List**.

➤　　Expand the width of your free-form surface by dragging a corner over to the right.

Create the two JLabels shown at the bottom of Figure 11.4.

➤　　Click the **JLabel** bean 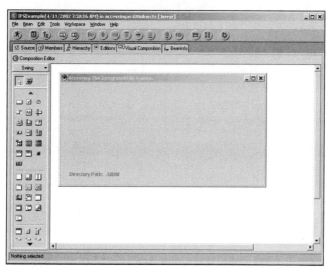, and drop it on the lower-left side of the free-form surface visual area.

➤　　Double-click the JLabel. Change the **text** property to **Directory Path:**.

➤　　Close the **Properties** sheet.

➤　　Expand the JLabel so that you can see all the text.

➤　　Click the **JLabel** bean again, and drop it next to the existing bean as shown in the figure.

➤　　Double-click the second JLabel. Change the **beanName** from **JLabel2** to **lbPath**.

➤　　Change the **text** property to **/QIBM**.

➤　　Close the **Properties** sheet.

➤　　Expand the JLabel so that you can see all the text.

Figure 11.4
Two Label Beans

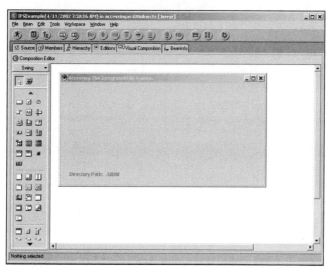

Using the AS/400 Details Pane

The AS400DetailsPane uses a table-type format, similar to a spreadsheet. Even though the pane shows no graphical hierarchy, you still have the ability to maneuver downward through a hierarchy of directories. Once you identify a file, you can select it to perform text-editing functions. You normally would probably use an **AS400ExplorerPane** bean with the **VIFSDirectory** bean. For some additional exposure, this chapter project uses the **AS400DetailsPane** bean.

Next, you'll add three beans from the AS/400 Toolbox as shown in Figure 11.5.

First, add an **AS400DetailsPane** bean. This bean is located about halfway through the bean list in the AS/400 Toolbox bean category.

➤　　Click to display the bean category drop-down list, and select the **AS/400 Toolbox** category. You may have to wait a minute.

➤　　Click the **AS400DetailsPane** bean 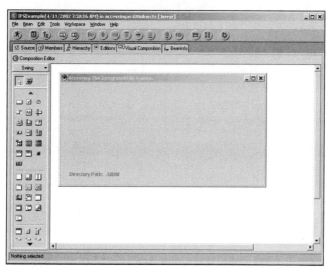, and drop it on the center of the free-form surface visual area.

➤　　Reduce the size of the AS400DetailsPane to match the figure.

Figure 11.5
AS400 and VIFSDirectory Beans

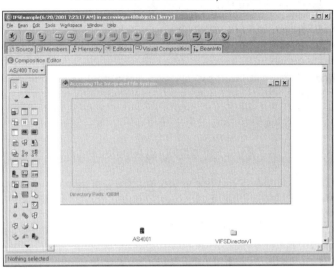

Second, add an **AS400** bean.

➤ Click the **AS400** bean ▪, and drop it on the free-form nonvisual surface as shown in the figure. You won't change any properties of this bean. You'll enter the AS/400 sign-on information at the sign-on prompt.

Third, add a **VIFSDirectory** bean. This bean is located close to the middle of the list in the AS/400 Toolbox bean category.

➤ Click the **VIFSDirectory** bean ▫, and drop it on the free-form nonvisual surface as shown in the figure. You won't change any properties of this bean.

Tips and Tricks

The *VIFSDirectory* bean has some useful properties. You can use the *setInclude()* method to specify whether directories, files, or both appear in the selected pane. The *setPattern()* method can be used as a filter for selecting file names based on a certain pattern. Wildcards such as "*" and "?" can be used in the patterns.

Connecting the AS/400 Beans

You are now going to set up four event-to-method connections and three parameter-from-property connections to implement the **setSystem()**, **setRoot()**, **setPath()**, and **load()** methods.

Event-to-Method Connection: setSystem()

```
connEtoM1: (IFSExample,initialize() → VIFSDirectory1,setSystem(com.ibm.as400.access.AS400))
```

In Chapter 10, you learned how to initiate the connection to the AS/400 before the main application screen appears. You did this by using the **initialize()** method. You'll go through similar steps using the **initialize()** method here in this chapter project.

Connect the **IFSExample** JFrame with a **setSystem(com.ibm.as400.access.AS400)** method.

➤ Select the **IFSExample** JFrame by clicking on the outside edge of the visual area of the free-form surface. *Caution: Make sure it is the outside edge of the JFrame.*

➢   Right-click the **IFSExample** JFrame.
➢   Click **Connect**.
➢   Click **Connectible Features**.
➢   Double-click the **initialize()** event.
➢   Click the spider-end pointer on the **VIFSDirectory** bean.
➢   Click **Connectible Features**.
➢   Click the **setSystem(com.ibm.as400.access.AS400)** method.
➢   Click **OK**.

Parameter-from-Property Connection

```
connPfromP1: (connEtoM1: (IFSExample,initialize() →
          VIFSDirectory1,setSystem(com.ibm.as400.access.AS400)),arg1 → AS4001,this)
```

Complete the connection by passing a value, or parameter, into the primary connection. The connection is expecting an **AS400** data type.

Identify the source property:

➢   Right-click the dashed line.
➢   Click **Connect**.
➢   Click **arg1**.

Identify the target property:

➢   Click the spider-end pointer on the **AS4001** bean.
➢   Click **this**.

Figure 11.6 shows what the connection should look like.

Figure 11.6
setSystem() Connections: connEtoM1 and connPfromP1

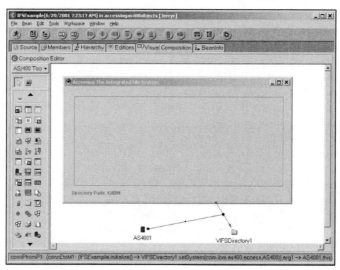

➢   Double-click each connection to verify that it is correct as shown in Figures 11.7 and 11.8.
➢   Close each **Properties** window.

Figure 11.7
Connection connEtoM1

Figure 11.8
Connection connPfromP1

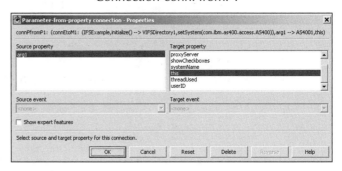

Event-to-Method Connection: setRoot()

```
connEtoM2: (IFSExample,initialize() → AS400DetailsPane1,setRoot(com.ibm.as400.vaccess.VNode))
```

In the previous chapter, you performed a **setRoot(VNode)** method using an AS400ExplorerPane to identify the AS/400 resource type. You are now going do another **setRoot(VNode)**, but with an AS400DetailsPane. You'll go through the same steps as before.

In this project, you'll be specifying an IFS directory resource. You'll accomplish this by specifying a **setRoot(VNode)** method and connecting it to the VIFSDirectory.

Connect the **IFSExample** JFrame with a **setRoot(VNode)** method.

➢ Select the **IFSExample** JFrame by clicking the outside edge of the visual area of the free-form surface.
➢ Right-click the **IFSExample** JFrame.
➢ Click **Connect**.
➢ Click **Connectible Features**.
➢ Double-click the **initialize()** event.
➢ Click the spider-end pointer on the **AS400DetailsPane1** bean, located in the middle of the visual area of the free-form surface.
➢ Click **Connectible Features**.
➢ Click the **setRoot(com.ibm.as400.vaccess.VNode)** method.
➢ Click **OK**.

Parameter-from-Property Connection

```
connPfromP2: (connEtoM2: (IFSExample,initialize() →
            AS400DetailsPane1,setRoot(com.ibm.as400.vaccess.VNode)),arg1 →
            VIFSDirectory1,this)
```

Complete the connection by passing a parameter into the primary connection. The connection is expecting a **VNode** data type.

Identify the source property:

➢ Right-click the dashed line.
➢ Click **Connect**.
➢ Click **arg1**.

Identify the target property:

➢ Click the spider-end pointer on the **VIFSDirectory** bean.
➢ Click **this**.

Figure 11.9 shows what the connection should look like.

Figure 11.9
setRoot() Connection: connEtoM2 and connPfromP2

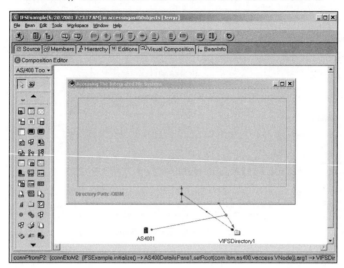

➢ Double-click each connection to verify that it is correct as shown in Figures 11.10 and 11.11.
➢ Close each **Properties** window.

Figure 11.10
Connection connEtoM2

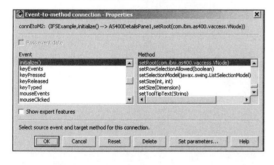

Figure 11.11
Connection connPfromP2

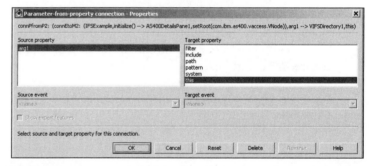

Event-to-Method Connection: setPath()

connEtoM3: (IFSExample,initialize() → VIFSDirectory1,setPath(java.lang.String))

The **setPath()** method specifies which directory is identified as the starting point for the directory selection. You'll be using the /QIBM directory as the starting point. Recall that you specified /**QIBM** in the JLabel **lbPath** you created earlier.

Connect the **IFSExample** JFrame with a **setPath(java.lang.String)** method.

➢ Select the **IFSExample** JFrame by clicking the outside edge of the visual area of the free-form surface.
➢ Right-click the **IFSExample** JFrame.
➢ Click **Connect**.
➢ Click **Connectible Features**.
➢ Double-click the **initialize()** event.

> Click the spider-end pointer on the **VIFSDirectory** bean.
> Click **Connectible Features**.
> Click the **setPath(java.lang.String)** method.
> Click **OK**.

Parameter-from-Property Connection

```
connPfromP3: (connEtoM3: (IFSExample,initialize() →
          VIFSDirectory1,setPath(java.lang.String)),arg1 → lbPath,this)
```

Complete the connection by passing a parameter into the primary connection. The connection is expecting a **String** data type.

Identify the source property:

> Right-click the dashed line.
> Click **Connect**.
> Click **arg1**.

Identify the target property:

> Click the spider-end pointer on the JLabel **lbPath** bean.
> Click **this**.

Figure 11.12 shows what the connection should look like.

Figure 11.12
setPath() Connection: connEtoM3 and connPfromP3

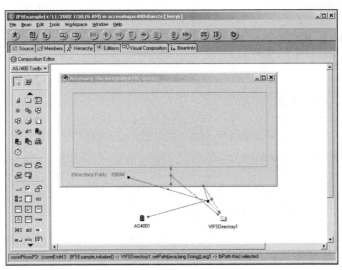

> Double-click each connection to verify that it is correct as shown in Figures 11.13 and 11.14.
> Close each **Properties** window.

Figure 11.13
setPath() Connection: connEtoM3

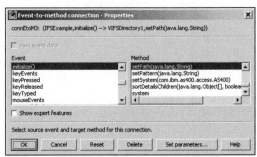

Figure 11.14
setPath() Connection: connPfromP3

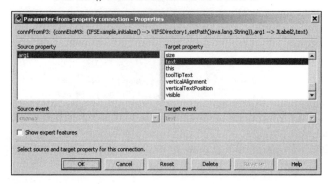

Event-to-Method Connection: load()

connEtoM4: (IFSExample,initialize() → VIFSDirectory1,load())

To load the contents of the AS400DetailsPane, you must explicitly call the **load()** method. Connect the **IFSExample** JFrame with a **load()** method.

➢   Select the **IFSExample** JFrame by clicking the outside edge of the visual area of the free-form surface.
➢   Right-click the **IFSExample** JFrame.
➢   Click **Connect**.
➢   Click **Connectible Features**.
➢   Double-click the **initialize()** event.
➢   Click the spider-end pointer on the **VIFSDirectory** bean.
➢   Click **Connectible Features**.
➢   Click the **load()** method.
➢   Click **OK**.

Figure 11.15 shows what the connection should look like.

Figure 11.15
load() connection: connEtoM4

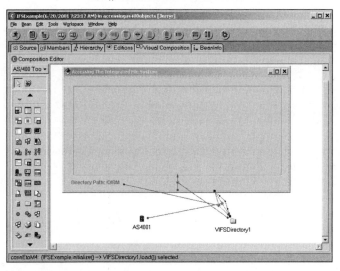

➢ Double-click the connection to verify that it is correct as shown in Figure 11.16.
➢ Close the **Properties** window.

Figure 11.16
Connection connEtoM4

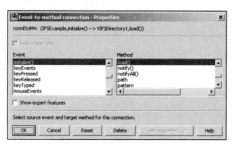

Accessing the IFS

Save your Java program.

➢ On the menu bar, click **Bean**.
➢ Click **Save Bean**.

To run this Java program, you need to successfully connect to the AS/400. Run your Java program.

➢ On the menu bar, click **Bean**.
➢ Click **Run**, and then click **Run Main**.
➢ Sign on to the AS/400.

After you've entered your sign-on information, it may take a few seconds before the application appears. Retrieving IFS directories takes some time. If you specify /QSYS.LIB, expect it to take some considerable time to load.

When the application appears, you'll see a window similar to the one shown in Figure 11.17. The window identifies all the directories and files contained within directory /QIBM.

Figure 11.17
Accessing the Integrated File System Application

Figure 11.18
Directory Actions

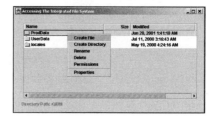

➢ Right-click the directory **ProdData**.

The resulting shortcut menu, shown in Figure 11.18, identifies the available actions for directories: **Create File**, **Create Directory**, **Rename**, **Delete**, **Permissions**, and **Properties**. Of course, you need the proper AS/400 authority to be able to execute these directory functions.

➢ Double-click directory ProdData. You should see a window similar to Figure 11.19, displaying the contents of the directory.

You are now going to traverse downward in the directory hierarchy of /QIBM.

➤   Double-click directory **HTTP**. Figure 11.20 shows the resulting window.

Figure 11.19
ProdData Directory

Figure 11.20
HTTP Directory

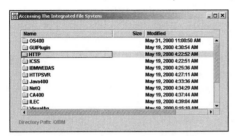

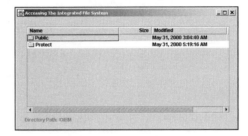

➤   Double-click directory **Public**. Figure 11.21 shows the resulting window.
➤   Double-click directory **jt400**. This one will take longer to load than the others. Figure 11.22 shows the resulting window.

Figure 11.21
Public Directory

Figure 11.22
jt400 Directory

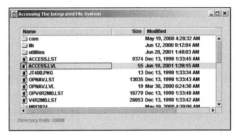

➤   *Right-click* file **ACCESS.LVL**.

The shortcut menu shown in Figure 11.23 identifies the available actions for files: **Edit**, **View**, **Rename**, **Delete**, **Permissions**, and **Properties**.

Figure 11.23
File Actions

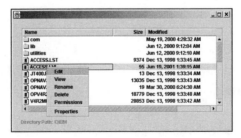

➤   Double-click file **ACCESS.LVL**.

A text editor window (Figure 11.24) appears, displaying the contents of file ACCESS.LVL. This text editor has full edit, view, rename, delete, and properties functions available to it. Behind the scenes, the **IFSTextFileDocument** bean is actually being executed. It was called from the **VIFSDirectory** bean.

Figure 11.24
IFSTextFileDocument Bean

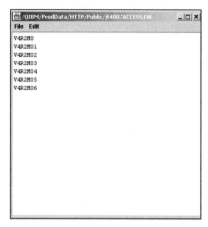

➢   Close your **Accessing The Integrated File System** application.

Summary

Another chapter down, and many more to go! Are you having fun? The detailed exercises are meant to reinforce the concepts you're learning but not be so complex that it takes you weeks to work through a chapter. In this chapter, you learned

- what the IFS is all about
- how to access the IFS
- how to use an AS400DetailsPane

Now you're ready to tackle one of the neatest functions on the AS/400: the local data area (LDA).

Chapter 12

Accessing a Local Data Area from Java

 ## Chapter Objectives

- ☐ Become familiar with the AS/400 Toolbox Local Data Area JavaBean
- ☐ Set and retrieve the AS/400 local data area
- ☐ Understand the use of the starting position and length settings
- ☐ Use multiple call parameters in connections

 ## Chapter Project

- ☐ A class will be created to display the contents of the AS/400 local data area (LDA).
- ☐ The class will let you set the LDA, get the LDA, and clear the LDA and let you specify where to position the setting and retrieval of the LDA.
- ☐ Figure 12.1 shows what the sample application will look like.

Figure 12.1
Chapter Project

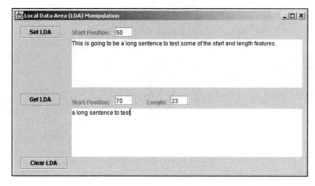

In this chapter, you'll learn how to update and retrieve data from an AS/400 local data area. The chapter also teaches you how to manipulate the local data area with the use of starting position and length parameters.

The AS/400 Local Data Area

The AS/400 local data area is one of the neatest functions on the system. It's such a simple function, yet most computer systems lack any equivalent.

An AS/400 data area object can be set up with different types of data and different lengths. The *local* data area, or LDA, represents a special type of AS/400 data area object. It is defined as 1,024 bytes of storage that a programmer or user can use and define. The LDA is present on any interactive job or batch job, whether you use it or not. You cannot create or delete a local data area. It is always present.

The LDA has no fields associated with it. You can use data structures inside your RPG, CL, and Cobol programs to define field structures within the LDA.

Many AS/400 programmers use the LDA as a way to pass parameters from one program to another. Others use it to store specific information about particular applications. Many use it to store standard printer spool file information and override information. The uses are virtually unlimited, restricted only by the programmer's imagination.

Some of the common AS/400 LDA commands are DSPDTAARA *LDA (display the LDA), CHGDTAARA *LDA (change the LDA), and RTVDTAARA *LDA (retrieve the data from the LDA). Figure 12.2 shows the results of a sample DSPDTAARA *LDA command.

Figure 12.2
*AS/400 DSPDTAARA *LDA Command*

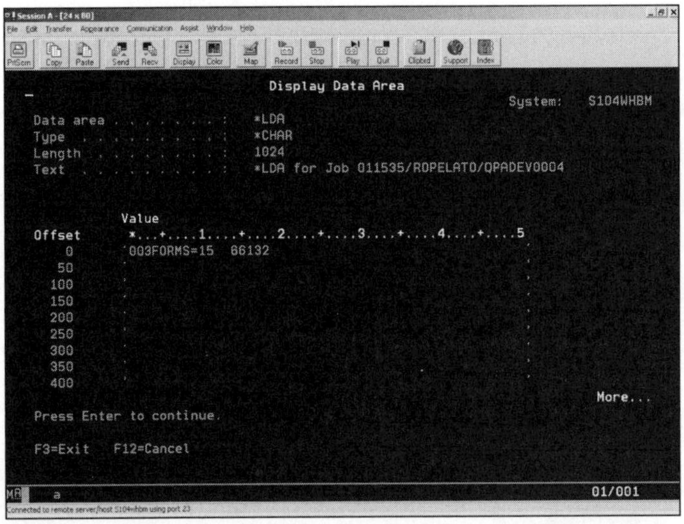

If you've never used the LDA, it's time you did, so let's begin the chapter project.

The Java **DataArea** class represents an AS/400 data area object. There is a **CharacterDataArea** class, a **DecimalDataArea** class, a **LogicalDataArea** class, and a **LocalDataArea** class. This chapter focuses on the **LocalDataArea** class or JavaBean.

As in previous chapters, you 're going to create a class that inherits properties from superclass **JFrame**. You'll store this class, called **LDAExample,** in the project **My AS/400 Access Projects** and in the package **accessingas400objects**.

➢ If the workbench isn't started, start it now.

➢ Expand the project **My AS/400 Access Projects** with a click.

➢ Select the package **accessingas400objects** with a click. Right-click to display the shortcut menu, select **Add**, and then select **Class**.

➤ Make sure the **Project** name is **My AS400 Access Projects**.
➤ Make sure the **Package** name is **accessingas400objects**.
➤ In the **Class name** field, type **LDAExample**.
➤ Click **Browse** to select a superclass.
➤ When the **Superclass** window appears, type **JFrame** in the **Pattern** field.
➤ In the **Type names** list, double-click **JFrame**. When you return to the SmartGuide, the **Superclass** field should contain **javax.swing.JFrame,** as shown in Figure 12.3.
➤ Select the **Browse the class when finished** check box.
➤ Select the **Compose the class visually** check box.
➤ Click **Finish** to complete the creation of the class.

Figure 12.3
Class LDAExample

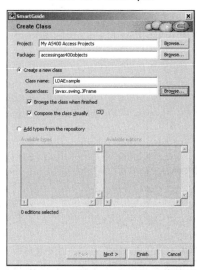

You should be inside the Visual Composition Editor. Change the title of the JFrame.

➤ On the menu bar, click **Tools**.
➤ Click **Beans List**.
➤ Double-click the **LDAExample** JFrame to display the **Properties** sheet.
➤ For the **title** property, type **Local Data Area (LDA) Manipulation**.
➤ Close the **Properties** sheet.
➤ Close the **Beans List**.
➤ Expand the width and height of your free-form surface by dragging a corner over to the right and down.

Now, create three JButtons as shown in Figure 12.4.

➤ Click the **JButton** bean ▢, and drop it in the upper-left corner of the free-from surface visual area, or JFrameContentPane.
➤ Double-click the JButton. Change the **beanName** from **JButton1** to **btSetLDA**.
➤ Change the **text** property to **Set LDA**.
➤ Close the **Properties** sheet.
➤ Click the **JButton** bean again, and drop it in the center-left portion of the visual area.
➤ Double-click the JButton. Change the **beanName** from **JButton1** to **btGetLDA**.

> Change the **text** to <u>**Get LDA**</u>.
> Close the **Properties** sheet.
> Click the **JButton** bean once more, and drop it in the lower-left corner of the visual area.
> Double-click the JButton. Change the **beanName** from **JButton1** to <u>**btClearLDA**</u>.
> Change the **text** to <u>**Clear LDA**</u>.
> Close the **Properties** sheet.
> Expand the button so that you can see all the text.

Figure 12.4
Screen Layout: Buttons and Text Areas

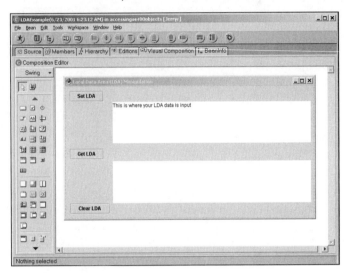

Create the two JTextAreas shown in the figure.

> Click the **JTextArea** bean , and drop it on the upper-right side of the visual area.
> Double-click the JTextArea. Change the **beanName** from **JTextArea1** to <u>**taInput**</u>.
> Change the **text** to <u>**This is where your LDA data is input**</u>.
> Change the **LineWrap** property to <u>**True**</u>.
> Close the **Properties** sheet.
> Click the **JTextArea** bean again, and drop it on the lower-right side of the visual area.
> Double-click the JTextArea. Change the **beanName** from **JTextArea1** to <u>**taOutput**</u>.
> Change the **LineWrap** property to <u>**True**</u>.
> Close the **Properties** sheet.

Create three JLabels as shown in Figure 12.5.

> Click the **JLabel** bean , and drop it in the upper-center portion of the visual area.
> Double-click the JLabel. Change the **beanName** from **JLabel1** to <u>**lbStartInput**</u>.
> Change the **text** to <u>**Start Position:**</u>.
> Close the **Properties** sheet.
> Expand the JLabel so that you can see all the text.
> Click the **JLabel** bean again, and drop it in the center of the visual area.
> Double-click the JLabel. Change the **beanName** from **JLabel1** to <u>**lbStartOutput**</u>.
> Change the **text** to <u>**Start Position:**</u>.

> ➤ Close the **Properties** sheet.
> ➤ Expand the JLabel so that you can see all the text.
> ➤ Click the **JLabel** bean once more, and drop it in the center of the visual area.
> ➤ Double-click the JLabel. Change the **beanName** from **JLabel1** to **lbLength**.
> ➤ Change the **text** to **Length:**.
> ➤ Close the **Properties** sheet.
> ➤ Expand the JLabel so that you can see all the text.

Figure 12.5

Screen Layout: Labels and Text Fields

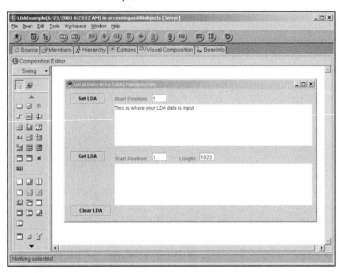

Create the three JTextFields shown in the figure.

> ➤ Click the **JTextField** bean ⊞, and drop it beside your first JLabel in the visual area.
> ➤ Double-click the JTextField. Change the **beanName** from **JTextField1** to **tfStartInput**.
> ➤ Change the **text** to **1**.
> ➤ Close the **Properties** sheet.
> ➤ Expand the JTextField to the size shown in the figure.
> ➤ Click the **JTextField** bean again, and drop it beside the second JLabel in the visual area.
> ➤ Double-click the JTextField. Change the **beanName** from **JTextField1** to **tfStartOutput**.
> ➤ Change the **text** to **1**.
> ➤ Close the **Properties** sheet.
> ➤ Expand the JTextField to the size shown in the figure.
> ➤ Click the **JTextField** bean once more, and drop it beside the third JLabel in the visual area.
> ➤ Double-click the JTextField. Change the **beanName** from **JTextField1** to **tfLength**.
> ➤ Change the **text** to **1023**.
> ➤ Close the **Properties** sheet.
> ➤ Expand the JTextField to the size shown in the figure.

The LocalDataArea Bean

Now, you're going to add a **LocalDataArea** bean. This bean is located about halfway through the list in the AS/400 Toolbox bean category.

➤   Click to display the bean category drop-down list, and select **AS/400 Toolbox**.

➤   Click the **LocalDataArea** bean 🔲, and drop it on the free-form *nonvisual* surface as shown in Figure 12.6. You won't change any properties of this bean.

Next, add an **AS400** bean.

➤   Click the **AS400** bean 🔲, and drop it on the free-form nonvisual surface as shown in the figure. You won't change any properties of this bean.

Figure 12.6
LocalDataArea and AS400 Beans

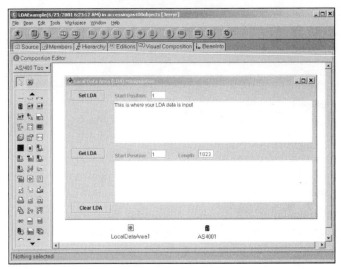

Save your Java program.

➤   On the menu bar, click **Bean**.
➤   Click **Save Bean**.

Connecting the AS/400 Beans

You are now going to set up one property-to-property connection, four event-to-method connections, and four parameter-from-property connections to connect the AS/400 beans.

Property-to-Property Connection: system

`connPtoP1: AS4001,this ←→ LocalDataArea1,system)`

Connect the **AS4001** bean with the **LocalDataArea1** bean as shown in Figure 12.7.

➤   Right-click the **AS4001** bean.
➤   Click **Connect**.
➤   Click **this**.
➤   Click the spider-end pointer on the **LocalDataArea1** bean.
➤   Click **Connectible Features**.
➤   Double-click the **system** property.

Figure 12.7

system() Connection

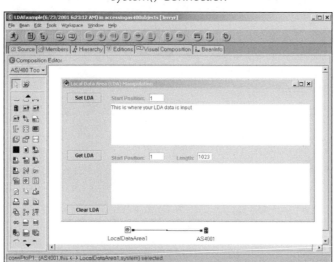

Event-to-Method Connection: write()

```
connEtoM1: (btSetLDA,actionPerformed → LocalDataArea1,write(java.lang.String, int))
```

The first event-to-method connection will let you write the contents of the input text area to the AS/400 LDA. It will use two parameters:

- the input text area
- the starting position at which to place the data in the LDA

Connect the **btSetLDA** JButton with a **write(java.lang.String, int)** method to the **LocalDataArea1** bean.

➤ Right-click the **btSetLDA** JButton.
➤ Click **Connect**.
➤ Click **actionPerformed**.
➤ Click the spider-end pointer on the **LocalDataArea1** bean.
➤ Click **Connectible Features**.
➤ Click the **write(java.lang.String, int)** method as shown in Figure 12.8. Make sure you click the write method that has the two parameters.
➤ Click **OK**.

Figure 12.8

Selection of write(java.lang.String, int) Connection

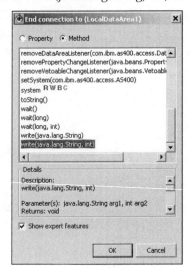

Parameter-from-Property Connection 1

```
connPfromP1: (connEtoM1: (btSetLDA,actionPerformed →
              LocalDataArea1,write(java.lang.String,int)),arg1 → taInput,text)
```

Complete the *first* parameter connection by passing a parameter into the primary connection. The connection is expecting a **String** data type.

Identify the source property:

➢   Right-click the dashed line.
➢   Click **Connect**.
➢   Click **arg1**.

Identify the target property:

➢   Click the spider-end pointer on the **taInput** JTextArea bean.
➢   Click **text**.

Figure 12.9 shows what the connection should look like. Notice that the main connection line is still a dashed line. That's because this connection expects two input parameters. You'll make the second parameter connection next.

Figure 12.9
write() Connections: connPfromP1 and connEtoM1

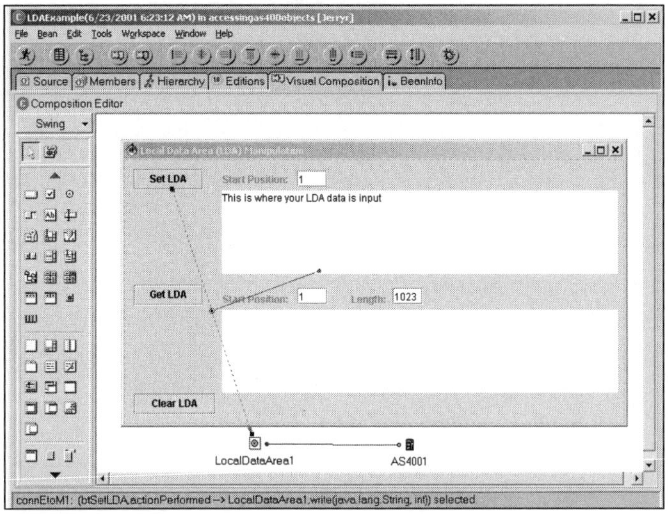

Parameter-from-Property Connection 2

```
connPfromP2: (connEtoM1: (btSetLDA,actionPerformed →
            LocalDataArea1,write(java.lang.String,int)),arg2 → tfStartInput,text)
```

Complete the *second* parameter connection by passing a parameter into the primary connection. The connection is expecting an **int** data type.

Identify the source property:

➢   Right-click the dashed line.
➢   Click **Connect**.
➢   Click **arg2**.

Identify the target property:

➢   Click the spider-end pointer on the **tfStartInput** JTextField bean.
➢   Click **text**.

Figure 12.10 shows what the connection should look like.

Figure 12.10
write() Connections: connPfromP1, connPfromP2, and connEtoM1

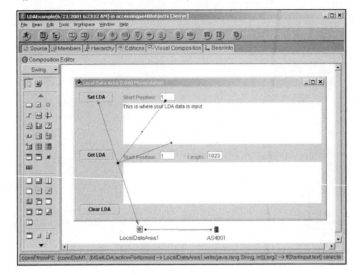

➤   Double-click each connection to verify that it is correct as shown in Figures 12.11, 12.12, and 12.13.
➤   Close each **Properties** window.

Figure 12.11
Connection connEtoM1

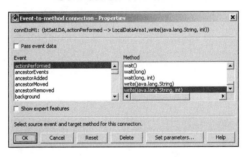

Figure 12.12
Connection connPfromP1

Figure 12.13
Connection connPfromP2

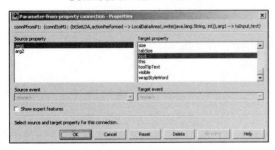
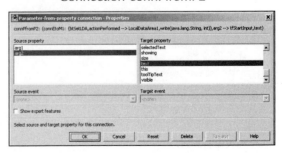

Event-to-Method Connection: read()

`connEtoM2: (btGetLDA,actionPerformed → LocalDataArea1,read(int,int))`

The second event-to-method connection will let you read the contents of the AS/400 LDA and put those contents into the output text area. The connection will use two parameters and will return a value. The two input parameters are

- the starting position, which specifies where in the LDA to begin retrieving data
- the offset or length, which defines how much data to retrieve from the LDA

The return value is the actual data selected and retrieved from the LDA.

Connect the **btGetLDA** JButton with a **read(int, int)** method to the **LocalDataArea1** bean.

➢ Right-click the **btGetLDA** JButton.
➢ Click **Connect**.
➢ Click **actionPerformed**.
➢ Click the spider-end pointer on the **LocalDataArea1** bean.
➢ Click **Connectible Features**.
➢ Click the **read(int, int)** method as shown in Figure 12.14.
➢ Before clicking **OK**, look at the parameters and return values specified in the Details section of the window. This is where the two input parameters and the return value are specified.
➢ Click **OK**.

Figure 12.14
Selection of read(int, int) Connection

Parameter-from-Property Connection 1

`connPfromP3: (connEtoM2: (btGetLDA,actionPerformed → LocalDataArea1,read(int,int)),arg1 →`
`        tfStartOutput,text)`

Complete the first parameter connection by passing a parameter into the primary connection. The connection is expecting an **int** data type.

Identify the source property:

➢   Right-click the dashed line.
➢   Click **Connect**.
➢   Click **arg1**.

Identify the target property:

➢   Click the spider-end pointer on the **tfStartOutput** JTextField bean.
➢   Click **text**.

Figure 12.15 shows what the connection should look like. Again, notice that the main connection line is still a dashed line. That's because the connection expects two input parameters.

Figure 12.15
read() Connections: connPfromP3 and connEtoM2

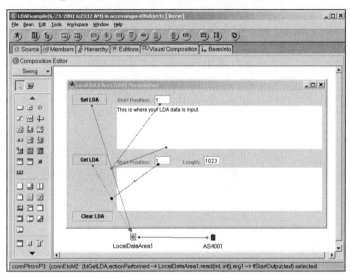

Parameter-from-Property Connection 2

```
connPfromP4: (connEtoM2: (btGetLDA,actionPerformed → LocalDataArea1,read(int,int)),arg2 →
            tfLength,text)
```

Complete the second parameter connection by passing a parameter into the primary connection. The connection is expecting an **int** data type.

Identify the source property:

➢   Right-click the dashed line.
➢   Click **Connect**.
➢   Click **arg2**.

Identify the target property:

➢   Click the spider-end pointer on the **tfLength** JTextField bean.
➢   Click **text**.

Figure 12.16 shows what the connection should look like. Notice that the connection line is no longer dashed. However, you still need to connect the text output area.

Figure 12.16
read() Connections: connPfromP3, connPfromP4, and connEtoM2

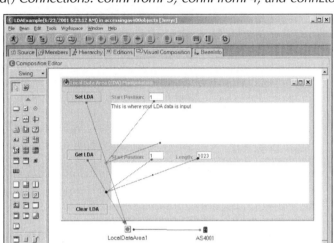

Event-to-Method Connection 3

```
connEtoM3: (connEtoM2: (btGetLDA,actionPerformed → LocalDataArea1,read(int,int)),
            normalResult → taOutput,text)
```

The third event-to-method connection connects the text output area. Complete this connection by returning the value from the LDA and placing it into the output text area. The return value is a **String** data type. The return value is identified as a **normal result**.

Identify the source property:

➢ Right-click the **connEtoM2** connection (just as if it were a dashed line). The **connEtoM2** connection connects the **btGetLDA** button and the **LocalDataArea1** bean.
➢ Click **Connect**.
➢ Click **normalResult**.

Identify the target property:

➢ Click the spider-end pointer on the **taOutput** JTextArea bean.
➢ Click **text**.

Figure 12.17 shows what the connection should look like.

Figure 12.17

read() Connections: connPfromP3, connPfromP4, connEtoM2, and connEtoM3

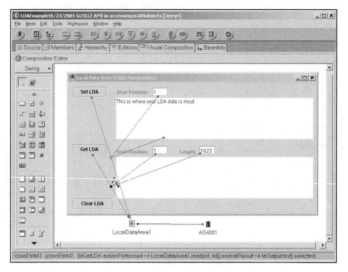

> Double-click each connection to verify that it is correct, as shown in Figures 12.18, 12.19, 12.20, and 12.21.
> Close each **Properties** window.

Figure 12.18

Connection: connEtoM2

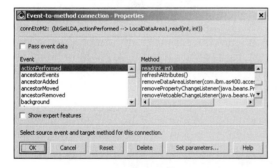

Figure 12.19

Connection: connPfromP3

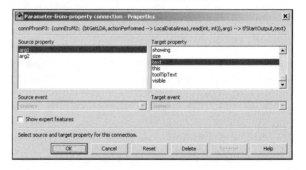

Figure 12.20

Connection: connPfromP4

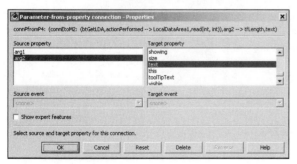

Figure 12.21

Connection: connEtoM3

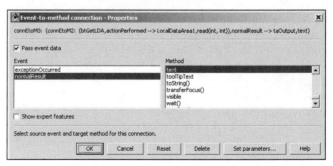

Event-to-Method Connection: clear()

`connEtoM4: (btClearLDA,actionPerformed → LocalDataArea1,clear())`

The fourth event-to-method connection will let you clear the contents of the AS/400 local data area. It blanks out all 1,024 characters of the LDA. There are no parameters.

Connect the **btClearLDA** JButton with a **clear()** method to the **LocalDataArea1** bean.

➢ Right-click the **btClearLDA** JButton.
➢ Click **Connect**.
➢ Click **actionPerformed**.
➢ Click the spider-end pointer on the **LocalDataArea1** bean.
➢ Click **Connectible Features**.
➢ Click the **clear()** method as shown in Figure 12.22.

Look at Figure 12.22. Do you see any parameter definitions or return values in the Details portion of the window? As you can see, the Details area lets you easily tell what parameters and return values are specified for each method. In this case, there are none.

➢ Click **OK**.

Figure 12.22
Selection of clear(int, int) Method

Figure 12.23 shows what the connection should look like.

➢ Double-click the connection, and verify that it is correct as shown in Figure 12.24.
➢ Close the **Properties** window.

Figure 12.23
clear() Connection: connEtoM4

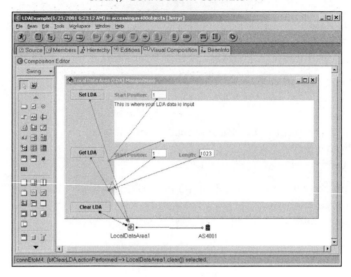

Figure 12.24
Connection connEtoM4

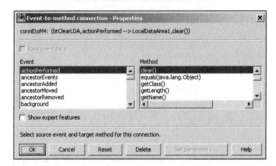

Accessing the AS/400 Local Data Area

Save your Java program.

> On the menu bar, click **Bean**.
> Click **Save Bean**.

To run this Java program, you need to successfully connect to the AS/400. Run your Java program.

> On the menu bar, click **Bean**.
> Click **Run**, and then click **Run Main**.

You should see the application appear as shown in Figure 12.25.

> Click the **Set LDA** button.
> Enter your sign-on information.
> Click the **Get LDA** button.

Figure 12.26 shows the output box with the retrieved LDA data.

Figure 12.25
Application Start

Figure 12.26
Updated Output Text Area

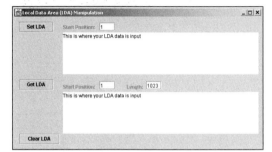

➢   Click the **Clear LDA** button.
➢   Click the **Get LDA** button.

Figure 12.27 shows the results of clearing the LDA. Why wasn't the text area cleared after you clicked the **Clear LDA** button? That's because the **Clear LDA** button clears only the contents of the AS/400 LDA, not the contents of the output text area.

➢   With the Delete key, erase all the text in the input area.
➢   In the input area, enter the following: **This is going to be a long sentence to test some of the start and length features.**
➢   As shown in Figure 12.28, change the input **Start Position** to **50**.
➢   Click the **Set LDA** button.
➢   Click the **Get LDA** button.

Figure 12.27
Cleared LDA

Figure 12.28
Newly Entered Input Data

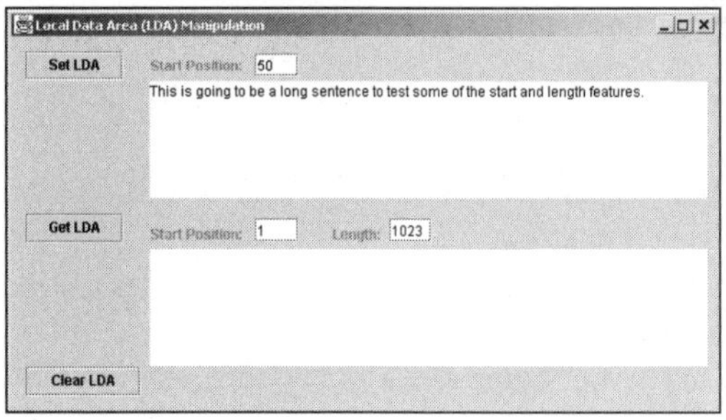

Figure 12.29 shows the results. What happened? The Set LDA operation began the placement of the data in the 50th position of the LDA. The Get LDA retrieved all the LDA data and displayed it in the output text area. It may not look like there are 50 blank spaces, but there are. It appears this way because of font properties.

Figure 12.29
Output Data with Offset of 50

> Click the **Clear LDA** button.
> Click the **Get LDA** button.
> Click the **Set LDA** button.
> As shown in Figure 12.30, change the output **Start Position** to **70** and the output **Length** to **23**.
> Click the **Get LDA** button.

Figure 12.31 shows the results. What happened? You cleared the LDA and then retrieved the blank LDA, thereby blanking out the output area on the screen. You then set the LDA again, this time putting the entire data string starting in the 50th position of the LDA. After changing the parameters, you requested a Get LDA. This time, the application pulled 23 bytes of the data string beginning in the 70th position of the LDA.

Figure 12.30   **Figure 12.31**
New Get LDA Parameters   *Data Pulled from the 70th Position for a Length of 23*

> Enter some different text strings and start and length parameters to get a good understanding of what is occurring.
> Close your **Local Data Area (LDA) Manipulation** application.

Congratulations! You just completed another Java application.

Summary

Local data areas are a valuable AS/400 function, both in the interactive and batch environments on the AS/400. They can also be a useful tool in the client/server environment. In this chapter you learned

- what AS/400 local data areas are and what they are used for
- how to use the **LocalDataArea** bean
- how to set, clear, and get a local data area on the AS/400
- how to use the start position and length parameters on the **LocalDataArea** bean
- how to use multiple call parameters in connections

The next chapter will be a fun one. You'll learn how to perform AS/400 database record-level access and how to work with database I/O handling. You'll be surprised how easy it is.

Unit 3

Working with AS/400 Databases from Java

Chapter 13

Using Record-Level Access

Chapter Objectives

- ☐ Understand record-level access concepts
- ☐ Become familiar with the AS/400 Toolbox Record List Form Pane
- ☐ Understand the use of file error handling

Chapter Project

- ☐ A class will be created to display the contents of any AS/400 database.
- ☐ The class will let you perform record-level access on a database file specified at run time.
- ☐ Figure 13.1 shows what the sample application will look like.

Figure 13.1
Chapter Project

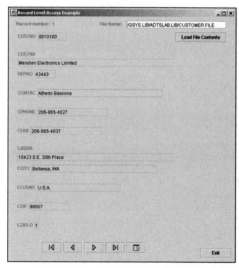

In Unit 3, which begins with this chapter, you'll become familiar with the different methods of accessing AS/400 database files. Each chapter will focus on accessing an AS/400 database using step-by-step examples. Chapter 13 begins with the use of database record-level access. This function is similar to accessing AS/400 files in RPG using the READ, READE, and CHAIN opcodes. Chapter 14 covers Java Database Connectivity (JDBC) and SQL access. Unit 4, which contains six chapters, will go into much more depth using record-level access.

To begin, you're going to create a new project named **My AS400 Database Projects**. The work accomplished in both Unit 3 chapters will be stored in this newly created project.

➢   If the workbench isn't started, start it now.
➢   In the workbench **All Projects** pane, right-click to display the shortcut menu, select **Add**, and then select **Project**.
➢   Make sure the **Create a new project named** option is selected. Type **My AS400 Database Projects** into the space provided.
➢   Click **Finish** to complete the creation of the project.

Once the project is created, you'll see it listed in the workbench upper pane. You are now going to create a package called **accessingas400databases**.

➢   Select the project **My AS400 Database Projects** with a click. Right-click to display the shortcut menu, select **Add**, and then select **Package**.
➢   Make sure the Project name is **My AS400 Database Projects**.
➢   Make sure the **Create a new package named** option is selected. Type **accessingas400databases** into the space provided.
➢   Click **Finish** to complete the creation of the package.

Once the package and project are created, you'll see them listed in the workbench **All Projects** pane, as shown in Figure 13.2.

Figure 13.2
Workbench Setup for Unit 3

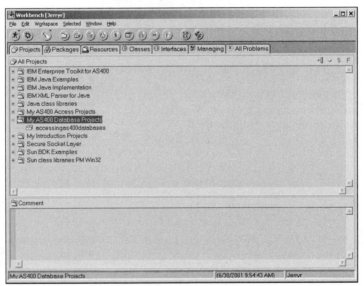

Record-Level Access

Distributed Data Management (DDM) record-level access is used to access records on the AS/400. The client program — your Java application — requests data from the AS/400 database by interfacing with the DDM host server. On the AS/400, the DDM server accesses the database and then returns the results (AS/400 records or an error message) to the client program. This means you can access records one at a time, by keyed values, sequentially, or by relative record number. Positioning within the file is also possible, just as you've done in RPG using the SETLL and SETGT opcodes. You can lock AS/400 files and use commit and rollback on database transactions. You can also delete records, members, or an entire database file.

When you use DDM record-level access, a TCP/IP socket connection accomplishes the interface communications. Each client creates a new server job on the AS/400. The AS/400 server job for record-level access is QRWTSRVR. You can view this server job in subsystem QSYSWRK using the WRKACTJOB (Work with Active Jobs) command. The user profile being used with the server job and communications function is QUSER.

Several AS/400 Toolbox JavaBeans work with record-level access to the AS/400. In this chapter, you'll use the **RecordListFormPane** JavaBean to accomplish record-level access. In later chapters, you'll learn about the **FormManager**, **ListManager**, **RecordIOManager**, and **RecordListTablePane** JavaBeans.

To enable DDM record-level access on the AS/400, several steps have to occur on the AS/400. There is a high possibility that most, if not all, of these steps are already in place on your system. Later in this chapter, if you experience difficulties with record-level access, review the following Tips and Tricks item.

Tips and Tricks

If you find that your DDM record-level access isn't working, these steps may resolve your problem.

1. At OS/400 V4R2 or later, enable server jobs by executing the following AS/400 command: STRHOSTSVR SERVER(*ALL).
2. Enable the DDM server: STRTCPSVR SERVER(*DDM).
3. Make sure you have the latest cumulative PTF package installed on your AS/400.
4. Verify that subsystem QCMN is started: STRSBS QCMN.
5. Verify that user profile QUSER is enabled.
6. Verify that you have free access to ports 446, 447, and 448. This access is usually controlled by the network administrator by means of a firewall.

You're going to create a class called **RecordLevelAccessExample** that inherits properties from superclass **JFrame**. You'll store your class in the project **My AS/400 Database Projects** and in the package **accessingas400databases**.

➢ If the workbench isn't started, start it now.
➢ Expand the project **My AS/400 Database Projects** with a click.
➢ Select the package **accessingas400databases** with a click. Right-click to display the shortcut menu, select **Add**, and then select **Class**.
➢ Make sure the **Project** name is **My AS400 Database Projects**.
➢ Make sure the **Package** name is **accessingas400databases**.
➢ In the **Class name** field, type **RecordLevelAccessExample**.
➢ Click **Browse** to select a superclass.
➢ When the **Superclass** window appears, type **JFrame** in the **Pattern** field.
➢ In the **Type names** list, double-click **JFrame**. When you return to the SmartGuide, the **Superclass** field should contain **javax.swing.JFrame,** as shown in Figure 13.3.
➢ Select the **Browse the class when finished** check box.
➢ Select the **Compose the class visually** check box.
➢ Click **Finish** to complete the creation of the class.

Figure 13.3
Class RecordLevelAccessExample

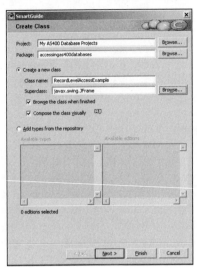

You should be inside the Visual Composition Editor. Change the title of the JFrame.

➢   On the menu bar, click **Tools**.
➢   Click **Beans List**.
➢   Double-click the **RecordLevelAccessExample** JFrame to display the **Properties** sheet.
➢   For the **title** property, type **Record Level Access Example**.
➢   Close the **Properties** sheet.
➢   Close the **Beans List**.
➢   Expand the height of your free-form surface by dragging a corner downward and to the right.

Create the two JButtons shown in Figure 13.4.

➢   Click the **JButton** bean 🔲, and drop it in the upper-right corner of the free-from surface visual area, or JFrameContentPane.
➢   Double-click the JButton. Change the **beanName** from **JButton1** to **btLoad**.
➢   Change the **text** to **Load File Contents**.
➢   Close the **Properties** sheet.
➢   Expand the button so that you can see all the text.
➢   Click the **JButton** bean again, and drop it in the lower-right corner of the visual area.
➢   Double-click the JButton. Change the **beanName** from **JButton1** to **btExit**.
➢   Change the **text** to **Exit**.
➢   Close the **Properties** sheet.

Figure 13.4

Screen Layout: Buttons, Labels, and Text Fields

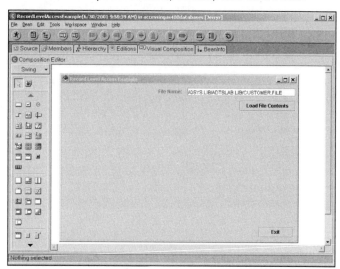

Now, create the JLabel and JTextField shown in the figure.

➤ Click the **JLabel** bean [Ab], and drop it on the upper center of the visual area.
➤ Change the **text** property to **File Name:** .
➤ Close the **Properties** sheet.
➤ Expand the JLabel so that you can see all the text.
➤ Click the **JTextField** bean [⊞], and drop it in the upper-right corner of the visual area.
➤ Double-click the JTextField. Change the **beanName** from **JTextField1** to **tfFileName**.
➤ Change the **text** to **/QSYS.LIB/ADTSLAB.LIB/CUSTOMER.FILE**. Or, if you don't have the CUSTOMER file in library ADTSLAB on your AS/400, you can substitute another AS/400 database file name and/or library.
➤ Close the **Properties** sheet.
➤ Expand the JTextField to the size shown in the figure.

Tips and Tricks

When using DDM record-level access, remember to specify your AS/400 file names in an Integrated File System (IFS) format (for more information about the IFS, see Chapter 11):

/QSYS.LIB	Use the standard AS/400 library structure
/xxxxxxxxxx.LIB	Identify the AS/400 library
/xxxxxxxxxx.FILE	Identify the AS/400 file name

Using the Record List Form Pane

The **RecordListFormPane** bean lets you quickly develop a record layout of a database file. At run time, this bean retrieves the file format and displays the results inside a pane. Navigational buttons let you select the first record, the last record, the next record, the prior record, and a refresh function.

If you've used IBM's Data File Utility (DFU) on the AS/400, you're already familiar with how easy it is to display the contents of each record on the screen. The RecordListFormPane is very similar. The main difference is that the RecordListFormPane provides no update capabilities, only a display function.

You're going to add a **RecordListFormPane** bean now. This bean is located about halfway through the list in the AS/400 Toolbox bean category.

➤   Click to display the bean category drop-down list, and select **AS/400 Toolbox**.
➤   Click the **RecordListFormPane** bean 🔲, and drop it on the center portion of the visual area as shown in Figure 13.5. As you can see, the RecordListFormPane has three parts: a record number identifier, five database navigational controls, and a database message area. You won't change any properties of this bean.
➤   Enlarge the RecordListFormPane to the size shown in the figure.

Figure 13.5
RecordListFormPane Bean

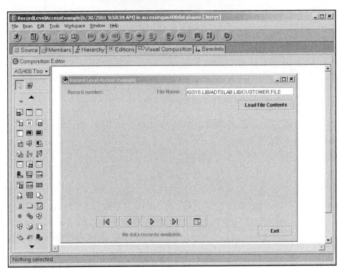

 Tips and Tricks

When using the *RecordListFormPane* JavaBean, you may want to specify keyed file access instead of sequential file access. To do so, change the *keyed* property to *True* on the *Properties* sheet for the *RecordListFormPane1* bean.

Now, add an **AS400** bean.

➤   Click the **AS400** bean 🔲, and drop it on the free-form nonvisual surface as shown in Figure 13.6. You won't change any properties of this bean.

Figure 13.6
AS400 and ErrorDialogAdapter Beans

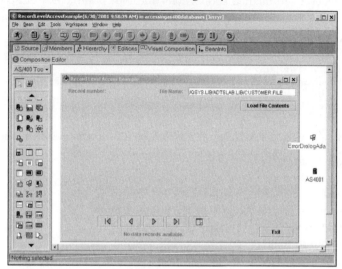

Using the Error Dialog Adapter

You've probably wondered about error handling in some of the earlier chapters of the book. The AS/400 Toolbox's **ErrorDialogAdapter** bean, in conjunction with an **addErrorListener()** method, is used to monitor for possible error conditions passed back from the AS/400. The ErrorDialogAdapter can be used in a variety of ways. In this chapter, you'll use it to monitor for file-related error conditions, such as "File not found." When an error occurs, the ErrorDialogAdapter is passed as a parameter into the error listener. A dialog box error message is then displayed, as shown in Figure 13.7. You'll use similar error handling in later chapters.

Figure 13.7
ErrorDialogAdapter

You're going to add an **ErrorDialogAdapter** bean now. This bean is located about halfway through the list in the AS/400 Toolbox bean category.

➢　Click the **ErrorDialogAdapter** bean , and drop it on the free-form nonvisual surface as shown above in Figure 13.6. You won't change any properties of this bean.

Save your Java program.

➢　On the menu bar, click **Bean**.
➢　Click **Save Bean**.

Connecting the AS/400 Beans

You're now going to set up six event-to-method connections and four parameter-from-property connections to connect the AS/400 beans.

Event-to-Method Connection: setSystem()

```
connEtoM1: (btLoad,actionPerformed →
           RecordListFormPane1,setSystem(com.ibm.as400.access.AS400))
```

The first event-to-method connection will let you connect to the AS/400 when the user clicks the **Load File Contents** button.

Connect the **btLoad** JButton with a **setSystem(com.ibm.as400.access.AS400)** method.

➢   Right-click the **btLoad** JButton.
➢   Click **Connect**.
➢   Click **actionPerformed**.
➢   Click the spider-end pointer on the **RecordListFormPane1** bean.
➢   Click **Connectible Features**.
➢   Click the **setSystem(com.ibm.as400.access.AS400)** method.
➢   Click **OK**.

Parameter-from-Property Connection

```
connPfromP1: (connEtoM1: (btLoad,actionPerformed →
            RecordListFormPane1,setSystem(com.ibm.as400.access.AS400)),arg1 → AS4001,this)
```

Complete the connection by passing a parameter into the primary connection. The connection is expecting an **AS400** data type.

Identify the source property:

➢   Right-click the dashed line.
➢   Click **Connect**.
➢   Click **arg1**.

Identify the target property:

➢   Click the spider-end pointer on the **AS4001** bean.
➢   Click **this**.

Figure 13.8 shows what the connection should look like.

Figure 13.8

setSystem() Connections: connEtoM1 and connPfromP1

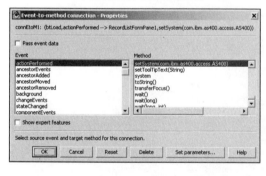

> Double-click each connection to verify that it is correct as shown in Figures 13.9 and 13.10.
> Close each **Properties** window.

Figure 13.9

Connection connEtoM1

Figure 13.10

Connection connPfromP1

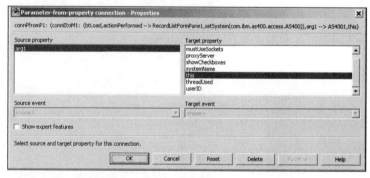

Event-to-Method Connection: setFileName()

`connEtoM2: (btLoad,actionPerformed → RecordListFormPane1,setFileName(java.lang.String))`

When the user clicks the **Load File Contents** button, the second event-to-method connection will specify the IFS file name to the RecordListFormPane. The user will be able to change the file name at run time and then reclick the **Load File Contents** button as many times as desired.

Connect the **btLoad** JButton with a **setFileName(java.lang.String)** method to the **RecordListFormPane1** bean.

> Right-click the **btLoad** JButton.
> Click **Connect**.
> Click **actionPerformed**.
> Click the spider-end pointer on the **RecordListFormPane1** bean.
> Click **Connectible Features**.

> Click the **setFileName(java.lang.String)** method.
> Click **OK**.

Parameter-from-Property Connection

```
connPfromP2: (connEtoM2: (btLoad,actionPerformed →
            RecordListFormPane1,setFileName(java.lang.String)),arg1 → tfFileName,text)
```

Complete the connection by passing a parameter into the primary connection. The connection is expecting a **String** data type.

Identify the source property:

> Right-click the dashed line.
> Click **Connect**.
> Click **arg1**.

Identify the target property:

> Click the spider-end pointer on the **tfFileName** JTextfield bean.
> Click **text**.

Figure 13.11 shows what the connection should look like.

Figure 13.11
setFileName() Connections: connEtoM2 and connPfromP2

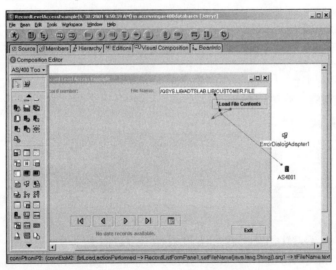

> Double-click each connection to verify that it is correct as shown in Figures 13.12 and 13.13.
> Close each **Properties** window.

Figure 13.12
Connection connEtoM2

Figure 13.13
Connection connPfromP2

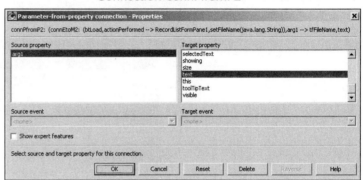

Event-to-Method Connection: load()

```
connEtoM3: (btLoad,actionPerformed → RecordListFormPane1,load())
```

The third event-to-method connection will let you load the contents of the database file, as well as the externally described database field definitions, into the RecordListFormPane.

Connect the **btLoad** JButton with a **load()** method to the **RecordListFormPane1** bean.

➤ Right-click the **btLoad** JButton.
➤ Click **Connect**.
➤ Click **actionPerformed**.
➤ Click the spider-end pointer on the **RecordListFormPane1** bean.
➤ Click **Connectible Features**.
➤ Click the **load()** method.
➤ Click **OK**.

Figure 13.14 shows what the connection should look like.

Figure 13.14
load() Connection connEtoM3

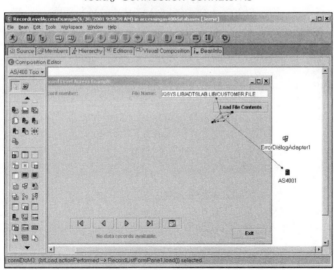

➤ Double-click the connection to verify that it is correct as shown in Figure 13.15.
➤ Close the **Properties** window.

Figure 13.15
Connection connEtoM3

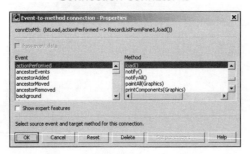

Event-to-Method Connection: close()

`connEtoM4: (btExit,actionPerformed → RecordListFormPane1,close())`

When the user clicks the **Exit** button, the fourth event-to-method connection will close the AS/400 database file specified in the RecordListFormPane.

Connect the **btExit** JButton with a **close()** method to the **RecordListFormPane1** bean.

➤ Right-click the **btExit** JButton.
➤ Click **Connect**.
➤ Click **actionPerformed**.
➤ Click the spider-end pointer on the **RecordListFormPane1** bean.
➤ Click **Connectible Features**.
➤ Click the **close()** method.
➤ Click **OK**.

Figure 13.16 shows what the connection should look like.

Figure 13.16
close() Connection connEtoM4

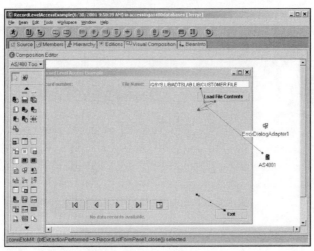

➢   Double-click the connection to verify that it is correct as shown in Figure 13.17.
➢   Close the **Properties** window.

Figure 13.17
Connection connEtoM4

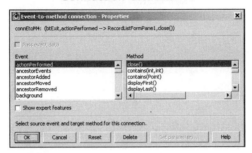

Event-to-Method Connection: dispose()

```
connEtoM5:  (btExit,actionPerformed  →  RecordLevelAccessExample,dispose())
```

When the user clicks the **Exit** button, the fifth event-to-method connection will dispose, or shut down, the **RecordLevelAccessExample** JFrame.

Connect the **btExit** JButton with a **dispose()** method to **RecordLevelAccessExample** JFrame.

➢   Right-click the **btExit** JButton.
➢   Click **Connect**.
➢   Click **actionPerformed**.
➢   Click the spider-end pointer on the outside edge of the visual area of the free-form surface, or **RecordLevelAccessExample** JFrame bean.
➢   Click **Connectible Features**.
➢   Click the **dispose()** method.
➢   Click **OK**.

Figure 13.18 shows what the connection should look like.

Figure 13.18
dispose() Connection connEtoM5

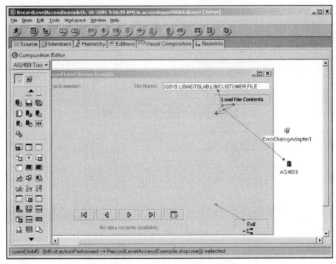

➢   Double-click the connection to verify that it is correct as shown in Figure 13.19.
➢   Close the **Properties** window.

Figure 13.19
Connection connEtoM5

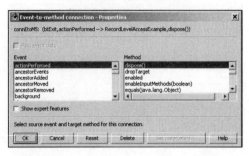

Event-to-Method Connection: addErrorListener()

```
connEtoM6: (RecordLevelAccessExample,windowOpened →
            RecordListFormPane1,addErrorListener(com.ibm.as400.vaccess.ErrorListener))
```

The sixth event-to-method connection will let you specify an error listener when the **RecordLevelAccessExample** window is opened. Connect the **RecordLevelAccessExample** JFrame with an **addErrorListener()** method.

➢   Select the **RecordLevelAccessExample** JFrame by clicking the outside edge of the visual area.
➢   Click **Connect**.
➢   Click **windowOpened**.
➢   Click the spider-end pointer on the **RecordListFormPane1** bean in the center of the screen.
➢   Click **Connectible Features**.
➢   Click the **addErrorListener(com.ibm.as400.vaccess.errorListener)** method, as shown in Figure 13.20.
➢   Click **OK**.

Figure 13.20
addErrorListener(com.ibm.as400.vaccess.ErrorListener)

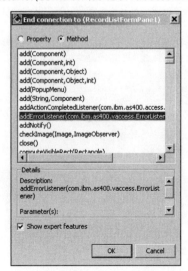

Figure 13.21 shows what the connection should look like.

Figure 13.21
addErrorListener() Connection connEtoM6

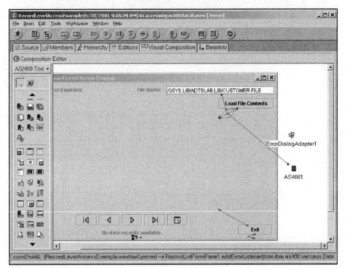

Parameter-from-Property Connection

```
connPfromP3: (connEtoM6: (RecordLevelAccessExample,windowOpened → RecordListFormPane1,
            addErrorListener (com.ibm.as400.vaccess.ErrorListener)),arg1 →
            ErrorDialogAdapter1,this)
```

Complete the connection by passing a parameter into the primary connection. The connection is expecting an **errorListener** data type.

Identify the source property:

➢   Right-click the dashed line.
➢   Click **Connect**.
➢   Click **arg1**.

Identify the target property:

➢   Click the spider-end pointer on the **ErrorDialogAdapter1** bean.
➢   Click **this**.

Figure 13.22 shows what the connection should look like.

➢   Double-click each connection to verify that it is correct as shown in Figures 13.23 and 13.24.
➢   Close each **Properties** window.

Figure 13.22

addErrorListener() Connection connPfromP3

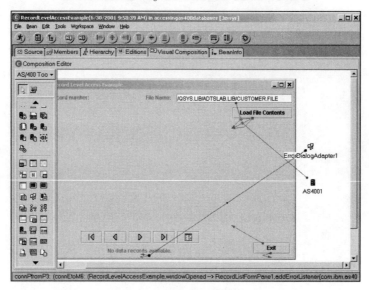

Figure 13.23

Connection connEtoM6

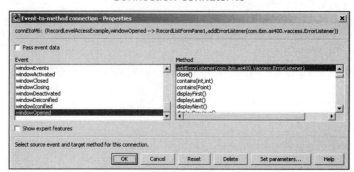

Figure 13.24

Connection connPfromP3

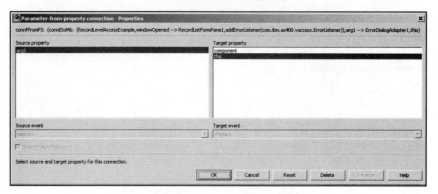

Save your Java program.

➢   On the menu bar, click **Bean**.
➢   Click **Save Bean**.

Review AS/400 Classes and Methods

Review the Java source code generated for the **connEtoM6(java.awt.event.WindowEvent)** method.

➢   Click the **Source** tab.
➢   In the **Elements** pane, click method **connEtoM6(java.awt.event.WindowEvent)**.

How are potential errors associated with the RecordListFormPane? As the code in Figure 13.25 shows, the **errorDialogAdapter1** parameter is passed to the **addErrorListener()** method. This is how the listener, the ErrorDialogAdapter, and the RecordListFormPane are all tied together. You'll learn more about error handling in later chapters.

Figure 13.25
Source Code for Method connEtoM6()

```
Source code: ConnEtoM6
private void connEtoM6(java.awt.event.WindowEvent arg1) {
    try {
        // user code begin {1}
        // user code end
        getRecordListFormPane1().addErrorListener(getErrorDialogAdapter1());
        // user code begin {2}
        // user code end
    } catch (java.lang.Throwable ivjExc) {
        // user code begin {3}
        // user code end
        handleException(ivjExc);
    }
}
```

Using Record-Level Access

To run this Java program, you need to successfully connect to the AS/400. Run the Java program.

➢   On the menu bar, click **Bean**.
➢   Click **Run**, and then click **Run Main**.

You should see the application appear as shown in Figure 13.26.

➢   Click the **Load File Contents** button.
➢   Enter your sign-on information, and wait a few seconds.

Figure 13.27 shows the results of retrieving the contents of file CUSTOMER in library ADTSLAB.

Figure 13.26
Application Start

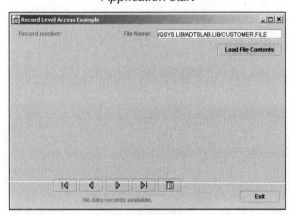

Figure 13.27
Results from CUSTOMER File

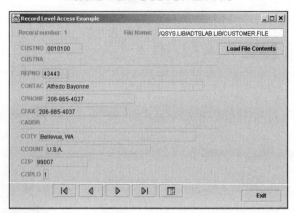

Look closely at the various fields shown on the display. Do you notice that two of the fields (CUSTNA and CADDR) aren't displayed completely? That's because the screen size isn't large enough to accommodate them. You're going to fix that problem now.

➢ Click the **Exit** button.
➢ Now that you're back in the VCE, expand the **RecordLevelAccessExample** JFrame downward. You may have to scroll down a couple times to complete this task.
➢ Expand the **RecordListFormPane** downward.

Now, run the program again.

➢ On the menu bar, click **Bean**.
➢ Click **Run**, and then click **Run Main**.
➢ Click the **Load File Contents** button.
➢ Enter your sign-on information, and wait a few seconds.

Figure 13.28 shows the results for file CUSTOMER. Notice that you can now see all the fields. Figure 13.29 shows the AS/400 Data Description Specifications (DDS) for the CUSTOMER file.

Figure 13.28
CUSTOMER File Results

Figure 13.29
CUSTOMER DDS

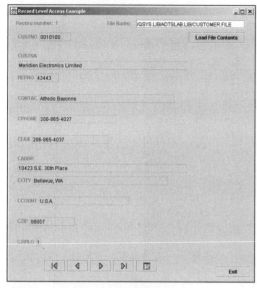

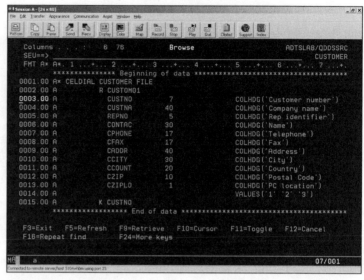

> Change the **File Name** entry so that it specifies the **PRODUCT** file rather than the CUSTOMER file. Use the same library, ADTSLAB.
> Click the **Load File Contents** button.
> Wait a few seconds.

Figure 13.30 shows the results. Notice that you now see all the fields of the PRODUCT file. Figure 13.31 shows the DDS for the PRODUCT file.

Figure 13.30
PRODUCT File Results

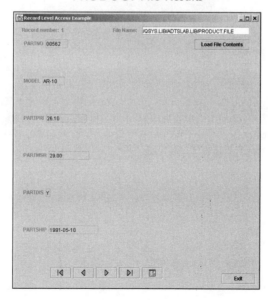

Figure 13.31
PRODUCT DDS

> ➤ Click the navigational control buttons at the bottom of your application window. Experiment with retrieving the previous, next, first, and last records.
> ➤ Change the **File Name** entry from the PRODUCT file to the **BILL** file. Use the same library, ADTSLAB.
> ➤ Click the **Load File Contents** button.

As Figure 13.32 shows, the error dialog box specifies that the file BILL does not exist in library ADTSLAB.

Figure 13.32
errorDialogAdapter

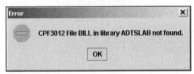

> ➤ Click the **Exit** button.

Congratulations! You just completed another Java application, and this one had error handling added to it. This was an easy application that let you access database records without writing a single line of code. It doesn't get much easier than that. An application like this is very limited in its use, but it can be a great tool from time to time.

Summary

In this chapter you learned

- what record-level access means
- how to use the **RecordListFormPane** bean and the **ErrorDialogAdapter** bean
- how to set up an AS/400 database error handler

The next chapter will take you through an example of accessing databases using SQL and JDBC. Have fun!

Chapter 14

Using SQL/JDBC

Chapter Objectives

- ☐ Understand SQL/JDBC concepts
- ☐ Become familiar with the AS/400 Toolbox SQL Result Set Table Pane
- ☐ Learn how to implement the **DriverManager** and **SQLConnection** beans

Chapter Project

- ☐ A class will be created to display the SQL results for any AS/400 database.
- ☐ The class will let you perform dynamic SQL query statements for any specified database file.
- ☐ Figure 14.1 shows what the sample application will look like.

Figure 14.1
Chapter Project

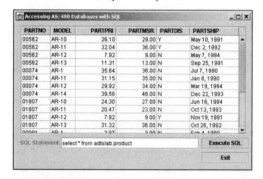

Structured Query Language (SQL) is an industry standard and a great language for accessing relational database records. On many systems, the only way to access a database is through SQL. Many AS/400 programmers haven't yet delved into using SQL. Instead, they've relied solely on record-level access through RPG and Cobol. Too bad for them, because they're missing out on a very powerful tool.

There's been much debate about when to use SQL versus record-level access. In general terms, selecting and processing a small amount of records is usually more efficient with record-level access methods, while SQL usually makes sense for larger amounts of records. There are no hard and fast rules, though. Most programmers have a favorite style of accessing records, and that's okay.

This chapter won't make you an SQL expert, but for those who've never used SQL, here are some simple examples:

A. This example selects all fields (columns) in each and every record (row) in the database file (table) CUSTOMER in library ADTSLAB.

```
select * from adtslab.customer
```

B. This example selects all fields in each and every record in database file CUSTOMER in library ADTSLAB that has a customer number (CUSTNO) less than 0010700.

```
select * from adtslab.customer where custno < '0010700'
```

C. In this example, only the customer name (CUSTNA) field is selected for every record in database file CUSTOMER in library ADTSLAB. All selected records are sorted in ascending order by customer name (CUSTNA).

```
select custna from adtslab.customer order by custna
```

You'll be using each of these examples, as well as some others, later on in the chapter project.

Java Database Connectivity

Open Database Connectivity (ODBC), developed by Microsoft, has been in use for a number of years. The concept of ODBC centered on allowing access to databases from any programming language by means of a standard protocol. Many AS/400 programmers and non-AS/400 programmers have used ODBC to access DB2 Universal Database for AS/400 (UDB/400) records.

When Java was developed, Sun Microsystems engineers wanted to improve and simplify ODBC. Java Database Connectivity (JDBC) was the result, and the rest is history.

JDBC provides all the constructs required to handle access to relational databases. JDBC is now an industry standard and allows access to a multitude of databases, including UDB/400. The AS/400 Toolbox implements the standard JDBC interface.

When you use the AS/400 Toolbox and JDBC, the AS/400 data types are automatically converted to Java data types. Another nice advantage of using JDBC is that it is very easy to switch the applications to point to another, non-AS/400 database. Let me make my allegiance known: Having personally used many other popular databases, I am still a huge fan of UDB/400. Enough said on that.

When you use JDBC, there are typically six major steps to create an application:

1. Register the AS/400 JDBC driver.
2. Connect to the AS/400 database.
3. Create SQL statements.
4. Execute SQL statements.
5. Retrieve the results of the SQL statements.
6. Close the statements and the AS/400 database connection.

You'll be using each of these steps in creating your application.

You are going to create a class called **SQLExample** that inherits properties from superclass **JFrame**. You'll store the class in the project **My AS/400 Database Projects** and in the package **accessingas400databases**.

➢   If the workbench isn't started, start it now.
➢   Expand the project **My AS/400 Database Projects** with a click.
➢   Select the package **accessingas400databases** with a click. Right-click to display the shortcut menu, select **Add**, and then select **Class**.
➢   Make sure the **Project** name is **My AS400 Database Projects**.
➢   Make sure the **Package** name is **accessingas400databases**.
➢   In the **Class name** field, type **SQLExample**.
➢   Click **Browse** to select a superclass.
➢   When the **Superclass** window appears, type **JFrame** in the **Pattern** field.
➢   In the **Type names** list, double-click **JFrame**. When you return to the SmartGuide, the **Superclass** field should contain **javax.swing.JFrame,** as shown in Figure 14.2.
➢   Select the **Browse the class when finished** check box.

➤ Select the **Compose the class visually** check box.
➤ Click **Finish** to complete the creation of the class.

Figure 14.2
SQLExample Class

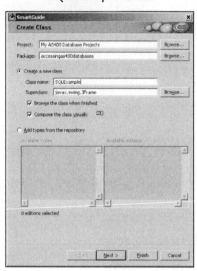

You should be inside the Visual Composition Editor. Change the title of the JFrame.

➤ On the menu bar, click **Tools**.
➤ Click **Beans List**.
➤ Double-click the **SQLExample** JFrame to display the **Properties** sheet.
➤ For the **title** property, type **Accessing AS/400 Databases with SQL**.
➤ Close the **Properties** sheet.
➤ Close the **Beans List**.
➤ Expand the height and width of your free-form surface by dragging a corner downward and to the right.

Now, create two JButtons as shown in Figure 14.3.

➤ Click the **JButton** bean ▦, and drop it in the lower-right corner of the free-from surface visual area, or JFrameContentPane.
➤ Double-click the JButton. Change the **beanName** from **JButton1** to **btExecute**.
➤ Change the **text** to **Execute SQL**.
➤ Close the **Properties** sheet.
➤ Expand the button so that you can see all the text.
➤ Click the **JButton** bean again, and drop it in the lower-right corner of the visual area.
➤ Double-click the JButton. Change the **beanName** from **JButton1** to **btExit**.
➤ Change the **text** to **Exit**.
➤ Close the **Properties** sheet.

Figure 14.3
Screen Layout: Buttons, Labels, and Text Fields

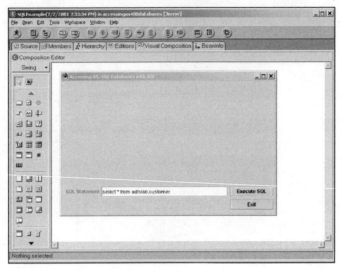

Create the JLabel and JTextField shown in the figure.

➢   Click the **JLabel** bean , and drop it in the lower-left corner of the visual area.
➢   Change the **text** to **SQL Statement:**.
➢   Close the **Properties** sheet.
➢   Expand the JLabel so that you can see all the text.
➢   Click the **JTextField** bean , and drop it on the lower-center portion of the visual area.
➢   Double-click the JTextField. Change the **beanName** from **JTextField1** to **tfSQLStatement**.
➢   Change the **text** to **select * from adtslab.customer**. If you don't have the CUSTOMER file in library ADTSLAB on your AS/400, substitute another AS/400 database file name and/or library.
➢   Close the **Properties** sheet.
➢   Expand the JTextField to the size shown in the figure.

Using the SQL Result Set Table Pane

The AS/400 Toolbox **SQLResultSetTablePane** bean lets you quickly develop an area for displaying the results of executed SQL query statements. At run time, the SQLResultSetTablePane formats the columns inside a pane. UDB/400 database names are displayed at the top of each column. You can attach an **ErrorDialogAdapter** bean as a listener to handle and display any error conditions from the SQL statements.

You're going to add an **SQLResultSetTablePane** bean now. This bean is located about halfway through the list in the AS/400 Toolbox bean category.

➢   Click to display the bean category drop-down list, and select **AS/400 Toolbox**.
➢   Click the **SQLResultSetTablePane** bean , and drop it on the center of the visual area. You won't change any properties of this bean.
➢   Resize the SQLResultSetTablePane to the size shown in Figure 14.4.

Figure 14.4
SQLResultSetTablePane Bean

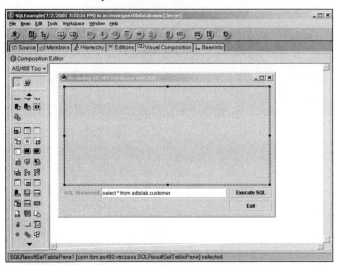

Next, you're going to add a **DriverManager** bean. This bean lets you register with the AS/400 the specific SQL/JDBC driver you're going to use for database access.

➢ In the upper-left corner of the VCE (above the AS/400 Toolbox beans), click the **Choose Bean** 🖳 button. The **Choose Bean** window appears.

➢ In the **Class name** field, type **Driver**, and then click **Browse** to select a class. The **Choose a valid class** window (Figure 14.5) appears.

➢ In the **Class Names** list, select **DriverManager**.

➢ Click **OK**.

➢ When you return to the **Choose Bean** window, the **Class name** field should now contain **java.sql.DriverManager**, as shown in Figure 14.6. Click **OK**.

➢ As shown in Figure 14.7, drop the **DriverManager** bean in the upper-right corner of the free-form nonvisual surface. You won't change any properties of this bean.

Figure 14.5
Choosing the Driver Manager

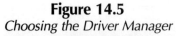

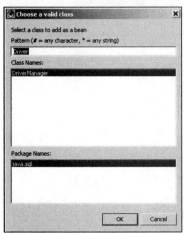

Figure 14.6
Selected Class

Figure 14.7
DriverManager Bean

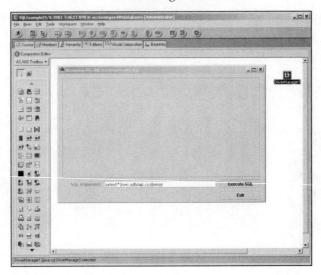

Now, you're going to add an **SQLConnection** bean. This bean is used to build the connection interface to the AS/400 database. It is located about halfway through the list in the AS/400 Toolbox bean category.

➢   Click the **SQLConnection** bean [image], and drop it on the free-form nonvisual surface as shown in Figure 14.8.

➢   Double-click the SQLConnection. As shown in Figure 14.9, change its **URL** property to **jdbc:as400::naming=sql;errors=full;date format = iso;**. Notice the difference between the colons and semicolons as you type the URL.

When you use a Web browser to surf the Internet, you specify a universal resource locator (URL) to find the particular Web site for which you're looking. In the **URL** property referenced above, you are specifying the proper syntax for the DriverManager to make the connection to the AS/400.

Figure 14.8
DriverManager, SQLConnection, and ErrorDialogAdapter Beans

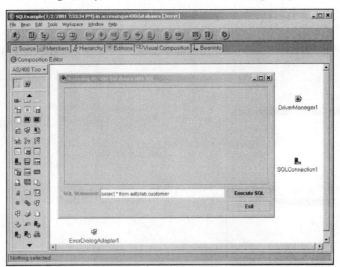

Figure 14.9
URL Property

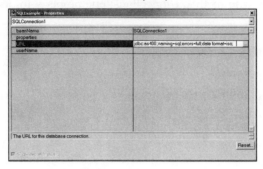

Using the Error Dialog Adapter

You used the ErrorDialogAdapter in Chapter 13. As you look at Figure 14.10, notice that the SQL error message is much more detailed than what you saw before. The ErrorDialogAdapter uses a dialog box window to display any error information. Some error messages are very short. Others are very detailed. When you use the ErrorDialogAdapter with SQL statements, the messages can be rather lengthy.

Figure 14.10
errorDialogAdapter

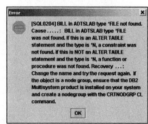

You're going to add an **ErrorDialogAdapter** bean now. This bean, too, is located about halfway through the list in the AS/400 Toolbox bean category.

➢ Click the **ErrorDialogAdapter** bean [icon], and drop it on the free-form nonvisual surface as shown in Figure 14.8. You won't change any properties of this bean.

Save your Java program.

➢ On the menu bar, click **Bean**.
➢ Click **Save Bean**.

Connecting the AS/400 Beans

You are now going to set up six event-to-method connections, one property-to-property connection, and two parameter-from-property connections.

Event-to-Method Connection: registerDriver()

```
connEtoM1: (SQLExample,windowOpened → DriverManager1,registerDriver(java.sql.Driver))
```

When the application begins, the AS/400 JDBC driver will be registered. Connect the **SQLExample** JFrame with a **registerDriver()** method.

➤ Select the **SQLExample** JFrame by clicking the outside edge of the visual area of the free-form surface.
➤ Click **Connect**.
➤ Click **windowOpened**.
➤ Click the spider-end pointer on the **DriverManager1** bean in the nonvisual area of the free-form surface.
➤ Click **Connectible Features**.
➤ Click the **registerDriver(java.sql.Driver)** method.
➤ Click **OK**.

Figure 14.11 shows what the connection should look like. Notice that it is not complete. To complete the connection, you need to specify the JDBC driver to be used. You'll do that next.

Figure 14.11
registerDriver() Connection: connEtoM1

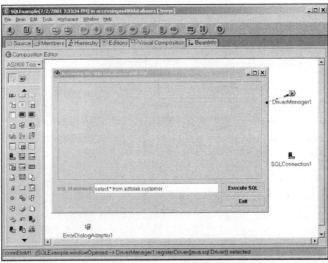

➤ Double-click the connection.
➤ Figure 14.12 shows the connection's **Properties** window. Instead of clicking **OK** here, click the **Set parameters** button. The **Constant Parameter Value Settings** window (Figure 14.13) is displayed.
➤ Click **driver**, and then click the **Details** button 🔲. The **Driver Implementor** window, shown in Figure 14.14, is displayed.
➤ Select the **Code String** option, and in the space provided, type the value **new com.ibm.as400.access.AS400JDBCDriver()**. Be sure to use this exact case.
➤ Click **OK**.

Figure 14.15 shows the new parameter value.

➢ Click **OK**.
➢ Click **OK**.

The connection should now be complete.

Figure 14.12
Connection connEtoM1

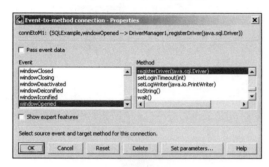

Figure 14.13
Constant Parameter Value Settings Window

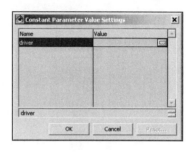

Figure 14.14
Driver Implementor Window

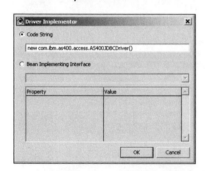

Figure 14.15
New Value Setting

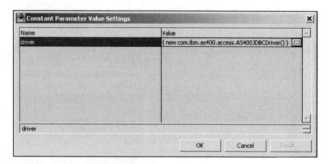

Property-to-Property Connection: SQLResultSetTablePane

```
connPtoP1: (SQLConnection1,this ↔ SQLResultSetTablePane1,connection)
```

Connect the **SQLConnection1** bean with the **SQLResultSetTablePane1** bean as shown in Figure 14.16. This is where the connection to the database on the AS/400 occurs.

➢ Right-click the **SQLConnection1** bean.
➢ Click **Connect**.
➢ Click **this**.
➢ Click the spider-end pointer on the **SQLResultSetTablePane1** bean.
➢ Click **Connectible Features**.
➢ Double-click the **connection()** method.
➢ Double-click the connection to verify that it is correct as shown in Figure 14.17.
➢ Close the **Properties** window.

Figure 14.16
SQLConnection() Connection: connPtoP1

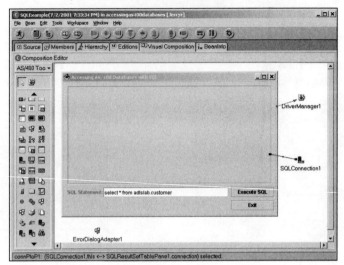

Figure 14.17
Connection connPtoP1

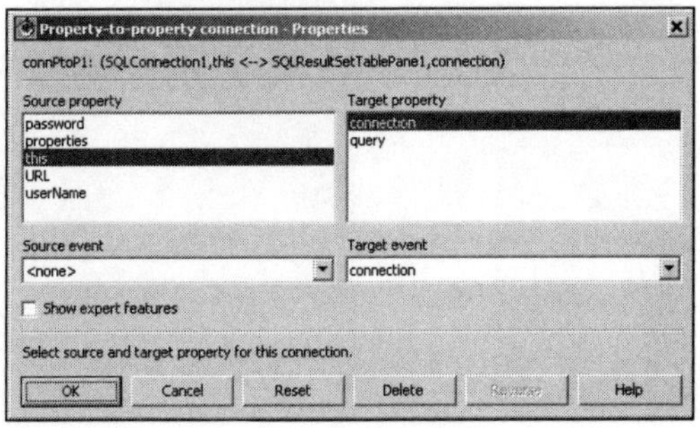

Event-to-Method Connection: setQuery()

```
connEtoM2: (btExecute,actionPerformed → SQLResultSetTablePane1,setQuery(java.lang.String))
```

This connection defines and prepares the SQL statements for execution. When the **Execute SQL** button is pressed, the query is set.

Connect the **btExecuteSQL** JButton with a **setQuery(java.lang.String)** method.

➤ Right-click the **btExecuteSQL** JButton.
➤ Click **Connect**.
➤ Click **actionPerformed**.
➤ Click the spider-end pointer on the **SQLResultSetTablePane1** bean.
➤ Click **Connectible Features**.
➤ Click the **setQuery(java.lang.String)** method.
➤ Click **OK**.

Parameter-from-Property Connection

```
connPfromP1: (connEtoM2: (btExecute,actionPerformed →
              SQLResultSetTablePane1,setQuery(java.lang.String)),arg1 → tfSQLStatement,text)
```

Complete the connection by passing a parameter into the primary connection. The connection is expecting a **String** data type.

Identify the source property:

➢   Right-click the dashed line.
➢   Click **Connect**.
➢   Click **arg1**.

Identify the target property:

➢   Click the spider-end pointer on the **tfSQLStatement** JTextField bean.
➢   Click **text**.

Figure 14.18 shows what the connection should look like.

Figure 14.18
SetQuery() Connection: connPfromP1

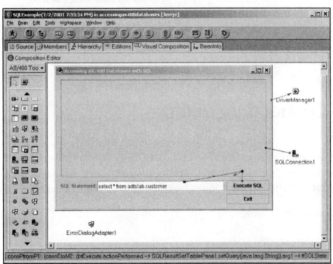

➢   Double-click each connection to verify that it is correct as shown in Figures 14.19 and 14.20.
➢   Close each **Properties** window.

Figure 14.19
Connection connEtoM2

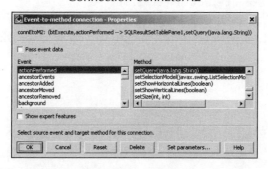

Figure 14.20
Connection connPfromP1

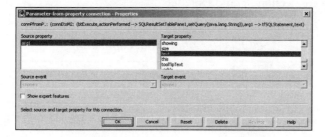

Event-to-Method Connection: load()

```
connEtoM3: (btExecute,actionPerformed → SQLResultSetTablePane1,load())
```

This connection lets you obtain and process the results of the SQL statements. The contents of the query, as well as the externally described database field definitions, are loaded into the SQLResultSetTablePane.

Connect the **btExecuteSQL** JButton with a **load()** method to the **SQLResultSetTablePane1** bean.

➢   Right-click the **btExecuteSQL** JButton.
➢   Click **Connect**.
➢   Click **actionPerformed**.
➢   Click the spider-end pointer on the **SQLResultSetTablePane1** bean.
➢   Click **Connectible Features**.
➢   Click the **load()** method.
➢   Click **OK**.

Figure 14.21 shows what the connection should look like.

➢   Double-click the connection to verify that it is correct as shown in Figure 14.22.
➢   Close the **Properties** window.

Figure 14.21
load() Connection: connEtoM3

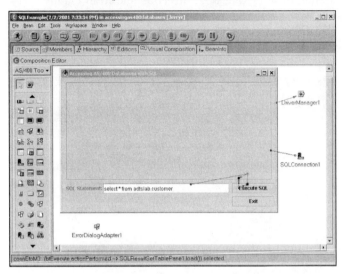

Figure 14.22
Connection connEtoM3

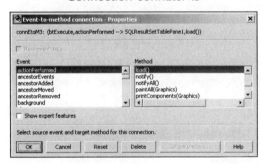

Event-to-Method Connection: close()

`connEtoM4: (btExit,actionPerformed → SQLResultSetTablePane1,close())`

When the **Exit** button is clicked, this connection will close the AS/400 database file specified in the SQL statements.

Connect the **btExit** JButton with a **close()** method to the **SQLResultSetTablePane1** bean.

> Right-click the **btExit** JButton.
> Click **Connect**.
> Click **actionPerformed**.
> Click the spider-end pointer on the **SQLResultSetTablePane1** bean.
> Click **Connectible Features**.
> Click the **close()** method.
> Click **OK**.

Figure 14.23 shows what the connection should look like.

➢ Double-click the connection to verify that it is correct as shown in Figure 14.24.
➢ Close the **Properties** window.

Figure 14.23
close() Connection: connEtoM4

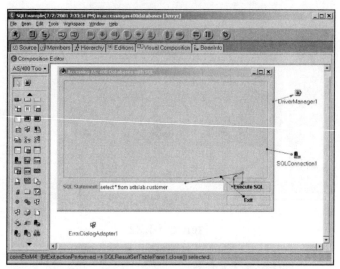

Figure 14.24
Connection connEtoM4

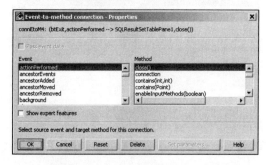

Event-to-Method Connection: dispose()

connEtoM5: (btExit,actionPerformed → SQLExample,dispose())

When the **Exit** button is clicked, this connection will dispose, or shut down, the **SQLExample** JFrame.
    Connect the **btExit** JButton with a **dispose()** method to the **SQLExample** JFrame.

➢ Right-click the **btExit** JButton.
➢ Click **Connect**.
➢ Click **actionPerformed**.
➢ Click the spider-end pointer on the outside edge of the visual area of the free-form surface, or **SQLExample** JFrame bean.
➢ Click **Connectible Features**.

> ➤ Click the **dispose()** method.
> ➤ Click **OK**.

Figure 14.25 shows what the connection should look like.

> ➤ Double-click the connection to verify that it is correct as shown in Figure 14.26.
> ➤ Close the **Properties** window.

Figure 14.25
dispose() Connection: connEtoM5

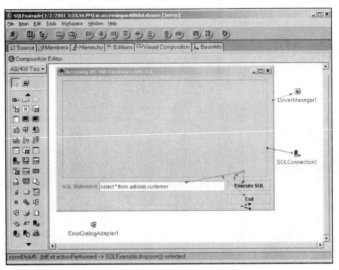

Figure 14.26
Connection connEtoM5

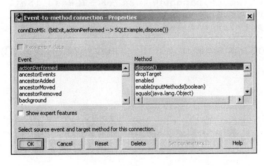

Event-to-Method Connection: addErrorListener()

```
connEtoM6: (SQLExample,windowOpened → SQLResultSetTablePane1,
          addErrorListener(com.ibm.as400.vaccess.ErrorListener))
```

This connection will let you specify a listener when the **SQLExample** window is opened. Connect the **SQLExample** JFrame with an **addErrorListener()** method.

> ➤ Select the **SQLExample** JFrame by clicking the outside edge of the visual area.
> ➤ Click **Connect**.

> Click **windowOpened**.
> Click the spider-end pointer on the **SQLResultSetTablePane1** bean in the center of the screen.
> Click **Connectible Features**.
> Click the **addErrorListener(com.ibm.as400.vaccess.errorListener)** method.
> Click **OK**.

Figure 14.27 shows what the connection should look like.

Figure 14.27
addErrorListener() Connection: connEtoM6

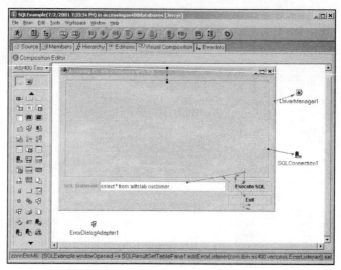

Parameter-from-Property Connection

```
connPfromP2: (connEtoM6: (SQLExample,windowOpened → SQLResultSetTablePane1,
            addErrorListener (com.ibm.as400.vaccess.ErrorListener)),arg1 →
            ErrorDialogAdapter1,this)
```

Complete the connection by passing a parameter into the primary connection. The connection is expecting an **errorListener** data type.

Identify the source property:

> Right-click the dashed line.
> Click **Connect**.
> Click **arg1**.

Identify the target property:

> Click the spider-end pointer on the **errorDialogAdapter1** bean.
> Click **this**.

Figure 14.28 shows what the connection should look like.

Figure 14.28

addErrorListener() Connection: connPfromP2

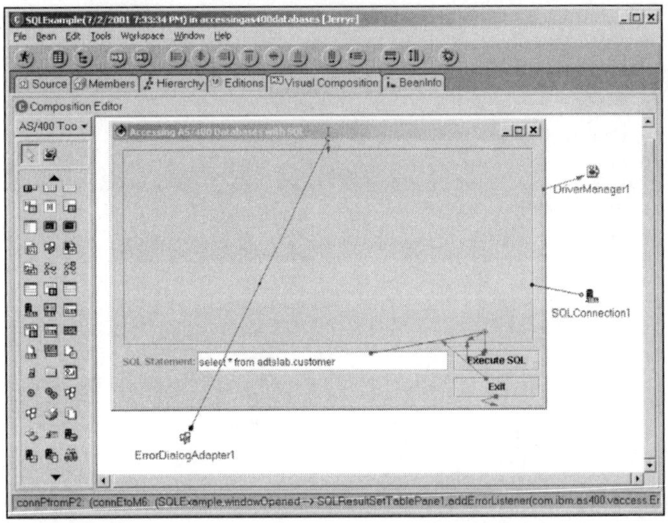

> Double-click each connection to verify that it is correct as shown in Figures 14.29 and 14.30.
> Close each **Properties** window.

Figure 14.29

Connection connEtoM6

Figure 14.30

Connection connPfromP2

Save your Java program.

> On the menu bar, click **Bean**.
> Click **Save Bean**.

Review AS/400 Classes and Methods

As you'll recall from earlier in the chapter, there are six steps to building a JDBC application. We're going to review the Java code associated with each of these steps. To review the generated Java source code:

> Click the **Source** tab.

Step 1: Register the AS/400 JDBC Driver

> In the **Elements** pane, click method **connEtoM1(java.awt.event.WindowEvent)**.

Figure 14.31 shows the registering of the AS/400 JDBC driver.

Figure 14.31

Source Code for Registering the AS/400 JDBC Driver

```
Source code: connEtoM1
private void connEtoM1(java.awt.event.WindowEvent arg1) {
    try {
        // user code begin {1}
        // user code end
        java.sql.DriverManager.registerDriver(new com.ibm.as400.access.AS400JDBCDriver());
        // user code begin {2}
        // user code end
    } catch (java.lang.Throwable ivjExc) {
        // user code begin {3}
        // user code end
        handleException(ivjExc);
    }
}
```

Step 2: Connect to the AS/400 Database

➢   In the **Elements** pane, click method **com.ibm.as400.vaccess.SQLConnection getSQLConnection()**.

The actual connecting to the AS/400 database takes place in method **connPtoP1SetTarget()** with the following line of code:

```
getSQLResultSetTablePane1().setConnection(getSQLConnection1())
```

Figure 14.32 shows the details of setting up the connection.

Figure 14.32

Source Code for Connecting to the AS/400 Database

```
Source code: getSQLConnection
private com.ibm.as400.vaccess.SQLConnection getSQLConnection1() {
    if (ivjSQLConnection1 == null) {
        try {
            ivjSQLConnection1 = new com.ibm.as400.vaccess.SQLConnection();
            ivjSQLConnection1.setURL("jdbc:as400:;naming=sql;errors=full;date format=iso;    ");
            // user code begin {1}
            // user code end
        } catch (java.lang.Throwable ivjExc) {
            // user code begin {2}
            // user code end
            handleException(ivjExc);
        }
    }
    return ivjSQLConnection1;
}
```

Step 3: Create SQL Statements

➢   In the **Elements** pane, click method **javax.swing.JTextField gettfSQLStatement()**.

Figure 14.33 shows the defining and preparing of the SQL statement.

Figure 14.33
Source Code for Creating the SQL Statement

```
Source code: getttfSQLStatement
private javax.swing.JTextField gettfSQLStatement() {
    if (ivjtfSQLStatement == null) {
        try {
            ivjtfSQLStatement = new javax.swing.JTextField();
            ivjtfSQLStatement.setName("tfSQLStatement");
            ivjtfSQLStatement.setText("select * from adtslab.customer");
            ivjtfSQLStatement.setBounds(102, 254, 311, 25);
            // user code begin {1}
            // user code end
        } catch (java.lang.Throwable ivjExc) {
            // user code begin {2}
            // user code end
            handleException(ivjExc);
        }
    }
    return ivjtfSQLStatement;
}
```

Step 4: Execute SQL Statements

➢   In the **Elements** pane, click method **connEtoM2(java.awt.event.ActionEvent)**.

Figure 14.34 shows the execution of the SQL statement.

Figure 14.34
Source Code for Executing SQL Statements

```
Source code: connEtoM2
private void connEtoM2(java.awt.event.ActionEvent arg1) {
    try {
        // user code begin {1}
        // user code end
        getSQLResultSetTablePane1().setQuery(gettfSQLStatement().getText());
        // user code begin {2}
        // user code end
    } catch (java.lang.Throwable ivjExc) {
        // user code begin {3}
        // user code end
        handleException(ivjExc);
    }
}
```

Step 5: Retrieve the Results of the SQL Statements

➢   In the **Elements** pane, click method **connEtoM3(java.awt.event.ActionEvent)**.

Figure 14.35 shows where the results are obtained.

Figure 14.35
Source Code for Retrieving SQL Results

```
Source code: connEtoM3
private void connEtoM3(java.awt.event.ActionEvent arg1) {
    try {
          // user code begin {1}
          // user code end
          getSQLResultSetTablePane1().load();
          // user code begin {2}
          // user code end
    } catch (java.lang.Throwable ivjExc) {
          // user code begin {3}
          // user code end
          handleException(ivjExc);
    }
}
```

Step 6: Close the Statements and Database Connection

➢   In the **Elements** pane, click method **connEtoM4(java.awt.event.ActionEvent)**.

Figure 14.36 shows the closing of the statement and database connection by way of closing the SQLResultSetTablePane1.

Figure 14.36
Source Code for Closing the Connection

```
Source code: connEtoM4
private void connEtoM4(java.awt.event.ActionEvent arg1) {
    try {
          // user code begin {1}
          // user code end
          getSQLResultSetTablePane1().close();
          // user code begin {2}
          // user code end
    } catch (java.lang.Throwable ivjExc) {
          // user code begin {3}
          // user code end
          handleException(ivjExc);
    }
}
```

Using SQL/JDBC

To demonstrate your Java application, you'll be using the CUSTOMER and PRODUCT files from the ADTSLAB library. If you need to review these files, see the file layouts located at the end of Chapter 13.

To run the Java program, you need to successfully connect to the AS/400. Run the Java program.

➢ On the menu bar, click **Bean**.
➢ Click **Run**, and then click **Run Main**.

You should be looking at the application as shown in Figure 14.37.

Figure 14.37
Application Start Execution

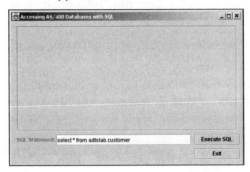

➢ Click the **Execute SQL** button.
➢ Enter your sign-on information, and wait a few seconds.

Cool stuff! Wasn't that fast? Figure 14.38 shows the results of the SQL statement selecting all (*) records from file CUSTOMER in library ADTSLAB. Notice the scroll bars.

Figure 14.38
CUSTOMER File Results

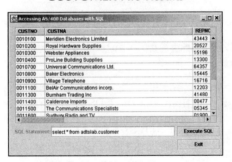

Now, you're going to enter another SQL statement. You'll select all records that have a customer number (CUSTNO) less than 0010700.

➢ In the **SQL Statement** field, type **select * from adtslab.customer where custno < '0010700'** .
➢ Click the **Execute SQL** button.

Figure 14.39 shows the results of all records less than 0010700. Did you notice that the selection and retrieval time was quite fast? Did you also notice that the vertical scroll bar disappeared when the records didn't fill the SQLResultSetTablePane?

Figure 14.39

Results from CUSTOMER File Where CUSTNO < 0010700

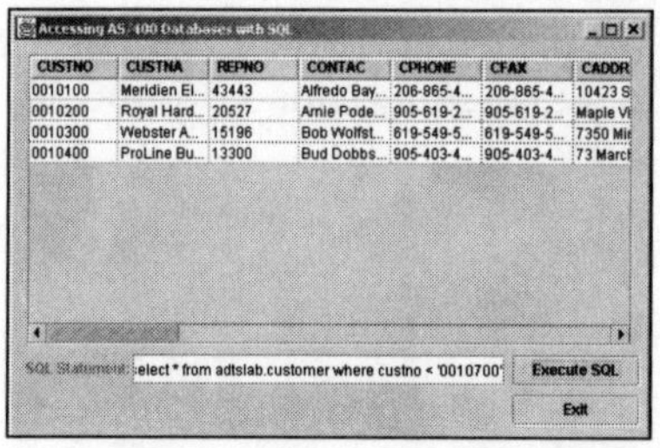

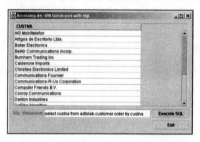

Now, select all the customer names (CUSTNA) from the CUSTOMER file and sort them. The only field shown will be customer name.

➤   In the **SQL Statement** field, type **select custna from adtslab.customer order by custna**.
➤   Click the **Execute SQL** button.

Figure 14.40 shows the customer name results. Notice which scroll bar disappeared this time! Because only one field is displayed, there's no need for a horizontal scroll bar. Also notice the sort order. It worked just as you specified.

Figure 14.40

Results from CUSTOMER File Where CUSTNA Is Only Field Selected

Now, you're going to change files. Select all records from the PRODUCT file in library ADTSLAB.

➤   In the **SQL Statement** field, type **select * from adtslab.product**.
➤   Click the **Execute SQL** button.

Figure 14.41 shows the results. Wasn't changing files easy? In later chapters, you'll learn how to display fields using field names that are more descriptive than just the DDS field name.

Figure 14.41

Results from PRODUCT File

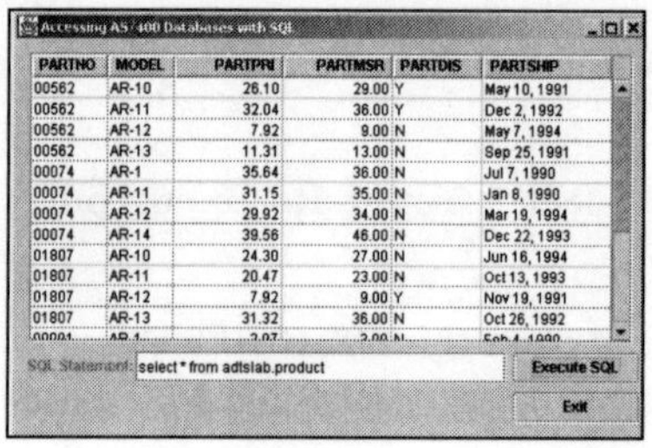

Let's see what an error message concerning SQL looks like.

➤ In the **SQL Statement** field, type **select * from adtslab.bill**.
➤ Click the **Execute SQL** button.

As Figure 14.42 shows, the error dialog box specifies that the file BILL does not exist in library ADTSLAB.

Figure 14.42
errorDialogAdapter

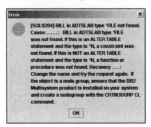

➤ Click the **Exit** button.

Again, congratulations! Did you notice that the look of the SQLResultSetTablePane was a little cleaner than that of the RecordListFormPane you coded in Chapter 13? In some of the upcoming chapters, you'll learn how to dress up these panes even more.

JDBC Performance

When the AS/400 Toolbox and JDBC classes were first released, performance wasn't as good as everyone would have liked. Since then, IBM has invested much time and effort in improving performance related to JDBC and UDB/400. Here are some tips for getting better performance when using JDBC:

- Stay on current releases of the AS/400 Toolbox. Considerable work and improvements are taking place.
- Keep in mind that because JDBC is based on ODBC, many of the performance issues related to ODBC apply to JDBC.
- Reuse connections when possible.
- Create efficient SQL in Select statements.
- Use prepared SQL statements when performing multiple executions.
- Use stored procedures to reduce I/O.
- Use proper record-blocking and package-caching strategies.

Summary

In this chapter you learned

- how to work with SQL and JDBC
- the six steps to building an SQL application
- how to use the **SQLResultSetTablePane**, **DriverManager**, **SQLConnection**, and **ErrorDialogAdapter** beans
- performance tips concerning JDBC

The next chapter will teach you how to do more record-level access with a prompt and display example. It will also introduce more techniques concerning error handling.

Unit 4

Building AS/400 Graphical Applications

Chapter 15

Building a Java AS/400 Prompt and Display

 ## Chapter Objectives

- ☐ Understand record-level access concepts
- ☐ Become familiar with the AS/400 Toolbox **FormManager** and **RecordIOManager** JavaBeans
- ☐ Learn how to implement error handling
- ☐ Understand layouts in the VCE

 ## Chapter Project

- ☐ A class will be created to prompt and display individual AS/400 database records.
- ☐ The class will let you position to records, read records, and perform direct access to records as well as report error conditions.
- ☐ Figure 15.1 shows what the sample class will look like.

Figure 15.1
Chapter Project

In Unit 4, which begins with this chapter, you'll become familiar with many different approaches to building graphical user interfaces that access AS/400 database records. The chapters in this unit are named using an AS/400 development flavor — in other words, their titles include words like "menu" and "subfile." The goal is to make it easier for you to convert your existing AS/400 knowledge to the functional equivalents in Java. We'll cover the Java equivalents of AS/400 prompt screens, menus, subfiles, and maintenance screens.

In Chapters 5 and 6, you learned how to implement a Model-View-Controller design in application development. In Chapters 15 through 20, the focus will be on using the VCE, the AS/400 Toolbox, and the interfacing of the two, and *not* with a Model-View-Controller design. When you begin the development process with your real-life applications, you should review Chapters 5 and 6 *before* designing your applications.

In Chapter 13, you learned the basics of database record-level access. In this chapter, you'll discover more details about how to use record-level access. You'll also learn some different techniques for handling errors such as attempts to read before the first record or past the last record in a file.

By number of pages, this chapter is the second longest of the book. Don't be alarmed, though; you'll cover it very quickly. *Do not skip this chapter.* Many of the error-handling techniques we'll cover here won't be repeated in other chapters, so this is *must-read* information. Besides, it will be a fun and fulfilling chapter for you.

To begin, you're going to create a new project named **My Graphical Applications**. The work accomplished in all the Unit 4 chapters will be stored in this newly created project.

➢ If the workbench isn't started, start it now.
➢ From the workbench **All Projects** pane, right-click to display the shortcut menu, select **Add**, and then select **Project**.
➢ Make sure the **Create a new project named** option is selected. Type **My Graphical Applications** in the space provided.
➢ Click **Finish** to complete the creation of the project.

Once the project is created, you'll see it listed in the workbench upper pane.

Now, create a package called **buildingas400graphics**.

➢ Select the project **My Graphical Applications** with a click. Right-click to display the shortcut menu, select **Add**, and then select **Package**.
➢ Make sure the **Project** name is **My Graphical Applications**.
➢ Make sure the **Create a new package named** option is selected. Type **buildingas400graphics** in the space provided.
➢ Click **Finish** to complete the creation of the package.

Once the package and the project are created, you'll see them listed in the workbench **All Projects** pane.

Data File Utility JavaBeans

The Enterprise Toolkit for AS/400 provides three Data File Utility (DFU) beans: the **FormManager**, **ListManager**, and **RecordIOManager** JavaBeans. If you use VisualAge for Java in your Java development, you'll probably use these three DFU beans as much as any other JavaBean in the Toolkit. These beans are very powerful and make it very easy to develop graphical applications that manipulate records within AS/400 databases. You'll use the **FormManager** and **RecordIOManager** JavaBeans in this chapter. You won't use the **ListManager** bean until you get to Chapter 17.

The **FormManager** bean lets you work with individual records, one at a time. The **ListManager** bean lets you work with multiple records at once, similar in function to an AS/400 subfile. The **RecordIOManager** bean lets you specify database attributes, retrieve database records, and control the opening and closing of the AS/400 database. Both the **FormManager** and **ListManager** beans have a property called **recordIOManager**, which is nothing more than an instance of the **RecordIOManager** bean. You'll use this property later in the chapter.

Form Manager

You use the **FormManager** bean to associate a form with an AS/400 database. Although you can work with only one record at a time, the form can have multiple JComponents (Swing components) associated with it. Each of these JComponents must have a single data element–type format, such as JFormattedTextField, JLabel, JTextArea, or JTextField. The number of JComponents will usually match the number of database fields you're mapping.

One important fact to remember is that the FormManager will map the database fields to the JComponent if the JComponent is named the same as the database field. For example, to correctly map a database field named PARTNO to a JTextField, you must also name the JTextField PARTNO. If you've ever used DDS names in an AS/400 display file, you know that the screen fields defined in the DDS can have exactly the same name as the database field. The advantage of doing this on the AS/400 is that you don't have to code any "move" functions to transfer the data from the database to the screen and vice versa. This is exactly how the **FormManager** bean works.

When you use the **FormManager** bean, you have to define a displayContainer. The displayContainer specifies the scope of JComponents associated with the database. If you have a database field named PARTNO and a JTextField named PARTNO but the JTextField isn't part of the displayContainer, no mapping of the two will occur. The displayContainer can be a pane or a frame.

To select records in the FormManager, you must specify a **recordIOManager** property.

Record IO Manager

The **RecordIOManager** bean is used primarily for adding, updating, and deleting records in the database. Typically, you'll use the **RecordIOManager** bean in conjunction with either the **FormManager** or the **ListManager** bean. Some of the functions associated with the **RecordIOManager** bean are

- opening and closing the database file
- retrieving records from the database — sequentially, by relative record number, or by key (similar to RPG's READ, READE, CHAIN, and READP opcodes)
- joining database files (logical join files are not supported)
- filtering database records (based on conditions of field data)
- positioning database pointers or cursors (similar to RPG's SETLL and SETGT opcodes)
- locking database files
- using commitment control
- writing, updating, and deleting database records (similar to RPG's WRITE, UPDATE, and DELETE opcodes)
- starting and ending journals

As you can see, **RecordIOManager** is a powerful JavaBean and is used in many different application scenarios.

When using the **RecordIOManager** bean, you can use AS/400 logical files only for retrieval functions. You must use AS/400 physical files with the add, update, and delete functions.

Prompt and Display Example

In this chapter project, you'll be using a product details physical file from the AS/400: file PRODDTL in library ADTSLAB. Figure 15.2 shows a DDS layout of the fields contained in file PRODDTL.

Figure 15.2
PRODDTL File Layout

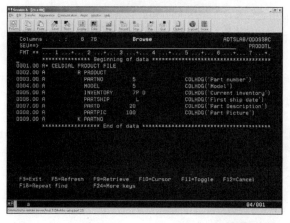

You're going to create another class, called **PromptAndDisplayExample**, that inherits properties from superclass **JFrame**. You'll store the class in the project **My Graphical Applications** and in the package **buildingas400graphics**.

➤   If the workbench isn't started, start it now.
➤   Expand the project **My Graphical Applications** with a click.
➤   Select the package **buildingas400graphics** with a click. Right-click to display the shortcut menu, select **Add**, and then select **Class**.
➤   Make sure the **Project** name is **My Graphical Applications**.
➤   Make sure the **Package** name is **buildingas400graphics**.
➤   In the **Class name** field, type **PromptAndDisplayExample**.
➤   Click **Browse** to select a superclass.
➤   When the **Superclass** window appears, type **JFrame** in the **Pattern** field.
➤   In the **Type names** list, double-click **JFrame**. When you return to the SmartGuide, the **Superclass** field should contain **javax.swing.JFrame**, as shown in Figure 15.3.
➤   Select the **Browse the class when finished** check box.
➤   Select the **Compose the class visually** check box.
➤   Click **Finish** to complete the creation of the class.

Figure 15.3
PromptAndDisplayExample Class

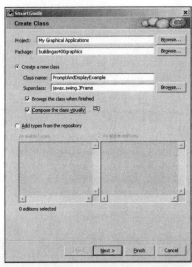

You should be inside the Visual Composition Editor. Change the title of the JFrame.

➤   On the menu bar, click **Tools**.
➤   Click **Beans List**.
➤   Double-click the **PromptAndDisplayExample** JFrame to display the **Properties** sheet.
➤   For the **title** property, type **Product Detail Prompt Example**.
➤   Close the **Properties** sheet.
➤   Close the **Beans List**.
➤   Expand the height and width of your free-form surface by dragging a corner downward and to the right.

Create the six JLabels shown in Figure 15.4.

➤ Click and drop six **JLabel** beans on the left side of the free-form surface visual area.
➤ Double-click each JLabel, and change the **text** property to **Part Number:**, **Model:**, **Description:**, **Inventory:**, **Ship Date:**, and **Picture:**, respectively.
➤ Close the **Properties** sheet.
➤ Expand the JLabels so that you can see all the text.

Figure 15.4
Screen Layout: Buttons, Labels, and Text Fields

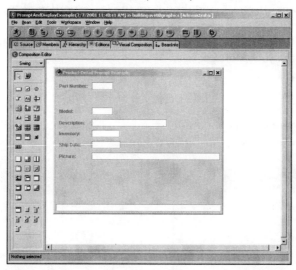

Next, you'll create the JComponents that will represent the AS/400 database fields. You'll name each JTextField with the associated AS/400 database field name. *You don't need to worry about case sensitivity.* Create the seven JTextFields shown in the figure.

➤ Click and drop six **JTextField** beans next to the labels on the visual area.
➤ Double-click each JTextField, and change the **beanName** property to **partno**, **model**, **partd**, **inventory**, **partship**, and **partpic**, respectively. Note that you are deliberately omitting the usual **tf** prefix so that the database field names match the names of the JTextField beans.
➤ Expand each JTextField to the size shown in the figure.
➤ Close the **Properties** sheet.
➤ Click the **JTextField** bean once more, and drop it at the bottom of the visual area. This field will be used as an error message box.
➤ Double-click the JTextField. Change the **beanName** from **JTextField7** to **msgArea**.
➤ Expand the JTextField to the size shown in the figure.
➤ Close the **Properties** sheet.

Next, protect all the fields except the **partno** field. Why should the fields be protected? This is just a simple display application, and users shouldn't expect to be able to change or maintain any screen values.

➤ Change the **editable** property to **False** on each JTextField except **partno**. In the VCE, these fields will now appear in gray instead of white, as shown in Figure 15.5.

Now, add the two JSeparator bars shown in the figure to help differentiate the various screen areas: the prompt area, the database fields, and the JButtons (which you'll add in a moment).

➤   Click the **JSeparator** bean 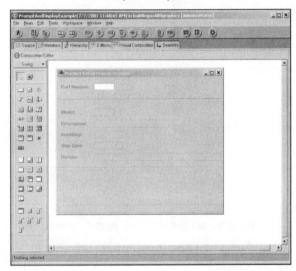, and drop it under the **Part Number** field. The **JSeparator** bean is the very last bean in the Swing categories.

➤   When you first drop the **JSeparator** bean, it appears as a box. You're only concerned about the top of the box. Widen the box, and move its top edge to the position where you want the separator to appear.

➤   Click the **JSeparator** bean again, and drop it under the **Picture** field.

➤   Again, resize the box and move the top edge to the position where you want the separator to appear.

Add a panel to contain all but one of the JButtons, as shown in Figure 15.6.

➤   In the VCE, click the **JPanel** bean 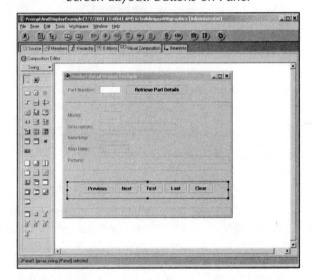, and drop it on the lower portion of the visual area.

➤   Click the JPanel. Expand it to the size shown in the figure.

➤   Double-click the JPanel to display the **Properties** sheet. Change the **layout** property to **FlowLayout** to switch to the FlowLayout Layout Manager.

➤   Close the **Properties** sheet.

Figure 15.5
Screen Layout: Separator Bars

Figure 15.6
Screen Layout: Buttons on Panel

Add five buttons to the JPanel as shown in the figure.

➤   Click and drop five **JButton** beans on the new JPanel. It doesn't matter where you drop them because the FlowLayout manager will position them automatically.

➤   Double-click each JButton to display the **Properties** sheet. Change the **beanName** property to **btPrevious**, **btNext**, **btFirst**, **btLast**, and **btClear**, respectively.

➤   Change the **text** property to **Previous**, **Next**, **First**, **Last**, and **Clear**, respectively.

➤   Close the **Properties** sheet.

Add another button at the top of the screen, as shown in the figure.

➤   Click the **JButton** bean again, and drop it on the upper-center portion of the visual area.

➤   Double-click the JButton. Change the **beanName** from **JButton1** to **btRetrieve**.

➤   Change the **text** to **Retrieve Part Details**.

➤   Close the **Properties** sheet.

➤   Expand the button so that you can see all the text.

Save your Java program.

➤ On the menu bar, click **Bean**.
➤ Click **Save Bean**.

Adding the FormManager Bean

Now, you're going to add a **FormManager** bean. This bean is the fifth bean in the AS/400 Toolbox bean category.

➤ Click to display the bean category drop-down list, and select **AS/400 Toolbox**.
➤ Click the **FormManager** bean █, and drop it on the nonvisual free-form surface, below the visual area.
➤ Double-click the FormManager.

Figure 15.7 shows the FormManager **Properties** sheet.

Figure 15.7
FormManager Properties Sheet

➤ Click the **Details** button 🔲 for the **recordIOManager** property.

Figure 15.8 shows the **recordIOManager** bean. Behind the scenes, you are going to create a new class to manage the PRODDTL file in the ADTSLAB library. This new class will be created automatically as you finish specifying the properties of the **recordIOManager** bean.

Figure 15.8
recordIOManager Bean

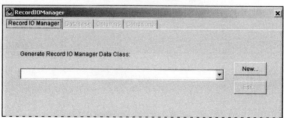

➤ Click **New**.
➤ As shown in Figure 15.9, type **buildingas400graphics** in the **Package** field.
➤ In the **Class Name** field, type **RIOProductDetailPRODDTL**.
➤ Click **OK**.

Figure 15.9
New Record IO Manager Data Class

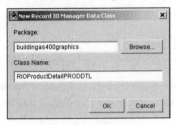

Figure 15.10 shows the **Database** tab of the **RecordIOManager** bean. You use this window to specify the database file, input/output attributes, and commitment control. It also identifies AS/400 sign-on information.

Tips and Tricks

The sign-on information supplied in the *RecordIOManager* bean doesn't do much for you. It serves only as a placeholder for sign-on information when selecting the fields in the database. This sign-on information has nothing to do with the sign-on information used when you execute your application. It is used only as convenience during development to retrieve the specifications database file.

Figure 15.10
Database Tab in RecordIOManager Bean

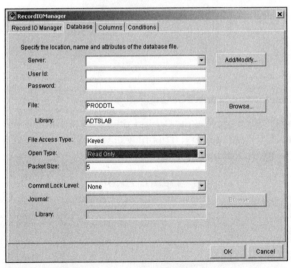

> As shown in the figure, type **PRODDTL** for the **File** name.
> For the **Library** name, type **ADTSLAB**.
> Change the **Open Type** value from **Read and Write** to **Read Only**.
> *Don't* click **OK**.

To go to the next step, you'll need to successfully connect to the AS/400.

> Click the **Columns** tab.

Notice that an AS/400 prompt appears. Up to this point in the book, you've used the AS/400 prompt only when executing your application. In this case, the RecordIOManager is attempting to retrieve all the AS/400 database field names defined in the PRODDTL file.

➢   Enter your sign-on information, and wait a few seconds.

Figure 15.11 shows the **Columns** tab of the **RecordIOManager** bean. Notice that all the field names defined in the database are shown on this screen. The left side of the screen lists all the available AS/400 database fields that can be used. The right side lists the database fields you are specifying to use in your application. You can use the **Add**, **Add All**, **Remove**, and **Remove All** buttons to manipulate the field (column) list on the right. Why might you not use all the database fields? There may be certain fields, such as customer credit card number and expiration information, to which a particular application shouldn't have access.

Figure 15.11
Columns Tab in RecordIOManager Bean

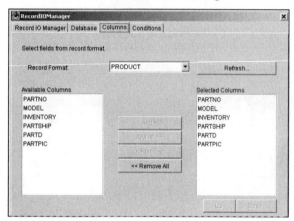

➢   Click the **Conditions** tab.

Figure 15.12 shows the **Conditions** tab of the **RecordIOManager** bean. Here, you specify sort order and the selection criteria for records in the database.

Figure 15.12
Conditions Tab in recordIOManager Bean

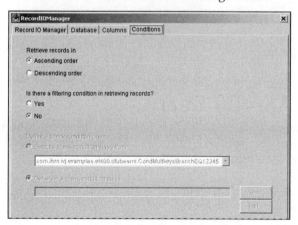

➤   Click **OK** to exit the **RecordIOManager** bean.

Tips and Tricks

Upon exiting the *recordIOManager* bean, you'll be returned to the *Properties* sheet. *Don't be in a big hurry to close the* Properties *sheet.* The information you supplied in the *RecordIOManager* bean goes through a compilation process. Give this process time to be completed. There have been known bugs in different versions of VisualAge for Java concerning this situation that could result in your workspace locking up.

➤   Wait until the compilation of the **recordIOManager** bean is completed. You'll know this has occurred when the class name (**buildingas400graphics.RIOProductDetailPRODDTL**) is filled in completely in the recordIOManager. Figure 15.13 shows the expanded **FormManager** bean with the **recordIOManager** property defined.

➤   Close the **Properties** sheet.

Figure 15.13
RecordIOManager Properties Sheet

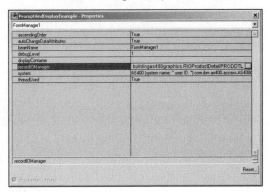

Now, you're going to add an **AS400** bean.

➤   Click the **AS400** bean 🔲, and drop it on the free-form nonvisual surface beside the **FormManager1** bean.
➤   Double-click the **AS4001** bean.
➤   For ease of use later on, fill in the **systemName** and **userID** properties.
➤   Close the **Properties** sheet.

Save your Java program.

➤   On the menu bar, click **Bean**.
➤   Click **Save Bean**.

Connecting the AS/400 Beans

You are now going to set up two property-to-property connections, five event-to-method connections, and eight event-to-code connections. Figure 15.14 shows both property-to-property connections and all but one of the event-to-method connections you'll be creating.

Figure 15.14
Chapter Project Connections

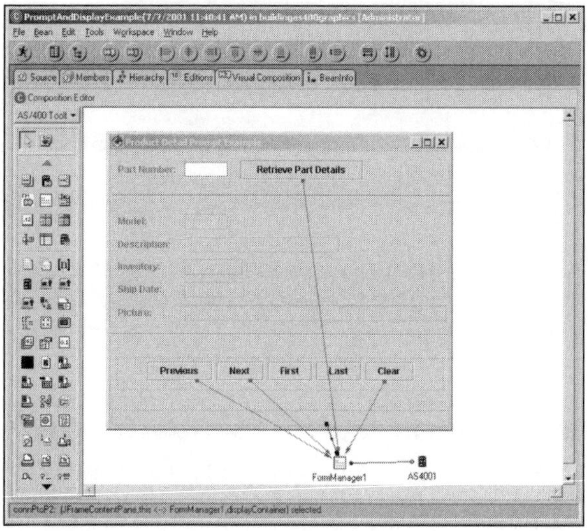

Property-to-Property Connection: system

connPtoP1: (AS4001,this ←→ FormManager1,system)

Connect the **AS4001** bean with the **FormManager1** bean.

➤ Right-click the **AS4001** bean.
➤ Click **Connect**.
➤ Click **this**.
➤ Click the spider-end pointer on the **FormManager1** bean.
➤ Click **Connectible Features**.
➤ Double-click the **system** property.

Event-to-Method Connection: readRecord()

connEtoM1: (btRetrieve,actionPerformed → FormManager1,readRecord())

This connection reads the record, similar to a CHAIN function in RPG. Connect the **btRetrieve** JButton with a **readRecord()** method.

➤ Right-click the **btRetrieve** JButton.
➤ Click **Connect**.
➤ Click **actionPerformed**.
➤ Click the spider-end pointer on the **FormManager1** bean.
➤ Click **Connectible Features**.
➤ Click the **readRecord()** method.
➤ Click **OK**.
➤ Double-click the connection to verify that it is correct as shown in Figure 15.15. Close the **Properties** window.

Figure 15.15
Connection connEtoM1

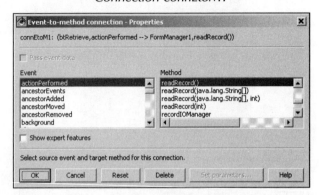

Event-to-Method Connection: readPreviousRecord()

connEtoM2: (btPrevious,actionPerformed → FormManager1,readPreviousRecord())

This connection reads the previous record, similar to a READP function in RPG. Connect the **btPrevious** JButton with a **readPreviousRecord()** method.

➢   Right-click the **btPrevious** JButton.
➢   Click **Connect**.
➢   Click **actionPerformed**.
➢   Click the spider-end pointer on the **FormManager1** bean.
➢   Click **Connectible Features**.
➢   Click the **readPreviousRecord()** method.
➢   Click **OK**.

Event-to-Method Connection: readNextRecord()

connEtoM3: (btNext,actionPerformed → FormManager1,readNextRecord())

This connection reads the next record, similar to a READ function in RPG. Connect the **btNext** JButton with a **readNextRecord()** method.

➢   Right-click the **btNext** JButton.
➢   Click **Connect**.
➢   Click **actionPerformed**.
➢   Click the spider-end pointer on the **FormManager1** bean.
➢   Click **Connectible Features**.
➢   Click the **readNextRecord()** method.
➢   Click **OK**.

Event-to-Method Connection: clearAllData()

connEtoM4: (btClear,actionPerformed → FormManager1,clearAllData())

This connection clears all the fields within a database record. Connect the **btClear** JButton with a **clearAllData()** method.

➢ Right-click the **btClear** JButton.
➢ Click **Connect**.
➢ Click **actionPerformed**.
➢ Click the spider-end pointer on the **FormManager1** bean.
➢ Click **Connectible Features**.
➢ Click the **clearAllData()** method.
➢ Click **OK**.

Property-to-Property Connection: displayContainer

connPtoP2: (JFrameContentPane,this ↔ FormManager1,displayContainer)

Next, you'll connect the **PromptAndDisplayExample** JFrame with the **displayContainer** property of the **FormManager1** bean. A displayContainer, you'll recall, is used to determine the scope or boundary of the database field mapping.

➢ Select the **PromptAndDisplayExample** JFrame by clicking the outside edge of the visual area.
➢ Click **Connect**.
➢ Click **this**.
➢ Click the spider-end pointer on the **FormManager1** bean.
➢ Click **displayContainer**. By defining the JFrame as the displayContainer, you are setting the displayContainer scope to include all the JFrame database fields.

Save your Java program.

➢ On the menu bar, click **Bean**.

Click **Save Bean**.
   To run the Java program, you need to successfully connect to the AS/400. Run the program.

➢ On the menu bar, click **Bean**.
➢ Click **Run**, and then click **Run Main**.

You should be looking at the application as shown in Figure 15.16.

Figure 15.16
Product Detail Prompt Example

➢   Click the **Next** button.
➢   Enter your sign-on information, and wait a few seconds.

Figure 15.17 shows the results of clicking **Next**.

➢   In the **Part Number** field, type **00005**.
➢   Click **Retrieve Part Details**.

Figure 15.18 shows the results of the **Retrieve Part Details** function.

Figure 15.17
Next Results

Figure 15.18
Retrieve Results

➢   Click **Clear**.
➢   Click **First**.

What happened? Nothing, because we haven't coded the **First** function yet. That's what you're going to do next. Close the **Product Detail Prompt Example** application.

Event-to-Code Connection: btFirst

```
connEtoC1: (btFirst,actionPerformed → PromptAndDisplayExample,
          void btFirst_ActionPerformed(java.awt.event.ActionEvent))
```

This connection, an event-to-code connection, will load the first record in the file. To accomplish this, you need to complete four tasks:

1. Clear all the data fields.
2. Position the file pointer to the first record in the file.
3. Read in the first record.
4. Handle any exception situations.

Create an event-to-code connection with the **btFirst** JButton.

➢   Right-click the **btFirst** JButton.
➢   Click **Connect**.
➢   Click **actionPerformed**.
➢   Click the spider-end pointer on the nonvisual free-form surface.
➢   Click **Event to Code**.

Your new event-to-code connection should appear as shown in Figure 15.19. Notice that VisualAge for Java named your new method **btFirst_ActionPerformed()**.

Figure 15.19
Connection connEtoC1

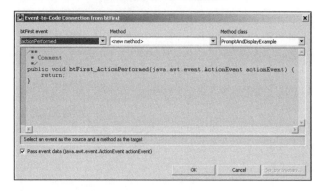

➤   Insert the Java code shown in Figure 15.20.

When you've finished typing the new Java code, your method should look identical to Figure 15.21. If you have any errors, you'll be prompted to fix them. Typically, the errors are due to misspelling, case-sensitivity problems, or missing semicolons. If errors are reported, look closely at your code and correct it.

Figure 15.20
Source Code for Getting the First Record

```
Source code: connEtoC1
    try {
        getFormManager1().clearAllData();
        getFormManager1().positionCursorToFirst();
        getFormManager1().readRecord();
        }
    catch (java.lang.Throwable ivjExc) {
        handleException(ivjExc);
    }
```

Figure 15.21
Connection connEtoC1

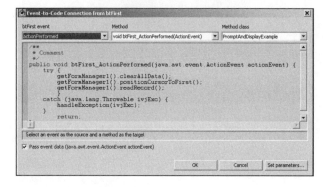

➤   Click **OK**.

When you exit this event-to-code connection, you'll notice that the new method is placed in the upper-right corner of the screen, as shown in Figure 15.22.

Figure 15.22
btFirst_ActionPerformed Connection: connEtoC1

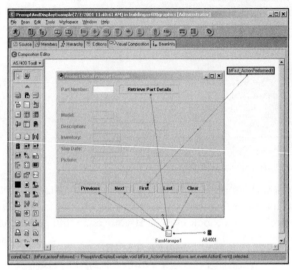

➢   Click and hold the **btFirst_ActionPerformed()** method, and drag it down closer to the **btFirst** button, as shown in Figure 15.23. As you add more of these event-to-code methods, this extra step will make your free-form surface look more organized.

Figure 15.23
Connection connEtoC1 in New Location

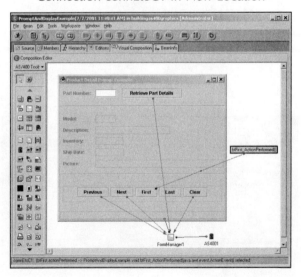

Event-to-Code Connection: btLast

```
connEtoC2: (btLast,actionPerformed → PromptAndDisplayExample,
            void btLast_ActionPerformed(java.awt.event.ActionEvent))
```

The steps required to create the connection to load the last record in the file are similar to those you took to load the first record. You need to complete four tasks:

1. Clear all the data fields.
2. Position the file pointer to the last record in the file.
3. Read in the last record.
4. Handle any exception situations.

Create an event-to-code connection with the **btLast** JButton.

➢   Right-click the **btLast** JButton.
➢   Click **Connect**.
➢   Click **actionPerformed**.
➢   Click the spider-end pointer on the nonvisual free-form surface.
➢   Click **Event to Code**.
➢   Insert the Java code shown in Figure 15.24. When you've finished typing the new Java code, your method should look identical to Figure 15.25.

Figure 15.24
Source Code for Getting the Last Record

```
Source code: connEtoC2
        try {
            getFormManager1().clearAllData();
            getFormManager1().positionCursorToLast();
            getFormManager1().readRecord();
            }
        catch (java.lang.Throwable ivjExc) {
            handleException(ivjExc);
        }
```

Figure 15.25
Connection connEtoC2

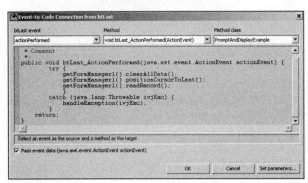

➤   Click **OK**.
➤   Click and hold the **btLast_ActionPerformed()** method, and drag it down closer to the **btLast** JButton, as shown in Figure 15.26.

Figure 15.26
connEtoC2 in New Location

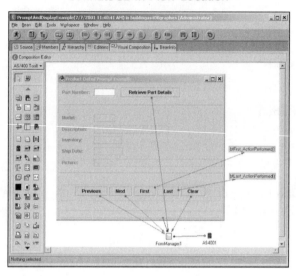

Save and then run your Java program.

➤   On the menu bar, click **Bean**.
➤   Click **Save Bean**.
➤   On the menu bar, click **Bean**.
➤   Click **Run**, and then click **Run Main**.
➤   Click the **Last** button.
➤   Enter your sign-on information, and wait a few seconds.

Figure 15.27 shows the results of clicking **Last**. You should see part number 00023, the last record in the file.

➤   Click the **First** button.

Figure 15.28 shows the results of clicking **First**. You should see part number 00001, the first record in the file.

Figure 15.27	**Figure 15.28**
Last Results	*First Results*

Error Handling

So far, things have been working well. In this section, you'll cause two error conditions to occur: reading past the first record in the file and reading past the last record in the file. Then, you'll add some methods to display error messages at the bottom of your application to handle these situations. This process will be similar to using the ERRMSG function in an AS/400 display file (*DSPF).

➤   Click the **Previous** button.

Figure 15.29 shows the results of clicking **Previous**. You should see an empty screen with no parts information.

Figure 15.29
Previous Results

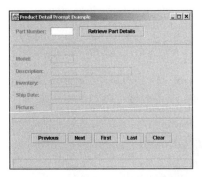

➤   Click **Previous** again.

Figure 15.30 shows the results. An exception occurred, causing your application to crash and the Console to appear. This normally is not what you want to have happen in your applications. The same thing would have happened if you had clicked the **Last** button and then the **Next** button.

➤   Close the **Product Detail Prompt Example** application.

Figure 15.30
Previous Results: Console Exception

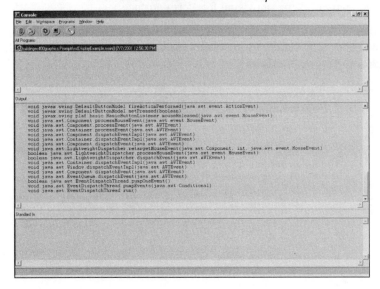

There are many ways to handle this error situation. Frequently, you may want to handle a specific exception without falling out to the standard **handleException()** method generated in VisualAge for Java. In this section, you're going to use two different approaches to handle this particular error scenario. The two approaches use events to accomplish the error handling. The events are the **exceptionOccurred** event and the **normalResult** event.

The first approach, using **exceptionOccurred**, doesn't quite accomplish the goals of full error handling, but it's important to understand what this method does and how it works. The second approach, **normalResult**, is a more complete and more proactive approach to error handling.

Tips and Tricks

The *normalResult* and *exceptionOccurred* events are not true Java events. They are special connections for use in the VCE. They generate the code to pass a return value to another connection. The *normalResult* event is fired when no exception is thrown from a method call. The *exceptionOccurred* event is fired when an exception is thrown from a method call.

Error Handling: btPrevious exceptionOccurred()

The first error-handling approach will use an **ExceptionOccurred()** method to handle the error situation of trying to read prior to the first record.

Event-to-Code Connection: exceptionOccurred()

```
connEtoC3: (btPrevious,actionPerformed →
            FormManager1,readPreviousRecord().exceptionOccurred →
            PromptAndDisplayExample,void connEtoM2_ExceptionOccurred())
```

This connection will let you pass an **ExceptionOccurred** argument — the error message — to the **connEtoM2_ExceptionOccurred()** method.

Create an event-to-code connection with connection **connEtoM2**.

➢   Right-click connection **connEtoM2**, the connection from the **btPrevious** JButton to the **FormManager1** bean.
➢   Click **Connect**.
➢   Click **exceptionOccurred**.

➢   Click the spider-end pointer on the nonvisual free-form surface.

➢   Click **Event to Code**.
➢   Insert the Java code shown in Figure 15.31. When you've finished typing the new Java code, your method should look identical to Figure 15.32.

Figure 15.31
Source Code for connEtoM2_ExceptionOccurred

```
Source code: connEtoM2_ExceptionOccurred
      getmsgArea().setText("Access Error:   " + arg1);
      getmsgArea().setBackground(java.awt.Color.red);
      getmsgArea().setForeground(java.awt.Color.white);
```

Figure 15.32

Connection connEtoM2_ExceptionOccurred

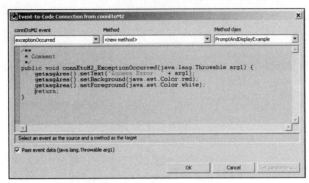

What did you just code? Basically, you are passing the error message that you would receive from the AS/400 to the **msgArea** JTextField. You created this JTextField earlier in the chapter. You have also changed the JTextField **msgArea** properties to use a background color of red and a foreground color of white when the message is displayed, identifying it as an error message.

➢   Click **OK**.

Your connection should look similar to that shown in Figure 15.33.

Figure 15.33

connEtoM2_ExceptionOccurred Connection connEtoC3

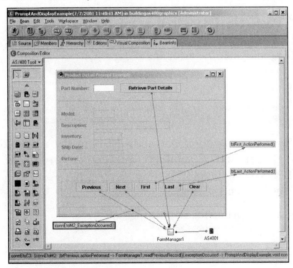

You are now going to test your new error-handling code. Save and then run the Java program.

➢   On the menu bar, click **Bean**.
➢   Click **Save Bean**.
➢   On the menu bar, click **Bean**.
➢   Click **Run**, and then click **Run Main**.
➢   Click the **First** button.
➢   Enter your sign-on information, and wait a few seconds.

The first part number in the file, 00001, appears.

➤   Click the **Previous** button.

You should see an empty screen with no parts information.

➤   Click **Previous** again.

Figure 15.34 shows the results. In this case, the error-handling approach didn't produce the ideal results. It did display an AS/400 CPF error message at the bottom of the screen stating what happened, but the program still crashed.

Figure 15.34
ExceptionOccurred() Error Message

➤   Close the **Product Detail Prompt Example** application.

Error Handling: btPrevious normalResult()

In this error-handling approach, you're going to take a more proactive stance to the error-handling coding. You'll use a **normalResult()** method to accomplish the error handling.

Event-to-Code Connection: normalResult()

```
connEtoC3: (btPrevious,actionPerformed → FormManager1,readPreviousRecord().normalResult →
            PromptAndDisplayExample,void connEtoM2_normalResult())
```

This connection lets you pass a **NormalResult** argument — the Boolean status — to the **connEtoM2_NormalResult()** method. If the Boolean status is false, an unsuccessful I/O operation occurred. This technique is similar to looking at the indicator status after an RPG I/O operation has been completed.

You are first going to delete the connection you just created.

➤   Right-click the **connEtoM2_ExceptionOccurred()** method.
➤   Click **Delete**.

Now, create another event-to-code connection with connection **connEtoM2**.

➤   Right-click connection **connEtoM2**, the connection from the **Previous** JButton to the **FormManager1** bean.
➤   Click **Connect**.
➤   Click **normalResult**.
➤   Click the spider-end pointer on the nonvisual free-form surface.
➤   Click **Event to Code**.
➤   Insert the Java code shown in Figure 15.35. When you've finished typing the new Java code, your method should look identical to Figure 15.36.

Figure 15.35

Source Code for connEtoM2_NormalResult

```
Source code: connEtoM2_NormalResult
      if (arg1 == false)
          {
              getmsgArea().setText("Beginning of File Reached");
              getmsgArea().setBackground(java.awt.Color.red);
              getmsgArea().setForeground(java.awt.Color.white);
              try {
                  getFormManager1().clearAllData();
                  getFormManager1().positionCursorToFirst();
                  getFormManager1().readRecord();
                  }
              catch (java.lang.Throwable ivjExc) {
                  handleException(ivjExc);
                  }
          }
```

Figure 15.36

Connection connEtoM2_NormalResult

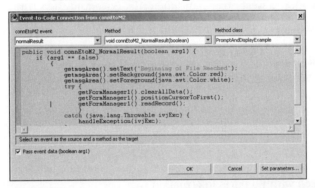

Notice that this Java code is similar to what you coded in the **ExceptionOccurred()** method. There are a few distinct differences, though. Instead of using the returned AS/400 error message, you have defined your own error message ("Beginning of File Reached"). The next difference is the use of the try/catch block. When using an I/O operation, you have to define a try/catch block to handle possible error conditions. The last difference is that you've used coding to reposition to the first record in the file whenever an attempt is made to read prior to the first record.

➤   Click **OK**.

Your connection should look similar to Figure 15.37.

Figure 15.37
connEtoM2_NormalResult Connection connEtoC3

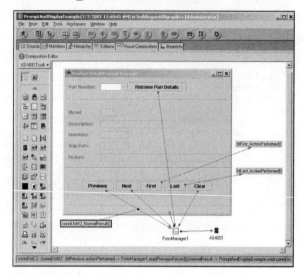

You are now going to test your newest error-handling code. Save and then run the Java program.

➢   On the menu bar, click **Bean**.
➢   Click **Save Bean**.
➢   On the menu bar, click **Bean**.
➢   Click **Run**, and then click **Run Main**.
➢   Click the **First** button.
➢   Enter your sign-on information, and wait a few seconds.

Just as before, the first part number in the file, 00001, appears.

➢   Click **Previous**.

You should see an empty screen with no parts information.

➢   Click **Previous** again.

Figure 15.38 shows the results. In this case, the error-handling approach *did* produce the ideal results. It displayed your user-friendly error message and didn't crash the program. However, you're not finished yet!

Figure 15.38
NormalResult() Error Message

➤ In the **Part Number** field, type **00005**.
➤ Click **Retrieve Part Details**.

Notice that the error message still appears on the screen. You need to fix this problem.

➤ Close the **Product Detail Prompt Example** application.

Clearing Error Messages with a Mouse Event

Event-to-Code Connection: mouseEvents()

```
connEtoC4: (PromptAndDisplayExample,mouseEvents →
          PromptAndDisplayExample,void promptAndDisplayExample_MouseEvents())
```

This connection will let you clear the **msgArea** JTextField whenever the mouse cursor is moved. The cursor movement is known as a *mouse event*. This approach works quite well in most cases. When a user has read the error message and is ready to act on it, he or she will usually move the mouse to make the correction. In later chapters, you'll see other approaches to clearing an error message.

Create an event-to-code connection with the **PromptAndDisplayExample** JFrame.

➤ Right-click the outside edge of the **PromptAndDisplayExample** JFrame.
➤ Click **Connect**.
➤ Click **Connectible Features**.
➤ Click the **mouseEvents** event.
➤ Click **OK**.
➤ Click the spider-end pointer on the nonvisual free-form surface.
➤ Click **Event to Code**.
➤ Insert the Java code shown in Figure 15.39. When you've finished typing the new Java code, your method should look identical to Figure 15.40.

This code will blank out the **msgArea** JTextField and restore the field to its original light-gray color. In essence, it clears the error message.

Figure 15.39
Source Code for promptAndDisplayExample_MouseEvents

```
Source code: promptAndDisplayExample_MouseEvents
    getmsgArea().setText("");
    getmsgArea().setBackground(java.awt.Color.lightGray);
```

Figure 15.40

promptAndDisplayExample_MouseEvents Connection

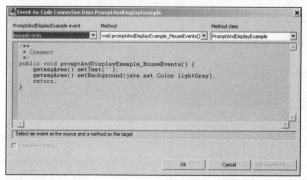

➤   Click **OK**.

Your connection should look similar to Figure 15.41.

Figure 15.41

promptAndDisplayExample_MouseEvents Connection connEtoC4

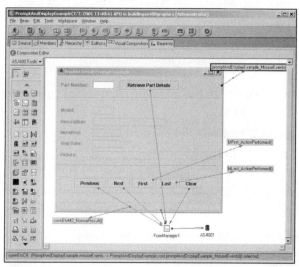

You are now going to test your mouse movements and the clearing of the error message. Save and then run your Java program.

➤   On the menu bar, click **Bean**.
➤   Click **Save Bean**.
➤   On the menu bar, click **Bean**.
➤   Click **Run**, and then click **Run Main**.
➤   Click the **First** button.
➤   Enter your sign-on information, and wait a few seconds.

The first part number in the file, 00001, appears.

➤   Click **Previous**.

You should see an empty screen with no parts information.

➢   Click **Previous** again.

You should see a screen with part number 00001 and the "Beginning of File Reached" error message displayed.

➢   Move the mouse.

Did you notice that as soon as you moved the mouse, even a very small bit, the error message disappeared? Wouldn't you agree that this is pretty cool stuff compared with the green-screen programming?

➢   Close the **Product Detail Prompt Example** application.

More Error Handling: Last Record and Invalid Part Number

Two more potential error situations exist that you'll want to handle in your application: attempts to read beyond the last record in the file and attempts to retrieve a part number that doesn't exist. In this section, you'll set up the connections to deal with these two types of errors.

Event-to-Code Connection: btNext normalResult()

```
connEtoC5: (btNext,actionPerformed → FormManager1,readNextRecord().normalResult →
          PromptAndDisplayExample,void connEtoM3_normalResult())
```

First, you're going to specify the error message handling that should occur if the **Next** button is clicked and an attempt is made to read past the end of the file. The code for this connection will be almost identical to the **connEtoM2_NormalResult()** method. The only differences will be an "End of File Reached" error message and positioning to the last record instead of the first.

Create an event-to-code connection with connection **connEtoM3**.

➢   Right-click connection **connEtoM3**, the connection from the **btNext** JButton to the **FormManager1** bean.
➢   Click **Connect**.
➢   Click **normalResult**.
➢   Click the spider-end pointer on the nonvisual free-form surface.
➢   Click **Event to Code**.
➢   Insert the Java code shown in Figure 15.42. Feel free to cut and paste from the **connEtoM2_NormalResult()** method. When you've finished typing the new Java code, your method should look identical to Figure 15.43.

Figure 15.42
Source Code for connEtoM3_NormalResult

```
Source code: connEtoM3_NormalResult
     if (arg1 == false)
        {
            getmsgArea().setText("End of File Reached");
            getmsgArea().setBackground(java.awt.Color.red);
            getmsgArea().setForeground(java.awt.Color.white);
            try {
                getFormManager1().clearAllData();
                getFormManager1().positionCursorToLast();
                getFormManager1().readRecord();
                }
            catch (java.lang.Throwable ivjExc) {
                handleException(ivjExc);
            }
        }
```

Figure 15.43

Connection connEtoM3_NormalResult

> Click **OK**.

Your connection should look similar to Figure 15.44.

Figure 15.44

connEtoM3_NormalResult Connection: connEtoC5

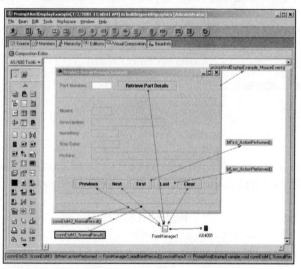

Event-to-Code Connection: btRetrieve normalResult()

```
connEtoC6: (btRetrieve,actionPerformed → FormManager1,readRecord().normalResult →
            PromptAndDisplayExample,void connEtoM1_normalResult())
```

This connection will specify the error message handling when the user clicks the **Retrieve Part Details** button and tries to retrieve an invalid part number. This connection will be similar to the error handling for the **First** and **Last** buttons.

Create an event-to-code connection with connection **connEtoM1**.

> Right-click connection **connEtoM1**, the connection from the **Retrieve Part Details** button to the **FormManager1** bean.
> Click **Connect**.

➢ Click **normalResult**.

➢ Click the spider-end pointer on the nonvisual free-form surface.

➢ Click **Event to Code**.

➢ Insert the Java code shown in Figure 15.45. When you've finished typing the new Java code, your method should look identical to Figure 15.46.

Figure 15.45
Source Code for connEtoM1_NormalResult

```
Source code: connEtoM1_NormalResult
    if (arg1 == false)
        {
            getmsgArea().setText("Part Number does not exist");
            getmsgArea().setBackground(java.awt.Color.red);
            getmsgArea().setForeground(java.awt.Color.white);
        }
```

Figure 15.46
connEtoM1_NormalResult Connection

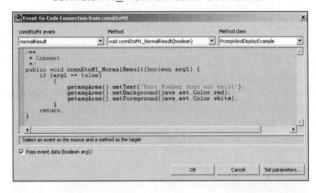

➢ Click **OK**.

Your connection should look similar to Figure 15.47.

Save the Java program.

➢ On the menu bar, click **Bean**.

➢ Click **Save Bean**.

Before you run the application, you're going to add a few other enhancements to your program.

Figure 15.47

connEtoM1_NormalResult Connection: connEtoC6

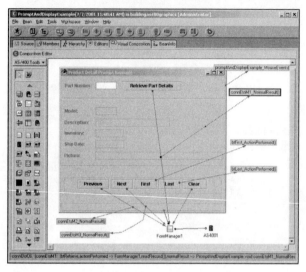

Shaping Connections

There will be times, especially when you use lots of event-to-code methods, when your nonvisual free-form surface area becomes very cluttered. You'll find many of your connection lines overlapping, making it difficult to easily understand what is connected to what. The VCE offers a neat little function that lets you rearrange connection lines. This function is easy to use. Look at Figure 15.48 and the **connEtoM3_NormalResult()** connection. Notice all the center points. By grabbing one of these center points and dragging your mouse, you can easily modify the visual appearance of the connection line.

Figure 15.48

Shaping Connection connEtoM3_NormalResult

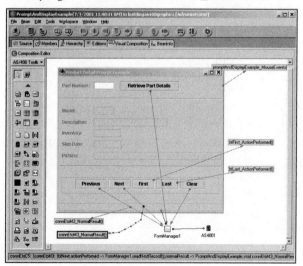

You are now going to experiment with changing one of your connections.

➢   Click the connection **connEtoC5 (connEtoM3_NormalResult())**. This is the **NormalResult** connection associated with the **Next** button.

➢   When the cross-hair pointer appears, click. While holding the mouse, drag it just a little.

Notice how the mouse movement reshaped the connection line and also created some additional connection center points. You can click any of these center points and drag the connection to create any shape you like. This ability comes in handy when you're trying to draw a connection line around or through other beans and/or connections.

Window Connections

In most applications, you'll probably want to perform certain functions based on the events of a window being either opened or closed. In this section, you'll accomplish two such functions: displaying the first record in the file when the application window first appears and closing the database file when the user exits the window.

Event-to-Method Connection: readNextRecord()

```
connEtoM5: (PromptAndDisplayExample,mouseEvents → FormManager1,readNextRecord())
```

Many times, you want a record or group of records to be already displayed when a screen first appears. This connection will do exactly that. It will make the AS/400 prompt appear before the application window is first opened. A call to the **readNextRecord()** method connected to the **windowOpened** event will cause this to occur. When the application window does open, you'll already have the first record loaded and displayed.

Create an event-to-method connection with the **PromptAndDisplayExample** JFrame.

➢   Right-click the outside edge of the **PromptAndDisplayExample** JFrame.
➢   Click **Connect**.
➢   Click **windowOpened**.
➢   Click the spider-end pointer on the **FormManager1** bean.
➢   Click **Connectible Features**.
➢   Click the **readNextRecord()** method.
➢   Click **OK**.

Event-to-Code Connection: windowClosed()

```
connEtoC7: (PromptAndDisplayExample,windowClosed → PromptAndDisplayExample,
           void promptAndDisplayExample_WindowClosed(java.awt.event.WindowEvent))
```

Notice that the sample application includes no **Exit** or **Close** JButton anywhere on the screen. The only way to end the application is to click the Windows **Close** button. You're going to use an event-to-code connection to perform the necessary shutdown functions for the application. This will consist of closing the database.

Create an event-to-code connection with the **PromptAndDisplayExample** JFrame.

➢   Right-click the outside edge of the **PromptAndDisplayExample** JFrame.
➢   Click **Connect**.
➢   Click **windowClosed**.
➢   Click the spider-end pointer on the nonvisual free-form surface.
➢   Click **Event to Code**.
➢   Insert the Java code shown in Figure 15.49.

Figure 15.49

Source Code for promptAndDisplayExample_WindowClosed

```
Source code: promptAndDisplayExample_WindowClosed
try {
    getFormManager1().closeFile();
    }
catch (java.lang.Throwable ivjExc) {
    handleException(ivjExc);
    }
```

This code will close the database file associated with the FormManager. Normally, you would also include a **dispose()** method to free up memory from the window. You won't be including the **dispose()** method here because you'll be using this application in the next chapter, and the **dispose()** method would cause you problems there if you included it.

➤   Click **OK**.

Your connection should look similar to that shown in Figure 15.50.

Figure 15.50

promptAndDisplayExample_WindowClosed Connection connEtoC7

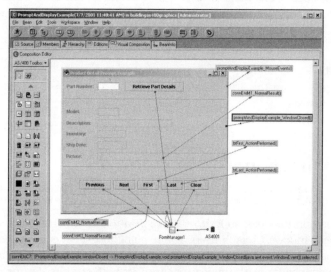

You're probably wondering when you'll be done with all these connections. You're there! That was the last connection in this chapter. Now you can reap the rewards of a completed application.

Using Prompt and Display

Save and then run your Java program.

➤   On the menu bar, click **Bean**.
➤   Click **Save Bean**.
➤   On the menu bar, click **Bean**.
➤   Click **Run**, and then click **Run Main**.

Notice that the AS/400 prompt appears immediately.

➤   Enter your sign-on information, and wait a few seconds.

Did you notice that the first record in the file was already loaded? That's because you associated the **readNextRecord()** method with the **windowOpened** event.

Now, test to see what happens when you enter an invalid part number.

➤   In the **Part Number** field, type **00055**.
➤   Click the **Retrieve Part Details** button.

Figure 15.51 shows the results. A nice error message — "Part Number does not exist" — is displayed. Notice that as soon as you move your cursor, the error message disappears.

Now, test to see what happens when you try to read past the end of the file.

➤   Click **Last**.
➤   Click **Next**.

Figure 15.52 shows the results. You should see a screen with part number 00023 (the last record in the file) and an error message stating that the end of file has been reached.

Figure 15.51	Figure 15.52
NormalResult() Error Message	*NormalResult() Error Message*

➤   Close the **Product Detail Prompt Example** application.

You've just completed a fairly complete prompt and display application, and you've seen a few ways to work with error handling. There are many variations of error handling. I hope this chapter sparked some ideas concerning how to work with errors. You could write some generic error classes whereby you pass an error message to a class and the class does the rest of the work of formatting and displaying the message. This technique would relieve you from having to write all the error handling for each possible error situation.

Spend some time on your error-routine standards to reduce your coding. Remember one of the strengths of Java: reusability.

Summary

In this chapter you learned

- how to work with errors using the **ExceptionOccurred()** and **NormalResult()** methods
- how to retrieve database records, both sequentially and using random access
- how to use the **FormManager** and **RecordIOManager** beans
- how to use several event-to-code connections
- how to reshape connection lines

The next chapter will teach you how to create menus and how to call classes that you've created.

Chapter 16

Building Java Menus

 ## Chapter Objectives

- ☐ Become proficient in building menus
- ☐ Understand the **JMenu**, **JMenuBar**, **JMenuItem**, and **JPopupMenu** JavaBeans
- ☐ Learn how to change the look and feel of Java components
- ☐ Learn how to build pop-up (shortcut) menus
- ☐ Become familiar with about boxes and splash screens

 ## Chapter Project

- ☐ Three classes will be created to build a menu interface, one function of which will be to call the program you created in Chapter 15.
- ☐ The classes will let you call the same program multiple times, as well as display an about box and a splash screen.
- ☐ Figure 16.1 shows what the sample classes will look like.

Figure 16.1
Chapter Project

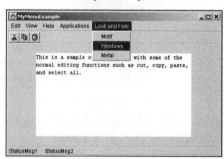

When most AS/400 developers think of menus, they think of a long, vertical list of numbered options. Many AS/400 developers have even taken the time to create full-blown, dynamic menu systems for users' ease of use in running applications. A few years ago, the AS/400 DDS and Screen Design Aid (SDA) began supporting menu functions. There are probably a few AS/400 shops that really embraced this new AS/400 function. Who they are, I don't know. The AS/400 menus never really caught on. I suspect that was because they just weren't as nice as a typical Windows menu interface. With Java, that can all change.

When we talk about menus in Java, it's possible to think in terms of our AS/400 menus, which call application programs. More likely, though, Java menus, which can be located on menu bars or appear as pop-up menus, are used to select options. These options can be used to call other programs, but they can also be used to enhance the functional capabilities related to a particular application.

If you look at typical Windows menus, you'll find options such as File, Edit, View, Insert, Format, Tools, Window, Help, and so on. You can incorporate all these options into menus created through Java. Associated with menus are toolbars that let you represent a menu option using a graphical icon, or button.

This chapter focuses on creating menus, menu bars, toolbars, and pop-up menus. You'll learn how to call other Java classes or applications and how to execute options from the menu bar and the toolbar. We'll also discuss how to change the look and feel of an application and how to build "about" dialog boxes and splash screens.

Menu-Related JavaBeans

Several JavaBeans are associated with menus. None of these beans are particular to the AS/400 Toolbox. These are standard JavaBeans. VisualAge for Java supports basic menu beans from the Abstract Window Toolkit (AWT), but this chapter focuses on Swing menu beans as provided in the **javax.swing** package. These Swing beans consist of the following:

Swing bean	Description
JMenu	Typically, a group of menu options represented on a menu bar, pop-up menu, or other type of menu
JMenuBar	A menu bar for a window
JMenuItem	A menu option that calls a method
JPopupMenu	A pop-up menu initiated with a right-click and positioned with the mouse cursor
JCheckBoxMenuItem	A menu option that toggles a state on or off
JRadioButtonMenuItem	One choice in a mutually exclusive group of menu options
JSeparator	A line that separates menu items
JToolBar	A graphical set of tool choices
JToolBarButton	A button on a toolbar
JToolBarSeparator	A visual separator between buttons on a toolbar

You're going to create a class called **MyMenuExample**. You will store this class in the project **My Graphical Applications** and in the package **buildingas400graphics**. You'll be using a different SmartGuide for this chapter: the **Create Application** SmartGuide. This application builder, shown in Figure 16.2, takes much of the work out of building a menu application, letting you easily specify common menus, menu items, and menu functions.

Figure 16.2

Create Application: MyMenuExample

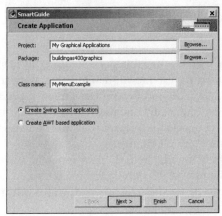

➢   If the workbench isn't started, start it now.

➢   Expand the project **My Graphical Applications**.

➢   Select the package **buildingas400graphics** with a click.

➢   Right-click to display the shortcut menu, select **Add**, and then select **Application**. The **Create Application** SmartGuide will appear.

➢   Make sure the **Project** name is **My Graphical Applications**.

➢   Make sure the **Package** name is **buildingas400graphics**.

➢   For the **Class name**, type **MyMenuExample**.

➢   Make sure the **Create Swing based application** option is selected.

➢   Click **Next** to complete the creation of the class.

Figure 16.3 shows the next window of the **Create Application** SmartGuide, the **Application Details** window.

➢   Clear the **Center and pack frame on screen** check box. When selected, this option makes your menus start out very small and centered on the screen. It requires the user to open up the window to use it — not a very good idea.

➢   Select the **Splash screen** check box. This option automatically creates a separate class called **MyMenuExampleSplashScreen** that is used to display an opening window for three seconds. As you'll see later, the default splash screen graphic is an image of a cow — yes, a cow.

➢   Select the **About dialog** check box. This option automatically creates a separate class called **MyMenuExampleAboutBox**. This class is nothing more than a standard about dialog box such as you'd see in any commercially developed software application.

Figure 16.3
Application Details

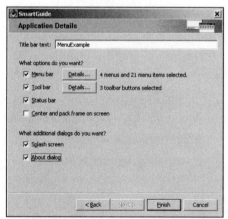

Notice that the **Application Details** window in Figure 16.3 says you're starting out with four menus, 21 menu items, and three toolbar buttons preselected. You're going to change that.

➢   Next to the **Menu bar** check box, click **Details**.

The **Menu Bar Details** window (Figure 16.4) is displayed. You're going to remove one of the preselected menus and several preselected menu items using the lists in this window. In the future, if you wanted to add some menu items as part of the builder, this is one place you could do so.

Figure 16.4
Menu Bar Details: Menus

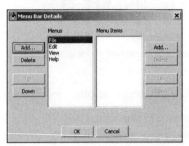

> In the **Menus** list, click **File**.
> Click the **Delete** button to remove the **File** menu.
> In the **Menus** list, click **Edit**. Notice the **Edit** menu items (e.g., Undo, Cut, Copy) and separators that appear in the **Menu Items** list on the right.
> In the **Menu Items** list, click **Undo**.
> Click the **Delete** button beside the **Menu Items** list.
> Click **Redo**.
> Click the **Delete** button.
> Click **-- Separator --**.
> Click the **Delete** button.
> Click **Find/Replace**.
> Click the **Delete** button.

When you're finished, the **Menu Bar Details** window should appear as shown in Figure 16.5.

Figure 16.5
Menu Bar Details: Menu Items

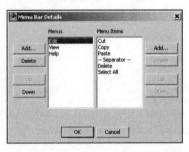

> Click **OK**.

You should be back at the **Application Details** window.

> Next to the **Tool bar** check box, click **Details**.

Figure 16.6 shows the standard toolbar functions you can select. You'll be accepting all three of the tools listed on the right side: the cut, copy, and paste buttons.

Figure 16.6
Tool Bar Details

> ➤ Click **OK**.

You should be back at the **Application Details** window. As Figure 16.7 shows, the window should now report that you have three menus, 11 menu items, and three toolbar buttons selected.

Figure 16.7
Application Details

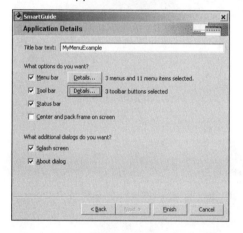

> ➤ Click **Finish**.

You should be inside the Visual Composition Editor, which will appear as shown in Figure 16.8. Notice that a lot of the work has already been done for you. Because it's a good idea to understand how to create menus and menu items directly in the VCE, you'll be adding some menus and menu items to what you see here. Keep in mind that you could have added all the following menus and menu items using the **Create Application** SmartGuide.

Figure 16.8
Initial Menu in VCE

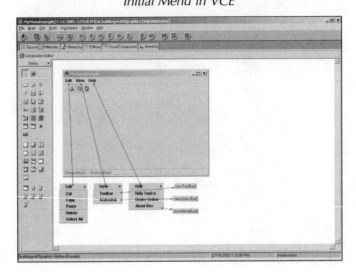

Add a JMenu as shown in Figure 16.9.

➢   Click the **JMenu** bean ⬜, and drop it on the menu bar as highlighted in the figure. This bean is located near the end of the Swing category list.

➢   Double-click the **JMenu1** JMenu. Change the **beanName** from **JMenu1** to <u>**mnApplications**</u>.

➢   Change the **text** to <u>**Applications**</u>.

➢   Close the **Properties** sheet.

Figure 16.9
JMenu1

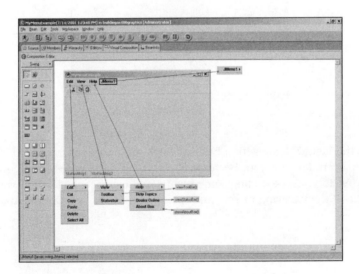

Add a JMenuItem as shown in Figure 16.10.

➢ Click the **JMenuItem** bean ⬜, and drop it on the **Applications** JMenu, as shown in the figure. This bean is located near the end of the Swing category list.

➢ Double-click the **JMenuItem1** JMenuItem. Change the **beanName** from **JMenuItem1** to **miPrompt**.

➢ Change the **text** to **Prompt Example**.

➢ Close the **Properties** sheet.

Figure 16.10

Prompt Example JMenuItem

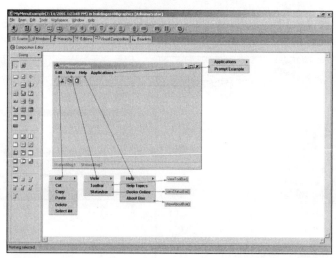

Calling Other Applications

In this section, you'll learn how to call another application or class that you've already created. Then, in the next section, we'll look at another approach to calling applications. There will be tradeoffs between the two approaches.

You just created a menu item called **Prompt Example**. When the user selects this menu item, you'll call the **PromptAndDisplayExample** application that you created in Chapter 15.

Add a **PromptAndDisplayExample** bean.

➢ In the upper-left corner of the VCE, click the **Choose Bean** 🖼 button. The **Choose Bean** window appears.

➢ In the **Class name** field, type **PromptAnd**. Then click **Browse** to select a class.

➢ Select class **PromptAndDisplayExample**, and click **OK**.

➢ Click **OK**.

➢ Drop the **PromptAndDisplayExample** bean on the upper-right area of the free-form nonvisual surface. You won't change any properties of this bean.

Event-to-Method Connection: show()

```
connEtoM1: (miPrompt,actionPerformed → PromptAndDisplayExample1,show())
```

This connection shows, or displays, the application specified as the bean. Connect the **Prompt Example** JMenuItem with a **show()** method.

➢ Right-click the **Prompt Example** JMenuItem.

➢ Click **Connect**.

➢ Click **actionPerformed**.

➤   Click the spider-end pointer on the **PromptAndDisplayExample1** bean.
➤   Click **Connectible Features**.
➤   Click the **show()** method.
➤   Click **OK**.

Your connection should appear as shown in Figure 16.11.

➤   Double-click the connection to verify that it is correct as shown in Figure 16.12.
➤   Close the **Properties** window.

Figure 16.11
PromptAndDisplayExample1 Connection

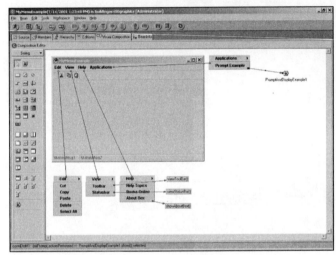

Figure 16.12
Connection connEtoM1

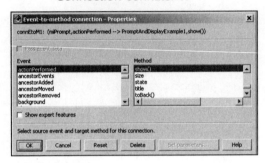

Save your Java program.

➤   On the menu bar, click **Bean**.
➤   Click **Save Bean**.

To run the Java program, you need to successfully connect to the AS/400. Run the program.

➤   On the menu bar, click **Bean**.
➤   Click **Run**, and then click **Run Main**.

You should notice the splash screen appear. It will be displayed for just three seconds. It's a picture of a cow, as shown in Figure 16.13. You'll learn more about splash screens later in this chapter.

Figure 16.13
Splash Screen

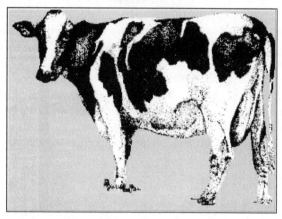

Once the splash screen goes away, you should be looking at the application as shown in Figure 16.14. Wasn't it fast to create?

Figure 16.14
MyMenuExample Application

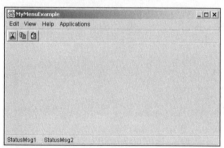

➢   On the menu bar, click **Applications** to display the **Applications** menu.
➢   Click the **Prompt Example** menu item.
➢   Enter your sign-on information, and wait a few seconds.

You should see your Chapter 15 application, the **Product Detail Prompt Example** window. Wasn't the process for calling another application easy to set up? Now, you're going to try calling the same application a second time without closing the first instance of the application. What will happen?

➢   Again, click **Applications**.
➢   Click **Prompt Example**.

Notice that nothing really happens. No second **Product Detail Prompt Example** window appeared, which is what you might have expected. In the next section, you'll learn how to make the application appear a second and even a third time.

➢   Close the **Product Detail Prompt Example** window.
➢   Close the **MyMenuExample** window.

Look and Feel

What's the big deal about look and feel? With Java, you can create applications that can run on multiple platforms: Windows, Macintosh, Unix, and Linux. Java is platform independent. Because Java may be spread out over multiple types of systems in a large organization, it can be beneficial to give your applications a graphical interface with which the user is already familiar. For example, a button in a Windows environment will look different from a button in a Macintosh environment.

VisualAge for Java supports several standard "look and feels." The *Motif* look and feel, which can be used on any operating system, is typical on Sun platforms. The *Windows* look and feel is used on Windows operating systems. The *Metal* look and feel is the same as the Java look and feel and can be used on any operating system. The *Mac* look and feel can be used only on Macintosh operating systems. Figures 16.15, 16.16, and 16.17 show the Motif, the Windows, and the Metal look and feel, respectively.

Figure 16.15
Motif Look

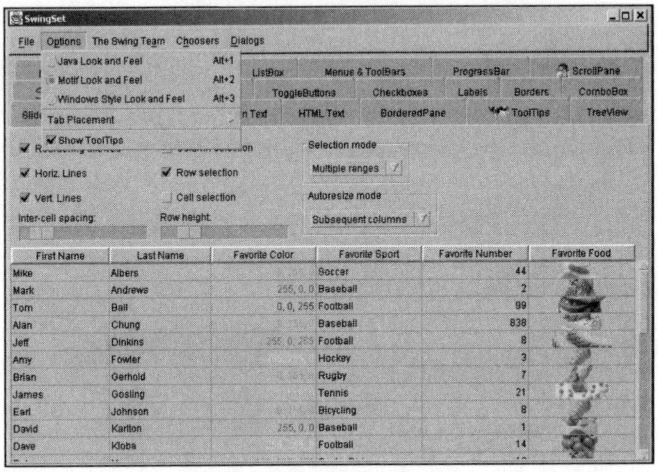

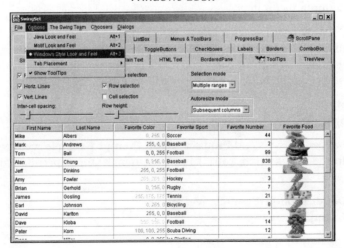

Figure 16.16
Windows Look

Figure 16.17
Metal Look

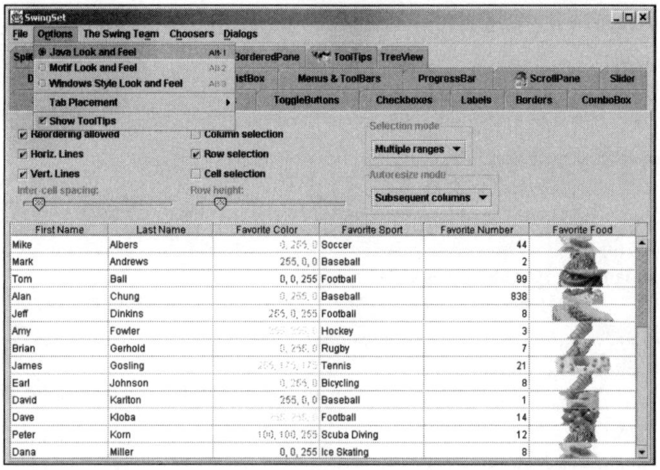

VisualAge for Java's **UIManager** (user interface manager) specifies the look and feel for an application. The Swing Java Foundation Class allows the specification or customization of its graphical components. This means you can change the look and feel whenever you like.

Tips and Tricks

To change the look and feel of an application before a VisualAge for Java VCE session is started, you would create a Swing properties file named *swing.properties.* The file could contain the following text:

```
swing.defaultlaf=com.sun.java.swing.plaf.windows.WindowsLookAndFeel
```

You would save the file in the *program\lib* directory of your VisualAge for Java installation.

Other look and feels could be defined as

```
swing.defaultlaf=com.sun.java.swing.plaf.motif.MotifLookAndFeel
```

or

```
swing.defaultlaf=com.sun.java.swing.plaf.metal.MetalLookAndFeel
```

Tips and Tricks

Here are some examples of the Java coding for various looks and feels.

Java look and feel:

```
UIManager.setLookAndFeel (
        UIManager.getCrossPlatformLookAndFeelClassName());
```

Native look for whatever platform the user runs the program on:

```
UIManager.setLookAndFeel (
        UIManager.getSystemLookAndFeelClassName());
```

Motif look and feel:

```
UIManager.setLookAndFeel (
        "com.sun.java.swing.plaf.motif.MotifLookAndFeel");
```

Windows look and feel (limited to Windows operating systems):

```
UIManager.setLookAndFeel (
        "com.sun.java.swing.plaf.windows.WindowsLookAndFeel");
```

Metal look and feel (also the Java look and feel):

```
UIManager.setLookAndFeel (
        "com.sun.java.swing.plaf.metal.MetalLookAndFeel");
```

Mac look and feel (limited to Mac operating systems):

```
UIManager.setLookAndFeel (
        "javax.swing.plaf.mac.MacLookAndFeel");
```

In the following example, you'll learn how to change the look and feel during program execution. First, add a **Look and Feel** JMenu as shown in Figure 16.18.

➢   Click the **JMenu** bean, and drop it on the menu bar.
➢   Double-click the JMenu. Change the **beanName** to **mnLookAndFeel**.
➢   Change the **text** to **Look and Feel**.
➢   Close the **Properties** sheet.

Your screen should look similar to Figure 16.18.

Figure 16.18
Look and Feel Menu

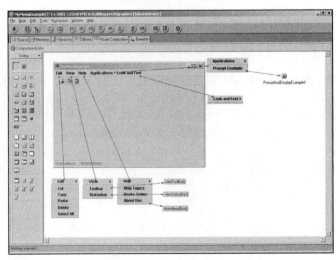

Now, add three JMenuItems as shown in Figure 16.19.

➢ Click the **JMenuItem** bean, and drop it on the **Look and Feel** JMenu.
➢ Double-click the JMenuItem.
➢ Change the **beanName** to **miMotif**.
➢ Change the **text** to **Motif**.
➢ Close the **Properties** sheet.
➢ Click the **JMenuItem** bean again, and drop it on the **Look and Feel** JMenu.
➢ Double-click the JMenuItem.
➢ Change the **beanName** to **miWindows**.
➢ Change the **text** to **Windows**.
➢ Close the **Properties** sheet.
➢ Click the **JMenuItem** bean once more, and drop it on the **Look and Feel** JMenu.
➢ Double-click the JMenuItem.
➢ Change the **beanName** to **miMetal**.
➢ Change the **text** to **Metal**.
➢ Close the **Properties** sheet.

Figure 16.19
Look and Feel Menu Items

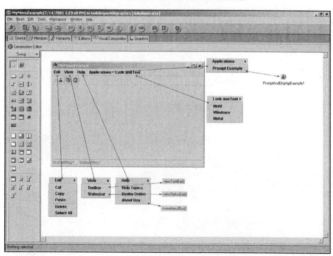

Event-to-Code Connection: setLookAndFeel() — Motif

```
connEtoC4: (miMotif,actionPerformed →
            MyMenuExample,void miMotif_ActionPerformed(java.awt.event.ActionEvent))
```

This connection will change the look and feel in the UI Manager to a **Motif** look and feel. It will then call the **PromptAndDisplayExample** application to demonstrate this new look and feel. You'll change the title on the application from **Product Detail Prompt Example** to **Motif Look**. When the **PromptAndDisplayExample** application is called, it is displayed in the upper-left corner of the screen. Depending on your screen resolution and screen size, you may have to adjust the **setLocation(10, 75)** method to fit the application window better on your screen.

Create an event-to-code connection with the **Motif** JMenuItem.

➢   Right-click the **Motif** JMenuItem.
➢   Click **Connect**.
➢   Click **actionPerformed**.
➢   Click the spider-end pointer on the nonvisual free-form surface.
➢   Click **Event to Code**.
➢   Insert the Java code shown in Figure 16.20. When you've finished typing the new Java code, your method
     should look identical to Figure 16.21.
➢   Click **OK**.

Figure 16.20
Source Code for Setting the Motif Look and Feel

```
Source code: connEtoC4
      try {
             UIManager.setLookAndFeel
                ("com.sun.java.swing.plaf.motif.MotifLookAndFeel");
          }
      catch (Exception e)
         {
         }
      PromptAndDisplayExample myPgm = new PromptAndDisplayExample();
      myPgm.setTitle("Motif Look");
      myPgm.setLocation(10, 75);
      myPgm.show();
```

Figure 16.21
Connection connEtoC4

Tips and Tricks

When you begin creating your event-to-code connections, you may notice that your first connection starts
with a *connEtoC4* designation. That's because the *Create Application* SmartGuide already created three
event-to-code connections with the *viewToolBar()*, *viewStatusBar()*, and *showAboutBox()* methods. You can
see these connections in Figure 16.8.

When you exit the event-to-code connection, you'll notice that the new method is placed in the upper-right corner of the screen.

➢ Click and hold the **miMotif_ActionPerformed()** method, and drag it down closer to the **Motif** MenuItem.

Event-to-Code Connection: setLookAndFeel() — Windows

```
connEtoC5: (miWindows,actionPerformed →
            MyMenuExample,void miWindows_ActionPerformed(java.awt.event.ActionEvent))
```

This connection will be almost identical to the previous one. It will change the look and feel in the UI Manager to a **Windows** look and feel. Again, you'll change the application title, this time to **Windows Look**. When the **PromptAndDisplayExample** application is called, it is displayed in the upper-right corner of the screen. Depending on your screen resolution and screen size, you may have to adjust the **setLocation(500, 75)** method to fit the application window better on your screen.

Create an event-to-code connection with the **Windows** JMenuItem.

➢ Right-click the **Windows** JMenuItem.
➢ Click **Connect**.
➢ Click **actionPerformed**.
➢ Click the spider-end pointer on the nonvisual free-form surface.
➢ Click **Event to Code**.
➢ Insert the Java code shown in Figure 16.22. When you've finished typing the new Java code, your method should look similar to Figure 16.23.
➢ Click **OK**.
➢ Click and hold the **miWindows_ActionPerformed()** method, and drag it down closer to the **Windows** MenuItem.

Figure 16.22
Source Code for Setting the Windows Look and Feel

```
Source code: connEtoC5
    try {
            UIManager.setLookAndFeel
                ("com.sun.java.swing.plaf.windows.WindowsLookAndFeel");
        }
    catch (Exception e)
        {
        }
        PromptAndDisplayExample myPgm = new PromptAndDisplayExample();
        myPgm.setTitle("Windows Look");
        myPgm.setLocation(500, 75);
        myPgm.show();
```

Figure 16.23
Connection connEtoC5

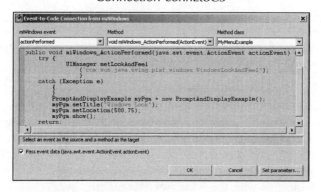

Event-to-Code Connection: setLookAndFeel() — Metal

```
connEtoC6: (miMetal,actionPerformed →
            MyMenuExample,void miMetal_ActionPerformed(java.awt.event.ActionEvent))
```

This connection will change the look and feel in the UI Manager to a **Metal** look and feel. Once again, you'll change the application title, this time to **Metal Look**. When the **PromptAndDisplayExample** application is called, it is displayed in the lower-left corner of the screen. Depending on your screen resolution and screen size, you may have to adjust the **setLocation(10, 400)** method to fit the application window better on your screen.

Create an event-to-code connection with the **Metal** JMenuItem.

➢   Right-click the **Metal** JMenuItem.
➢   Click **Connect**.
➢   Click **actionPerformed**.
➢   Click the spider-end pointer on the nonvisual free-form surface.
➢   Click **Event to Code**.
➢   Insert the Java code shown in Figure 16.24. When you've finished typing the new Java code, your method should look identical to Figure 16.25.
➢   Click **OK**.
➢   Click and hold the **miMetal_ActionPerformed()** method, and drag it down closer to the **Metal** MenuItem.

Figure 16.24
Source Code for Setting the Metal Look and Feel

```
Source code: connEtoC6
      try {
                UIManager.setLookAndFeel
                    ("com.sun.java.swing.plaf.metal.MetalLookAndFeel");
            }
      catch (Exception e)
            {
            }
      PromptAndDisplayExample myPgm = new PromptAndDisplayExample();
      myPgm.setTitle("Metal Look");
      myPgm.setLocation(10, 400);
      myPgm.show();
```

Figure 16.25

Connection connEtoC6

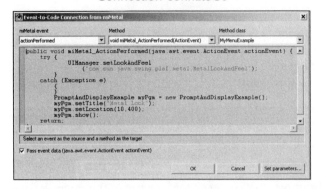

Your look and feel menu and connections should appear as shown in Figure 16.26.

Figure 16.26

Look and Feel Connections: connEtoC4, connEtoC5, and connEtoC6

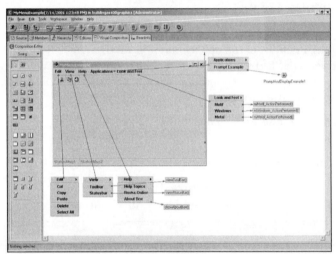

Event-to-Method Connection: dispose()

connEtoM2: (MyMenuExample,windowClosed → MyMenuExample,dispose())

This connection disposes, or shuts down, the application. Connect the **MyMenuExample** JFrame with a **dispose()** method.

➢   Right-click the outside edge of the **MyMenuExample** JFrame.

➢   Click **Connect**.

➢   Click **windowClosed**.

➢   Click the spider-end pointer on the nonvisual free-form surface.

➢   Click **Connectible Features**.

➢   Click the **dispose()** method.

➢   Click **OK**.

Your connection should appear as shown in Figure 16.26. It is the connection line (along the right edge of the JFrame) that points upward to no other JavaBean.

Save and then run your Java program.

➢   On the menu bar, click **Bean**.
➢   Click **Save Bean**.
➢   On the menu bar, click **Bean**.
➢   Click **Run**, and then click **Run Main**.

Your **MyMenuExample** application should now be displayed.

➢   On the menu bar, click **Look and Feel** to display the **Look and Feel** menu.
➢   Click the **Motif** menu item.
➢   Enter your sign-on information, and wait a few seconds.

The **PromptAndDisplayExample** application should appear in the upper-left corner. Notice that the window title is **Motif Look** and not **Product Detail Prompt Example**. That's because you specified the **setTitle("Motif Look")** method. Did you notice that the look is much different than anything you've done in the previous chapters? This is the Motif look and feel.

➢   On the menu bar, click **Look and Feel** again.
➢   Click **Windows**.

Did you notice that another instance of the application appeared? Why is it located on the upper-right side of your screen? That's because you specified the **setLocation (500, 75)** method. Why weren't you prompted for an AS/400 sign-on? Because you already had a connection open to the AS/400. Did you notice a different look? Also, notice that the window title is now **Windows Look**.

➢   On the menu bar, click **Look and Feel** again.
➢   Click **Metal**.

Even though it's a bit cluttered, your screen should now look similar to Figure 16.27.

Figure 16.27
Look and Feel Open Applications

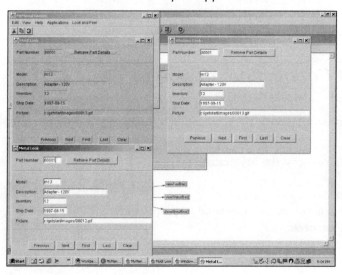

At this point, if you were to issue a WRKACTJOB (Work with Active Jobs) command on the AS/400 side, what would you see? You'd see under subsystem QUSRWRK and job QZSOSIGN three QUSER sign-ons — one for each AS/400 application currently running. Keep in mind that the **MyMenuExample** application, by itself, does not connect to the AS/400 and therefore doesn't appear on the AS/400 side as a running application.

As you can see, this function of multiple instances can be a handy thing from a user perspective. On the negative side, it can also be system resource issue.

You can play with each of the windows. Notice that you can set the **Part Number** value to different or the same records in the various windows. When you're ready to exit, just close the **MyMenuExample** window and not each of the **Look and Feel** windows.

➢   Close the **MyMenuExample** window.

All four windows closed at once! Pretty cool!

Earlier, I mentioned that there are tradeoffs between the two ways of calling applications. By restricting a user to calling an application only once at the same time, you may be limiting user flexibility and productivity. On the other hand, by letting users call applications multiple times, you can easily run into problems with system resources, such as a lack of memory. You need to weigh the advantages of allowing or not allowing multiple calls to the same application in your particular situation.

Edit Menu Functions

If you're a big user of Windows applications, you're probably very familiar with some of the standard **Edit** menu functions, such as **Undo**, **Redo**, **Cut**, **Copy**, **Paste**, **Delete**, **Select All**, and **Find/Replace**. In this section, you'll learn how to implement the most common of these functions in your Java application.

Create a JTextArea as shown in Figure 16.28.

➢   Click the **JTextArea** bean 🖳, and drop it on the center of the free-form surface visual area.

Figure 16.28
JTextArea

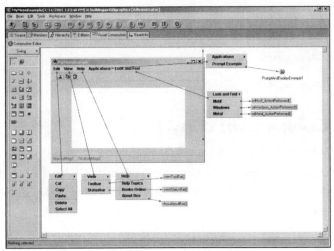

Event-to-Method Connection: cut()

`connEtoM3: (CutMenuItem,actionPerformed → JTextArea1,cut())`

When the user clicks the **Edit** menu's **Cut** JMenuItem, this connection calls the **cut()** method to perform a cut function within the JTextArea. Connect the **Cut** JMenuItem with a **cut()** method.

➢ Right-click the **Cut** JMenuItem.
➢ Click **Connect**.
➢ Click **actionPerformed**.
➢ Click the spider-end pointer on the **JTextArea1** bean.
➢ Click **Connectible Features**.
➢ Click the **cut()** method.
➢ Click **OK**.

Your connection should appear as shown in Figure 16.29. This figure also shows the next four connections you're going to create to enable the other **Edit** menu options.

Figure 16.29
Edit Menu Connections

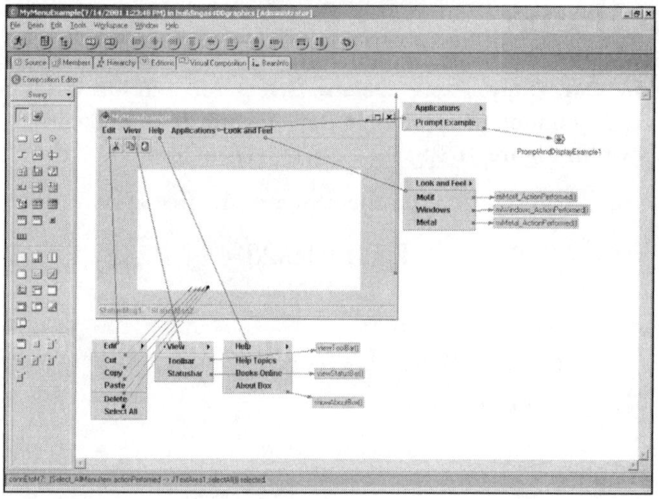

Event-to-Method Connection: copy()

`connEtoM4: (CopyMenuItem,actionPerformed → JTextArea1,copy())`

When the user clicks the **Edit** menu's **Copy** JMenuItem, this connection calls the **copy()** method to perform a copy function within the JTextArea. Connect the **Copy** JMenuItem with a **copy()** method.

➢ Right-click the **Copy** JMenuItem.
➢ Click **Connect**.
➢ Click **actionPerformed**.
➢ Click the spider-end pointer on the **JTextArea1** bean.
➢ Click **Connectible Features**.
➢ Click the **copy()** method.
➢ Click **OK**.

Event-to-Method Connection: paste()

`connEtoM5: (PasteMenuItem,actionPerformed → JTextArea1,paste())`

When the user clicks the **Edit** menu's **Paste** JMenuItem, this connection calls the **paste()** method to perform a paste function within the JTextArea. Connect the **Paste** JMenuItem with a **paste()** method.

➢ Right-click the **Paste** JMenuItem.
➢ Click **Connect**.
➢ Click **actionPerformed**.
➢ Click the spider-end pointer on the **JTextArea1** bean.
➢ Click **Connectible Features**.
➢ Click the **paste()** method.
➢ Click **OK**.

Event-to-Method Connection: cut()

`connEtoM6: (DeleteMenuItem,actionPerformed → JTextArea1,cut())`

The delete function is usually used for deletion operations other than cut. In this example, you'll use the delete function to perform the same function as the cut operation. When the user clicks the **Edit** menu's **Delete** JMenuItem, this connection calls the **cut()** method to perform a cut function within the JTextArea. Connect the **Delete** JMenuItem with a **cut()** method.

➢ Right-click the **Delete** JMenuItem.
➢ Click **Connect**.
➢ Click **actionPerformed**.
➢ Click the spider-end pointer on the **JTextArea1** bean.
➢ Click **Connectible Features**.
➢ Click the **cut()** method.
➢ Click **OK**.

Event-to-Method Connection: selectAll()

`connEtoM7: (Select_AllMenuItem,actionPerformed → JTextArea1,selectAll())`

When the user clicks the **Edit** menu's **Select All** JMenuItem, this connection calls the **selectAll()** method to perform a select all function within the JTextArea. Connect the **Select All** JMenuItem with a **selectAll()** method.

➢ Right-click the **Select All** JMenuItem.
➢ Click **Connect**.
➢ Click **actionPerformed**.
➢ Click the spider-end pointer on the **JTextArea1** bean.
➢ Click **Connectible Features**.
➢ Click the **selectAll()** method.
➢ Click **OK**.

Event-to-Method Connection: cut()

`connEtoM8:  (CutButton,actionPerformed  →  JTextArea1,cut())`

When the user clicks the **Cut** toolbar button ![cut icon], this connection calls the **cut()** method to perform a cut function within the JTextArea. Connect the **Cut** button with a **cut()** method.

➤   Right-click the **Cut** button.
➤   Click **Connect**.
➤   Click **actionPerformed**.
➤   Click the spider-end pointer on the **JTextArea1** bean.
➤   Click **Connectible Features**.
➤   Click the **cut()** method.
➤   Click **OK**.

Your connection should appear as shown in Figure 16.30. This figure also shows the next two connections you're going to create to enable the other two toolbar buttons.

Figure 16.30
Toolbar Connections

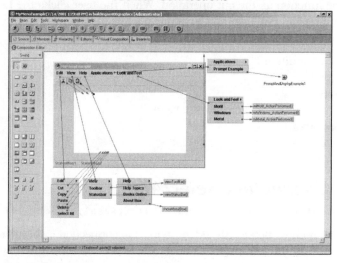

Event-to-Method Connection: copy()

`connEtoM9:  (CopyButton,actionPerformed  →  JTextArea1,copy())`

When the user clicks **Copy** toolbar button ![copy icon], this connection calls the **copy()** method to perform a copy function within the JTextArea. Connect the **Copy** button with a **copy()** method.

➤   Right-click the **Copy** button.
➤   Click **Connect**.
➤   Click **actionPerformed**.
➤   Click the spider-end pointer on the **JTextArea1** bean.
➤   Click **Connectible Features**.
➤   Click the **copy()** method.
➤   Click **OK**.

Event-to-Method Connection: paste()

`connEtoM10: (PasteButton,actionPerformed → JTextArea1,paste())`

When the user clicks the **Paste** toolbar button , this connection calls the **paste()** method to perform a paste function within the JTextArea.

Connect the **Paste** button with a **paste()** method.

➢   Right-click the **Paste** button.
➢   Click **Connect**.
➢   Click **actionPerformed**.
➢   Click the spider-end pointer on the **JTextArea1** bean.
➢   Click **Connectible Features**.
➢   Click the **paste()** method.
➢   Click **OK**.

Save and then run your Java program.

➢   On the menu bar, click **Bean**.
➢   Click **Save Bean**.
➢   On the menu bar, click **Bean**.
➢   Click **Run**, and then click **Run Main**.
➢   In the **JTextArea**, type the following: **This is a sample of how to work with some of the normal editing functions such as cut and paste.**

Figure 16.31 shows the **MyMenuExample** application.

Figure 16.31
MyMenuExample Application

Perform a cut and paste function from the toolbar.

➢   With the mouse, highlight and select the words "normal editing" within the JTextArea.
➢   On the toolbar, click the **Cut** button.
➢   Move the mouse cursor to the end of the sentence in the JTextArea.
➢   On the toolbar, click the **Paste** button.

Figure 16.32 shows the results of the cut and paste.

Figure 16.32
Toolbar Cut and Paste

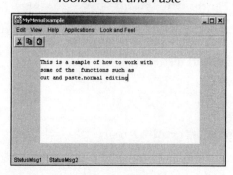

Now, perform a select all and delete function from the **Edit** menu.

➤   On the menu bar, click **Edit** to display the **Edit** menu.
➤   Click the **Select All** menu item.
➤   Click **Edit** again.
➤   Click **Delete**.

Notice that the JTextArea is now blank again.
   Try out the toggles on the **View** menu.

➤   On the menu bar, click **View** to display the **View** menu.
➤   Click the **Toolbar** menu item.

The toolbar should have disappeared.

➤   Click **View** again.
➤   Click **Toolbar** again.

The toolbar should have reappeared.

➤   Repeat the steps you just did, only this time use the **View** menu's **Statusbar** menu item.

Pop-Up Menus

Pop-up menus (also known as shortcut menus) are used to associate a hidden menu with a particular component on the screen. To activate a pop-up menu, the user performs a right-click on the mouse. The pop-up menu is then displayed at the cursor position where the mouse was when the right-click occurred. The cursor position is defined down to the pixel level.
   To activate a pop-up menu, a few steps are required:

1. Detect a right mouse button release with an **isPopupTrigger()** method.
2. Retrieve the window component with a **getComponent()** method.
3. Display the pop-up menu with a **show()** method.

The steps in this section will show you how to implement a pop-up menu. The menu items created in this example do nothing. They're used only to show what the menu items would look like on a real pop-up menu.
   Add a JMenu as shown in the lower-right corner of Figure 16.33.

➤   Click the **JPopupMenu** bean ▣, and drop it on the nonvisual free-form surface. This bean is located near the end of the Swing category list.
➤   Double-click JPopupMenu1. Change the **beanName** from **JPopupMenu1** to **mnMyPopUpMenu**.

➤   Change the **label** to <u>**My Popup Menu**</u>.
➤   Close the **Properties** sheet.

Figure 16.33
Popup Menu

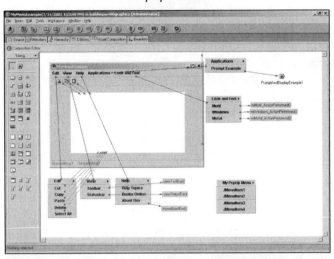

Add the four JMenuItems shown in the figure.

➤   Click the **JMenuItem** bean, and drop it on the **My Popup Menu** JMenu.
➤   Create three more JMenuItems on the **My Popup Menu** JMenu.
➤   Don't change any of the properties.

Add the JSeparator shown in the figure.

➤   Click the **JSeparator** bean, and drop it on the **My Popup Menu** JMenu, dividing the JMenuItems as shown.
➤   Don't change any of the properties.

  Save your Java program.

➤   On the menu bar, click **Bean**.
➤   Click **Save Bean**.

Event-to-Code Connection: mouseReleased()

```
connEtoC7: (JTextArea1,mouseReleased →
           MyMenuExample,void jTextArea1_MouseReleased(java.awt.event.MouseEvent,
           javax.swing.JPopupMenu pop))
```

This connection will determine whether the right mouse button has been pressed (implying that the pop-up menu should be displayed). It will also determine whether, if the right mouse button was pressed, the mouse cursor was within the JTextArea boundaries. Create an event-to-code connection with the JTextArea and a **mouseReleased()** method.

➤   Right-click JTextArea1.
➤   Click **Connect**.
➤   Click **Connectible Features**.
➤   Click the **mouseReleased()** method.
➤   Click the spider-end pointer on the nonvisual free-form surface.

➢   Click **Event to Code**.
➢   *Replace* the code displayed with the Java code shown in Figure 16.34. When you've finished typing the new Java code, your method should look similar to Figure 16.35.

Figure 16.34
Source Code for MouseReleased() Method

```
Source code: connEtoC7
    public void jTextArea1_MouseReleased(java.awt.event.MouseEvent mouseEvent,
                                         javax.swing.JPopupMenu pop) {
        if ((mouseEvent.isPopupTrigger()))
            ivjmnMyPopUpMenu.show(mouseEvent.getComponent(),
                                           mouseEvent.getX(),
                                           mouseEvent.getY());
        return;
    }
```

Figure 16.35
Connection connEtoC7

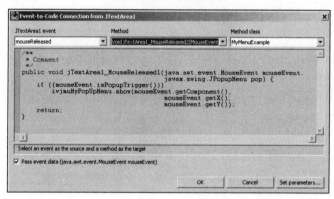

Notice that you have an additional parameter defined in the method as **javax.swing.JPopupMenu pop**. This is the mnMyPopUpMenu being passed as a parameter to the **mouseReleased()** method. Also notice the conditional statement that tests the mouse for a right-click:

```
if ((mouseEvent.isPopupTrigger()))
```

If this condition is true, the second step is executed to determine the component where the mouse was clicked.

➢   Click **OK**.

Note that you now have an incomplete connection on the screen.

Parameter-from-Property Connection

```
connPfromP1: (connEtoC7: (JTextArea1,mouseReleased → MyMenuExample,void
              jTextArea1_MouseReleased(java.awt.event.MouseEvent,javax.swing.JPopupMenu)),arg2 →
              MnMyPopUpMenu,this)
```

Complete the connection by passing the parameter into the primary connection. The connection is expecting to receive a **JPopupMenu** type.

Identify the source property:

➢   Right-click the dashed line.
➢   Click **Connect**.
➢   Click **pop**.

Identify the target property:

➢   Click the spider-end pointer on the **mnMyPopUpMenu** JPopupMenu bean.
➢   Click **this**.

Figure 16.36 shows what the connection should look like.

Figure 16.36
MouseReleased Connection: connPfromP1

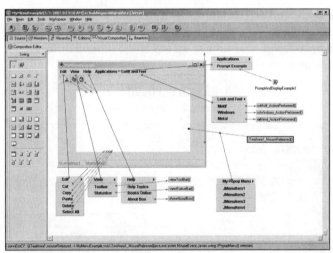

Submenus

Now, you'll add another menu (a submenu) to the **My Popup Menu** JPopupMenu. This exercise will show you how to add secondary menus to a primary menu.

Add another JMenu as shown in Figure 16.37.

➢   Click the **JMenu** bean, and drop it on top of the **My Popup Menu** JPopupMenu.
➢   Don't change any of the properties.

Figure 16.37
JMenu1 Menu

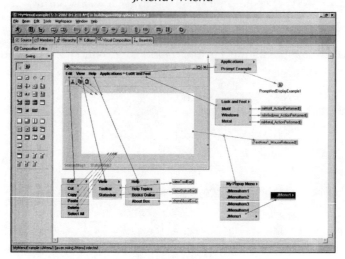

Add two JMenuItems as shown in Figure 16.38.

➢   Click the **JMenuItem** bean, and drop it on top of the **JMenu1** JMenu that you created in the previous step.
➢   Don't change any of the properties.
➢   Click the **JMenuItem** bean again, and drop it on top of the **JMenu1** JMenu.
➢   Don't change any of the properties.

Figure 16.38
JMenu1 Menu Items

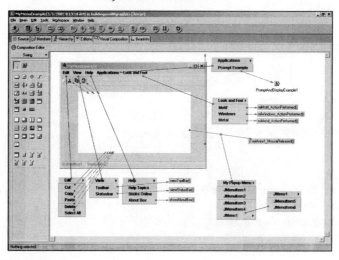

Save and then run your Java program.

➢   On the menu bar, click **Bean**.
➢   Click **Save Bean**.
➢   On the menu bar, click **Bean**.
➢   Click **Run**, and then click **Run Main**.

➤   With the cursor inside the JTextArea, right-click. (If you try right-clicking outside the JTextArea, even if you're off by just one pixel, the pop-up menu won't work.)

The pop-up menu will be displayed.

➤   Click **JMenu1**.

The secondary menu **JMenu1** should appear, as shown in Figure 16.39.

Figure 16.39
Pop-up Menu and Submenu

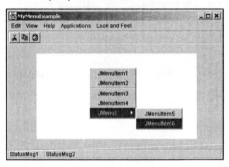

About Box

In most commercially developed software, an *about box* is usually present that typically identifies the software release level, copyright information, and other information related to the software. When you first created your menu application using the **Create Application** SmartGuide, you selected the **About dialog** check box. When you did that, the SmartGuide created a separate class called **MyMenuExampleAboutBox**. If you were to look at the classes in the **MyGraphicalApplications** package, you would see class **MyMenuExampleAboutBox** contained there.

     To display the about box in your application:

➤   Click **Help** on the application menu bar.
➤   Click **About Box**.

Figure 16.40 shows what the about box looks like. It's a dialog box. You can't do anything further until you click **OK**.

Figure 16.40
About Box

➤   Click **OK**.
➤   Close the **MyMenuExample** application.
➤   Close the VCE.

Back at the workbench, you should see three classes associated with MyMenuExample.

➤   At the workbench, double-click class **MyMenuExampleAboutBox**.

Once inside the VCE, experiment with some of the components on the about box. As you can see, creating and/or changing an about box is easy.

➤   Close the VCE.

Splash Screen

Along with the about box, most commercially developed software features a *splash screen* that appears as the application first starts. When you created the menu application with the **Create Application** SmartGuide, you selected the **Splash screen** check box. When you did that, the SmartGuide created a separate class called **MyMenuExampleSplashScreen**.

➤   At the workbench, double-click class **MyMenuExampleSplashScreen**.

Once inside the VCE, your screen should appear similar to Figure 16.41. There's not much code associated with this class.

Figure 16.41
Splash Screen

➤   Double-click the picture of the cow.
➤   Click the **Details** button 🔲 for the **icon** property.

Figure 16.42 shows the **Icon** window, which names the directory where the graphic of the cow is located. Using this window, you could easily change from the cow to any other graphic you'd like to use.

Figure 16.42
Splash Screen Graphic

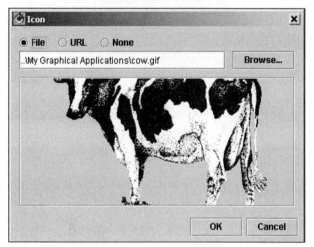

➢   Close the VCE.

Summary

In this chapter you learned

- how to build a menu with menu items
- what it takes to change the look and feel of a Java program
- the use of the standard **Edit** functions
- how to use toolbars
- how to produce pop-up menus
- how about boxes and splash screens work

The next chapter is a fairly short one that will introduce you to the **JTable**, **JTableColumn**, and **ListManager** JavaBeans — three beans that let you emulate the function of AS/400 subfiles. As you'll see, this is really easy and fun stuff.

Chapter 17

Building Simple Java Subfile Equivalents

Chapter Objectives

❑ Understand how to build a subfile equivalent using a **JTable** bean
❑ Understand the components that make up a JTable
❑ Become familiar with the AS/400 Toolbox **ListManager** bean
❑ Learn how to use the horizontal scroll bar

Chapter Project

❑ A class will be created to list all records from an AS/400 database in a list format, similar to a load-all subfile.
❑ Figure 17.1 shows what the sample class will look like.

Figure 17.1
Chapter Project

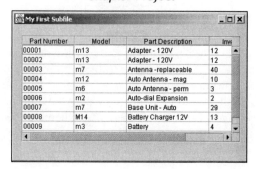

Compared with the past couple of chapters, this chapter is a short one. It walks you through the steps required to build a powerful subfile equivalent. On the AS/400, subfiles can be one of the more complex topics. In this chapter, you'll be surprised at how easy it is to set up a Java subfile equivalent, the JTable. In later chapters, you'll learn more about JTables.

If you're not familiar with AS/400 subfiles, don't worry. You needn't be a subfile expert to code this chapter's project. A few subfile terms are simply mentioned throughout the chapter to make the concepts easier to understand.

JTable and JFormattedTable

The Swing **JTable** JavaBean is the closest equivalent to implementing an AS/400 subfile. The chapter project window in Figure 17.1 shows an example of a JTable. It's nothing more than a list of records presented in a two-dimensional table format. The rows are the database records, and the columns are the individual fields within the record.

In Chapter 5, you learned how to use the Enterprise Toolkit for AS/400 **JFormattedTextField** bean. As you may recall, this bean is similar to the Swing **JTextField** bean but provides additional AS/400-related editing and formatting capabilities. Similarly, the Enterprise Toolkit for AS/400 **JFormattedTable** bean is much like the Swing **JTable** bean, but with some major differences. The **JFormattedTable** bean supports AS/400 edit codes, edit words, formatting, and verification of data capabilities. It also has auto record advance, data types, data length, and decimal point specification. Whenever the **JTable** bean is mentioned in this chapter, the same concepts apply to the **JFormattedTable** bean.

In an AS/400 subfile, you have two important record format types: SFL and SFLCTL. The SFL type contains the subfile records. The SFLCTL type controls functions related to the subfile records. A JTable is very similar. It has two components: the ScrollPaneTable and the JScrollPane. The ScrollPaneTable is similar to the AS/400 SFL type; it's where automatic scrolling of the data occurs. The JScrollPane is similar to the AS/400 SFLCTL type. Internally, a JScrollPane is made up of nine components: a viewport, two scroll bars, a row header, a column header, and four corner components. Normally, you don't need to worry about the details of these nine components.

List Manager

In Chapter 15, you learned about the **FormManager** and **RecordIOManager** beans. The FormManager works with one record at a time. Like the FormManager, the **ListManager** bean, which you'll use in this chapter, lets you work with multiple records at once. Using the **ListManager** bean, you can employ a number of methods to access the entire database file or a specified number of records. These operations are similar to the AS/400 subfile concepts of a load-all subfile versus a load-a-page-at-a-time subfile. This chapter covers the simple equivalent of a load-all subfile.

The ListManager works with components that allow the handling of multiple records at a time, including JTable, JFormattedTable, JComboBox, and JList. Just as the FormManager lets you map AS/400 database fields to the various components named by the database fields, so too does the ListManager. You'll typically use the **TableColumn** bean to map the AS/400 database fields. If you don't use a TableColumn, VisualAge for Java selects and displays all fields that are specified in the RecordIOManager.

When you use the **ListManager** bean, you must define a displayContainer to specify the scope of JComponents associated with the database. Typically, you'll use the JTable's JScrollPane to define the displayContainer. To select records in the ListManager, you must specify a **recordIOManager** property.

Subfile Example

In this chapter project, you'll be using a product details physical file from the AS/400. It will be file PRODDTL in library ADTSLAB. You used this file in Chapter 15.

You're going to create another class, called **SubfileExample**, that inherits properties from superclass **JFrame**. You'll store the class in the project **My Graphical Applications** and in the package **buildingas400graphics**.

➢　If the workbench isn't started, start it now.

➢　Expand the project **My Graphical Applications** with a click.

➢　Select the package **buildingas400graphics** with a click. Right-click to display the shortcut menu, select **Add**, and then select **Class**.

➢　Make sure the **Project** name is **My Graphical Applications**.

➢　Make sure the **Package** name is **buildingas400graphics**.

➤ In the **Class name** field, type **SubfileExample**.
➤ Click **Browse** to select a superclass.
➤ When the **Superclass** window appears, type **JFrame** in the **Pattern** field.
➤ In the **Type names** list, double-click **JFrame**. When you return to the SmartGuide, the **Superclass** field should contain **javax.swing.JFrame**, as shown in Figure 17.2.
➤ Select the **Browse the class when finished** check box.
➤ Select the **Compose the class visually** check box.
➤ Click **Finish** to complete the creation of the class.

Figure 17.2
SubfileExample Class

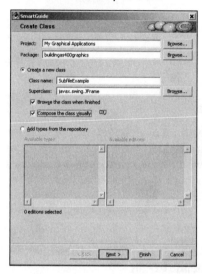

You should be inside the Visual Composition Editor. Change the title of the JFrame.

➤ On the menu bar, click **Tools**.
➤ Click **Beans List**.
➤ Double-click the **SubfileExample** JFrame to display the **Properties** sheet.
➤ For the **title** property, type **My First Subfile**.
➤ Close the **Properties** sheet.
➤ Close the **Beans List**.

Next, create a JTable as shown in Figure 17.3.

➤ In the **Swing** bean category, click and drop a **JTable** bean on the center of the free-form surface visual area.
➤ Resize the JTable so that it appears similar to the figure.

Tips and Tricks

Be careful when resizing or moving a JTable. A JTable is made up of a JScrollPane (outer area) and a ScrollPaneTable (inner area). To move or resize, be sure to select the JScrollPane. If you accidentally select the ScrollPaneTable instead, you can really impact (negatively) the use of your table. Tip: If you make a mistake, you can always use the *Edit* menu's *Undo* option.

Figure 17.3
JTable Outline

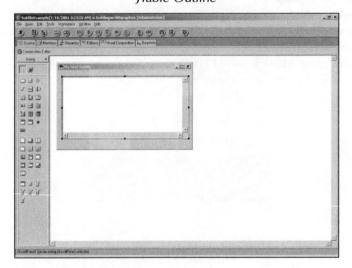

Because of the intricacies involved with managing and manipulating the different layers of components, it's helpful to have the beans list open when working with JTables or JFormattedTables. It's sometimes desirable to work with the beans list when working with JTables. It makes it easier to select the right component. You may want to leave your beans list open throughout this chapter project. You're going to open the beans list now to see the components that make up the JTable.

➢   On the menu bar, click **Tools**.
➢   Click **Beans List**.
➢   Click the plus sign (+) to expand the **JFrameContentPane** bean.
➢   Click the + to expand the **JScrollPane1** bean.

Figure 17.4 shows the beans list with the expanded JTable. The JScrollPane and the ScrollPaneTable are two components that together make up the **JTable** bean.

Figure 17.4
Beans List

Now, add the **AS400** bean.

➢ In the **AS/400 Toolbox** bean category, click the **AS400** bean ▣, and drop it on the nonvisual free-form surface as shown in Figure 17.5.
➢ Double-click the **AS4001** bean.
➢ For ease of use later on, fill in the **systemName** and **userID** properties.
➢ Close the **Properties** sheet.

Figure 17.5
ListManager and AS400 Beans

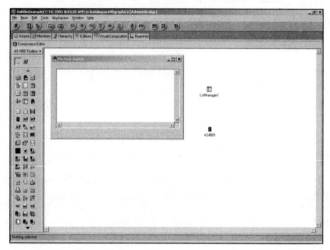

Next, add a **ListManager** bean. This bean is the eleventh bean in the **AS/400 Toolbox** bean category. This **ListManager** bean will use the same **recordIOManager** property you used in Chapter 15.

➢ Click the **ListManager** bean ▣, and drop it on the nonvisual free-form surface as shown in the figure.
➢ Double-click the **ListManager1** bean.
➢ Click the **recordIOManager** property's **Details** button ▣.
➢ In the **Generate Record IO Manager Data Class** list, select class **Buildingas400graphics.RIOProduct DetailPRODDTL** as shown in Figure 17.6.
➢ Click **OK**.
➢ Wait until the compilation of the **recordIOManager** bean is completed. You'll know this has occurred when the class name is completely filled in for the **recordIOManager** property.
➢ Close the **Properties** sheet.

Figure 17.6
RIOProductDetailPRODDTL Class

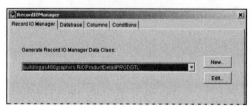

Save the Java program.

➢ On the menu bar, click **Bean**.
➢ Click **Save Bean**.

Connecting the AS/400 Beans

You are now going to set up two property-to-property connections and two event-to-method connections to connect the AS/400 beans.

Property-to-Property Connection: system

`connPtoP1: (AS4001,this ←→ ListManager1,system)`

Connect the **AS4001** bean with the **ListManager1** bean.

> ➢ Right-click the **AS4001** bean.
> ➢ Click **Connect**.
> ➢ Click **this**.
> ➢ Click the spider-end pointer on the **ListManager1** bean.
> ➢ Click **Connectible Features**.
> ➢ Double-click the **system** property.

Property-to-Property Connection: displayContainer

`connPtoP2: (JScrollPane1,this ←→ ListManager1,displayContainer)`

Connect the JScrollPane with the **displayContainer** property of the **ListManager1** bean. (Recall that a displayContainer determines the scope or boundary of the database field mapping.)

> ➢ Select the **JScrollPane1** bean by clicking the outside edge of the JTable.
> ➢ Click **Connect**.
> ➢ Click **this**.
> ➢ Click the spider-end pointer on the **ListManager1** bean.
> ➢ Click **displayContainer**.

Your connection should appear as shown in Figure 17.7.

Figure 17.7

displayContainer Connection: connPtoP2

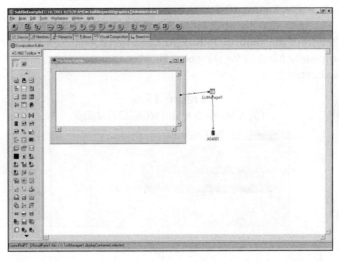

Tips and Tricks

When designing screen flow, you may want to present the user with an AS/400 prompt screen before the application screen appears. To accomplish this, simply specify an *initialize()* event associated with an AS/400 method. The next connection shows you how to do this.

Event-to-Method Connection: readAllRecords()

connEtoM1: (SubfileExample,initialize → ListManager1,readAllRecords())

This connection reads all records within the AS/400 database file, similar to a subfile load-all routine. The only drawback to the load-all approach is that if the file is very large, loading all of it can take some time. Chapter 19 discusses this consideration further.

This connection will force the AS/400 sign-on screen to appear before the application screen appears, due to the connection to the **initialize()** method. The **readAllRecords()** method will be executed before the application is first displayed. This, in essence, will show a full JTable (subfile) when the application first appears.

Create an event-to-method connection with the **SubfileExample** JFrame and the **readAllRecords()** method.

➤ Right-click the outside edge of the **SubfileExample** JFrame.
➤ Click **Connect**.
➤ Click **Connectible Features**.
➤ Click the **initialize()** event.
➤ Click **OK**.
➤ Click the spider-end pointer on the **ListManager1** bean.
➤ Click **Connectible Features**.
➤ Click the **readAllRecords()** method.
➤ Click **OK**.

Your connection should appear as shown in Figure 17.8.

➤ Double-click the connection to verify that it is correct as shown in Figure 17.9.
➤ Close the **Properties** window.

Figure 17.8	**Figure 17.9**
ReadAllRecords() Connection: connEtoM1	*Connection connEtoM1*

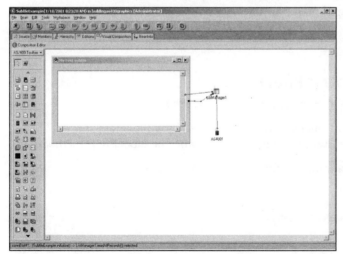

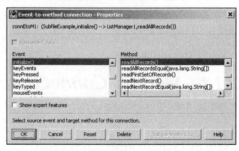

Save the Java program.

➢ On the menu bar, click **Bean**.
➢ Click **Save Bean**.

To run this Java program, you need to successfully connect to the AS/400. Run the program.

➢ On the menu bar, click **Bean**.
➢ Click **Run**, and then click **Run Main**.

You should be looking at the application as shown in Figure 17.10. Notice that all the database fields defined in your **RecordIOManager** bean are displayed.

Figure 17.10
My First Subfile

Wasn't that easy? Not bad for writing absolutely no lines of code. There are a few things to notice. Look at each of the columns, or database fields. See how they're all scrunched together? Even though there are more columns that you can't fully see, there's no horizontal scroll bar.

➢ With your mouse, drag the vertical scroll bar downward.

Does it work? Yes, it does (although there aren't many records in this file, so your scrolling activity won't be too impressive).

➢ Click one of the records (rows) in the PARTPIC column.

Notice that you have to move your cursor over to the end of the field to see all the data contained in this particular row-column intersection. That's okay. Your new application has a few shortcomings. You'll fix these in the sections to follow.

➢ Close the application.

Event-to-Method Connection: closeFile()

connEtoM2: (SubfileExample,windowClosed → ListManager1,closeFile())

When the application window closes, this connection will close the AS/400 database file.
    Create an event-to-method connection with the **SubfileExample** JFrame and the **closeFile()** method.

➢ Right-click the outside edge of the **SubfileExample** JFrame.
➢ Click **Connect**.
➢ Click **windowClosed**.
➢ Click the spider-end pointer on the **ListManager1** bean.
➢ Click **Connectible Features**.

➤ Click the **closeFile()** method.
➤ Click **OK**.

Your connection should appear as shown in Figure 17.11.

➤ Double-click the connection to verify that it is correct as shown in Figure 17.12.
➤ Close the **Properties** window.

Figure 17.11
closeFile() Connection: connEtoM2

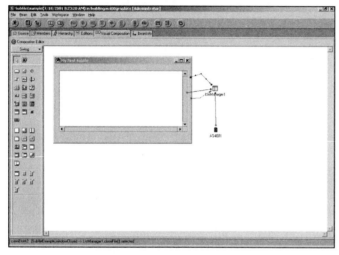

Figure 7.12
Connection connEtoM2

If you don't have the beans list open, do the following:

➤ On the menu bar, click **Tools**.
➤ Click **Beans List**.

You're going to look at the properties of the **JScrollPane1** bean now.

➤ In the **Beans List**, double-click the **JScrollPane1** bean.
➤ When the **Properties** sheet (Figure 17.13) appears, look at the **preferredSize** property.

Figure 17.13
JScrollPane1 Properties

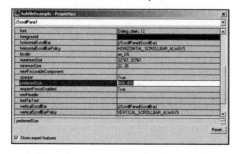

Notice that the **preferredSize** value of JScrollPane1 is 468, 418. (Your number may differ slightly based on your screen size and settings.) This value signifies a size of 468 pixels (x-coordinates) across by 418 pixels (y-coordinates) high.

➢ In the **Beans List**, double-click the **ScrollPaneTable** bean.
➢ Write down the **preferredSize** setting of the ScrollPaneTable. Figure 17.14 shows a **preferredSize** setting of 385, 171. You'll use this value later in the chapter.

Figure 17.14
ScrollPaneTable Properties

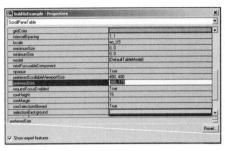

Table Columns

A **TableColumn** bean represents all the attributes associated with a column (field) in a JTable. These attributes include width, resize options, minimum and maximum widths, and renderers and editors that can be used to edit the value of the data in a column. The TableColumn is also where you define the header information of the data as well as the database mapping of the database field.

You can reposition or switch each TableColumn in the VCE. You can also do this at run time. To move a TableColumn, you simply click on the column and drag it to where you'd like it to be. You can't resize a table column with the mouse; you have to change the column's **width** and **minWidth** properties by specifying the pixel size.

Create a TableColumn as shown in Figure 17.15.

➢ In the **Swing** bean category, click the **TableColumn** bean ▦, and drop it on the left side of the JTable.

Figure 17.15
TableColumn

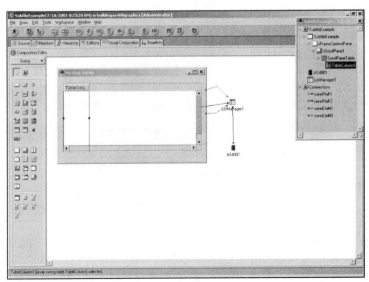

Look at the beans list shown in the figure. VisualAge for Java placed the **TableColumn1** bean under the **ScrollPaneTable** bean.

➢ In the **Beans List**, double-click the **TableColumn1** bean to display its **Properties** sheet.
➢ Change the **headerValue** property to **Part Number**. This text will appear as the column heading on the TableColumn.
➢ Change the **identifier** property to **{"partno"}**. It doesn't matter whether you use upper or lower case, but be sure to include the double quotation marks (") around the database field name.

The **Properties** sheet in Figure 17.16 shows what these properties should look like.

➢ Close the **Properties** sheet.

When you close the **Properties** sheet, the column header value doesn't automatically change. You have to click another component before this occurs. Create four more **TableColumn** beans.

➢ In the **Swing** bean category, click four more **TableColumn** beans, and drop them on the JTable as shown in Figure 17.17.
➢ Change the **headerValue** property to **Model**, **Part Description**, **Inventory**, and **Picture Location**, respectively.
➢ Change the **identifier** property to **{"model"}**, **{"partd"}**, **{"inventory"}**, and **{"partpic"}**, respectively. Be sure to include the double quotation marks around each database field name.
➢ Close the **Properties** sheet.

Figure 17.16
TableColumn1 Properties

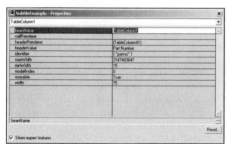

Figure 17.17
TableColumns

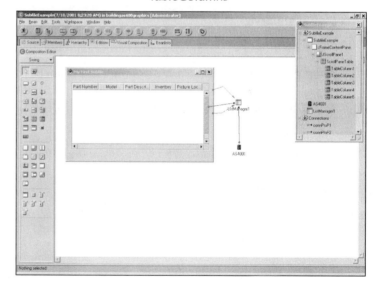

Save and then run your Java program.

➢ On the menu bar, click **Bean**.
➢ Click **Save Bean**.
➢ On the menu bar, click **Bean**.
➢ Click **Run**, and then click **Run Main**.

You should be looking at the application as shown in Figure 17.18.

Figure 17.18
My First Subfile

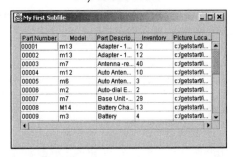

Did you notice that not all the database fields defined in the RecordIOManager are displayed? The shipped date is missing. That's because you used a **TableColumn** bean. As soon as you use one **TableColumn** bean, the layout of the columns (database fields) switches from the RecordIOManager to the definition of the **TableColumn** beans.

Look at Figure 17.18. Notice that all the columns are the same width, even though the data contained in each column is larger or smaller than the column width. In the next section, you'll learn how to specify a fixed length for each column, which, by default, activates the horizontal scroll bar.

➢   Close the application.

Tips and Tricks
To activate the horizontal scroll bar, the *autoResizeMode* property on the ScrollPaneTable must be set to *AUTO_RESIZE_OFF*.

Set up the ScrollPaneTable to allow the horizontal scroll bar to appear.

➢   In the **Beans List**, double-click the **ScrollPaneTable** bean.
➢   Change the **autoResizeMode** property to **AUTO_RESIZE_OFF** by clicking the **Details** button and selecting **AUTO_RESIZE_OFF**, as shown in Figure 17.19.

Specify a fixed length for each column in the JTable.

➢   In the **Beans List**, double-click the **TableColumn1** (or **Part Number**) bean.
➢   Change the **minWidth** property to **60**.
➢   Change the **width** property to **60**.

Figure 17.20 shows the new properties of TableColumn1.

Figure 17.19	Figure 17.20
ScrollPaneTable Properties	TableColumn1 Properties

> ➢ In the **Beans List**, double-click the **TableColumn2** (or **Model**) bean.
> ➢ Change the **minWidth** property to **60**.
> ➢ Change the **width** property to **60**.
> ➢ In the **Beans List**, double-click the **TableColumn3** (or **Part Description**) bean.
> ➢ Change the **minWidth** property to **150**.
> ➢ Change the **width** property to **150**.
> ➢ In the **Beans List**, double-click the **TableColumn4** (or **Inventory**) bean.
> ➢ Change the **minWidth** property to **60**.
> ➢ Change the **width** property to **60**.
> ➢ In the **Beans List**, double-click the **TableColumn5** (or **Picture**) bean.
> ➢ Change the **minWidth** property to **150**.
> ➢ Change the **width** property to **150**.
> ➢ Close the **Properties** sheets.

If you add up all the fixed-length fields (60 + 60 + 150 + 60 + 150), the total is 480. For the horizontal scroll bar to work correctly, the **preferredSize** property of the ScrollPaneTable must be set to a *minimum* of 480 for the x-coordinate.

Change the ScrollPaneTable x-coordinate.

> ➢ In the **Beans List**, double-click the **ScrollPaneTable** bean.
> ➢ Earlier, you wrote down your ScrollPaneTable **preferredSize** setting. Change the **preferredSize** property from the original setting (the book example was 385, 171) to **480, 171** as shown in Figure 17.21.
> ➢ Close the **Properties** sheet.

Save and then run your Java program.

> ➢ On the menu bar, click **Bean**.
> ➢ Click **Save Bean**.
> ➢ On the menu bar, click **Bean**.
> ➢ Click **Run**, and then click **Run Main**.

Figure 17.22 shows the new column sizes. Notice the horizontal scroll bar. You can experiment with the scroll bars and see how you like them.

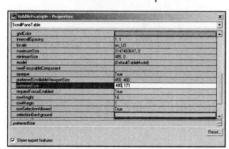

Figure 17.21
ScrollPaneTable Properties

Figure 17.22
My First Subfile

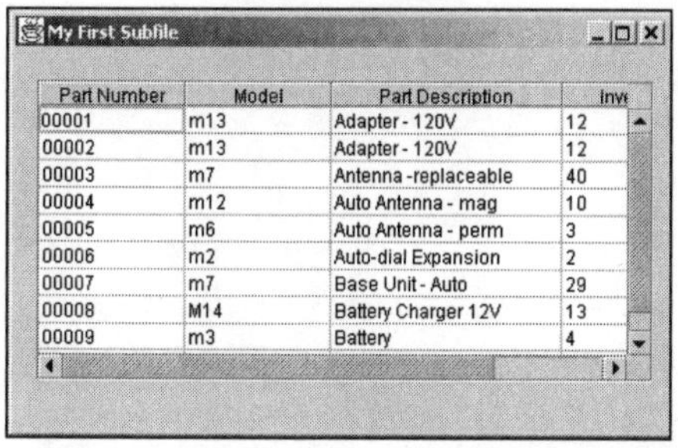

With that, you've created a JTable, or subfile equivalent. You have to admit this was pretty easy to accomplish. In Chapters 19 and 20, you'll learn more about JTables.

Summary

In this chapter you learned

- how to create a JTable
- how to select the various components that make up a JTable
- how to use a **ListManager** bean
- how to manipulate the horizontal scroll bar

Take a break before you start the next chapter. It's the longest one in the book. The chapter project will show you how to implement a database maintenance program. You'll learn some neat features that will come in handy as you begin development in VisualAge for Java.

Chapter 18

Building Java GUI Database Maintenance Applications

 ## Chapter Objectives

- ☐ Understand add, update, and delete record-level access concepts
- ☐ Learn how to customize JButtons
- ☐ Learn how to print from Java
- ☐ Become proficient at edit checks and error handling
- ☐ Understand dialog boxes

 ## Chapter Project

- ☐ A class will be created to maintain a database file on the AS/400 with edit checking and error handling.
- ☐ This class will let you navigate records using graphical buttons and let you clear, add, change, delete, and print database records.
- ☐ Figure 18.1 shows what the sample class will look like.

Figure 18.1
Chapter Project

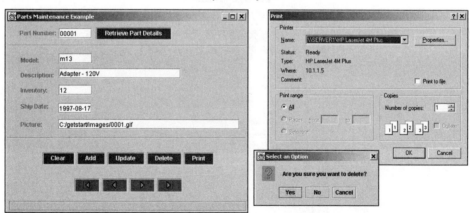

Take a break for a few minutes before you begin this chapter. It's the longest one in the book. There's some great information here. You'll get a complete, step-by-step guide to building a full-blown database maintenance program. You'll notice many similarities between the chapter project in this chapter and that in Chapter 15. But even though some of the steps are the same as in Chapter 15, you'll see that there are many subtle differences. I promise the next chapter will be much shorter.

Maintenance Example

You could easily write a Java database maintenance program using a few simple methods such as **addRecord()**, **updateRecord()**, and **deleteRecord()**. As you probably already know, edit checking and error handling can be 90 percent of the code in a maintenance program. This chapter project walks you through a couple of approaches to these tasks.

Another topic we'll tackle here is printing. There aren't too many in-depth discussions about printing from Java. Printing is probably one of Java's weaker points. In this chapter, you'll learn some simple ways to perform the equivalent of a Windows Print Screen function and how to call the standard Windows Print API.

As in previous chapters, you'll be using the product details physical file from the AS/400, file PRODDTL in library ADTSLAB. Your first step is to create another class, called **PartsMaintenanceExample**, that inherits properties from superclass JFrame. You'll store this class in the project **My Graphical Applications** and in the package **buildingas400graphics**.

➢ If the workbench isn't started, start it now.
➢ Expand the project **My Graphical Applications** with a click.
➢ Select the package **buildingas400graphics** with a click. Right-click to display the shortcut menu, select **Add**, and then select **Class**.
➢ Make sure the **Project** name is **My Graphical Applications**.
➢ Make sure the **Package** name is **buildingas400graphics**.
➢ In the **Class name** field, type **PartsMaintenanceExample**.
➢ Click **Browse** to select a superclass.
➢ When the **Superclass** window appears, type **JFrame** in the **Pattern** field.
➢ In the **Type names** list, double-click **JFrame**. When you return to the SmartGuide, the **Superclass** field should contain **javax.swing.JFrame**, as shown in Figure 18.2.
➢ Select the **Browse the class when finished** check box.
➢ Select the **Compose the class visually** check box.
➢ Click **Finish** to complete the creation of the class.

Figure 18.2
PartsMaintenanceExample Class

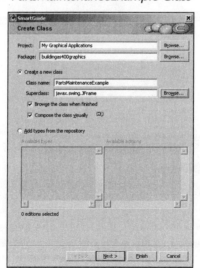

You should be inside the Visual Composition Editor. Change the title of the JFrame.

➢ On the menu bar, click **Tools**.
➢ Click **Beans List**.
➢ Double-click the **PartsMaintenanceExample** JFrame to display the **Properties** sheet.
➢ For the **title** property, type **Parts Maintenance Example**.
➢ Close the **Properties** sheet.
➢ Close the **Beans List**.
➢ Expand the height and width of your free-form surface by dragging a corner downward and to the right.

Now, create two JPanels as shown in Figure 18.3.

➢ Click the **JPanel** bean ▢, and drop it on the lower portion of the visual area of the free-form surface. This will be the upper JPanel.
➢ Resize JPanel1 to match the figure.
➢ Double-click the JPanel to display the **Properties** sheet.
➢ Change the **layout** property to **FlowLayout**.
➢ Close the **Properties** sheet.
➢ Click the **JPanel** bean again, and drop it below the other JPanel on the visual area.
➢ Resize this JPanel to match the figure.
➢ Double-click JPanel2 to display the **Properties** sheet.
➢ Change the **layout** property to **FlowLayout**.
➢ Close the **Properties** sheet.

Figure 18.3
JPanel Layout

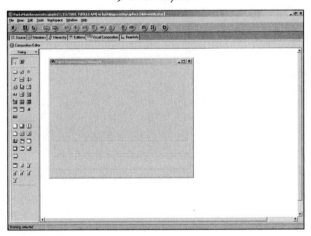

Customized JButtons, Icons, and Animation

Rarely does an AS/400 programmer ever think about using animation or customizing a button on the screen to use a graphical image as opposed to a standard button look. If you've ever seen any of Sun Microsystems' demo programs, you've probably noticed the *duke* figurines. Figure 18.4 shows what these images look like.

Figure 18.4
Duke Animation Characters

It's easy to simulate animation simply by swapping different graphical images such as these back and forth. For example, you could change the image of a button from a *sleeping duke* image to a *waving hand duke* image. You could program this change to occur whenever the user moves the mouse over the button. You could also change the image when the user holds down the mouse button. In today's programming environment, there are plenty of off-the-shelf graphical images you can buy. If you have in-house designers, they can probably create some great images for your applications.

In this section, you're going to learn how to use graphical images in your application. In Chapter 15, you created JButtons titled **First**, **Previous**, **Next**, and **Last**. Here, you'll learn how to change those navigational buttons to appear more graphical instead of being text oriented.

You'll have to do a little setup work to be able to retrieve the correct graphical images. You need to copy four graphical icons (.gif files) using Windows Explorer, the DOS command line, or whatever method you choose. The four file names are FirstIcon.gif, PreviousIcon.gif, NextIcon.gif, and LastIcon.gif. The source directory is

```
C:\Program Files\IBM\VisualAge for Java\IDE\tools\com-ibm-ivj-et400\com\ibm\as400\vaccess
```

The target directory is

```
C:\Program Files\IBM\VisualAge for Java\IDE\Project_Resources\My Graphical Applications
```

➢   Copy the four .gif files from the source directory to the target directory. Use your preferred method of copying.

> **Note:** *If for some reason, you can't find or copy the above .gif files, you can copy any .gif file available on your system.*

Now, add four buttons to the lower JPanel as shown in Figure 18.5. These buttons will be the navigational icons used to maneuver through the database.

➢   Click and drop four **JButton** beans 🔲 on the lower JPanel, JPanel2. It doesn't matter where on the JPanel you drop them because the FlowLayout Layout Manager will position them automatically.

➢   Double-click each JButton to display the **Properties** sheet. Change the **beanName** property to **btFirst**, **btPrevious**, **btNext**, and **btLast**, respectively.

➢   Change the **text** property by blanking out all the text contained there. Do this for all four JButtons.

➢   Change the **background** property to **DarkGray** on all four JButtons. To do so, click the **background** property's **Details** button 🔲. Then select the **Basic** option, and click the **DarkGray** color. Click **OK**.

Figure 18.5
JButtons

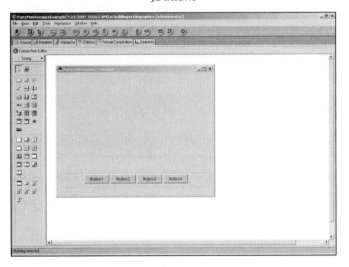

➤ On the first JButton, change the **icon** property. To do so, click the **icon** property's **Details** button, select the **Icon** window's **File** option, and click **Browse** to select a graphics file. Then, as shown in Figure 18.6, double-click file **FirstIcon**. Figure 18.7 shows the **Icon** window as it appears once you've made this selection.

➤ Click **OK**.

➤ Make a similar same change for the other three JButtons, selecting file **PreviousIcon**, **NextIcon**, and **LastIcon**, respectively.

Figure 18.6
Available Icons

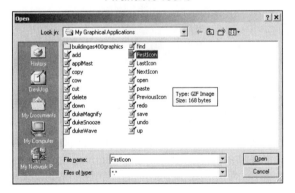

Figure 18.7
Selected Icon

Next, specify the hover text that will appear when the user moves the mouse over the navigational tools.

➢ Change the **toolTipText** property to **First Record**, **Previous Record**, **Next Record**, and **Last Record**, respectively.

➢ Close the **Properties** sheets.

Your newly customized JButtons should look similar to Figure 18.8.

Figure 18.8
Customized Navigational JButtons

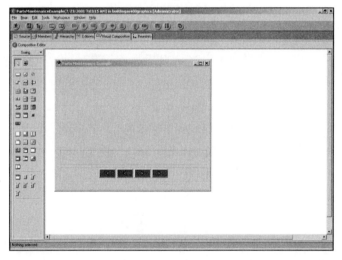

Next, add five buttons to the upper JPanel. These buttons will be used as the operational buttons to perform the database functions of clear, add, update, delete, and print. Figure 18.9 shows what the buttons will look like when you've completed the following steps.

➢ Click and drop five **JButton** beans on the upper JPanel (JPanel1). It doesn't matter where you drop them because the FlowLayout manager will position them automatically.

➢ Double-click each JButton to display the **Properties** sheet. Change the **beanName** property to **btClear**, **btAdd**, **btUpdate**, **btDelete**, and **btPrint**, respectively.

➢ Change the **text** property to **Clear**, **Add**, **Update**, **Delete**, and **Print**, respectively.

➢ Change the **background** property to **Blue** on all five JButtons. To do so, click the **background** property's **Details** button, select **Basic**, and click the **Blue** color. Then click **OK**.

➢ Change the **foreground** property to **White** on all five JButtons. To do so, click the **foreground** property's
   Details button, select **Basic**, and click the **White** color. Then click **OK**.
➢ Close the **Properties** sheets.

Figure 18.9
Customized Operational JButtons

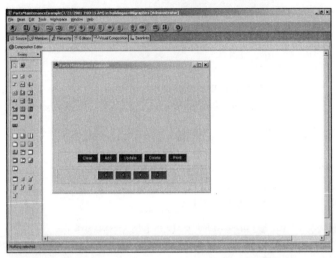

Now, at the top of the screen, add a button to retrieve the parts details. Figure 18.10 shows what this button
will look like when you've completed the following steps.

➢ Click and drop a **JButton** bean on the upper portion of the visual area.
➢ Double-click the JButton to display the **Properties** sheet.
➢ Change the **beanName** property to **btRetrieve**.
➢ Change the **text** property to **Retrieve Part Details**.
➢ Change the **background** property to **Blue**.
➢ Change the **foreground** property to **White**.
➢ Close the **Properties** sheet.
➢ Expand the button so that you can see all the text.

Figure 18.10
Customized Retrieve JButton

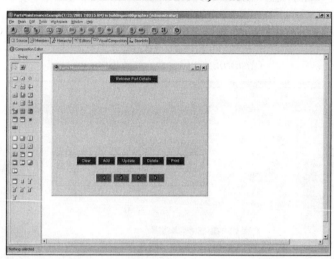

Next, create the six JLabels shown in Figure 18.11.

➤ Click and drop six **JLabel** beans on the left side of the visual area.
➤ Double-click each JLabel, and change the **text** property to **Part Number:**, **Model:**, **Description:**, **Inventory:**, **Ship Date:**, and **Picture:**, respectively.
➤ Close the **Properties** sheets.
➤ Expand the JLabels so that you can see all the text.

Figure 18.11
Screen Layout: Buttons, Labels, and Text Fields

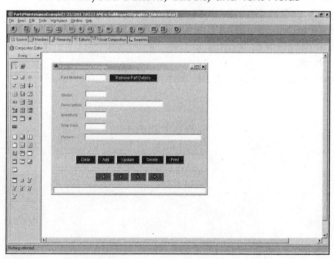

Next, you'll create the JComponents that will represent the AS/400 database fields. You'll do this by way of a JTextField. You'll name each JTextField using the associated AS/400 database field name. You needn't to worry about case sensitivity.

Create the seven JTextFields shown above in Figure 18.11.

> Click and drop six **JTextField** beans 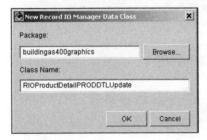 beside the labels on the visual area.
> Double-click each JTextField, and change the **beanName** property to **partno**, **model**, **partd**, **inventory**, **partship**, and **partpic**, respectively. Remember, you're deliberately omitting the **tf** prefix so that the database fields match up with the names of the **JTextField** beans.
> Expand the JTextFields to match the figure.
> Close the **Properties** sheets.
> Click the **JTextField** bean again, and drop it at the bottom of the visual area. This field will be used as a message area.
> Double-click the JTextField. Change the **beanName** to **msgArea**.
> Expand the JTextField to match the figure.
> Close the **Properties** sheet.

Save the Java program.

> On the menu bar, click **Bean**.
> Click **Save Bean**.

Specifying the Form Manager

Now, you're going to add a **FormManager** bean. This bean is the fifth bean in the AS/400 Toolbox bean category.

> Click to display the bean category drop-down list, and select **AS/400 Toolbox**.
> Click the **FormManager** bean □, and drop it on the nonvisual free-form surface.
> Double-click the FormManager.
> Click the **recordIOManager** property's **Details** button.

You're going to create a new class to manage file PRODDTL in library ADTSLAB. This class will allow reads and writes of the database file.

> Click **New**.
> In the **Package** field, type **buildingas400graphics**, as shown in Figure 18.12.
> In the **Class Name** field, type **RIOProductDetailPRODDTLUpdate**.
> Click **OK**. The **Database** tab of the **RecordIOManager** bean is displayed.
> In the **File** field, type **PRODDTL**.
> In the **Library** field, type **ADTSLAB**.
> *Don't* click OK.

Figure 18.12
New Record IO Manager Data Class

To go to the next step, you need to successfully connect to the AS/400.

> Click the **Columns** tab.
> Enter your sign-on information, and wait a few seconds.

> After the database fields appear, click **OK**. Doing so selects all the fields.
> Wait until the compilation of the **recordIOManager** bean is completed. You'll know this has occurred when the class name is filled in completely in the recordIOManager.
> Close the **Properties** sheet.

Now, add the **AS400** bean.

> Click the **AS400** bean 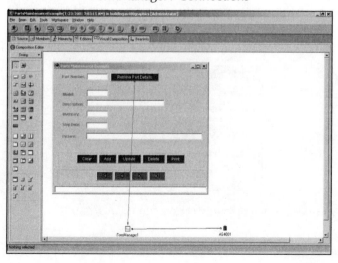, and drop it on the free-form nonvisual surface.
> Double-click the **AS4001** bean.
> For ease of use later on, fill in the **systemName** and **userID** properties.
> Close the **Properties** sheet.

Save the Java program.

> On the menu bar, click **Bean**.
> Click **Save Bean**.

Connecting the AS/400 Beans

You're going to set up two property-to-property connections, seven event-to-method connections, and eleven event-to-code connections. Most of these connections will focus on handling the database maintenance functions (retrieve, clear, add, update, delete, and print) and the database navigational functions (first, previous, next, and last).

Property-to-Property Connection: system

```
connPtoP1: (AS4001,this ←→ FormManager1,system)
```

Connect the **AS4001** bean with the **FormManager1** bean as shown in Figure 18.13.

> Right-click the **AS4001** bean.
> Click **Connect**.
> Click **this**.
> Click the spider-end pointer on the **FormManager1** bean.
> Click **Connectible Features**.
> Double-click the **system** property.

Figure 18.13
FormManager1 Connections

Event-to-Method Connection: readRecord()

```
connEtoM1: (btRetrieve,actionPerformed → FormManager1,readRecord())
```

This connection, also shown in Figure 18.13, is created to retrieve the part number that the user enters. The connection reads the record, similar to a CHAIN function in RPG. Connect the **btRetrieve** JButton with a **readRecord()** method.

> ➤ Right-click the **btRetrieve** JButton.
> ➤ Click **Connect**.
> ➤ Click **actionPerformed**.
> ➤ Click the spider-end pointer on the **FormManager1** bean.
> ➤ Click **Connectible Features**.
> ➤ Click the **readRecord()** method.
> ➤ Click **OK**.
> ➤ Double-click the connection to verify that it is correct as shown in Figure 18.14.
> ➤ Close the **Properties** window.

Figure 18.14
Connection connEtoM1

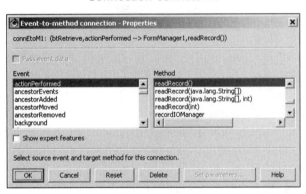

Event-to-Method Connection: readPreviousRecord()

`connEtoM2: (btPrevious,actionPerformed → FormManager1,readPreviousRecord())`

Figure 18.15 shows the next three connections you'll create. The first connection you'll add reads the previous record, similar to a READP function in RPG. Connect the **btPrevious** JButton with a **readPrevious()** method.

➢ Right-click the **btPrevious** JButton.
➢ Click **Connect**.
➢ Click **actionPerformed**.
➢ Click the spider-end pointer on the **FormManager1** bean.
➢ Click **Connectible Features**.
➢ Click the **readPreviousRecord()** method.
➢ Click **OK**.

Figure 18.15
Connections

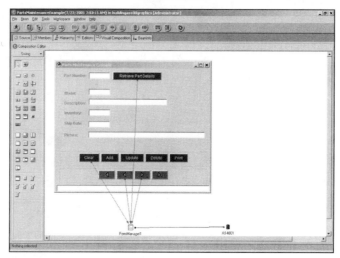

Event-to-Method Connection: readNextRecord()

`connEtoM3: (btNext,actionPerformed → FormManager1,readNextRecord())`

This connection reads the next record, similar to a READ function in RPG. Connect the **btNext** JButton with a **readNextRecord()** method.

➢ Right-click the **btNext** JButton.
➢ Click **Connect**.
➢ Click **actionPerformed**.
➢ Click the spider-end pointer on the **FormManager1** bean.
➢ Click **Connectible Features**.
➢ Click the **readNextRecord()** method.
➢ Click **OK**.

Event-to-Method Connection: clearAllData()

`connEtoM4: (btClear,actionPerformed → FormManager1,clearAllData())`

This connection clears all the fields within a database record. Connect the **btClear** JButton with a **clearAllData()** method.

- ➤ Right-click the **btClear** JButton.
- ➤ Click **Connect**.
- ➤ Click **actionPerformed**.
- ➤ Click the spider-end pointer on the **FormManager1** bean.
- ➤ Click **Connectible Features**.
- ➤ Click the **clearAllData()** method.
- ➤ Click **OK**.

Property-to-Property Connection: displayContainer

`connPtoP2: (PartsMaintenanceExample,this ↔ FormManager1,displayContainer)`

Next, you'll connect the **PartsMaintenanceExample** JFrame with the FormManager1 **displayContainer** property as shown in Figure 18.16. Recall that a displayContainer determines the scope or boundary of the database field mapping.

- ➤ Select the **PartsMaintenanceExample** JFrame by clicking the outside edge of the visual area.
- ➤ Click **Connect**.
- ➤ Click **this**.
- ➤ Click the spider-end pointer on the **FormManager1** bean.
- ➤ Click **displayContainer**.

Your connection should appear as shown in the figure. You may need to adjust the position of the connection by dragging the center point. As you'll see later, there are going to be a lot of connections displayed on the non-visual area.

Figure 18.16
displayContainer Connection: connPtoP2

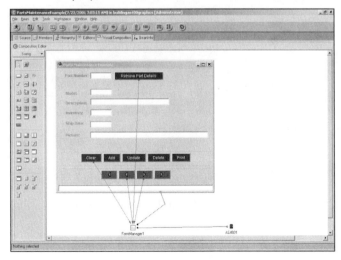

Save the Java program.

➤   On the menu bar, click **Bean**.
➤   Click **Save Bean**.

Printing an Application Snapshot

It's often beneficial to print a screen snapshot and send it directly to the printer. In this section, you'll do exactly that. Most standard Windows applications let you perform this printing function, but doing so requires a few steps:

1. Press the Print Screen key, which saves a copy of the screen snapshot in the Windows Clipboard.
2. Paste the contents of the Clipboard into another application (e.g., Microsoft Word).
3. Print the contents of the application using the normal print function.

This can be a cumbersome way to get a screen snapshot. The upcoming code shows you how to do the same thing with fewer steps for the user. *You will probably use this small snippet of print code over and over again. You may want to place a bookmark on this page.*

Event-to-Code Connection: btPrint

```
connEtoC1: (btPrint,actionPerformed →
            PartsMaintenanceExample,void btPrint_ActionPerformed(java.awt.event.ActionEvent))
```

This connection will capture a screen snapshot and then call the standard Windows Print API. Caution: This method works only on Windows operating systems; for your application to be completely portable, you'll have to rework this approach for other platforms.

To accomplish the Print Screen function, the following programming steps are required:

1. Retrieve the print job object.
2. Retrieve the graphics image.
3. Print the graphics image.
4. Dispose, or free up, the memory allocation.
5. End the print job.

Create an event-to-code connection with the **btPrint** JButton.

➤   Right-click the **btPrint** JButton.
➤   Click **Connect**.
➤   Click **actionPerformed**.
➤   Click the spider-end pointer on the nonvisual free-form surface.
➤   Click **Event to Code**.
➤   Insert the Java code shown in Figure 18.17 into the new method named **btPrint_ActionPerformed()**.
      When you've finished typing the new Java code, your method should look identical to Figure 18.18.

Figure 18.17
Source Code for Printing a Screen Snapshot

```
Source code: connEtoC1
    java.awt.PrintJob job = java.awt.Toolkit.getDefaultToolkit().getPrintJob(null,"",null);
    java.awt.Graphics g = job.getGraphics();
    ivjJFrameContentPane.printAll(g);
    g.dispose();
    job.end();
```

Figure 18.18
Connection connEtoC1

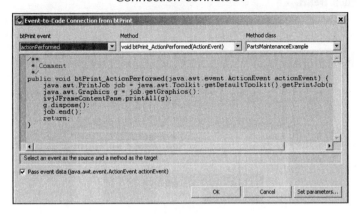

➢   Click **OK**.

If you have any errors, you'll be prompted to fix them. Typically, the errors are due to misspelling, case-sensitivity problems, or missing semicolons. If errors are reported, look closely at your code and correct it.

➢   Click and hold the **btPrint_ActionPerformed()** method, and drag it down closer to the **btPrint** button as shown in Figure 18.19.

As you add more of these event-to-code methods, this extra step will make your free-form surface look more organized. You'll be implementing quite a few event-to-code methods in this chapter.

Figure 18.19
btPrint_ActionPerformed Connection: connEtoC1 in New Location

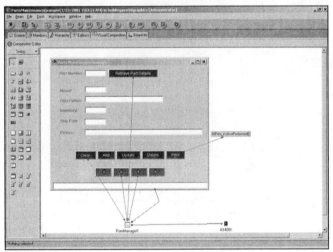

Save the Java program.

➢   On the menu bar, click **Bean**.
➢   Click **Save Bean**.

To test the print function, you must have access to a printer. Run the Java program.

➢   On the menu bar, click **Bean**.
➢   Click **Run**, and then click **Run Main**.
➢   When the application appears, click the **Print** button.

Figure 18.20 shows the results of clicking **Print**. As you can see, the standard Windows printer interface appears.

Figure 18.20
Windows Printer Interface

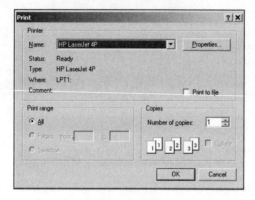

➢   Select the correct printer, and then click **OK**. (The printer must support graphics.)

A copy of Figure 18.21 should be printed. You have to admit that was pretty easy! When data is displayed in the fields on the screen, you can click the **Print** button and the data will be printed as well.

Figure 18.21
Printout

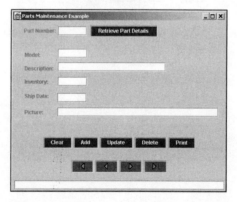

➢   Close the application.

Method Creation: Manual Entry

There are many ways to create your own methods in VisualAge for Java. In Chapter 5, you learned how to create method features. You've also learned how to create event-to-code methods or class methods. You can create methods manually as well.

To manually create a method, you can use the **Create Method** SmartGuide, but it's actually just as easy to type in the method manually. The SmartGuide is useful for adding a **main()** method or adding an existing method from the repository.

The general steps to create a method manually are:

1. Bring up the class's **Source** pane in the workbench.
2. Insert your new method just below the class definition.
3. Save your code. At this point, VisualAge for Java takes your newly entered code and positions it in the source code where it should be. Your new method is then listed under the class, just like any other method.

This section shows you how to create methods manually. You will create two methods: one to display an error message and another to determine whether an edit error occurred. We'll also discuss handling edit checks.

Manual Method Creation: displayErrorMessage()

The first method you're going to create is a **displayErrorMessage(String message)** method. In Chapter 15, you created several event-to-code methods in which the same sections of code were duplicated over and over. You're going to create a new method that is passed a message and displays the message on the screen. You'll use this method later in the chapter for quite a few of your event-to-code connections.

You could improve this method and create it as a standalone class, with some additional parameters for x-coordinate and y-coordinate, background and foreground colors, and so on. Most AS/400 programmers will feel very comfortable with this approach to displaying an error message. Some people would advocate using a dialog box to accomplish this function. Later in the chapter, you'll learn about dialog boxes.

➢ Go to the workbench window.

➢ In the **All Projects** pane, select the **PartsMaintenanceExample** class, as shown in Figure 18.22.

Figure 18.22
PartsMaintenanceExample Class

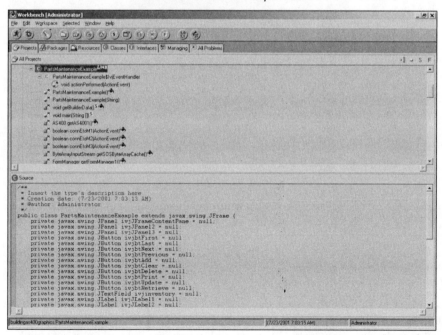

In the lower part of the screen, the **Source** pane displays the source code for the class. You're going to add your new method right after the class definition.

➢   Insert the Java code shown in Figure 18.23 immediately after the **PartsMaintenanceExample** class definition. The source code you're adding displays a red and white error message. Figure 18.24 shows what the source code should look like and where it should appear after you've entered it into the **Source** pane.

Figure 18.23
Source Code for displayErrorMessage() Method

```
Source code: displayErrorMessage
    public void displayErrorMessage(String message) {
        getmsgArea().setText(message);
        getmsgArea().setBackground(java.awt.Color.red);
        getmsgArea().setForeground(java.awt.Color.white);
        return;
    }
```

Figure 18.24
displayErrorMessage() Source Code

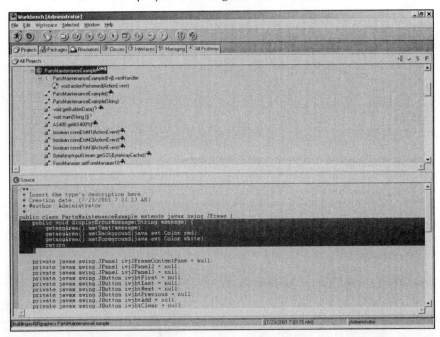

➢   Right-click in the **Source** pane to display the shortcut menu.
➢   Click **Save**.

After a few seconds, you'll notice that your new source code is gone. VisualAge for Java removed your new method and positioned it in the source code at the appropriate place. The **Source** pane for the **PartsMaintenanceExample** class now looks the way it did before you entered your new method.

➤ In the upper pane of the workbench, scroll down through all the methods until you find the **displayErrorMessage()** method.

➤ Click the **displayErrorMessage()** method.

As you can see in Figure 18.25, your new method is accessible just like any other method. In the **Source** pane, you can see the new source code you just entered.

Figure 18.25
New Method: displayErrorMessage()

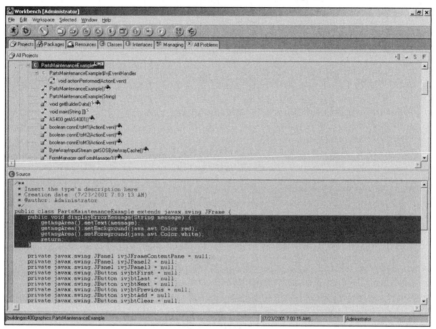

Error Handling: Edit Checks

Author's note: As I wrote this section of the book, I vacillated on the best approach to performing everyday edit checks in a maintenance program. In an object-oriented development approach, a Java purist would use encapsulation, getters, and setters to perform edit checks on data entities. This approach would entail creating a method for each data element and throwing an exception if an error occurred. A separate class would be created to handle each exception. From a practical development standpoint, where most AS/400 developers are trying to get an application out the door as quickly as possible, it would be much easier to put all the edit checks into one method. Hence my dilemma. Which approach should I use? I decided to show you a quick example of how to set up the class using a pure object-oriented approach. Then, inside our chapter project, I show you how to put all the edit checks into one method, similar to what most RPG programmers are already used to doing.

Setters, Exceptions, and the Try/Catch Approach

The following example shows how to use a setter method to perform an edit check and generate the possible resulting error. We're going to use a fruit validation example. Assume you want to verify that a fruit's description is one of these values: Banana, Orange, Apple, Strawberry, or Peach. (The example could just as easily be valid months of the year, valid state codes, valid country codes, or some other category of values.) Figure 18.26 shows the logic for a setter function. If an invalid fruit description occurs, an **InvalidFruitException** is thrown. If there is no error, **FRUIT** — which is defined as a private class variable — receives the correct value of the fruit. Figure 18.27 shows the exception class that passes the error message to the parent via the **super()** method. Figure 18.28 shows an example of how you would execute the edit check with a try/catch combination.

The argument in support of using this approach is that it encapsulates all the error handling within the business entity. In AS/400 terms, this entity could be a physical file, such as the product file.

Figure 18.26
Setter Logic

```
Source code: setFruit
public void setFruit(String fruit) throws InvalidFruitException {
    String fruits[ ] = ("Banana", "Orange", "Apple", "Strawberry", "Peach");
    for (int cnt=0; cnt<fruits.length;I++) {
        if (fruit.equals(fruits[cnt])) {
            FRUIT = fruit;
            return;
        }
    }
    throw new InvalidFruitException(fruit);
}
```

Figure 18.27
Exception Logic

```
Source code: InvalidFruitException
public class InvalidFruitException extends Exception {
    public InvalidFruitException(String fruitDescription)  {
        super("Invalid Fruit Description:  " + fruitDescription);
    }
}
```

Figure 18.28
Edit Check Logic

```
Source code:
try {
    currentEntity.setFruit(fruit);
}
catch (InvalidFruitException err) {
    displayErrorMessage(err.toString());
}

public class InvalidFruitException extends Exception {
    public InvalidFruitException(String fruitDescription)  {
        super("Invalid Fruit Description:  " + fruitDescription);
    }
}
```

Manual Method Creation: editChecks()

Arguing in support of the second approach — putting all the edit checks into one method — you could say that, typically, one application should maintain an entity and all the edits should be contained within that application. A design like this can make the edit checks much easier to find. This approach works and is easier from an RPG perspective, but it's not as clean in the object-oriented programming world. The approach described above supports object-oriented programming.

You're going to create a new method to perform edit checks. If an error is encountered, an error message is sent to method **displayErrorMessage()**. The return value, **passed**, is a Boolean value signifying whether the edits were passed. If the edits are passed, the appropriate **Add** or **Update** function is executed.

This example performs an edit check for a mandatory entry of part number and model. (Additional edit checks are possible beyond the ones used in this example.) If no part number is entered or no model is entered, a **requestFocus()** method (position cursor) is executed and an error message is sent.

➢   Go to the workbench window.

➢   Select the **PartsMaintenanceExample** class.

You're going to create your new method right after the class definition.

➢   Insert the Java code shown in Figure 18.29 immediately after the **PartsMaintenanceExample** class definition. This code contains your typical conditional "if" statements for doing edit checks. A Boolean flag is initially set to false. If all the edit checks are passed, a true Boolean condition is returned to the caller. Figure 18.30 shows what the source code should look like after you've entered it in the **Source** pane.

Figure 18.29
Source Code for editChecks()

```
Source code: editChecks
    public boolean editChecks() {
        boolean passed = false;
        if (getpartno().getText().equals("")) {
            ivjpartno.requestFocus();
            displayErrorMessage("Part Number Required");
        }
        else
            if (getmodel().getText().equals("")) {
            ivjmodel.requestFocus();
            displayErrorMessage("Model Required");
            }
        else
            passed = true;
    return passed;
}
```

Figure 18.30
editChecks() Source Code

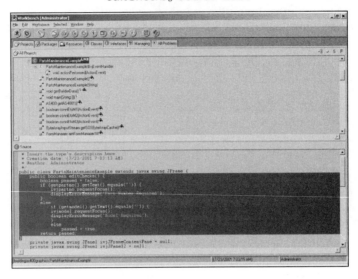

➢   Right-click in the **Source** pane to display the shortcut menu.

➢   Click **Save**.

After a few seconds, notice that your source code is gone.

➢   In the workbench, scroll down through the methods until you find the **editChecks()** method.

➢   Click the **editChecks()** method.

As you can see in Figure 18.31, your new method is accessible just like any other method. Your new source code is displayed in the **Source** pane.

Figure 18.31
New Method: editChecks()

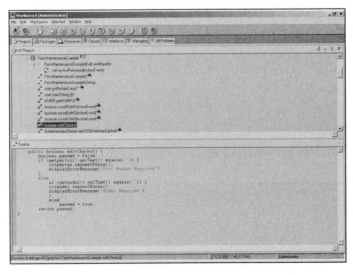

Tips and Tricks

The manual entry approaches also works if you need to copy in a method from another class. You could just use the cut and paste functions to perform the copy.

Navigational Button Connections

Now, it's time to complete the connections for the rest of the navigational JButtons: **First**, **Last**, **Previous**, and **Next**.

Event-to-Code Connection: btFirst

```
connEtoC2: (btFirst,actionPerformed →
            PartsMaintenanceExample,void btFirst_ActionPerformed(java.awt.event.ActionEvent))
```

This connection will load the first record in the file. Create an event-to-code connection with the **btFirst** JButton.

➢   Right-click the **btFirst** JButton.
➢   Click **Connect**.
➢   Click **actionPerformed**.
➢   Click the spider-end pointer on the nonvisual free-form surface.
➢   Click **Event to Code**.
➢   Insert the Java code shown in Figure 18.32. This code clears the database buffer, positions to the first record in the database, and then reads the first record. When you've finished typing the new Java code, your method should look identical to Figure 18.33.

Figure 18.32
Source Code for Getting the First Record

```
Source code: connEtoC2
    try {
        getFormManager1().clearAllData();
        getFormManager1().positionCursorToFirst();
        getFormManager1().readRecord();
        }
    catch (java.lang.Throwable ivjExc) {
        handleException(ivjExc);
    }
```

Figure 18.33
Connection connEtoC2

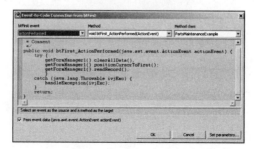

➢   Click **OK**.
➢   Click and hold the **btFirst_ActionPerformed()** method, and drag it down closer to the **btFirst** JButton as shown in Figure 18.34.

Figure 18.34
btFirst_ActionPerformed Connection: connEtoC2

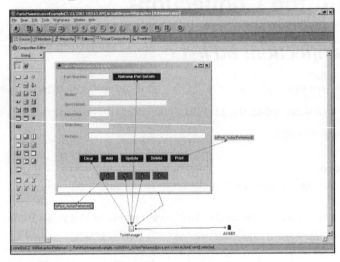

Event-to-Code Connection: btLast

```
connEtoC3: (btLast,actionPerformed →
            PartsMaintenanceExample,void btLast_ActionPerformed(java.awt.event.ActionEvent))
```

This connection will load the last record in the file. Create an event-to-code connection with the **btLast** JButton.

➢   Right-click the **btLast** JButton.
➢   Click **Connect**.
➢   Click **actionPerformed**.
➢   Click the spider-end pointer on the nonvisual free-form surface.
➢   Click **Event to Code**.
➢   Insert the Java code shown in Figure 18.35. This code clears the database buffer, positions to the last record in the database, and then reads the last record. When you've finished typing the new Java code, your method should look identical to Figure 18.36.

Figure 18.35

Source Code for Getting the Last Record

```
Source code: connEtoC3
        try {
                getFormManager1().clearAllData();
                getFormManager1().positionCursorToLast();
                getFormManager1().readRecord();
                }
        catch (java.lang.Throwable ivjExc) {
                handleException(ivjExc);
        }
```

Figure 18.36

Connection connEtoC3

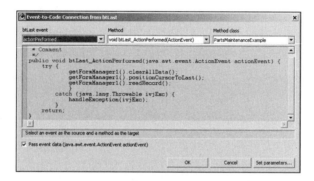

➤ Click **OK**.

➤ Click and hold the **btLast_ActionPerformed()** method, and drag it down closer to the **btLast** JButton.

Event-to-Code Connection: btPrevious normalResult()

```
connEtoC4: (connEtoM2: (btPrevious,actionPerformed →
            FormManager1,readPreviousRecord()),normalResult →
            PartsMaintenanceExample,void connEtoM2_NormalResult(boolean))
```

This connection will let you pass a **NormalResult** argument — the Boolean status — to the **connEtoM2_Normal Result()** method. If the Boolean status is false, an unsuccessful I/O operation occurred. This technique is similar to looking at the indicator status after an RPG I/O operation has been completed.

Create an event-to-code connection with the **readPreviousRecord()** connection, **connEtoM2**.

➤ Right-click connection **connEtoM2**, which is the connection from the **Previous** JButton to the FormManager1.

➤ Click **Connect**.

➤ Click **normalResult**.

➤ Click the spider-end pointer on the nonvisual free-form surface.

➤ Click **Event to Code**.

➤ Insert the Java code shown in Figure 18.37. This code determines whether the beginning of file has been reached. If it has, the code clears the database buffer, positions to the first record in the database, and then reads the first record. Otherwise, an error message is displayed. When you've finished typing the new Java code, your method should look identical to Figure 18.38.

Figure 18.37
Source Code for connEtoM2_NormalResult

```
Source code: connEtoM2_NormalResult
    if (arg1 == false) {
            displayErrorMessage("Beginning of File Reached");
            try {
                getFormManager1().clearAllData();
                getFormManager1().positionCursorToFirst();
                getFormManager1().readRecord();
                }
            catch (java.lang.Throwable ivjExc) {
                handleException(ivjExc);
            }
                }
```

Figure 18.38
connEtoM2_NormalResult Connection

> Click **OK**.
> Click and hold the **connEtoM2_NormalResult()** method, and drag it down closer to the **btPrevious** JButton.

Event-to-Code Connection: btNext normalResult()

```
connEtoC5: (connEtoM3: (btNext,actionPerformed →
            FormManager1,readNextRecord()),normalResult →
            PartsMaintenanceExample,void connEtoM3_NormalResult(boolean))
```

This connection will let you pass a **NormalResult** argument — the Boolean status — to the **connEtoM3_Normal Result()** method. If the Boolean status is false, an unsuccessful I/O operation occurred.

Create an event-to-code connection with the **readNextRecord()** connection, **connEtoM3**.

> Right-click connection **connEtoM3**, which is the connection from the **Next** JButton to the FormManager1.
> Click **Connect**.
> Click **normalResult**.
> Click the spider-end pointer on the nonvisual free-form surface.
> Click **Event to Code**.
> Insert the Java code shown in Figure 18.39. This code determines whether the end of file has been reached. If it has, the code clears the database buffer, positions to the last record in the database, and then reads the last record. Otherwise, an error message is displayed. When you've finished typing the new Java code, your method should look identical to Figure 18.40.

Figure 18.39
Source Code for connEtoM3_NormalResult

```
Source code: connEtoM3_NormalResult
    if (arg1 == false)      {
            displayErrorMessage("End of File Reached");
            try {
                getFormManager1().clearAllData();
                getFormManager1().positionCursorToLast();
                getFormManager1().readRecord();
                }
            catch (java.lang.Throwable ivjExc) {
                handleException(ivjExc);
            }
        }
```

Figure 18.40
Connection connEtoC5

➢   Click **OK**.
➢   Click and hold the **connEtoM3_NormalResult()** method, and drag it down closer to the **btNext** JButton.

Maintenance Button Connections

Next, you're going to connect the **Add** and **Update** buttons. (You'll connect the **Delete** button later, in the section covering dialog boxes.) You could easily have coded an event-to-method connection to accomplish this — for example, using an **addRecord()** method. The only problem is that you still would have had to code the edit check. The following event-to-code connections include the logic to test for edit checks.

Event-to-Code Connection: btAdd

```
connEtoC6: (btAdd,actionPerformed →
            PartsMaintenanceExample,void btAdd_ActionPerformed(java.awt.event.ActionEvent))
```

This connection will add a record to the database if the edit checks pass. This operation is similar to a WRITE opcode in RPG. Because the file isn't defined with UNIQUE keys, there is no checking to see whether the keyed record already exists.

Create an event-to-code connection with the **btAdd** JButton.

➢   Right-click the **btAdd** JButton.
➢   Click **Connect**.
➢   Click **actionPerformed**.

➤ Click the spider-end pointer on the nonvisual free-form surface.

➤ Click **Event to Code**.

➤ Insert the Java code shown in Figure 18.41. This code determines whether the edit checks passed. If they did, the code adds the record to the database and then clears the database buffer. When you've finished typing the new Java code, your method should look identical to Figure 18.42.

Figure 18.41

Source Code for Adding a Record

```
Source code: connEtoC6
    if (editChecks() == true) {
    try {
        getFormManager1().addRecord();
        getFormManager1().clearAllData();
        }
    catch (java.lang.Throwable ivjExc) {
        handleException(ivjExc);
        }
    }
```

Figure 18.42

Connection connEtoC6

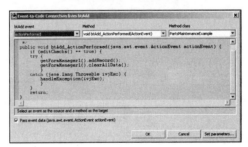

➤ Click **OK**.

Your screen should look similar to Figure 18.43.

Figure 18.43
btAdd_ActionPerformed Connection: connEtoC6

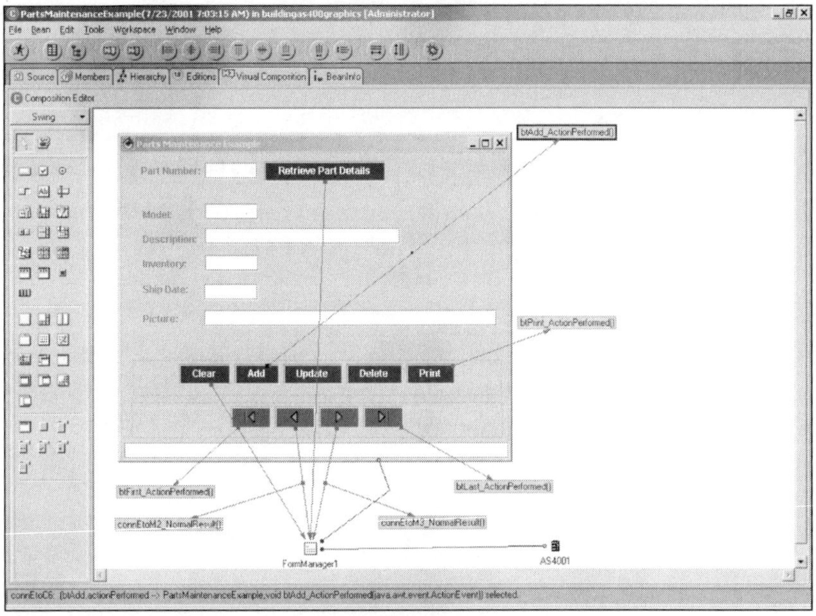

Event-to-Code Connection: btUpdate

```
connEtoC7: (btUpdate,actionPerformed →
            PartsMaintenanceExample,void
            btUpdate_ActionPerformed(java.awt.event.ActionEvent))
```

This connection will update an existing record in the database if the edit checks pass. This operation is similar to an UPDATE opcode in RPG. Because the file isn't defined with UNIQUE keys, there is no checking to see whether the keyed record was changed or whether the keyed record already exists.

Create an event-to-code connection with the **btUpdate** JButton.

➢   Right-click the **btUpdate** JButton.
➢   Click **Connect**.
➢   Click **actionPerformed**.
➢   Click the spider-end pointer on the nonvisual free-form surface.
➢   Click **Event to Code**.
➢   Insert the Java code shown in Figure 18.44. This code determines whether the edit checks passed. If they did, the code updates the record to the database and then clears the database buffer. When you've finished typing the new Java code, your method should look identical to Figure 18.45.

Figure 18.44

Source Code for Updating a Record

```
Source code: connEtoC7
    if (editChecks() == true) {
    try {
        getFormManager1().updateRecord();
        getFormManager1().clearAllData();
        }
    catch (java.lang.Throwable ivjExc) {
        handleException(ivjExc);
        }
    }
```

Figure 18.45

Connection connEtoC7

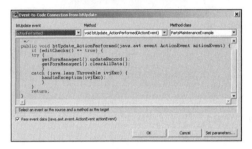

> Click **OK**.
> Click and hold the **btUpdate_ActionPerformed()** method, and drag it down closer to the **btUpdate** button.

Save your Java program.

> On the menu bar, click **Bean**.
> Click **Save Bean**.

Event-to-Code Connection: btRetrieve normalResult()

```
connEtoC8: (connEtoM1: (btRetrieve,actionPerformed →
        FormManager1,readRecord()),normalResult →
        PartsMaintenanceExample,void connEtoM1_NormalResult(boolean))
```

This connection will let you pass a **NormalResult** argument — the Boolean status — to the **connEtoM1_NormalResult()** method. If the Boolean status is false, an unsuccessful I/O operation occurred.

Create an event-to-code connection with the **readRecord()** connection, **connEtoM1**.

> Right-click connection **connEtoM1**, which is the connection from the **Retrieve Part Details** JButton to the FormManager1.
> Click **Connect**.
> Click **normalResult**.
> Click the spider-end pointer on the nonvisual free-form surface.

➢ Click **Event to Code**.

➢ Insert the Java code shown in Figure 18.46. This code determines a part number was entered and displays an error message if one was not. When you've finished typing the new Java code, your method should look identical to Figure 18.47.

Figure 18.46
Source Code for connEtoM1_NormalResult

```
Source code: connEtoM1_NormalResult
    if (arg1 == false)
        {
            displayErrorMessage("Part Number does not exist");
        }
```

Figure 18.47
connEtoM1_NormalResult Connection

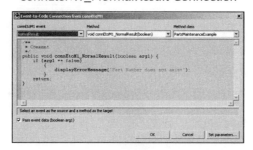

➢ Click **OK**.

➢ Click and hold the **connEtoM1_NormalResult()** method, and drag it down to the center of the screen as shown in Figure 18.48.

➢ Click connection **connEtoM1**, and drag it to the right, to the position shown in the figure.

When you have many visual connections, as you do in this chapter project, it's sometimes worth the effort to rearrange your connections like this to make it easier to distinguish what the various connections do.

Figure 18.48
connEtoM1_NormalResult Connection: connEtoC8

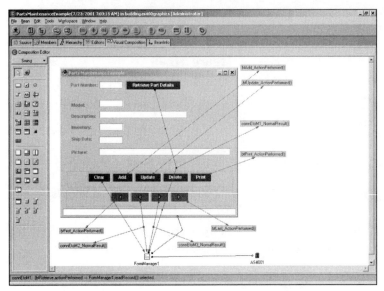

Initialize Connection

One connection is needed to connect the **initialize()** event and cause the AS/400 prompt to appear.

Event-to-Method Connection: readNextRecord()

connEtoM5: (PartsMaintenanceExample,initialize → FormManager1,readNextRecord())

When the application is first initialized, a **readNextRecord()** method connected to the **initialize()** event will cause the AS/400 prompt to appear. The AS/400 prompt appears before your application window appears.

Create an event-to-method connection with the **PartsMaintenanceExample** JFrame.

➢ Right-click the outside edge of the **PartsMaintenanceExample** JFrame.
➢ Click **Connect**.
➢ Click **Connectible Features**.
➢ Click the **initialize()** event.
➢ Click the spider-end pointer on the **FormManager1** bean.
➢ Click **Connectible Features**.
➢ Click the **readNextRecord()** method.
➢ Click **OK**.

Your connection should appear as shown in Figure 18.49.

Figure 18.49

connEtoM5 readNextRecord() Connection

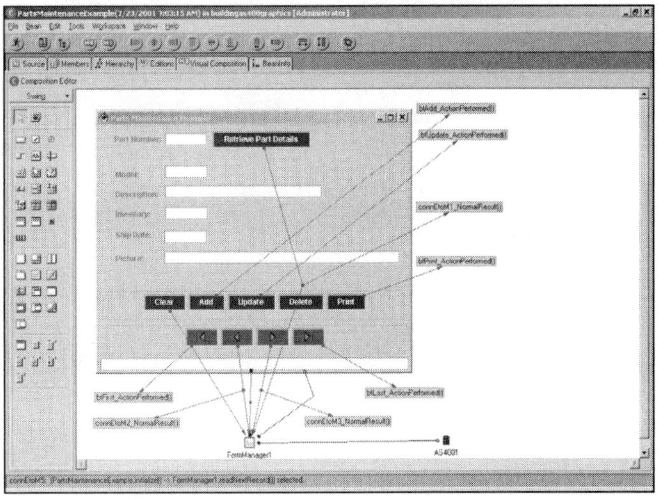

Window Connections

In most applications, you'll probably perform certain functions based on the events of a window being either opened or closed. In this section, you'll create the connections to handle these functions for the application.

Event-to-Code Connection: closeFile()

```
connEtoC9: (PartsMaintenanceExample,windowClosed →
            PartsMaintenanceExample,void
            partsMaintenanceExample_WindowClosed(java.awt.event.WindowEvent))
```

The sample application includes no **Exit** or **Close** JButton anywhere on the screen. To end the program, the user must click the Windows **Close** button. You're going to use an event-to-code connection to perform the necessary shutdown functions for the application: closing the database and disposing of the window.

Create an event-to-code connection with the **PartsMaintenanceExample** JFrame.

➤ Right-click the outside edge of the **PartsMaintenanceExample** JFrame.
➤ Click **Connect**.
➤ Click **windowClosed**.
➤ Click the spider-end pointer on the nonvisual free-form surface.
➤ Click **Event to Code**.
➤ Insert the Java code shown in Figure 18.50. This code closes the database file and then disposes of the window in memory. When you've finished typing the new Java code, your method should look identical to Figure 18.51.

Figure 18.50
Source Code for partsMaintenanceExample_WindowClosed

```
Source code: partsMaintenanceExample_WindowClosed
    try {
        getFormManager1().closeFile();
        }
    catch (java.lang.Throwable ivjExc) {
        handleException(ivjExc);
        }
    dispose();
```

Figure 18.51
Connection connEtoC9

➢ Click **OK**.

➢ Click and hold the **partsMaintenanceExample_WindowClosed()** method, and drag it to the upper-right corner of the screen as shown in Figure 18.52.

➢ Click the connection you just created (**connEtoC9**), and drag it to the top of the screen as shown in the figure. You may have to shape the connection a couple of times to get the correct connection line.

Figure 18.52
partsMaintenanceExample_WindowClosed() Connection: connEtoC9

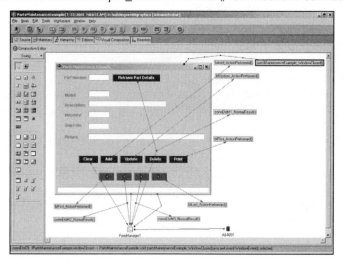

Mouse Events Connection

You are now going to create an event connection so that whenever the user moves the mouse, the event will automatically cause the message area to be cleared.

Event-to-Code Connection: mouseEvents()

```
connEtoC10: (PartsMaintenanceExample,mouseEvents →
            PartsMaintenanceExample,void partsMaintenanceExample_MouseEvents())
```

Create an event-to-code connection with the **PartsMaintenanceExample** JFrame.

➤ Right-click the outside edge of the **PartsMaintenanceExample** JFrame.
➤ Click **Connect**.
➤ Click **Connectible Features**.
➤ Click the **mouseEvents()** event.
➤ Click the spider-end pointer on the nonvisual free-form surface.
➤ Click **Event to Code**.
➤ Insert the Java code shown in Figure 18.53. This code clears the error message field and restores the field to its original gray color. When you've finished typing the new Java code, your method should look identical to Figure 18.54.

Figure 18.53
Source Code for partsMaintenanceExample_MouseEvents

```
Source code: partsMaintenanceExample_MouseEvents
    getmsgArea().setText("");
    getmsgArea().setBackground(java.awt.Color.lightGray);
```

Figure 18.54
Connection connEtoC10

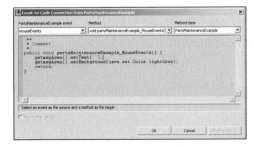

➤ Click **OK**.
➤ Click and hold the **partsMaintenanceExample_MouseEvents()** method, and drag it to the upper-right corner of the screen as shown in Figure 18.55.
➤ Click connection **connEtoC10**, and drag it to the top as shown in the figure.

Figure 18.55

partsMaintenanceExample_MouseEvents Connection connEtoC10

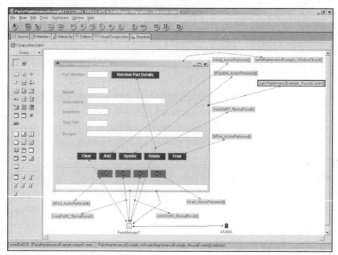

Event-to-Method Connection: requestFocus()

`connEtoM6: (PartsMaintenanceExample,windowOpened → partno,requestFocus())`

This connection will position the cursor in the **Part Number** field when the application begins execution. Connect the **partno** JTextField with a **requestFocus()** method.

- ➢ Right-click the outside edge of the **PartsMaintenanceExample** JFrame.
- ➢ Click **Connect**.
- ➢ Click **windowOpened**.
- ➢ Click the spider-end pointer on the **partno** JTextField.
- ➢ Click **Connectible Features**.
- ➢ Click the **requestFocus()** method.
- ➢ Click **OK**.

Your connection should appear as shown in Figure 18.56.

Figure 18.56
requestFocus() Connection: connEtoM6

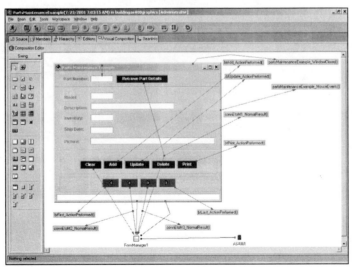

Now, add two separator bars to distinguish the part number prompt area of the screen, the database fields, and the JButtons.

➤ Click the **JSeparator** bean █, and drop it under the **Part Number** field as shown in Figure 18.57. The **JSeparator** bean is the very last bean in the **Swing** bean category.

➤ Click the **JSeparator** bean again, and drop it under the **Picture** field as shown in the figure.

Figure 18.57
JSeparators

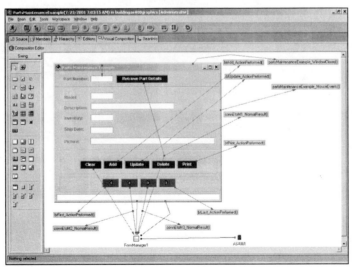

Using the Maintenance Application

Take a break. You can save and run your program now. Everything is done except the delete function. The best is saved for last!

➤   On the menu bar, click **Bean**.
➤   Click **Save Bean**.

Make sure you're connected to the AS/400. Run your Java program.

➤   On the menu bar, click **Bean**.
➤   Click **Run**, and then click **Run Main**.

Notice that the AS/400 prompt appears immediately.

➤   Enter your sign-on information, and wait a few seconds.

Did you notice that when the first record was loaded, the cursor was blinking inside the **Part Number** field? That's because of the **requestFocus()** method (the equivalent of an AS/400 DDS position cursor function) you associated with the **windowOpened** event.

Now you'll perform some tests.

➤   Click the **Clear** button.
➤   Once all the fields are blank, click the **Add** button.

What happens? As Figure 18.58 shows, you received an error message stating that a part number is required. This error message came from the **editCheck()** method. Notice that the cursor is blinking inside the **Part Number** field. That's because of the **requestFocus()** method.

➤   In the **Part Number** field, type **98765**.
➤   Click the **Add** button.

Figure 18.59 shows what happens. This time, you receive an error message stating that a model is required. Again, this error message came from the **editCheck()** method. Where is the cursor blinking? Inside the **Model** field.

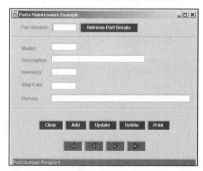

Figure 18.58	**Figure 18.59**
Edit Check on Part Number	*Edit Check on Model*

Complete the add function as shown in Figure 18.60.

➤   In the **Model** field, type **WB01**.
➤   In the **Description** field, type **Wire Basket**.
➤   In the **Inventory** field, type **0**.
➤   In the **Ship Date** field, type **2001-06-04**.

> ➤   Leave the **Picture** field blank.
> ➤   Click **Add**.

You've just added a new record to your database! You'll delete this record later in the chapter.

Figure 18.60
New Record

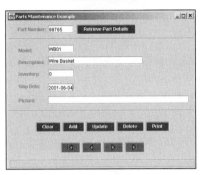

You could add all kinds of additional edit checks to your program. You could also change the JTextFields to JFormattedTextFields to gain additional edit-checking capabilities that you're familiar with on the AS/400. To review these functions, see Chapter 4.

Deletion Confirmation with JOptionPane

It would have been easy to create an event-to-method connection to simply delete a record. But good system design calls for you to confirm a deletion operation. In other words, you should prompt the user to make sure he or she actually wants to delete the record. In this section, you'll create a confirmation message using a standard **JOptionPane** bean.

JOptionPanes are powerful beans that make it easy to display a standard dialog box. You can use a JOptionPane in a variety of ways — to display a confirmation message, an error message, or some other kind of information.

The **JOptionPane** bean can be a little tricky to set up, with all its parameters and available methods. Once you get used to all the variations, though, it can be a great programming aide. This JavaBean provides four different categories of dialogs:

Dialog	Description
showConfirmDialog()	Prompts for a confirmation. The prompt can use Yes, No, and Cancel.
showInputDialog()	Prompts for user input.
showMessageDialog()	Informs the user that some action or event has occurred.
showOptionDialog()	Provides a combination of the above three dialog options.

These dialogs are all modal, which means that the user must respond to the dialog box before proceeding in the application. Sometimes, when used incorrectly, modal dialogs can be a poor programming choice.

Two parameters of the **JOptionPane** bean are worth mentioning:

- The *parentComponent* identifies the parent of the dialog box. The parent's screen helps position the dialog box when it pops up on the screen.
- The *descriptive message* is the message that appears in the dialog box. The message is an **Object** type, but **String** types are usually used.

You're going to create a confirmation dialog box using the **showConfirmDialog()** method. It will display **Yes**, **No**, and **Cancel** JButtons. The parentComponent will be the **PartsMaintenanceExample** JFrame. You'll pass the string "Are you sure you want to delete?" as the descriptive message.

Add a JOptionPane to confirm a deletion request as shown in Figure 18.61.

➤   In the **Swing** bean category, click the **JOptionPane** bean 🔲, and drop it on the right side of the visual area.
➤   Double-click the JOptionPane to display the **Properties** sheet.
➤   Click the **border** property's **Details** button. You're going to change this property to give the pane a more pronounced border.
➤   In the **Border Implementor** window (Figure 18.62), click to display the **Bean Implementing Interface** drop-down list. Select **EtchedBorder**, as shown in the figure.
➤   Click **OK**.

Figure 18.61
JOptionPane

Figure 18.62
EtchedBorder

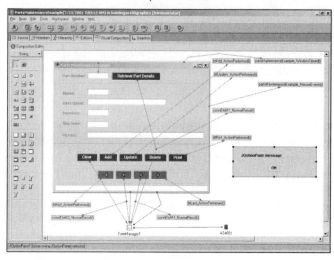

For the JOptionPane's **messageType** property, you can specify one of the following values:

- ERROR_MESSAGE
- INFORMATION_MESSAGE
- WARNING_MESSAGE
- QUESTION_MESSAGE
- PLAIN_MESSAGE

Depending on which option you select, a different graphical icon (e.g., an exclamation point, a question mark) will appear on the JOptionPane. You'll be selecting a WARNING_MESSAGE.

➤   Change the **messageType** property to **WARNING_MESSAGE**.

For the **optionType** property, you can specify one of the following values:

- DEFAULT_OPTION
- YES_NO_OPTION
- YES_NO_CANCEL_OPTION
- OK_CANCEL_OPTION
- an option of your own creation

Depending on which option you select, different buttons will appear on the JOptionPane. You'll be selecting a YES_NO_CANCEL_OPTION.

➢   Change the **optionType** property to **YES_NO_CANCEL_OPTION**.
➢   Close the **Properties** sheet.

Your JOptionPane should now look similar to Figure 18.63. Notice that you have a graphical icon, an etched border, and three new buttons.

Figure 18.63
JOptionPane: YES_NO_CANCEL_OPTION

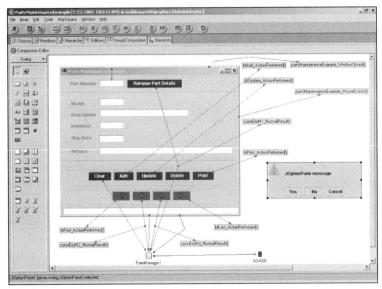

Event-to-Method Connection: showConfirmDialog()

`connEtoM7: (btDelete,actionPerformed → JOptionPane1,showConfirmDialog(Component, Object))`

When the user clicks the **Delete** button, this connection will prompt for a confirmation by displaying a dialog box. Connect the **btDelete** JButton with a **showConfirmDialog()** method.

➢   Right-click the **btDelete** JButton.
➢   Click **Connect**.
➢   Click **actionPerformed**.
➢   Click the spider-end pointer on JOptionPane1.
➢   Click **Connectible Features**.
➢   Click **showConfirmDialog(Component, Object)**.

Notice that your connection is a dashed line. To complete the connection, you must accomplish two more tasks.

First, you're going to make the connection for the second parameter of the **showConfirmDialog()** method, the **Object** parameter. For this parameter, you'll pass the string "Are you sure you want to delete?"

➢   Double-click the dashed connection line.

You should see the event-to-method window shown in Figure 18.64.

Figure 18.64
Connection connEtoM7

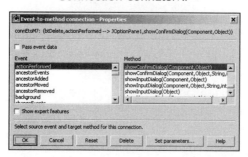

- ➤ Click **Set parameters**.
- ➤ Click **message**.
- ➤ Type **"Are you sure you want to delete?"**. Be sure to include the double quotation marks.
- ➤ Click **OK**.
- ➤ Click **OK**.

Notice that the message you just entered doesn't appear in the JOptionPane. Don't worry. It will appear when you run the application because the message is passed at run time.

Parameter-from-Property Connection

```
connPfromP1: (connEtoM7: (btDelete,actionPerformed →
            JOptionPane1,showConfirmDialog(Component,Object)),arg1 →
            JFrameContentPane,this)
```

Notice that the connection still isn't complete. You need to make the connection for the first parameter of the **showConfirmDialog()** method, the **Component** parameter. You'll pass the **PartsMaintenanceExample** JFrame for this parameter.

- ➤ Right-click the dashed connection **connEtoM7**.
- ➤ Click **connect**.
- ➤ Click **parentComponent**.
- ➤ Click the spider-end pointer on the outside edge of the **PartsMaintenanceExample** JFrame.
- ➤ Click **this**.
- ➤ For ease of distinction, drag your connection so that it appears as shown in Figure 18.65. (In the figure, look for the small angled connection near the bottom-right corner of the JFrame.)

Figure 18.65

showConfirmDialog() connPfromP1

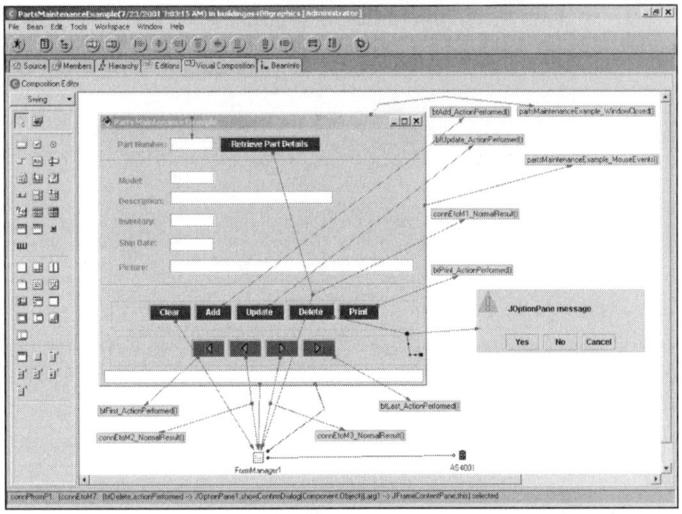

Event-to-Code Connection: connEtoM7_NormalResult(int)

```
connEtoC11: (connEtoM7: (btDelete,actionPerformed →
            JOptionPane1,showConfirmDialog(Component,Object)),normalResult →
            PartsMaintenanceExample,void connEtoM7_NormalResult(int))
```

This connection will let you test for the results of the user selecting the Yes, No, Cancel, or Close window event. Create an event-to-code connection with the **normalResult()** method.

➢   Click connection **connEtoM7**. This is the connection from the **btDelete** JButton to the JOptionPane.
➢   Click **Connect**.
➢   Click **normalResult**.
➢   Click the spider-end pointer on the nonvisual free-form surface.
➢   Click **Event to Code**.
➢   Insert the Java code shown in Figure 18.66. This code determines whether **Yes** was clicked, confirming a deletion. If the deletion is confirmed, the record is deleted from the database and the database buffer is cleared. When you've finished typing the new Java code, your method should look identical to Figure 18.67.

Figure 18.66

Source Code for connEtoM7_NormalResults

```
Source code: connEtoM7_NormalResult
    if (arg1 == ivjJOptionPane1.YES_OPTION) {
        try {
            getFormManager1().deleteRecord();
            getFormManager1().clearAllData();
            }
        catch (java.lang.Throwable ivjExc) {
            handleException(ivjExc);
            }
```

Figure 18.67
Connection connEtoC11

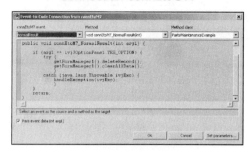

Tips and Tricks

To test the results of a JOptionPane, you could use *if* statements such as the following to determine which key was pressed in the JOptionPane:

```
if (arg1 == ivjJOptionPane1.YES_OPTION)
if (arg1 == ivjJOptionPane1.NO_OPTION)
if (arg1 == ivjJOptionPane1.CANCEL_OPTION)
```

➢   Click **OK**.
➢   Click and hold the **connEtoM7_NormalResult()** method, and drag it just under the JOptionPane as shown in Figure 18.68.

Figure 18.68
connEtoM7_normalResult Connection connEtoC11

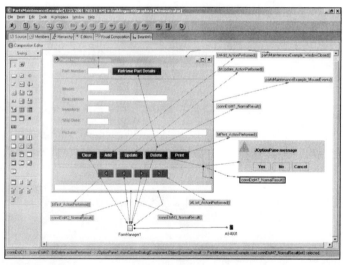

Congratulations! You're probably thinking that this has been a long chapter. You're right, it has. It's time to test your delete and deletion-confirmation functions now, and then it's on to the next chapter.

Save and then run the Java program.

➢   On the menu bar, click **Bean**.
➢   Click **Save Bean**.
➢   On the menu bar, click **Bean**.
➢   Click **Run**, and then click **Run Main**.
➢   Enter your sign-on information, and wait a few seconds.

Test the update function.

➢ When the application appears, type **98765** in the **Part Number** field.
➢ Click **Retrieve Part Details**.
➢ Change the **Description** to **Painting Basket**.
➢ Click **Update**.
➢ When the application appears, type **98765** in the **Part Number** field.
➢ Click **Retrieve Part Details**.

The application should have displayed the record with the new part description in it.

Test the delete function.

➢ Click **Delete**.

You should see the deletion-confirmation dialog box shown in Figure 18.69.

Figure 18.69
Deletion Confirmation Dialog Box

➢ Click **Cancel**.

Your 98765 record should still be there.

➢ Click **Delete**.
➢ Click **Yes** to confirm the deletion.

Your record is now deleted.

Feel free to spend some time playing with this program. For example, try changing a key value, the part number. The program will let you.

➢ Close the **Parts Maintenance Example** application.

You've just completed a fairly complete maintenance application. You've also seen a few more ways of working with error handling. I hope this chapter has given you a great foundation for building more complex maintenance applications.

You undoubtedly noticed that you ended up with quite a few connections. With some careful placement in the VCE, it's easy to visually understand what is occurring inside the program.

Summary

In this chapter you learned

- how to customize JButtons and simulate the animation of a button
- how to create a method by manually typing in the code
- how to print from Java
- how to use different methods of performing edit checks
- how to work with dialog boxes
- how to maintain a database record with add, update, and delete functions
- how to position the cursor to an error message

The next chapter will teach you how to do the equivalent of subfile maintenance.

Chapter 19

Building Java Maintenance Applications: Subfile Load-All

Chapter Objectives

- ❏ Understand how to use multiple JTables on the same screen
- ❏ Maintain database files through a JTable
- ❏ Learn how to use the **DefaultListSelectionModel** class
- ❏ Build a **String[] key** value

Chapter Project

- ❏ A class will be created to list parts and part orders from two separate AS/400 database files. The part orders will be maintainable.
- ❏ Figure 19.1 shows what the sample class will look like.

Figure 19.1
Chapter Project

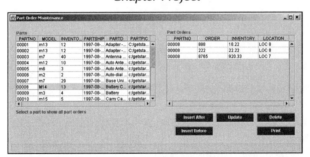

In this chapter, you'll learn how to maintain a database file through a JTable, using a subfile-like maintenance screen. You'll use two JTables to build a part order maintenance application. Both of these JTables are similar to a load-all type of subfile. In the next chapter, you'll learn how to load a JTable in page-at-a-time style.

There are many ways to implement JTables in programming an application. With the foundation you're receiving in Chapters 17 through 20, you should be able to handle most JTable development scenarios. You may have to mix and match different sections from each chapter to build your own unique JTable environments.

I have a personal opinion regarding the use of JTables (subfiles) for maintaining database records. I believe most database file maintenance functions are best accomplished using a single-record-at-a-time approach, which means not using a JTable. But there are many situations in which using a JTable to maintain the database records makes great sense. This chapter covers how to accomplish that.

I've deliberately omitted certain topics here that we've already covered in earlier chapters, including edit checks, error handling, TableColumns, and deletion-confirmation pop-ups. When you're finished with this chapter, you should be able to incorporate anything you've learned in the book up to this point.

You've used file PRODDTL from library ADTSLAB numerous times throughout the book. You'll use it again in this chapter. You'll also use another file from library ADTSLAB, the PARTORDER file. This file is nothing more than a list of part orders for each part. Both files are keyed by part number (PARTNO). Figure 19.2 shows the DDS layout of the PARTORDER file.

Figure 19.2
PARTORDER File

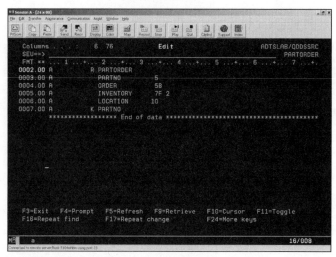

Part Order Maintenance Example

You're going to create a class called **OrderMaintenanceSubfileExample** that inherits properties from superclass **JFrame**. You'll store this class in the project **My Graphical Applications** and in the package **buildingas400graphics**.

➢ If the workbench isn't started, start it now.
➢ Expand the project **My Graphical Applications** with a click.
➢ Select the package **buildingas400graphics** with a click. Right-click to display the shortcut menu, select **Add**, and then select **Class**.
➢ Make sure the **Project** name is **My Graphical Applications**.
➢ Make sure the **Package** name is **buildingas400graphics**.
➢ In the **Class name** field, type **OrderMaintenanceSubfileExample**.
➢ Click **Browse** to select a superclass.
➢ When the **Superclass** window appears, type **JFrame** in the **Pattern** field.
➢ In the **Type names** list, double-click **JFrame**. When you return to the SmartGuide, the **Superclass** field should contain **javax.swing.JFrame**, as shown in Figure 19.3.
➢ Select the **Browse the class when finished** check box.
➢ Select the **Compose the class visually** check box.
➢ Click **Finish** to complete the creation of the class.

Figure 19.3
OrderMaintenanceSubfileExample Class

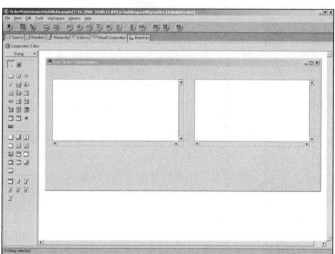

You should be inside the Visual Composition Editor. Change the title of the JFrame.

➢ On the menu bar, click **Tools**.
➢ Click **Beans List**.
➢ Double-click the **OrderMaintenanceSubfileExample** JFrame to display the **Properties** sheet.
➢ For the **title** property, type **<u>Part Order Maintenance</u>**.
➢ Close the **Properties** sheet.
➢ Close the **Beans List**.
➢ Expand the JFrame to the right and downward as shown in Figure 19.4.

Figure 19.4
JTable Outline

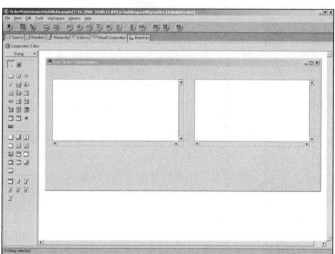

Next, create the two JTables shown in the figure.

➢ In the **Swing** bean category, click and drop two **JTable** beans ▦ on the left side of the free-form surface visual area.

➢ Resize each JTable so that it appears similar to the figure. Make sure you resize the JScrollPane, not the ScrollPaneTable. (Recall from Chapter 17 that a JTable has two components: the JScrollPane and the ScrollPaneTable.) You can use the beans list to accomplish this.

Now, create the three JLabels shown in Figure 19.5.

➢ Click and drop three **JLabel** beans ▣ on the visual area, placing them as shown in the figure.

➢ Double-click each JLabel, and change the **text** property to **Parts**, **Part Orders**, and **Select a part to show all part orders**, respectively.

➢ On the first two labels, change the **foreground** property to **DarkGray**. To do so, double-click the label, click the **Details** button ▣, select **Basic**, click the color **DarkGray**, and then click **OK**.

➢ Close the **Properties** sheet.

➢ Expand the JLabels so that you can see all the text.

Figure 19.5
Screen Layout: JTables, JLabels, and JTextFields

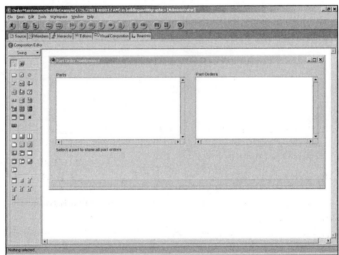

Create the JTextField shown at the bottom of the figure.

➢ Click the **JTextField** bean ▣, and drop it on the lower portion of the visual area. This field will be used as a message area.

➢ Double-click the JTextField. Change the **beanName** from **JTextField1** to **msgArea**.

➢ Change the **background** property to **LightGray**. To do so, double-click the JTextField, click the **Details** button, select **Basic**, click the color **LightGray**, and then click **OK**.

➢ Change the **editable** property to **False**.

➢ Expand the JTextField to match the figure.

➢ Close the **Properties** sheet.

Add an **AS400** bean.

➤   Click to display the bean category drop-down list, and select **AS/400 Toolbox**.
➤   Click the **AS400** bean 🔲, and drop it on the free-form nonvisual surface as shown in Figure 19.6.
➤   Double-click the **AS4001** bean.
➤   Fill in the properties **systemName** and **userID**.
➤   Close the **Properties** sheet.

Figure 19.6
AS400, ListManager, and DefaultListSelectionModel Beans

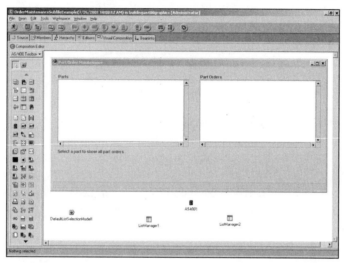

Now, you're going to add two **ListManager** beans. You'll set up one of these beans to manage the PRODDTL file and the other to manage the PARTORDER file. You'll use the existing class of **RIOProductDetailPRODDTL** as the RecordIOManager for the PRODDTL file. You created this class in earlier chapters. You'll also create a new class, **RIOPartOrdersPARTORDERUpdate**, as the RecordIOManager for the PARTORDER file.

➤   Click the **ListManager** bean 🔲, and drop it on the nonvisual free-form surface as shown above in Figure 19.6.
➤   Double-click the **ListManager1** bean.
➤   Click the **recordIOManager** property's **Details** button.
➤   Click to display the drop-down list, and select the class **Buildingas400graphics.RIOProductDetailPRODDTL**.
➤   Click **OK**.
➤   Wait until the compilation of the **RecordIOManager** bean is completed. You'll know this has occurred when the class name is filled in completely on the **recordIOManager** property.
➤   Close the **Properties** sheet.

Now, create the new class to manage the PARTORDER file. This class will allow reads and writes of the file.

➤   Click the **ListManager** bean again, and drop it on the nonvisual free-form surface as shown above in Figure 19.6.
➤   Double-click the **ListManager2** bean.
➤   Click the **recordIOManager** property's **Details** button.
➤   Click **New**.

➢ As shown in Figure 19.7, type **buildingas400graphics** in the **Package** field.
➢ In the **Class Name** field, type **RIOPartOrdersPARTORDERUpdate**.
➢ Click **OK**. The **Database** tab of the **RecordIOManager** bean is displayed.
➢ In the **File** field, type **PARTORDER**.
➢ In the **Library** field, type **ADTSLAB**.
➢ *Don't* click **OK**.

Figure 19.7
New Record IO Manager Data Class

To go to the next step, you need to successfully connect to the AS/400.

➢ Click the **Columns** tab.
➢ Enter your sign-on information, and wait a few seconds.
➢ After the database fields appear, click **OK**.
➢ Wait until the compilation of the **RecordIOManager** bean is completed. You'll know this has occurred when the class name is filled in completely on the **recordIOManager** property.
➢ Close the **Properties** sheet.

DefaultListSelectionModel

You use the **DefaultListSelectionModel** class to enable selecting records (rows) in a JTable. The **valueChanged** event signals that the selection of a record has occurred; processing of that record can then follow. You can set the selection mode so that the user can define either single or multiple selections.

You're going to add a **DefaultListSelectionModel** bean, or class. You won't find this class in the bean palette. You must retrieve it using the **Choose Bean** button.

➢ In the upper-left corner of the VCE, click the **Choose Bean** button.
➢ In the **Choose Bean** window's **Class name** field, type **DefaultList**. Then click **Browse** to select a class.
➢ In the **Choose a Valid Class** window's **Class names** list, select **DefaultListSelectionModel**.
➢ Click **OK**. When you return to the **Choose Bean** window, the **Class name** field should contain **javax.swing.DefaultListSelectionModel**, as shown in Figure 19.8.
➢ Click **OK**.

Figure 19.8
Choose Bean Window

➢ Using the crosshair pointer, drop the **DefaultListSelectionModel** bean on the lower-left nonvisual free-form surface as shown above in Figure 19.6. Notice that the new bean icon is identified with the same symbol as the **Choose Bean** button.

➢ Double-click the **DefaultListSelectionModel1** bean to display the **Properties** sheet.

➢ Change the **selectionMode** property to **0**. This value signifies that the user is limited to selecting a single row (record) in the JTable.

➢ Close the **Properties** sheet.

Save the Java program.

➢ On the menu bar, click **Bean**.

➢ Click **Save Bean**.

Connecting the AS/400 Beans

You are now going to set up five property-to-property connections, five event-to-method connections, and three event-to-code connections.

Property-to-Property Connection: system

connPtoP1: (AS4001,this ↔ ListManager1,system)

Connect the **AS4001** bean with the **ListManager1** bean.

➢ Right-click the **AS4001** bean.

➢ Click **Connect**.

➢ Click **this**.

➢ Click the spider-end pointer on the **ListManager1** bean.

➢ Click **Connectible Features**.

➢ Double-click the **system** property.

Property-to-Property Connection: system

connPtoP2: (AS4001,this ↔ ListManager2,system)

Connect the **AS4001** bean with the **ListManager2** bean.

➢ Right-click the **AS4001** bean.

➢ Click **Connect**.

➢ Click **this**.

➢ Click the spider-end pointer on the **ListManager2** bean.

➢ Click **Connectible Features**.

➢ Double-click the **system** property.

Property-to-Property Connection: selectionModel

connPtoP3: (DefaultListSelectionModel1,this ↔ ScrollPaneTable,selectionModel)

Connect the **DefaultListSelectionModel1** bean with the left **JScrollPane** bean.

➢ Right-click the **DefaultListSelectionModel1** bean.

➢ Click **Connect**.

➢ Click **this**.

➢ Click the spider-end pointer on the center of the left **JScrollPane** bean (i.e., on the ScrollPaneTable).
➢ Click **Connectible Features**.
➢ Double-click the **selectionModel** property. Be careful to choose the **selection<u>Model</u>**, not the **selection<u>Mode</u>**, property.

Your connection should appear as shown in Figure 19.9.

➢ Double-click the connection to verify that it is correct as shown in Figure 19.10.
➢ Close the **Properties** window.

<table>
<tr><td align="center">**Figure 19.9**</td><td align="center">**Figure 19.10**</td></tr>
<tr><td align="center">*selectionModel Connection: connPtoP3*</td><td align="center">*Connection connPtoP3*</td></tr>
</table>

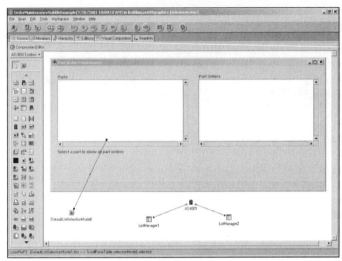

Property-to-Property Connection: displayContainer

```
connPtoP4: (JScrollPane1,this ↔ ListManager1,displayContainer)
```

Connect the **JScrollPane1** bean with the ListManager1 **displayContainer** property as shown in Figure 19.11.

➢ Select JScrollPane1 by clicking the outside edge of the left JTable.
➢ Click **Connect**.
➢ Click **this**.
➢ Click the spider-end pointer on the **ListManager1** bean.
➢ Click **displayContainer**.

Figure 19.11
displayContainer Connections: connPtoP4 and connPtoP5

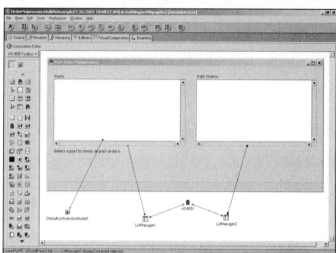

Property-to-Property Connection: displayContainer

connPtoP5: (JScrollPane2,this ⟷ ListManager2,displayContainer)

Connect the **JScrollPane2** bean with the ListManager2 **displayContainer** property as shown above in Figure 19.11.

➢   Select JScrollPane2 by clicking the outside edge of the right JTable.
➢   Click **Connect**.
➢   Click **this**.
➢   Click the spider-end pointer on the **ListManager2** bean.
➢   Click **displayContainer**.

Save the Java program.

➢   On the menu bar, click **Bean**.
➢   Click **Save Bean**.

Event-to-Method Connection: readAllRecords()

connEtoM1: (OrderMaintenanceSubfileExample,initialize() → ListManager1,readAllRecords())

This connection will read all the records in the AS/400 database file, similar to a subfile load-all routine. The connection will force the AS/400 sign-on prompt to appear before the application screen appears, due to the connection to the **initialize()** method. The **readAllRecords()** method will be executed before the application first appears. This, in essence, will show a full JTable (subfile) of the parts file (PRODDTL) when the application first appears.

Create an event-to-method connection with the **OrderMaintenanceSubfileExample** JFrame and the **readAllRecords()** method.

➢   Right-click the outside edge of the **OrderMaintenanceSubfileExample** JFrame.
➢   Click **Connect**.
➢   Click **Connectible Features**.

➢   Click the **initialize()** event.
➢   Click **OK**.
➢   Click the spider-end pointer on the **ListManager1** bean.
➢   Click **Connectible Features**.
➢   Click the **readAllRecords()** method.
➢   Click **OK**.

Your connection should appear as shown in Figure 19.12.

➢   Double-click the connection to verify that it is correct as shown in Figure 19.13.
➢   Close the **Properties** window.

Figure 19.12
Initialize() Connection: connEtoM1

Figure 19.13
Connection connEtoM1

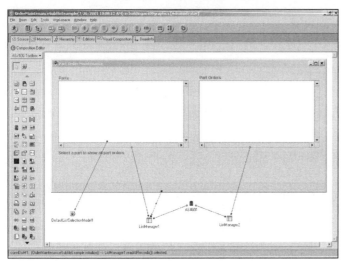

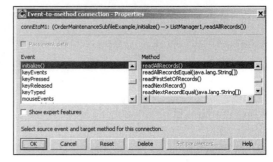

Event-to-Code Connection: closeFile()

```
connEtoC1: (OrderMaintenanceSubfileExample,windowClosed → OrderMaintenanceSubfileExample,void
           orderMaintenanceSubfileExample_WindowClosed(java.awt.event.WindowEvent))
```

Once again your application has no **Exit** or **Close** JButton anywhere on the screen. The only way to end the application is to click the Windows **Close** button. You're going to use an event-to-code connection to perform the necessary shutdown functions for the application: closing the two databases and disposing of the window.

Create an event-to-code connection with the **OrderMaintenanceSubfileExample** JFrame.

➢   Right-click the outside edge of the **OrderMaintenanceSubfileExample** JFrame.
➢   Click **Connect**.
➢   Click **windowClosed**.
➢   Click the spider-end pointer on the nonvisual free-form surface.
➢   Click **Event to Code**.
➢   Insert the Java code shown in Figure 19.14. When you've finished typing the new Java code, your method should look identical to Figure 19.15.
➢   Click **OK**.

Figure 19.14
Source Code for orderMaintenanceSubfileExample_WindowClosed

```
Source code: orderMaintenanceSubfileExample_WindowClosed
try {
    getListManager1().closeFile();
    getListManager2().closeFile();
    dispose();
}
 catch (java.lang.Throwable ivjExc) {
    handleException(ivjExc);
}
```

Figure 19.15
Connection connEtoC1

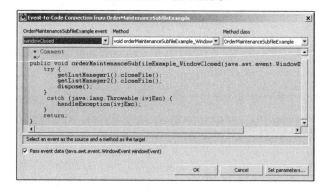

Defining a KLIST Equivalent

You may want to bookmark the following connection. There will be many times, including for this chapter's application, when you want to accomplish the equivalent of an RPG Chain operation with a key value. The following section of code shows you how to do this.

Event-to-Code Connection: valueChanged

```
connEtoC2: (DefaultListSelectionModel1,valueChanged → OrderMaintenanceSubfileExample,void
        defaultListSelectionModel1_ValueChanged javax,swing.event.ListSelectionEvent))
```

The **valueChanged** event triggers the action to take place when a parts record (row) is selected in the first, or left, JTable. When the record is selected, the following steps will be taken:

1. To retrieve all the part order records, set up a **String[]** key value. This step is similar to building a KLIST in RPG.
2. With the new **String[] key** value (the part number), attempt to read a record from the parts order (PARTORDER) file. This step is similar to a CHAIN operation in RPG.
3. If a record is found in the parts order file that matches the part number from the parts file, then
    a. Clear any possible error messages.
    b. Clear the part orders JTable.
    c. Read all matched part orders. This step is similar to an RPG READE operation inside a loop.
4. If no record is found in the parts order file that matches the part number from the parts file, display an error message stating "No orders exist for part number *xxxxx*".

Create an event-to-code connection with the **DefaultListSelectionModel1** bean.

➤ Right-click the **DefaultListSelectionModel1** bean.
➤ Click **Connect**.
➤ Click **Connectible Features**.
➤ Click the **valueChanged** event.
➤ Click the spider-end pointer on the nonvisual free-form surface.
➤ Click **Event to Code**.
➤ Insert the Java code shown in Figure 19.16. This code first sets up the key to be used to retrieve the related part orders. Next, it checks to see whether there are any related part orders. If there are, it reads all the related records into the scrollpane. If there are no part orders, it displays a red and white error message.
➤ Click **OK**.

Figure 19.17 shows what this connection should look like.

Figure 19.16
Source Code for defaultListSelectionModel_ValueChanged

```
Source code: defaultListSelectionModel1_ValueChanged
  String[] key = new String[1];
  key[0] = (String)getScrollPaneTable().getValueAt(getScrollPaneTable().getSelectedRow(), 0);
  try {
    if (getListManager2().readRecord(key) == true) {
        getmsgArea().setText(" ");
        getmsgArea().setBackground(java.awt.Color.lightGray);
        getListManager2().clearAllData();
        getListManager2().readAllRecordsEqual(key);
    }
    else {
        getListManager2().clearAllData();
        getmsgArea().setText("No orders exist for part number " + key[0]);
        getmsgArea().setBackground(java.awt.Color.red);
        getmsgArea().setForeground(java.awt.Color.white);
    }
  }
  catch (java.lang.Throwable ivjExc) {
    handleException(ivjExc);
  }
```

Figure 19.17
defaultListSelectionModel_ValueChanged() Connection: connEtoC2

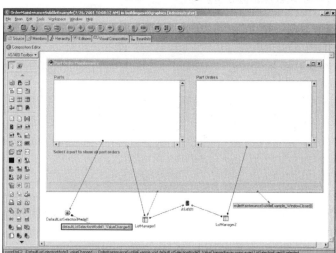

Save the Java program.

➤ On the menu bar, click **Bean**.
➤ Click **Save Bean**.

To run the Java program, you need to successfully connect to the AS/400. Run the program.

➤ On the menu bar, click **Bean**.
➤ Click **Run**, and then click **Run Main**.

Notice that the AS/400 prompt appears immediately.

➤ Enter your sign-on information, and wait a few seconds. It may take just a little longer than what you've experienced in the past.

You should see the application as shown in Figure 19.18. Notice that all the database fields defined in the RecordIOManager for the parts file are displayed. Why are the columns all scrunched together? That's because you haven't defined any TableColumns. If you want to define TableColumns, review the previous chapter.

Figure 19.18
Part Order Maintenance

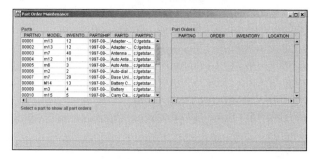

➤ Click part number **00008**. A few seconds may pass before anything occurs.

Figure 19.19 shows what happened. All the part orders associated with part number 00008 were loaded into the JTable on the right side of the screen. Pretty cool! That wasn't too difficult.

Figure 19.19
Part Orders Loaded

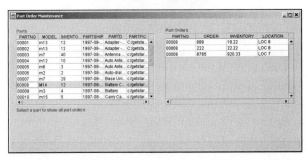

Now, you're going to see what happens when no part orders are associated with a part number.

➤   On the left side of the screen, click part number **00007**.

As Figure 19.20 shows, two things should have happened. The part orders JTable was cleared, and an error message appeared: "No part orders exist for part number 00007."

Figure 19.20
Error Message for No Part Orders

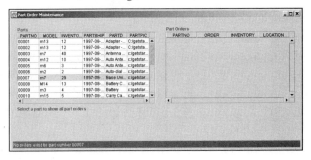

➤   Click part number **00005**.

As Figure 19.21 shows, notice that the error message disappeared. That's because you included code to clear the error message in the **DefaultListSelectionModel1_ValueChanged()** event-to-code connection.

Figure 19.21
Error Message Cleared

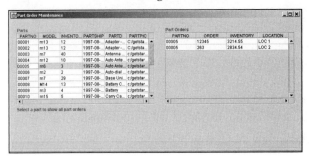

Before we continue, feel free to play around. You can't hurt anything.

➢ Close the **Part Order Maintenance** application.

You still have some work to do. Create the five JButtons shown in Figure 19.22.

➢ Return to the **Swing** bean category.
➢ Click and drop five **JButton** beans ▣ in the lower-right corner of the visual area as shown in the figure.
➢ Double-click each JButton to display the **Properties** sheet. Change the **beanName** property to **btInsertAfter**, **btInsertBefore**, **btUpdate**, **btDelete**, and **btPrint**, respectively.
➢ Change the **text** property to **Insert After**, **Insert Before**, **Update**, **Delete**, and **Print**, respectively.
➢ Change the **background** property to **DarkBlue** on all five JButtons.
➢ Change the **foreground** property to **White** on all five JButtons.
➢ Verify that the **font** property is bold on all five JButtons.
➢ Close the **Properties** sheet. Expand the JButtons so that you can see all the text.

Figure 19.22
JButtons

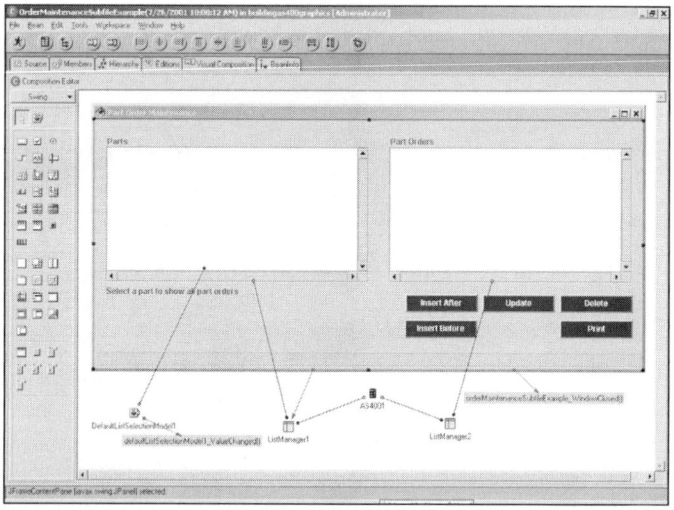

More Connections

Now, you're going to create the connections to perform the functions of the JButtons you just added.

Event-to-Code Connection: btPrint

```
connEtoC3: (btPrint,actionPerformed → OrderMaintenanceSubfileExample,void
            btPrint_ActionPerformed(java.awt.event.ActionEvent))
```

This connection will capture a screen snapshot and then call the standard Windows Print API.

Create an event-to-code connection with the **btPrint** JButton.

➢ Right-click the **btPrint** JButton.
➢ Click **Connect**.
➢ Click **actionPerformed**.
➢ Click the spider-end pointer on the nonvisual free-form surface.
➢ Click **Event to Code**.

➢ Insert the Java code shown in Figure 19.23 into the new method named **btPrint_ActionPerformed()**.When you've finished typing the new Java code, your method should look identical to Figure 19.24.

➢ Click **OK**.

➢ Click and hold the **btPrint_ActionPerformed()** method, and drag it down closer to the **btPrint** JButton, as shown in Figure 19.25.

Figure 19.23
Source Code for Printing a Screen Snapshot

```
Source code: connEtoC3
    java.awt.PrintJob job = java.awt.Toolkit.getDefaultToolkit().getPrintJob(null,"",null);
    java.awt.Graphics g = job.getGraphics();
    ivjJFrameContentPane.printAll(g);
    g.dispose();
    job.end();
```

Figure 19.24
Connection connEtoC3

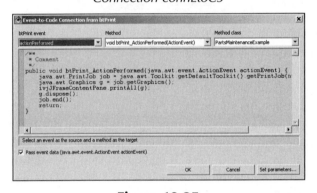

Figure 19.25
btPrint_ActionPerformed Connection: connEtoC3 in New Location

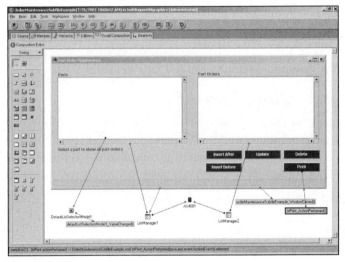

Event-to-Method Connection: insertAfterCurrentRecord()

`connEtoM2: (btInsertAfter,actionPerformed → ListManager2,insertAfterCurrentRecord())`

This connection inserts a record into the parts order file when the user clicks the **Insert After** button. It also inserts a blank record into the JTable (displayContainer).

Create an event-to-method connection with the **btInsertAfter** JButton and the **insertAfterCurrentRecord()** method. The **insertAfterCurrentRecord()** method is a standard record-handling method within the **ListManager** bean.

➢ Right-click the **btInsertAfter** JButton.
➢ Click **Connect**.
➢ Click **actionPerformed**.
➢ Click the spider-end pointer on the **ListManager2** bean.
➢ Click **Connectible Features**.
➢ Click the **insertAfterCurrentRecord()** method.
➢ Click **OK**.
➢ Double-click the connection to verify that it is correct as shown in Figure 19.26.
➢ Close the **Properties** window.

Figure 19.26
Connection connEtoM2

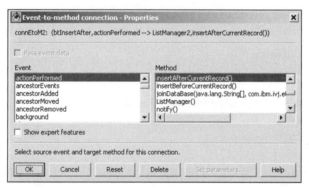

Event-to-Method Connection: insertBeforeCurrentRecord()

`connEtoM3: (btInsertBefore,actionPerformed → ListManager2,insertBeforeCurrentRecord())`

This connection inserts a record into the parts order file when the user clicks the **Insert Before** button. It also inserts a blank record into the JTable (displayContainer).

Create an event-to-method connection with the **btInsertBefore** JButton and the **insertBeforeCurrentRecord()** method. The **insertBeforeCurrentRecord()** method is a standard record-handling method within the **ListManager** bean.

➢ Right-click the **btInsertBefore** JButton.
➢ Click **Connect**.
➢ Click **actionPerformed**.
➢ Click the spider-end pointer on the **ListManager2** bean.
➢ Click **Connectible Features**.
➢ Click the **insertBeforeCurrentRecord()** method.
➢ Click **OK**.

➤ Double-click the connection to verify that it is correct as shown in Figure 19.27.
➤ Close the **Properties** window.

Figure 19.27
Connection connEtoM3

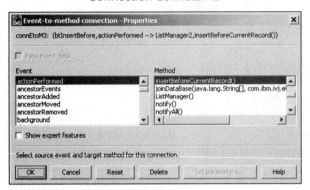

Event-to-Method Connection: updateRecord()

`connEtoM4: (btUpdate,actionPerformed → ListManager2,updateRecord(int))`

This connection updates an existing record in the parts order file when the user clicks the **Update** JButton.
Create an event-to-method connection with the **btUpdate** JButton and the **updateRecord()** method.

➤ Right-click the **btUpdate** JButton.
➤ Click **Connect**.
➤ Click **actionPerformed**.
➤ Click the spider-end pointer on the **ListManager2** bean.
➤ Click **Connectible Features**.
➤ Click the **updateRecord(int)** method.
➤ Click **OK**.
➤ Double-click the connection to verify that it is correct as shown in Figure 19.28.
➤ Close the **Properties** window.

Figure 19.28
Connection connEtoM4

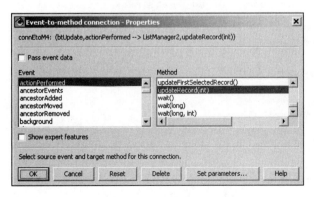

Parameter-from-Property Connection

```
connPfromP1: (connEtoM4: (btUpdate,actionPerformed →
              ListManager2,updateRecord(int)),arg1 → ScrollPaneTable1,selectedRow)
```

Notice that the connection is incomplete. To complete it, you need to make the connection for the parameter of the **updateRecord(int)** method. The **int** parameter needs to be the row designator of the selected record in the part orders JTable.

➤ Right-click the dashed connection **connEtoM4**.
➤ Click **Connect**.
➤ Click **row**.
➤ Click the spider-end pointer on the outside edge of the **OrderMaintenanceSubfileExample** JFrame.
➤ Click the spider-end pointer on the center of the right **JScrollPane** bean (i.e., on ScrollPanelTable1).
➤ Click **selectedRow**.

Your connection should appear as shown in Figure 19.29.

➤ Double-click the connection to verify that it is correct as shown in Figure 19.30.
➤ Close the **Properties** window.

Figure 19.29
selectedRow Connection: connPfromP1

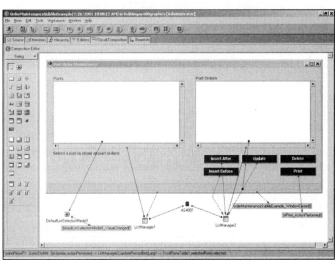

Figure 19.30
Connection connPfromP1

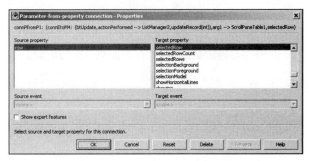

Event-to-Method Connection: deleteRecord()

`connEtoM5: (btDelete,actionPerformed → ListManager2,deleteSelectedRecords())`

This connection can delete one or more records from the parts order file when the user clicks the **Delete** button.
Create an event-to-method connection with the **btDelete** JButton and the **deleteSelectedRecords()** method.

➤ Right-click the **btDelete** JButton.
➤ Click **Connect**.
➤ Click **actionPerformed**.
➤ Click the spider-end pointer on the **ListManager2** bean.
➤ Click **Connectible Features**.
➤ Click the **deleteSelectedRecords()** method.
➤ Click **OK**.

Your connection should appear as shown in Figure 19.31.

➤ Double-click the connection to verify that it is correct as shown in Figure 19.32.
➤ Close the **Properties** window.

Figure 19.31
deleteSelectedRecords() Connection: connEtoM5

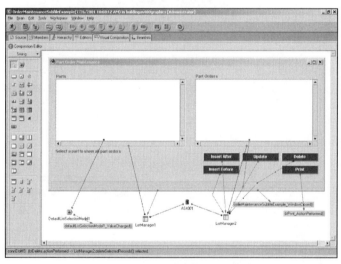

Figure 19.32
Connection connEtoM5

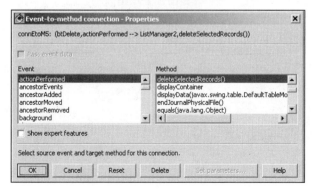

Save and then run the Java program.

➢   On the menu bar, click **Bean**.

➢   Click **Save Bean**.

➢   On the menu bar, click **Bean**.

➢   Click **Run**, and then click **Run Main**.

➢   Enter your sign-on information, and wait a few seconds.

You should see the application as shown in Figure 19.33.

Figure 19.33
Part Order Maintenance

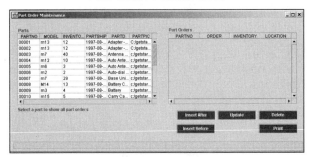

➢   Click part number **00006**.

As shown in Figure 19.34, you should have received an error message stating that no part orders exist for part number 00006. That is correct. Now, you're going to enter a new part order.

➢   Click **Insert After**.

You should see a blank record in the part orders JTable, as shown in Figure 19.34.

Figure 19.34
Blank Insert Record

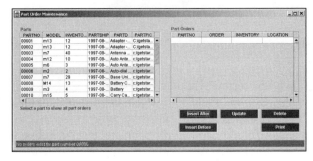

Enter the new part order information shown in Figure 19.35.

➢   In the **PARTNO** field, enter **00006**.

➢   In the **ORDER** field, enter **001**.

➢   In the **INVENTORY** field, enter **0**.

➢   In the **LOCATION** field, enter **Bldg A.**.

➢   Click the **Update** button.

Figure 19.35
Newly Entered Part Order

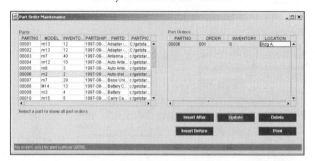

➢   Click part number **00007**.

You should have received an error message stating that 00007 has no part orders. That is correct. Now let's see what you have under part number 00006.

➢   Click part number **00006**.

There's your new record! You should see the same screen as shown in Figure 19.36.

Figure 19.36
Retrieved Part Order

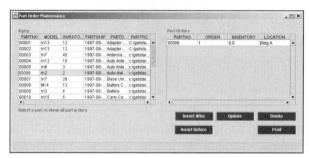

➢   In the **Part Orders** JTable, click part number **00006**, order number **1**.
➢   Click **Delete**.

Figure 19.37 shows what happened. The record is gone. Did you notice that no deletion-confirmation message appeared? That's because you didn't add that section of code to this program. To create a deletion confirmation, you'd need to add something similar to what you did in Chapter 18.

Figure 19.37
Deleted Part Order

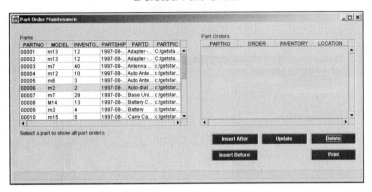

If you had multiple records to delete, you could do so by holding down the Shift key and selecting the desired records. Then when you clicked the **Delete** button, the application would delete all the selected records at once.

Spend some time getting familiar with all the functions you just programmed. Try the **Update**, **Print**, and **Insert Before** buttons.

➤   Close the **Part Order Maintenance** application.

Congratulations on completing your first maintenance subfile equivalent! You may want to add some coding to perform certain functions after the **Delete** key, the **Update** key, or one of the **Insert** keys is clicked. To do so, you would need to change the appropriate event-to-method connection to an event-to-code connection and then add in the Java code.

Summary

In this chapter you learned

- how to use multiple JTables and ListManagers on the same screen
- how to maintain a database using a JTable
- how to use the **DefaultListSelectionModel** class
- how to select a record by key, using the information from another database file
- how to set up a **String[] key** value

The next chapter will show you how to code the equivalent of a page-at-a-time subfile.

Chapter 20

Building Java Maintenance Applications: Subfile Page-at-a-Time

 Chapter Objectives

- [ ] Understand how to use load-page-at-a-time concepts
- [ ] Use position-to functions in a JTable
- [ ] Become familiar with SetOfRecords methods
- [ ] Learn how to implement graphical icons for page-up/page-down functions

 Chapter Project

- [ ] A class will be created to list parts one page at a time.
- [ ] Figure 20.1 shows what the sample class will look like.

Figure 20.1
Chapter Project

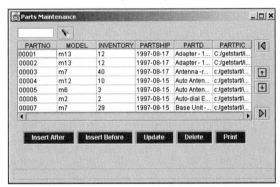

When developing AS/400 subfiles, 99 out of 100 times I use a "load-a-page-at-a-time" design. Such subfiles are more complicated to write than load-all subfiles, but in most cases they are more effective. One feature of the page-at-a-time concept is the ability to reload the screen, either up or down, always knowing that you're getting the most current set of data. This ability is most important when you're dealing with very dynamic database files.

Another feature I really enjoy seeing built into subfiles or JTables is a "position-to" function. This function helps a user quickly find the database record for which he or she is looking. There are many ways to implement a position-to function. You'll be creating such a function using one approach in this chapter.

Personal biases aside, the two design weaknesses I dislike most when using a subfile or JTable are

- having to wait while a large database is loaded (load-all concept)
- not being able to quickly reach the record I'm looking for. In a JTable, this entails using the scroll bar to get there. Scroll bars work great on small files, but they can be cumbersome on large database files.

In this chapter, you'll overcome these two design weaknesses. You're going to create the equivalent of a page-at-a-time JTable. Instead of using a vertical scroll bar, you'll use a page-up/page-down function. You could implement this function by testing for the particular Page Up or Page Down keystroke. Instead, you'll create graphical buttons depicting an up arrow and a down arrow to implement the page-up and page-down concepts.

Enjoy the chapter. It's a fun one!

Parts Maintenance Example

In this chapter project, you'll be using the product details physical file from the AS/400, file PRODDTL in library ADTSLAB. You've already used this file in previous chapters.

You're going to create a class called **PartsMaintenanceSubfileExample** that inherits properties from superclass **JFrame**. You'll store the class in the project **My Graphical Applications** and in the package **buildingas400graphics**.

➤   If the workbench isn't started, start it now.
➤   Expand the project **My Graphical Applications** with a click.
➤   Select the package **buildingas400graphics** with a click. Right-click to display the shortcut menu, select **Add**, and then select **Class**.
➤   Make sure the **Project** name is **My Graphical Applications**.
➤   Make sure the **Package** name is **buildingas400graphics**.
➤   In the **Class name** field, type **PartsMaintenanceSubfileExample**.
➤   Click **Browse** to select a superclass.
➤   When the **Superclass** window appears, type **JFrame** in the **Pattern** field.
➤   In the **Type names** list, double-click **JFrame**. When you return to the SmartGuide, the **Superclass** field should contain **javax.swing.JFrame,** as shown in Figure 20.2.
➤   Select the **Browse the class when finished** check box.
➤   Select the **Compose the class visually** check box.
➤   Click **Finish** to complete the creation of the class.

You should be inside the Visual Composition Editor. Change the title of the JFrame.

➤   On the menu bar, click **Tools**.
➤   Click **Beans List**.
➤   Double-click the **PartsMaintenanceSubfileExample** JFrame to display the **Properties** sheet.
➤   For the **title** property, type **Parts Maintenance**.
➤   Close the **Properties** sheet.
➤   Close the **Beans List**.
➤   Expand the JFrame to the right and downward as shown in Figure 20.3.

Create a JTable as shown in the figure.

➤   In the **Swing** bean category, click and drop a **JTable** bean ⊞ on the center of the free-form surface visual area.
➤   Resize the JTable so that it appears similar to the figure. Be sure to resize the JScrollPane, not the ScrollPaneTable.

Figure 20.2
PartsMaintenanceSubfileExample Class

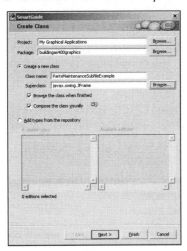

Figure 20.3
JTable Outline

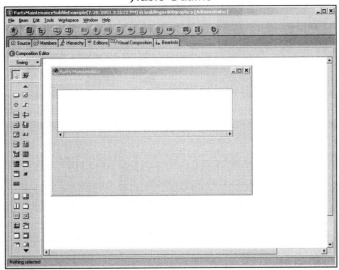

You won't be using the JTable's vertical scroll bar in this chapter. Instead, you'll define your own JButtons that will replace this scroll bar's functionality. Disable the vertical scroll bar by taking the following steps.

➤ Click the outside edge of the **JTable** to display the **Properties** sheet.
➤ Change the **verticalScrollBarPolicy** property to **VERTICAL_SCROLLBAR_NEVER**.
➤ Close the **Properties** sheet.

Create the two JTextFields shown in Figure 20.4.

➤ Click the **JTextField** bean ▣, and drop it on the upper portion of the visual area.
➤ Double-click the JTextField. Change the **beanName** from **JTextField1** to **partno**.

➤ Change the **toolTipText** property to **Enter Part Number**. As the user moves the mouse pointer across this input field, this hover text will appear.

➤ Expand the JTextField to the size shown in the figure.

➤ Close the **Properties** sheet.

➤ Click the **JTextField** bean again, and drop it on the lower portion of the visual area.

➤ Double-click the JTextField. Change the **beanName** from **JTextField1** to **msgArea**. This field will be used as a message area.

➤ Change the **background** property to **LightGray**.

➤ Change the **editable** property to **False**.

➤ Expand the JTextField to the size shown in the figure.

➤ Close the **Properties** sheet.

Figure 20.4
Screen Layout: JTextFields

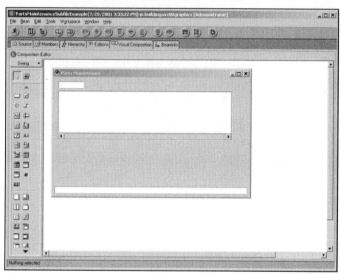

Add five JButtons to the JFrame as shown in Figure 20.5. These buttons will be the navigational icons used to maneuver through the database: a retrieve, first, page up, page down, and last button. You learned about customizing JButtons in Chapter 18. You'll customize each of these JButtons to appear as a graphical icon.

➤ Click and drop five **JButton** beans ▣ on the visual area as shown in the figure.

➤ Double-click each JButton to display the **Properties** sheet. Change the **beanName** property to **btRetrieve**, **btFirst**, **btPageUp**, **btPageDn**, and **btLast**, respectively.

➤ Change the **text** property by blanking out or clearing all the text contained there. Do this on all five JButtons.

➤ On the first JButton, change the **icon** property. To do so, click the property's **Details** button ▣. Then select the **Icon** window's **File** option, and click **Browse** to choose an icon file.

➤ As shown in Figure 20.6, double-click file **find**. This choice will cause the find.gif graphic (a flashlight image) to appear on the face of the **btRetrieve** JButton.

➤ Click **OK**.

➤ Make a similar change for the other four JButtons, selecting file **FirstIcon**, **up**, **down**, and **LastIcon**, respectively.

Figure 20.5
JButtons

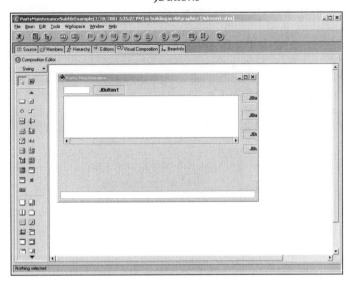

Figure 20.6
Available Icons

➢ Change the JButtons' **toolTipText** property to **<u>Find Part</u>**, **<u>First Record</u>**, **<u>Page Up</u>**, **<u>Page Down</u>**, and **<u>Last Record</u>**, respectively. When the user hovers over the navigational tools, the appropriate toolTipText will be displayed.

➢ Close the **Properties** sheet.

➢ Resize your buttons so that they look as shown in Figure 20.7. You may need to align the buttons to get them to appear as shown.

Figure 20.7

Customized Navigational JButtons

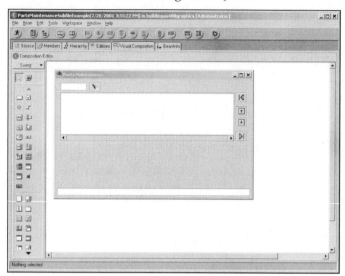

Next, create a JPanel as shown in Figure 20.8.

➢   Click the **JPanel** bean 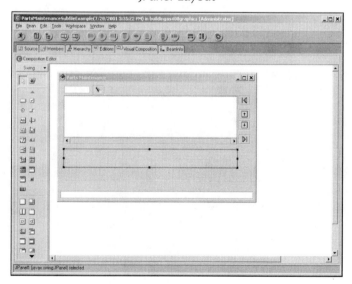, and drop it on the lower portion of the visual area.
➢   Resize the JPanel to match the size shown in the figure.
➢   Double-click the JPanel to display the **Properties** sheet.
➢   Change the **layout** property to **FlowLayout**.
➢   Close the **Properties** sheet.

Figure 20.8

JPanel Layout

Next, you're going to add five buttons to the newly created JPanel. These buttons will serve as the operational buttons to perform the insert after, insert before, update, delete, and print database functions. Figure 20.9 shows what the buttons will look like after you've completed the following steps.

➢   Click and drop five **JButton** beans on the JPanel. It doesn't matter where you drop them because the **FlowLayout** Layout Manager will position them automatically.
➢   Double-click each JButton to display the **Properties** sheet.
➢   Change the **beanName** property to **btInsertAfter**, **btInsertBefore**, **btUpdate**, **btDelete**, and **btPrint**, respectively.
➢   Change the **text** property to **Insert After**, **Insert Before**, **Update**, **Delete**, and **Print**, respectively.
➢   Change the **background** property to **Blue** on all five JButtons.
➢   Change the **foreground** property to **White** on all five JButtons.
➢   Close the **Properties** sheet.

Figure 20.9
Customized Operational JButtons

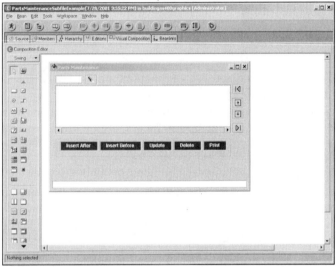

Save the Java program.

➢   On the menu bar, click **Bean**.
➢   Click **Save Bean**.

Now you're going to add an **AS400** bean.

➢   Click to display the bean category drop-down list, and select **AS/400 Toolbox**.
➢   Click the **AS400** bean 🔲, and drop it on the free-form nonvisual surface as shown in Figure 20.10.
➢   Double-click the **AS4001** bean.
➢   For ease of use later on, fill in the **systemName** and **userID** properties.
➢   Close the **Properties** sheet.

Figure 20.10
AS400 and ListManager Beans

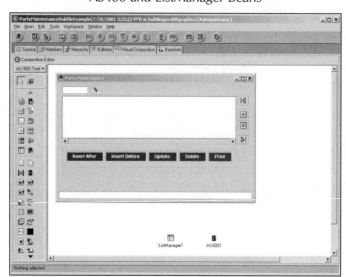

Packet Size: Subfile Size

When working with AS/400 subfiles, you need to define the subfile size — that is, the number of records that appear within the subfile. Similarly, you need to define a JTable's size by specifying what is called a *packet size*. The packet size determines how many physical records the application retrieves from the database to load into the JTable. The packet size is not actually defined on the JTable; it is defined in the **RecordIOManager** bean, the bean that controls the retrieving of records from the database file.

In previous chapters, you used methods such as **readRecord()** and **readNextRecord()** to retrieve database records. In this chapter, you'll be exposed to some new methods that use *sets*, such as the method **readNextSetOfRecords()**. As you can probably guess, these methods retrieve a set, or group, of records at a time. The packet size determines how many records are retrieved in a set.

You're going to add a **ListManager** bean now. You'll use this bean to manage the PRODDTL file. You'll create a new class called **RIOProductDetailPRODDTLSubfileUpdate** as the RecordIOManager for this file. The new class will allow reads and writes of PRODDTL. You'll also change the packet size to 7. With this value, the application will retrieve seven records at a time when you use the various **readxxxSetOfRecords()** methods.

➤   Click the **ListManager** bean ▣, and drop it on the nonvisual free-form surface as shown above in Figure 20.10.
➤   Double-click the **ListManager1** bean.
➤   Click the **recordIOManager** property's **Details** button.
➤   Click **New**.
➤   As shown in Figure 20.11, type **buildingas400graphics** in the **Package** field.
➤   In the **Class Name** field, type **RIOProductDetailPRODDTLSubfileUpdate**.
➤   Click **OK**. The **Database** tab of the **RecordIOManager** bean is displayed.

Figure 20.11
New Record IO Manager Data Class

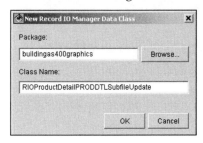

Set up the database information as shown in Figure 20.12.

➢   In the **File** field, type **PRODDTL**.
➢   In the **Library** field, type **ADTSLAB**.
➢   Change the **Packet Size** value to **7**.
➢   *Don't* click **OK**.

Figure 20.12
Database Specification

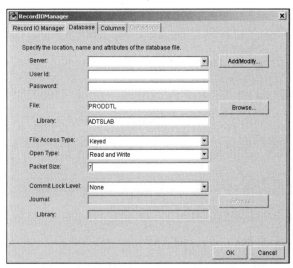

To go to the next step, you need to successfully connect to the AS/400.

➢   Click the **Columns** tab.
➢   Enter your sign-on information, and wait a few seconds.
➢   After the database fields appear, click **OK**.
➢   Wait until the compilation of the **RecordIOManager** bean has been completed. You'll know this has occurred when the class name is filled in completely in the **recordIOManager** property.
➢   Close the **Properties** sheet.

Save the Java program.

➢   On the menu bar, click **Bean**.
➢   Click **Save Bean**.

Connecting the AS/400 Beans

You are now going to set up two property-to-property connections, five event-to-method connections, eight event-to-code connections, and one parameter-from-property connection.

Property-to-Property Connection: system

`connPtoP1: (AS4001,this ↔ ListManager1,system)`

Connect the **AS4001** bean with the **ListManager1** bean.

➢   Right-click the **AS4001** bean.
➢   Click **Connect**.
➢   Click **this**.
➢   Click the spider-end pointer on the **ListManager1** bean.
➢   Click **Connectible Features**.
➢   Double-click the **system** property.

Property-to-Property Connection: displayContainer

`connPtoP2: (JScrollPane1,this ↔ ListManager1,displayContainer)`

Connect the JScrollPane with the **ListManager1** bean's **displayContainer** property as shown in Figure 20.13.

➢   Select JScrollPane1 by clicking the outside edge of the JTable.
➢   Click **Connect**.
➢   Click **this**.
➢   Click the spider-end pointer on the **ListManager1** bean.
➢   Click **displayContainer**.

Figure 20.13
displayContainer Connection: connPtoP2

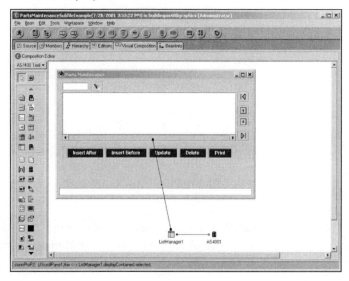

Event-to-Method Connection: readFirstSetOfRecords()

```
connEtoM1: (PartsMaintenanceSubfileExample,initialize() →
            ListManager1,readFirstSetOfRecords())
```

The **readFirstSetOfRecords()** method is similar to the **readFirstRecord()** method. The only difference is that **readFirstRecord()** reads only one record. The **readFirstSetOfRecords()** method begins reading at the first record of the file and continues reading until either the packet size or the end-of-file is reached. Remember, the packet size is defined in the **RecordIOManager** bean. In this chapter project, seven records are read.

This connection displays an AS/400 prompt screen and then reads the first seven records before the application screen appears. Create an event-to-method connection with the **PartsMaintenanceSubfileExample** JFrame and the **readFirstSetOfRecords()** method.

➤   Right-click the outside edge of the **PartsMaintenanceSubfileExample** JFrame.
➤   Click **Connect**.
➤   Click **Connectible Features**.
➤   Click the **initialize()** event.
➤   Click **OK**.
➤   Click the spider-end pointer on the **ListManager1** bean.
➤   Click **Connectible Features**.
➤   Click the **readFirstSetOfRecords()** method.
➤   Click **OK**.
➤   Double-click the connection to verify that it is correct as shown in Figure 20.14.
➤   Close the **Properties** window.

Figure 20.14
Connection connEtoM1

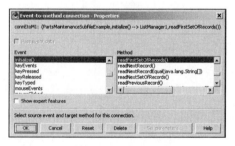

Event-to-Code Connection: windowClosed

```
connEtoC1: (PartsMaintenanceSubfileExample,windowClosed →
            PartsMaintenanceSubfileExample,void
            partsMaintenanceSubfileExample_WindowClosed
            (java.awt.event.WindowEvent))
```

As in previous chapters, notice that there is no **Exit** or **Close** JButton anywhere on the application screen. The only way to end this application is to click the Windows **Close** button. You're going to use an event-to-code connection to perform the necessary shutdown functions for the application: closing the database and disposing of the window.

Create an event-to-code connection with the **PartsMaintenanceSubfileExample** JFrame.

➤   Right-click the outside edge of the **PartsMaintenanceSubfileExample** JFrame.
➤   Click **Connect**.

➢ Click **windowClosed**.
➢ Click the spider-end pointer on the nonvisual free-form surface.
➢ Click **Event to Code**.
➢ Insert the Java code shown in Figure 20.15. When you've finished typing the new Java code, your method should look identical to Figure 20.16.
➢ Click **OK**.

Figure 20.15
Source Code for partsMaintenanceSubfileExample_WindowClosed

```
Source code: partsMaintenanceSubfileExample_WindowClosed
    try {
        getListManager1().closeFile();
        }
    catch (java.lang.Throwable ivjExc) {
        handleException(ivjExc);
        }
    dispose();
```

Figure 20.16
Connection connEtoC1

Save the Java program.

➢ On the menu bar, click **Bean**.
➢ Click **Save Bean**.

To run the Java program, you need to successfully connect to the AS/400. Run the program.

➢ On the menu bar, click **Bean**.
➢ Click **Run**, and then click **Run Main**.

Notice that the AS/400 prompt appears immediately.

➢ Enter your sign-on information, and wait a few seconds.

You should see the application as shown in Figure 20.17. Notice that all the database fields defined in the RecordIOManager are displayed. Why are the columns all scrunched together? That's because you haven't defined any TableColumns. If you want to define TableColumns, review Chapter 18.

Most likely, you don't see all seven of the records (rows) that you defined in the packet size. That's because you haven't made the JTable the exact size for viewing all seven rows. The JTable in Figure 20.17 displays only five records. Also notice that none of your navigational or maintenance JButtons work. That's because you haven't defined any events yet.

Change the size of the JTable so that you can see all seven records, as shown in Figure 20.18.

➤   Close the **Parts Maintenance** application.
➤   Click JScrollPane1 (not the ScrollPaneTable). Resize the JScrollPane until you can see all seven records. You may have to try this a few times until you get the size of the JScrollPane exactly the way you want it.

Figure 20.17
Parts Maintenance

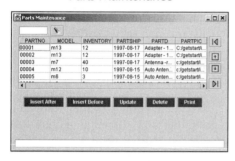

Figure 20.18
Resized JTable

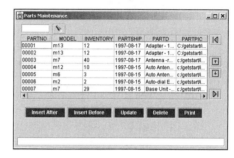

Save and then run the Java program again.

➤   On the menu bar, click **Bean**.
➤   Click **Save Bean**.
➤   On the menu bar, click **Bean**.
➤   Click **Run**, and then click **Run Main**.

Your screen should look similar to Figure 20.18, with all seven records visible in the JTable.

Test your toolTipText.

➤   Hold the mouse pointer over any of the navigational buttons. You should see the toolTipText appear on each JButton.
➤   Close the **Parts Maintenance** application.

Manual Entry of Source Code

Next, you're going to manually add the **displayErrorMessage()** method that you used in Chapter 18. You'll also be adding a static variable.

➤   Go to the workbench window.
➤   In the **All Projects** pane, select the **PartsMaintenanceSubfileExample** class.

You'll create your new method in the **Source** pane, right after the class definition.

➤   Insert the Java code shown in Figure 20.19 immediately after the **PartsMaintenanceSubfileExample** class definition. Figure 20.20 shows what the source code should look like after you've entered it in the **Source** pane.
➤   Right-click to display the shortcut menu.
➤   Click **Save**.

Figure 20.19
Source Code for displayErrorMessage() Method

```
Source code: displayErrorMessage
public void displayErrorMessage(String message) {
    getmsgArea().setText(message);
    getmsgArea().setBackground(java.awt.Color.red);
    getmsgArea().setForeground(java.awt.Color.white);
    return;
}
```

Figure 20.20
displayErrorMessage() Source Code

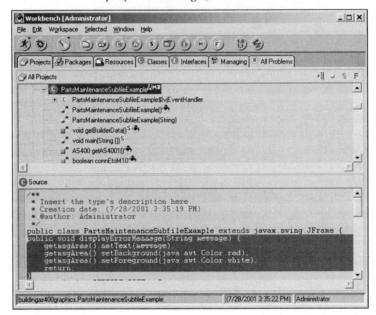

After a few seconds, notice that your source code is gone. VisualAge for Java removed your new method and positioned it in the source code at the appropriate place. The **Source** pane for the **PartsMaintenanceSubfileExample** class now looks as it did before you entered the new method.

Creating a Static Variable or Class Variable

When dealing with an AS/400 page-at-a-time subfile, the most complex part of the logic is handling the beginning-of-file and end-of-file. Coding the subfile correctly requires some good programming logic to make the subfile work flawlessly. In this section, you'll use a *static final* variable and a **getRecordNumber(int)** method to make this complex logic look easy.

In Java, you can define a variable as static. This means that all objects of the class will share the same value for the static variable. This also lets you access the variable without specifying the object. Static variables are also known as *class variables*.

You can also specify a variable as final, meaning that it is a constant (never-changing) variable.

You're going to create a static final variable to define the size of the JTable. Then, if you ever need to change the subfile size, you can simply change the static variable and the recordIOManager packet size, and you won't have to change any logic, especially the complex beginning-of-file and end-of-file logic.

➤ Go to the workbench window.
➤ Select the **PartsMaintenanceSubfileExample** class.

Add a new static integer called **SUBFILE_SIZE**.

➤ Insert the Java code shown in Figure 20.21 immediately after the **PartsMaintenanceSubfileExample** class definition. Notice the syntax. Static final variables, or constants, are normally defined using all uppercase letters. with an underscore separating the words. Figure 20.22 shows what the source code should look like after you've entered it in the **Source** pane.
➤ Right-click to display the shortcut menu.
➤ Click **Save**.

Figure 20.21
Source Code for a Static Variable

```
Source code: Static variable
        static final int SUBFILE_SIZE = 7;
```

Figure 20.22
static int Source Code

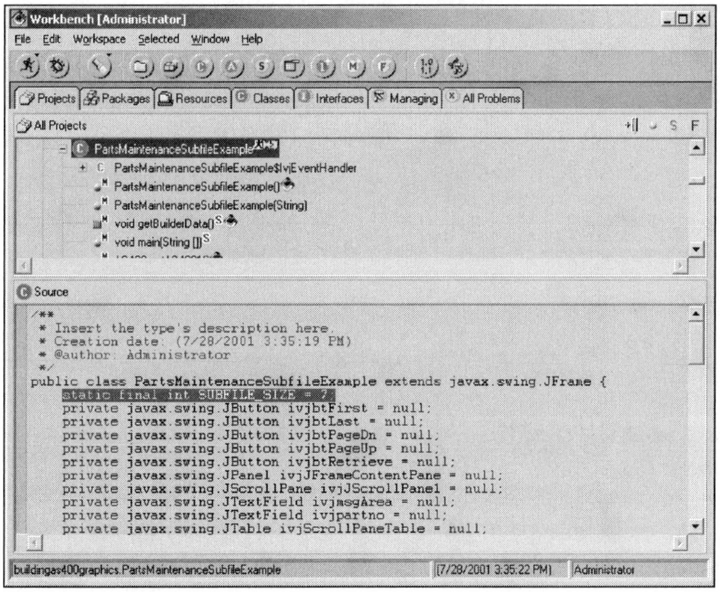

Page Up and Page Down

If you've written a subfile, you know that getting the page-up and page-down functions to do exactly what you want in all situations can be a little tricky. In this section, you'll create two connections that will execute the Java code necessary to perform the function of a user pressing the Page Up and Page Down keys.

Event-to-Code Connection: btPageDn

```
connEtoC2 (btPageDn,actionPerformed →
           PartsMaintenanceSubfileExample,void
           btPageDn_ActionPerformed(java.awt.event.ActionEvent))
```

When the user clicks the down arrow, this connection will emulate a Page Down function. When coding this function, you need to test for an end-of file condition. You also need to handle the situation in which the user tries paging down past the end of the file. Does this sound familiar to coding a page-at-a-time subfile? It should; the logic is exactly the same.

Create an event-to-code connection with the **btPageDn** JButton.

➢ Right-click the **btPageDn** JButton.
➢ Click **Connect**.
➢ Click **actionPerformed**.
➢ Click the spider-end pointer on the nonvisual free-form surface.
➢ Click **Event to Code**.
➢ Insert the Java code shown in Figure 20.23 into the new method named **btPageDn_ActionPerformed()**.
   When you've finished typing the new Java code, your method should look identical to Figure 20.24.

In this section of code, you're using a **getRecordNumber(int)** method. This method returns the record number associated with the last record in the last retrieved set of records. It's a little tricky to test for the end-of-file condition, and I personally don't like the way it is implemented in the bean. You don't test for the last record of the set; you test for the last record minus 1 of the set. This can be a little confusing. In this example, an end-of-file condition test is made for the sixth record (SUBFILE_SIZE − 1 = 6), not the seventh record. If a value less than zero (0) is returned, this indicates that no more records are available; an "End of file reached" message is therefore displayed. If more records are available, the next set of records is retrieved.

Figure 20.23

Source Code for Performing a Page Down Function

```
Source code: connEtoC2
    try {
        if (getListManager1().getRecordNumber(SUBFILE_SIZE − 1) < 0)
            displayErrorMessage("End of file reached");
        else
            getListManager1().readNextSetOfRecords();
    }
    catch (java.lang.Throwable ivjExc) {
        handleException(ivjExc);
    }
```

Figure 20.24

Connection connEtoC2

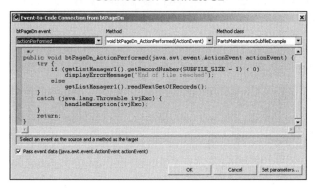

➢ Click **OK**.

➢ Click and hold the **btPageDn_ActionPerformed()** method, and drag it down closer to the **btPageDn** JButton.

Event-to-Code Connection: btPageUp

```
connEtoC3 (btPageUp,actionPerformed →
          PartsMaintenanceSubfileExample,void
          btPageUp_ActionPerformed(java.awt.event.ActionEvent))
```

When the user clicks the up arrow, this connection will emulate a Page Up function. When coding this function, you need to test for a beginning-of file condition. You also need to handle the situation in which the user tries paging up past the beginning of the file. This is the opposite of the logic for the previous connection with **btPageDn**.

Create an event-to-code connection with the **btPageUp** JButton.

➢ Right-click the **btPageUp** JButton.

➢ Click **Connect**.

➢ Click **actionPerformed**.

➢ Click the spider-end pointer on the nonvisual free-form surface.

➢ Click **Event to Code**.

➢ Insert the Java code shown in Figure 20.25 into the new method named **btPageUp_ActionPerformed()**. When you've finished typing the new Java code, your method should look identical to Figure 20.26.

In this section of code, you're again using the **getRecordNumber(int)** method that you used in the previous section. Determining a beginning-of-file condition is just about as difficult as determining an end-of-file condition. To test for beginning-of-file, you need to test the 0th record. In this example, we have seven records per subfile. If a value less than 8 (SUBFILE_SIZE + 1 = 8) is returned, this indicates there are no more records available, and a "Beginning of file reached" message is therefore displayed. If more records are available, the previous set of records is retrieved.

Figure 20.25
Source Code for Performing a Page Up Function

```
Source code: connEtoC3
    try {
        if (getListManager1().getRecordNumber(0) < SUBFILE_SIZE + 1) {
            getListManager1().readFirstSetOfRecords();
            displayErrorMessage("Beginning of file reached");
        }
        else
            getListManager1().readPreviousSetOfRecords();
    }
    catch (java.lang.Throwable ivjExc) {
            handleException(ivjExc);
    }
```

Figure 20.26
Connection connEtoC3

➢ Click **OK**.
➢ Click and hold the **btPageUp_ActionPerformed()** method, and drag it down closer to the **btPageUp** JButton.

Navigational and Retrieve Button Connections

Now, you need to complete the connections for the remaining navigational JButtons (**btFirst** and **btLast**), as well as the connection for the **btRetrieve** JButton.

Event-to-Code Connection: btFirst

```
connEtoC4 (btFirst,actionPerformed →
        PartsMaintenanceSubfileExample,void
        btFirst_ActionPerformed(java.awt.event.ActionEvent))
```

This connection will load the first set of records from the file — that is, the first seven records from file PRODDTL.
    Create an event-to-code connection with the **btFirst** JButton.

➢ Right-click the **btFirst** JButton.
➢ Click **Connect**.
➢ Click **actionPerformed**.

➤ Click the spider-end pointer on the nonvisual free-form surface.

➤ Click **Event to Code**.

➤ Insert the Java code shown in Figure 20.27 into the new method named **btFirst_ActionPerformed()**. When you've finished typing the new Java code, your method should look identical to Figure 20.28.

In this section of code, you position the cursor to the first record. The only problem is that if you try to execute a **readNextSetOfRecords()** method at this point, the application will start reading with the second record. To avoid this problem, you need to perform a **positionCursorToPrevious()** so that the actual cursor is set before the first record. When you then perform the **readNextSetOfRecords()**, reading starts with the first record and continues through the seventh record, as specified by the packet size in the **RecordIOManager** bean.

Figure 20.27
Source Code for Loading the First Page

```
Source code: connEtoC4
    try {
        getListManager1().positionCursorToFirst();
        getListManager1().positionCursorToPrevious();
        getListManager1().readNextSetOfRecords();
    }
    catch (java.lang.Throwable ivjExc) {
            handleException(ivjExc);
    }
```

Figure 20.28
Connection connEtoC4

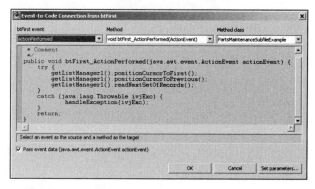

➤ Click **OK**.

➤ Click and hold the **btFirst_ActionPerformed()** method, and drag it down closer to the **btFirst** JButton.

Event-to-Code Connection: btLast

```
connEtoC5 (btLast,actionPerformed →
        PartsMaintenanceSubfileExample,void
        btLast_ActionPerformed(java.awt.event.ActionEvent))
```

This connection will load the last record from the file. When the JTable content is displayed, you'll see only one record in the table, the last record in file PRODDTL.

Create an event-to-code connection with the **btLast** JButton.

➢   Right-click the **btLast** JButton.
➢   Click **Connect**.
➢   Click **actionPerformed**.
➢   Click the spider-end pointer on the nonvisual free-form surface.
➢   Click **Event to Code**.
➢   Insert the Java code shown in Figure 20.29 into the new method named **btLast_ActionPerformed()**. When you've finished typing the new Java code, your method should look identical to Figure 20.30.

Figure 20.29
Source Code for Loading the Last Page

```
Source code: connEtoC5
    try {
        getListManager1().positionCursorToLast();
        getListManager1().positionCursorToPrevious();
        getListManager1().readNextSetOfRecords();
    }
    catch (java.lang.Throwable ivjExc) {
            handleException(ivjExc);
    }
```

Figure 20.30
Connection connEtoC5

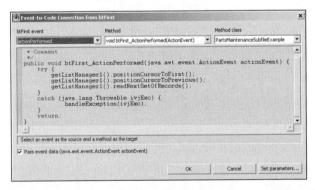

In this section of code, you position the cursor to the last record. The only problem is that if you try to execute a **readNextSetOfRecords()** method at this point, the application won't read the last record. To avoid this problem, you perform a **positionCursorToPrevious()** so that the actual cursor is set to the record immediately before the last record. When you then perform the **readNextSetOfRecords()**, the last record in the file is read.

➢   Click **OK**.
➢   Click and hold the **btLast_ActionPerformed()** method, and drag it down closer to the **btLast** JButton.

Event-to-Code Connection: btRetrieve

```
connEtoC6 (btRetrieve,actionPerformed →
            PartsMaintenanceSubfileExample,void
            btRetrieve_ActionPerformed(java.awt.event.ActionEvent))
```

This connection will find the selected record and then load the selected record and the next six records from the file.

Create an event-to-code connection with the **btRetrieve** JButton.

➢   Right-click the **btRetrieve** JButton.
➢   Click **Connect**.
➢   Click **actionPerformed**.
➢   Click the spider-end pointer on the nonvisual free-form surface.
➢   Click **Event to Code**.
➢   Insert the Java code shown in Figure 20.31 into the new method named **btRetrieve_ActionPerformed()**.

Figure 20.31
Source Code for Retrieving Record and Loading the Page

```
Source code: connEtoC6
  String[] key = new String[1];
  key[0] = (String)ivjpartno.getText();
  try {
      getListManager1().clearAllData();
      if (getListManager1().readRecord(key) == true) {
          getListManager1().positionCursorToPrevious();
          getListManager1().readNextSetOfRecords();
      }
      else {
          displayErrorMessage("Part not found");
          getListManager1().readFirstSetOfRecords();
      }
  }
  catch (java.lang.Throwable ivjExc) {
          handleException(ivjExc);
  }
```

In this section of code, you position the cursor to the record matching the input from the **partno** JTextField. If the record is found, you position to the previous record and then read the next set of records. If the record is not found, you display a "Part not found" error message and display the first set of records from the file in the JTable.

➢   Click **OK**.
➢   Click and hold the **btRetrieve_ActionPerformed()** method, and drag it down to the location shown in Figure 20.32.

Figure 20.32

btRetrieve_ActionPerformed Connection: connEtoC6

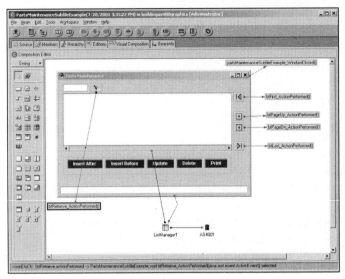

Mouse Events Connection

Next, you're going to create an event connection so that whenever the user moves the mouse, the event automatically clears the message area.

Event-to-Code Connection: mouseEvents

```
connEtoC7: (PartsMaintenanceExample,mouseEvents →
            PartsMaintenanceExample,void
            partsMaintenanceExample_MouseEvents())
```

Create an event-to-code connection with the **PartsMaintenanceSubfileExample** JFrame.

➢ Right-click the outside edge of the **PartsMaintenanceSubfileExample** JFrame.
➢ Click **Connect**.
➢ Click **Connectible Features**.
➢ Click the **mouseEvents()** event.
➢ Click the spider-end pointer on the nonvisual free-form surface.
➢ Click **Event to Code**.
➢ Insert the Java code shown in Figure 20.33. This code clears the error message field and restores it to its original gray color. When you've finished typing the new Java code, your method should look identical to Figure 20.34.

Figure 20.33

Source Code for partsMaintenanceSubfileExample_MouseEvents

```
Source code: partsMaintenanceSubfileExample_MouseEvents
        getmsgArea().setText("");
        getmsgArea().setBackground(java.awt.Color.lightGray);
```

Figure 20.34
Connection connEtoC7

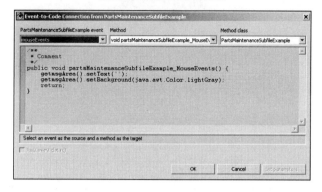

➤   Click **OK**.

➤   Click and hold the **partsMaintenanceSubfileExample_MouseEvents()** method, and drag it to the lower-right corner of the screen as shown in Figure 20.35.

Figure 20.35
partsMaintenanceSubfileExample_MouseEvents Connection: connEtoC7

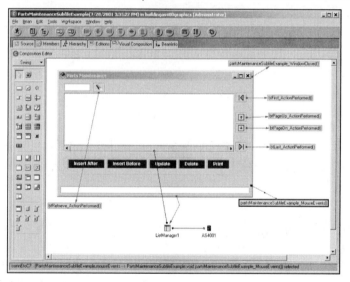

Save and then run your Java program.

➤   On the menu bar, click **Bean**.

➤   Click **Save Bean**.

➤   On the menu bar, click **Bean**.

➤   Click **Run**, and then click **Run Main**.

Test the page-down function.

➤   Click the **btPageDn** JButton.

Your screen should look similar to Figure 20.36. The first record should be part number 00008.

Figure 20.36
Second Page

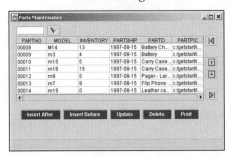

Page down to the last page.

➤   Click the **btPageDn** JButton.
➤   Click the **btPageDn** JButton.

You should see a screen similar to Figure 20.37. The first record should be part number 00022.

Figure 20.37
Last Page

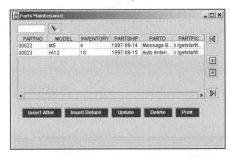

What happens if you try to page down past the last page?

➤   Click the **btPageDn** JButton.

You should have received the error message "End of file reached," as shown in Figure 20.38. If you continue clicking the **btPageDn** JButton, you'll continue to receive the same error message.

Page up to the first page, and then try to go beyond it.

➤   Click the **btPageUp** JButton.
➤   Click the **btPageUp** JButton.
➤   Click the **btPageUp** JButton.
➤   Click the **btPageUp** JButton.

You should see a screen similar to Figure 20.39, displaying the error message "Beginning of file reached." If you continue clicking the **btPageUp** JButton, you'll continue to receive the same error message.

Figure 20.38
End-of-File Message

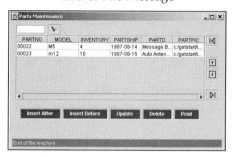

Figure 20.39
Beginning-of-File Message

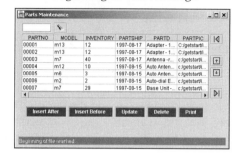

Now, test the retrieve button.

➢   In the part number JTextField, type **00019**.
➢   Click the **btRetrieve** JButton.

You should see a screen similar to Figure 20.40. Notice that the JTable was positioned to part number 00019. The rest of the page was then loaded.

➢   In the part number JTextField, type **03213**.
➢   Click the **btRetrieve** JButton.

Look at Figure 20.41. Did you notice the error message displayed? It is "Part not found." Also notice that the file was repositioned to the first page in the JTable.

Figure 20.40
Repositioning

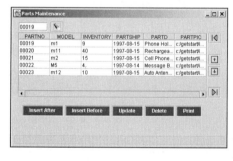

Figure 20.41
Attempted Reposition

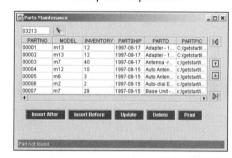

Test the first and last arrow buttons.

➢   Click the **btFirst** JButton.

You should be looking at the first page of records.

➢   Click the **btLast** JButton.

Now, you're looking at the last record.

➢   Close the **Parts Maintenance** application.

Maintenance Buttons

In this section, you'll complete the connections to process the maintenance JButtons: **Insert After**, **Insert Before**, **Update**, **Delete**, and **Print**.

Event-to-Method Connection: insertAfterCurrentRecord()

```
connEtoM2: (btInsertAfter,actionPerformed →
            ListManager1,insertAfterCurrentRecord())
```

This connection inserts a record into the PRODDTL file when the user clicks the **Insert After** button. It also inserts a blank record into the JTable (displayContainer).

Create an event-to-method connection with the **btInsertAfter** JButton and the **insertAfterCurrentRecord()** method.

> Right-click the **btInsertAfter** JButton.
> Click **Connect**.
> Click **actionPerformed**.
> Click the spider-end pointer on the **ListManager1** bean.
> Click **Connectible Features**.
> Click the **insertAfterCurrentRecord()** method.
> Click **OK**.
> Double-click the connection to verify that it is correct as shown in Figure 20.42.
> Close the **Properties** window.

Figure 20.42
Connection connEtoM2

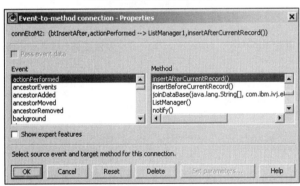

Event-to-Method Connection: insertBeforeCurrentRecord()

```
connEtoM3: (btInsertBefore,actionPerformed →
            ListManager1,insertBeforeCurrentRecord())
```

This connection inserts a record into the PRODDTL file when the user clicks the **Insert Before** button. It also inserts a blank record into the JTable (displayContainer).

Create an event-to-method connection with the **btInsertBefore** JButton and the **insertBeforeCurrentRecord()** method.

> Right-click the **btInsertBefore** JButton.
> Click **Connect**.
> Click **actionPerformed**.
> Click the spider-end pointer on the **ListManager1** bean.

➤   Click **Connectible Features**.
➤   Click the **insertBeforeCurrentRecord()** method.
➤   Click **OK**.
➤   Double-click the connection to verify that it is correct as shown in Figure 20.43.
➤   Close the **Properties** window.

Figure 20.43
Connection connEtoM3

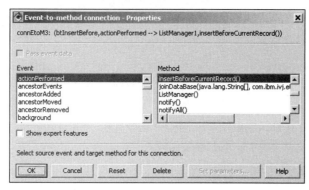

Event-to-Method Connection: updateRecord()

```
connEtoM4: (btUpdate,actionPerformed →
           ListManager1,updateRecord(int))
```

This connection updates an existing record in the PRODDTL file when the user clicks the **Update** button. Create an event-to-method connection with the **btUpdate** JButton and the **updateRecord()** method.

➤   Right-click the **btUpdate** JButton.
➤   Click **Connect**.
➤   Click **actionPerformed**.
➤   Click the spider-end pointer on the **ListManager1** bean.
➤   Click **Connectible Features**.
➤   Click the **updateRecord(int)** method.
➤   Click **OK**.
➤   Double-click the connection to verify that it is correct as shown in Figure 20.44.
➤   Close the **Properties** window.

Figure 20.44
Connection connEtoM4

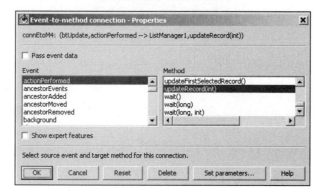

Parameter-from-Property Connection

```
connPfromP1: (connEtoM4: (btUpdate,actionPerformed →
               ListManager1,updateRecord(int)),arg1 →
               ScrollPaneTable1,selectedRow)
```

Notice that the connection is not yet complete. You need to make the connection for the parameter of the **updateRecord(int)** method. The **int** parameter must be the row designator of the selected record in the part maintenance JTable.

➢   Right-click the dashed connection **connEtoM4**.
➢   Click **connect**.
➢   Click **row**.
➢   Click the spider-end pointer on the center outside edge of the **PartsMaintenanceSubfileExample** JFrame.
➢   Click the spider-end pointer on the center of the **JScrollPane** bean (i.e., on the ScrollPaneTable).
➢   Click **selectedRow**.

Your connection should appear as shown in Figure 20.45.

➢   Double-click the connection to verify that it is correct as shown in Figure 20.46.
➢   Close the **Properties** window.

Figure 20.45
selectedRow Connection: connPfromP1

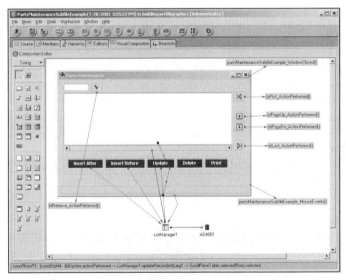

Figure 20.46
Connection connPfromP1

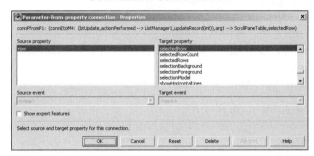

Event-to-Method Connection: deleteRecord()

```
connEtoM5:  (btDelete,actionPerformed →
             ListManager1,deleteSelectedRecords(int))
```

This connection can delete one or more records from the PRODDTL file when the user clicks the **Delete** button. Create an event-to-method connection with the **btDelete** JButton and the **deleteSelectedRecords()** method.

- ➤ Right-click the **btDelete** JButton.
- ➤ Click **Connect**.
- ➤ Click **actionPerformed**.
- ➤ Click the spider-end pointer on the **ListManager1** bean.
- ➤ Click **Connectible Features**.
- ➤ Click the **deleteSelectedRecords()** method.
- ➤ Click **OK**.
- ➤ Double-click the connection to verify that it is correct as shown in Figure 20.47.
- ➤ Close the **Properties** window.

Figure 20.47
Connection connEtoM5

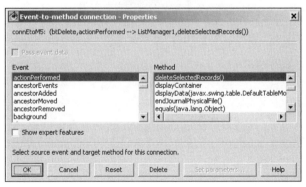

Event-to-Code Connection: btPrint

```
connEtoC8: (btPrint,actionPerformed →
             PartsMaintenanceSubfileExample,void
             btPrint_ActionPerformed(java.awt.event.ActionEvent))
```

This connection will capture a screen snapshot and then call the standard Windows Print API. You used this same section of code in Chapters 18 and 19.

Create an event-to-code connection with the **btPrint** JButton.

➤   Right-click the **btPrint** JButton.
➤   Click **Connect**.
➤   Click **actionPerformed**.
➤   Click the spider-end pointer on the nonvisual free-form surface.
➤   Click **Event to Code**.
➤   Insert the Java code shown in Figure 20.48 into the new method named **btPrint_ActionPerformed()**.
     When you've finished typing the new Java code, your method should look identical to Figure 20.49.

Figure 20.48
Source Code for Printing a Screen Snapshot

```
Source code: connEtoC8
    java.awt.PrintJob job = java.awt.Toolkit.getDefaultToolkit().getPrintJob(null,"",null);
    java.awt.Graphics g = job.getGraphics();
    ivjJFrameContentPane.printAll(g);
    g.dispose();
    job.end();
```

Figure 20.49
Connection connEtoC8

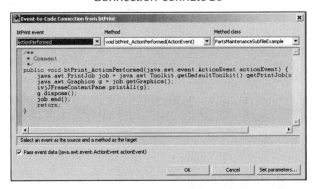

➤   Click **OK**.
➤   Click and hold the **btPrint_ActionPerformed()** method, and drag it down closer to the **btPrint** button.

Save and then run the Java program.

➤   On the menu bar, click **Bean**.
➤   Click **Save Bean**.

> ➤ On the menu bar, click **Bean**.
> ➤ Click **Run**, and then click **Run Main**.
> ➤ Enter your sign-on information, and wait a few seconds.

Test the **Insert After** button.

> ➤ Click or highlight part number **00004**.
> ➤ Click the **Insert After** button.

Enter the new part information shown in Figure 20.50.

> ➤ In the **PARTNO** field, enter **00335**.
> ➤ In the **MODEL** field, enter **m01**.
> ➤ In the **INVENTORY** field, enter **0**.
> ➤ In the **PARTSHIP** field, enter **2001-06-10**.
> ➤ In the **PARTD** field, enter **Cut**.
> ➤ Click the **Update** JButton.

Now, retrieve the new part.

> ➤ In the part number JTextField, enter **00335**.
> ➤ Click the **btRetrieve** JButton.

Figure 20.51 shows that the new record is placed at the end of the file.

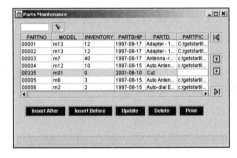

Figure 20.50
Insert After Record

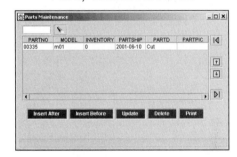

Figure 20.51
Newly Entered Part Order

Delete the new record.

> ➤ Click part number **00335**.
> ➤ Click **Delete**.

Figure 20.52 shows the results. The record is gone. No deletion-confirmation message appeared because you didn't add that section of code to the program. To create a deletion confirmation, you'd need to add something similar to what you did in Chapter 18.

Figure 20.52
Deleted Part

If you had multiple records to delete, you could do so by holding down the Shift key and selecting the desired records. Then when you clicked the **Delete** button, the application would delete all the selected records at once.

Spend some time getting familiar with all the functions you just programmed. Try the **Update**, **Print**, and **Insert Before** buttons.

➢   Close the **Parts Maintenance** application.

Congratulations on completing your page-at-a-time maintenance subfile! You may want to add some coding to perform certain functions after the **Delete**, **Update**, or one of the **Insert** keys is clicked. Some code to refresh the subfile (JTable) might be a useful feature. To make any of these changes, you'd need to change the appropriate event-to-method connection to an event-to-code connection and then add in the Java code.

There are many ways to implement JTables (subfiles) in programming an application. With the foundation you've received in Chapters 17 through 20, you should be able to handle most JTable development scenarios. You may have to mix and match different sections from each chapter to build your own unique JTable environments.

Summary
In this chapter you learned

- how to load a JTable using page-at-a-time logic
- how to emulate page-up/page-down functions
- how to use a find/position-to function with a JTable
- how to work with the SetOfRecords methods

In the next chapter, you'll learn how to use the Enterprise Toolkit for AS/400 to call an RPG program with passed parameters.

Unit 5

ET/400, Work, and Execution Environments

Chapter 21

Creating Java-to-RPG Program Calls Using Enterprise Toolkit for AS/400

 ## Chapter Objectives

☐ Understand the **Create Program Call** SmartGuide

☐ Learn how to use version control

☐ Learn how to pass parameters and receive completion messages

 ## Chapter Project

☐ You will version and modify a prior chapter project. You will also add a Print function that calls an AS/400 RPG print program.

☐ Figures 21.1A and 21.1B show what the sample class and its output will look like.

Figure 21.1A
Chapter Project — Screen 1 of 2

Figure 21.1B
Chapter Project — Screen 2 of 2

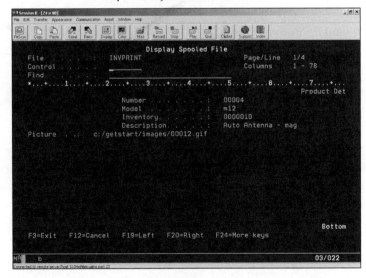

The Enterprise Toolkit for AS/400 (ET/400) provides SmartGuides to speed up the process of creating Java classes. Two of these aids are the **Create Program Call** SmartGuide and the **Convert Display File** SmartGuide. Earlier versions of VisualAge for Java included a SmartGuide to create subfiles as well. That guide has been discontinued.

To access the ET/400 SmartGuides, you must have the Enterprise Version of VisualAge for Java. You'll use the **Create Program Call** SmartGuide in this chapter and work with the **Convert Display File** SmartGuide in Chapter 22.

Create Program Call SmartGuide

The **Create Program Call** SmartGuide generates a new class that contains all the necessary methods and variables to perform a call function to an AS/400 program. The class can be executed on a desktop workstation, a network station client, or the AS/400 server. In this chapter, you'll use this newly generated class to call an AS/400 RPG print program, PRTINVR, located in library ADTSLAB. Your Java program will pass the part number to the RPG program.

Figure 21.2 shows the source code for program PRTINVR. You don't need to write this RPG program. It should already exist in library ADTSLAB.

Figure 21.2
RPG Program PRTINVR

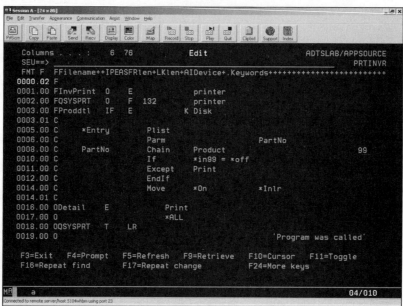

RPG program PRTINVR creates two spool files. Spool file QSYSPRT prints a "Program was called" message. Spool file INVPRINT, shown above in Figure 21.1B, prints most of the database values for the part number passed to the RPG program. You're going to add a **Print** button to the **PromptAndDisplayExample** class that you created in Chapter 15. This button will initiate the call to the RPG program.

You'll begin by starting the **Create Program Call** SmartGuide as shown in Figure 21.3.

➤   If the workbench isn't started, start it now.
➤   In the workbench **All Projects** pane, right-click the project **My Graphical Applications** to display the shortcut menu. Select **Tools**, then select **ET/400**, and then select **Create Program Call**. Wait a few seconds.

Figure 21.3
Create Program Call SmartGuide Option

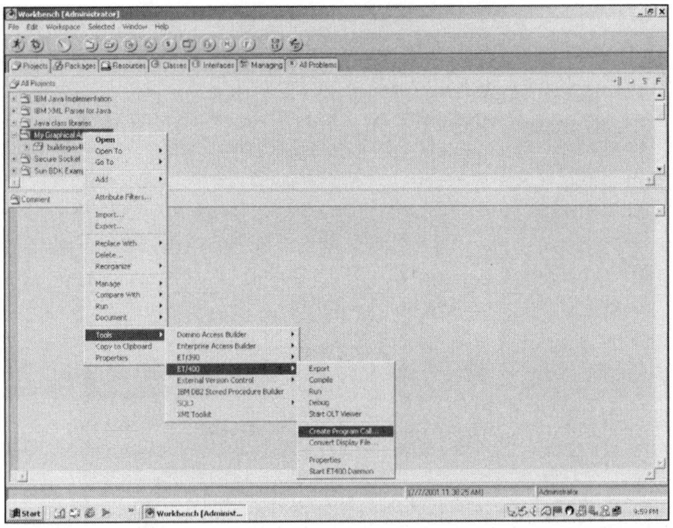

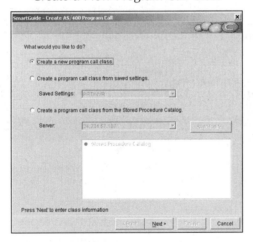

Figure 21.4 shows the first screen of the SmartGuide, which gives you three options from which to choose. You'll normally select the first option, which is to create a new class. You can also create a class from a previously created class or from a stored procedure catalog on the AS/400.

Figure 21.4
Create a New Program Call Class

➢   Make sure the **Create a new program call class** option is selected.
➢   Click **Next**.

You use the next screen of the SmartGuide (Figure 21.5) to specify the server, name, and library of the program you want to call and to enter the specifications for creation of the class.

➢   Select the appropriate server name from the **Server** drop-down list.
➢   In the **Program** field, enter **PRTINVR**.
➢   In the **Library** field, enter **ADTSLAB**.

> ➤ In the **Class** field, enter **PRTINVR**.
> ➤ Click **Browse** to select a project, and select the project **My Graphical Applications**.
> ➤ Click **Browse** to select a package, and select the package **buildingas400graphics**.
> ➤ Click **Next**.

Figure 21.6 shows the next screen, where you define the AS/400 program parameters. The definitions you specify here need to match the parameters defined in the RPG *ENTRY PLIST.

Figure 21.5
Specify Program and Class Information

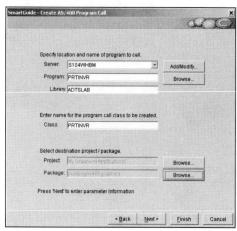

Figure 21.6
Specify AS/400 Program Parameters

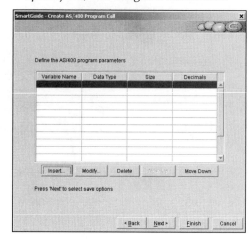

Data Type Definition

The following table describes the data types and lengths supported by the **Create Program Call** SmartGuide when defining program parameters.

Data type	Length
Character	0 to 16,711,568 bytes
Graphic	0 to 16,711,568 bytes
Binary	1 to 9 digits
Integer	5 or 10 digits
Packed Decimal	1 to 30 digits
Unsigned	5 or 10 digits
Float	4 or 8 digits
Date	Not specified; assumed default of 10 digits
Time	Not specified; assumed default of 8 digits
TimeStamp	Not specified; assumed default of 26 digits

> ➤ On the parameters screen of the SmartGuide, click **Insert**.
> ➤ As shown in Figure 21.7, type **Partno** in the **Name** field, **Character** in the **Type** field, and **5** in the **Size** field.
> ➤ Click **OK**.

Figure 21.7
Insert Program Parameter

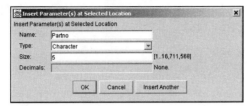

Notice that the parameter you just created matches the *ENTRY PLIST from the RPG program shown earlier in Figure 21.2. Your screen should look identical to Figure 21.8.

Figure 21.8
New Program Parameter

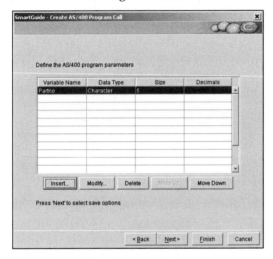

Tips and Tricks
When specifying program parameters in the *Create Program Call* SmartGuide, you can define a maximum of 35 parameters (or arguments) on a call to an AS/400 program.

➤   Click **Next**.
➤   When the final screen appears, click **Finish**.

Your new class, called PRTINVR, has now been generated. That was pretty easy! You should now be back at the workbench.

➤   Click the **PRTINVR** class.
➤   Look in the **Source** pane to see the Java code that was automatically generated for you. Figure 21.9 shows this code.
➤   Expand class **PRTINVR** to view its methods, as shown in Figure 21.10.

Look closely at methods **getCompletionMsg()**, **setPartnoAsString()**, and **runProgram()**. You'll use these three methods later in the chapter.

Figure 21.9
PRTINVR Class

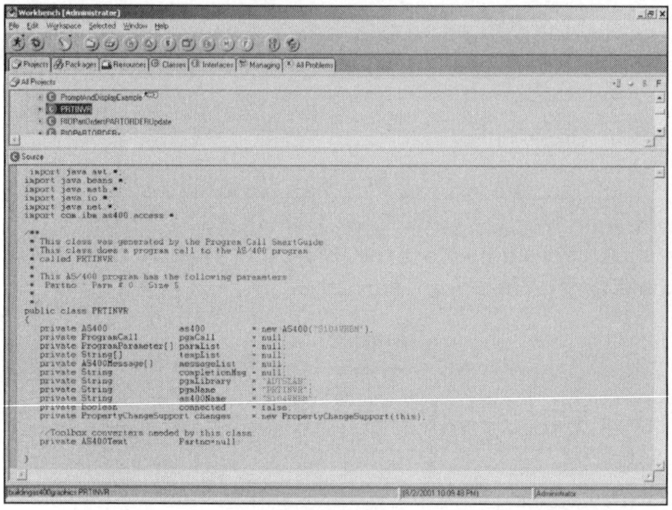

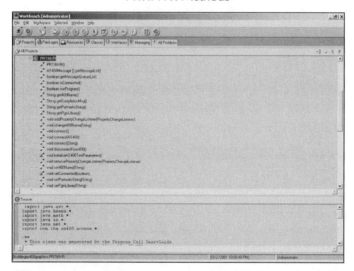

Figure 21.10
PRTINVR Methods

Version Control

As a starting point for this chapter's project, you're going to use the **PromptAndDisplayExample** class from Chapter 15's chapter project. Before you make any changes or additions to this class, you will save a *version* of the class. That way, if you need to go back to the original **PromptAndDisplayExample** class later, you can do so. This practice is called *version control* or *versioning*.

You may have used the concept of versioning on the AS/400, perhaps in the form of creating different source physical files and/or libraries to store different versions of your programs. You may have purchased a configuration management or version control software package. Regardless of what you've used in the past, versioning with VisualAge for Java and its repository is quite a bit different.

In VisualAge for Java version control, you version program elements, not files. Methods, projects, packages, and types can all be versioned. When you create a new version of your code, you create a new *edition*. There are four types of editions: versioned editions, open editions, released editions, and scratch editions.

Whenever you reach a point where you want to save off a snapshot of your Java code, you create a *versioned edition*. Versioned editions cannot be modified directly. They are frozen, or unchangeable. To change a versioned program element, you must create an *open edition*. Open editions have a timestamp associated with the creation date.

You also have *released editions*, which can be part of a public use strategy. You use this type of edition when you're ready to release your code to the general public, install it, or make it available to a company user group or department.

Scratch editions are used by programmers within the user workspace. These editions are never contained within the repository. They are created from versioned editions and used only for projects and packages. They are primarily used for temporary work.

All editions except scratch editions reside in the repository. You can load or work with only one edition at a time in the workspace. You can exchange the current edition for another edition whenever you need to. To do so, you right-click to display the shortcut menu and select the **Replace With** menu item. At this point you have two options: **Previous Edition** or **Another Edition**. That's how easy exchanging editions is.

You are now going to version Chapter 15's chapter project.

➢　From the workbench, click to expand the **My Graphical Applications** project.
➢　Expand the **buildingas400graphics** package.
➢　Right-click the **PromptAndDisplayExample** class to display the shortcut menu.
➢　Click **Manage**.
➢　Click **Version**.

Figure 21.11 shows the **Versioning Selected Items** window. It provides three options for versioning:

• **Automatic** — This is the recommended option. It automatically creates new edition names, and VisualAge for Java assigns a unique name to each program element you're versioning.
• **One Name** — This option specifies a common version name for all program elements.
• **Name Each** — This option lets you explicitly name each program element.

Figure 21.11
Versioning Selected Items

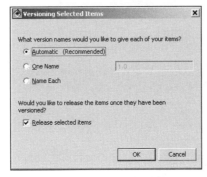

Accept the default option, **Automatic**, and click **OK**.

To see your version names:

➢　On the workbench menu bar, click **Window**.
➢　Click **Show Edition Names**. You can toggle this menu option on and off.

Notice that the class name displayed in the workbench is now **PromptAndDisplayExample 1.0**, while the other classes all have a creation date and time. The **PromptAndDisplayExample 1.0** class is now a released edition. You can't change it at this point. All you can do is create a new open edition.

There are two ways to create an open edition of the **PromptAndDisplayExample** class so that you can make changes. You can open the class normally and edit it; then, when you try to exit, you'll be prompted to create a new open edition. Or you can explicitly create a new open edition. That is what you'll do next.

Explicitly create a new open edition.

➤ From the workbench, right-click the **PromptAndDisplayExample 1.0** class to display the shortcut menu.
➤ Click **Manage**.
➤ Click **Create Open Edition**.

Notice that the 1.0 disappears and is replaced by today's date and time. You now have an open edition that you can work with just as you've done throughout the book. If you were to version the class again, the next edition number would be 1.1.

PRTINVR Class

Now, you're going to add a **PRTINVR** class bean to the **PromptAndDisplayExample** class.

➤ From the workbench, double-click the **PromptAndDisplayExample** class.

You should be inside the Visual Composition Editor, looking at a screen similar to Figure 21.12. This is the class you created in Chapter 15.

Figure 21.12
PromptAndDisplayExample

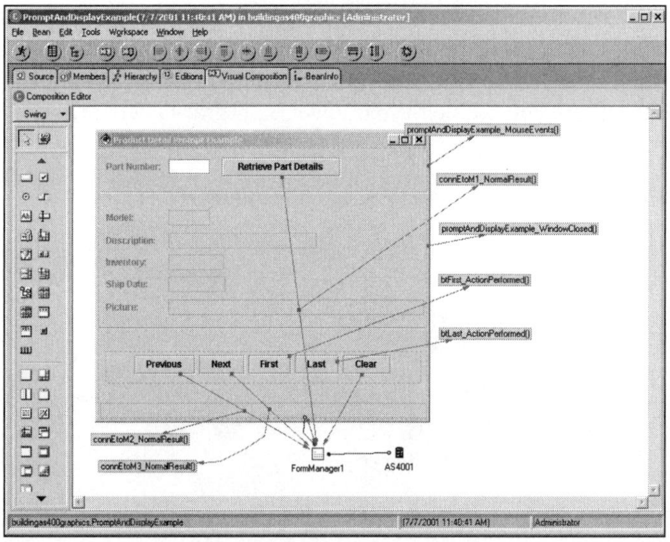

Use the **Choose Bean** button to retrieve the **PRTINVR** class.

➤ In the upper-left corner of the VCE, click the **Choose Bean** button 🖼.
➤ In the **Choose Bean** window's **Class name** field, type **PRTINVR**. Then click **Browse** to select a class.
➤ In the **Choose a Valid Class** window's **Class names** list, select **buildingas400graphics.PRTINVR**.
➤ Click **OK**.

➤   As shown in Figure 21.13, enter **CallPRTINVRProgram** in the **Choose Bean** window's **Name** field.
➤   Click **OK**.

Figure 21.14 shows the **CallPRTINVRProgram** bean.

Figure 21.13
PRTINVR Bean

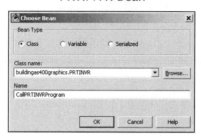

Figure 21.14
CallPRTINVRProgram Bean

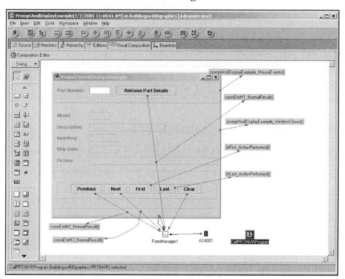

Now, add a new button, **Print**, to the JPanel as shown in Figure 21.15.

➤   Click the **JButton** bean ⬜, and drop it on the JPanel as shown in the figure.
➤   Double-click the JButton to display the **Properties** sheet.
➤   Change the **beanName** property to **btPrint**.
➤   Change the **text** property to **Print**.
➤   Close the **Properties** sheet.

Figure 21.15
Print JButton

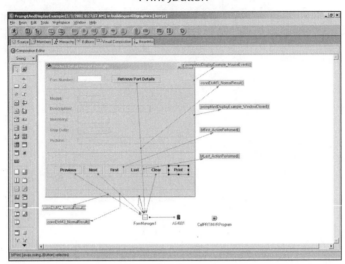

Connecting the AS/400 Beans

You are now going to set up one event-to-method connection, one parameter-from-property connection, and one event-to-code connection. The event-to-method and parameter-from-property connections will actually connect to the AS/400. The event-to-code connection will call the RPG program and return a completion message.

Event-to-Method Connection: connect()

`connEtoM6: (btPrint,actionPerformed → CallPRTINVRProgram,connect(com.ibm.as400.access.AS400)`

This connection will set up the connection to the AS/400. Connect the **btPrint** JButton with a **connect(com.ibm.as400.access.AS400)** method.

> Right-click the **btPrint** JButton.
> Click **Connect**.
> Click **actionPerformed**.
> Click the spider-end pointer on the **CallPRTINVRProgram** bean.
> Click **Connectible Features**.
> Click the **connect(com.ibm.as400.access.AS400)** method.
> Click **OK**.

Your connection should appear as shown in Figure 21.16. Notice that it is incomplete at this point.

> Double-click the connection to verify that it is correct as shown in Figure 21.17.
> Close the **Properties** window.

Figure 21.16
CallPRTINVRProgram Connection

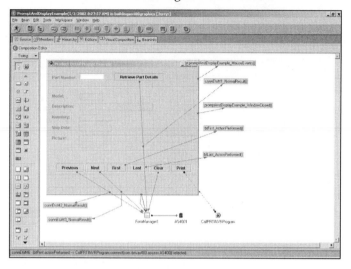

Figure 21.17
connect() Connection: connEtoM6

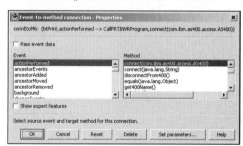

Parameter-from-Property Connection

```
connPfromP1: (connEtoM6: (btPrint,actionPerformed →
              CallPRTINVRProgram,connect(com.ibm.as400.access.AS400)) arg1 → AS4001,this)
```

Complete the connection by passing the parameter into the primary connection. The connection is expecting an **AS400** object type.

Identify the source property:

➢   Right-click the dashed line.
➢   Click **Connect**.
➢   Click **obj**.

Identify the target property:

➢   Click the spider-end pointer on the **AS4001** bean.
➢   Click **this**.

Figure 21.18 shows what the connection should look like.

Figure 21.18
Print Connection: connPfromP1

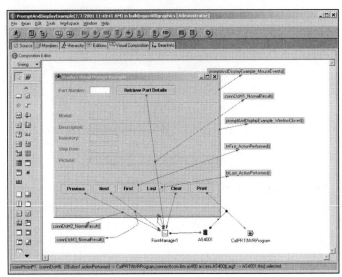

Event-to-Code Connection: btPrint

```
connEtoC8: (btPrint,actionPerformed → PromptAndDisplayExample,void
          btPrint_ActionPerformed(java.awt.event.ActionEvent))
```

This connection will execute the Java code necessary to call the PRTINVR program. To accomplish this, you need to complete four tasks:

1. Pass the Partno value to the RPG program on the AS/400.
2. Run, or execute, the RPG program.
3. Receive a completion message from the AS/400.
4. Display the completion message on the screen.

   Create an event-to-code connection with the **btPrint** JButton.

➢   Right-click the **btPrint** JButton.
➢   Click **Connect**.
➢   Click **actionPerformed**.
➢   Click the spider-end pointer on the nonvisual free-form surface.
➢   Click **Event to Code**.
➢   Insert the Java code shown in Figure 21.19. When you've finished typing the new Java code, your method should look identical to Figure 21.20.

Figure 21.19

Source Code for Calling the PRTINVR RPG Program

```
Source code: connEtoC8
    try {
        getCallPRTINVRProgram().setPartnoAsString(getpartno().getText());
        getCallPRTINVRProgram().runProgram();
        getmsgArea().setText(getCallPRTINVRProgram().getCompletionMsg());
        getmsgArea().setBackground(java.awt.Color.red);
        getmsgArea().setForeground(java.awt.Color.white);
    }
    catch (java.lang.Throwable ivjExc) {
        handleException(ivjExc);
    }
```

Figure 21.20

Connection connEtoC8

> Click **OK**.
> Click and hold the **btPrint_ActionPerformed()** method, and drag it down closer to the **btPrint** JButton as shown in Figure 21.21.

Figure 21.21

btPrint_ActionPerformed Connection: connEtoC8

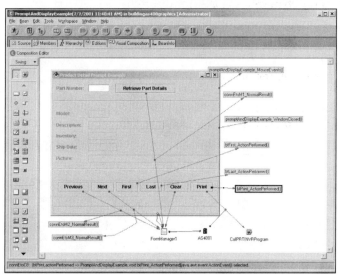

Save the Java program.

> On the menu bar, click **Bean**.
> Click **Save Bean**.

Make sure you're connected to the AS/400. Run the Java program.

> On the menu bar, click **Bean**.
> Click **Run**, and then click **Run Main**.
> Enter your sign-on information, and wait a few seconds.
> In the **Part Number** field, enter **00004**.
> Click the **Retrieve Part Details** button.

Figure 21.22 shows the results of clicking **Retrieve Part Details**. You should see part number 00004.

> Click the **Print** button.

Figure 21.23 shows the results of clicking **Print**. You should see the completion message "Program called ok." This message was passed back from the AS/400 operating system, not the RPG program.

Figure 21.22	**Figure 21.23**
Part Number Retrieved	*Completion Message*

> If you're not signed on to the AS/400, go ahead and sign on now from your normal Client Access sign-on screen. Be sure to use the same sign-on name you used earlier.
> At a command-entry line, type **WRKSPLF**.

You should see a Work with All Spooled Files screen similar to Figure 21.24. Two spool files should be listed.

Figure 21.24
Work with All Spooled Files Screen

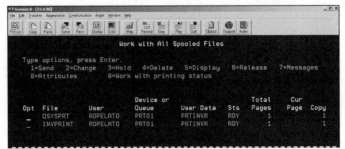

> ➤ Type option **5** to display the **QSYSPRT** spool file. Figure 21.25 shows this file.
> ➤ Type option **5** to display the **INVPRINT** spool file. Figure 21.26 shows this file.

Figure 21.25
Spool File QSYSPRT

Figure 21.26
Spool File INVPRINT

Congratulations! You've just called an AS/400 RPG program from a Java program. That was really pretty easy, wasn't it? How would you accomplish some of the common override functions that might be associated with a print program or a batch program? You could just as easily call a CL program that performed overrides, preprocessing of a database, a submission to batch, and so on. There's nothing different about calling a CL program as opposed to the RPG program you used in this chapter.

Summary

In this chapter you learned

- how to use the **Create Program Call** SmartGuide
- how to do versioning
- how to pass parameters to an AS/400 RPG program
- how to call an AS/400 RPG program
- how to receive a completion message back from the AS/400

The next chapter will teach you how to convert an existing AS/400 display file to Java.

Chapter 22

Converting Display Files to Java Using Enterprise Toolkit for AS/400

 ## Chapter Objectives

❑ Understand the basics of using the **Convert Display File** SmartGuide
❑ Become familiar with Java generation rules

At times, you may want to convert typical AS/400 screens to a graphical user interface for use in your Java applications. The Enterprise Toolkit for AS/400's (ET/400's) **Convert Display File** SmartGuide can be a quick solution for performing this conversion. To use the SmartGuide, you need the Enterprise Version of VisualAge for Java. Figure 22.1 shows a sample converted screen.

Figure 22.1
Converted Display File

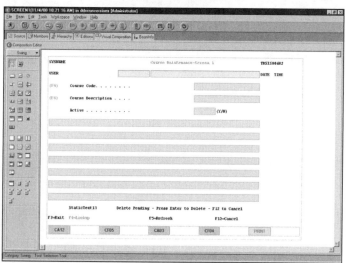

As you'll probably find, the **Convert Display File** SmartGuide isn't the perfect solution for converting AS/400 screens. Once the conversion is completed, you still have much work to do to interface with the logic. The Smart-Guide can sometimes be a handy tool for migrating DDS fields to a Java environment, but at other times it can actually slow the process of GUI design. The generated GUI screen often looks quite different from the original AS/400 screen and requires a complete overhaul. I often prefer to start from scratch rather than use the SmartGuide. Nevertheless, the **Convert Display File** SmartGuide can be a handy tool in certain circumstances, so in this chapter we take a quick look at the basics of its use. *You won't be coding any project in this chapter. This will be a read-along chapter only.*

Display File Conversion

Figure 22.2 shows a simple AS/400 screen that will be the example used in this chapter. This sample screen is a simple course-maintenance screen. The DDS includes two record formats, SCREEN1 and SCREEN2. There are four command keys: F3, F4, F5, and F12. A PRINT keyword is defined in the DDS. The "Copy Mode" shown at the top of the screen is nothing more than a variable.

Figure 22.2
AS/400 Screen

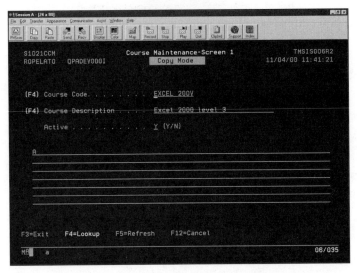

The process for converting a DDS display file to Java is fairly straightforward. The SmartGuide does most of the work for you. To start the process, you take the steps depicted in Figure 22.3. From the workbench, you right-click to display the shortcut menu. Then you select **Tools**, **ET/400**, and **Convert Display File** as shown to start the SmartGuide.

Figure 22.3
Menu Selection of Convert Display File

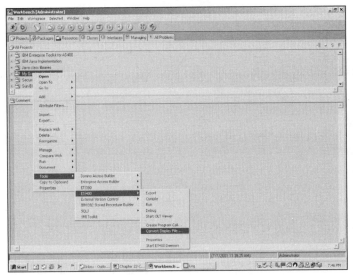

On the first screen of the SmartGuide, shown in Figure 22.4, you specify the AS/400 on which the display file resides and select the display file and record format(s) that you want to convert. You can specify a particular library or accept the default *LIBL. To display a list of files or libraries, you click on the server in the navigational tree. You'll then be prompted to sign on to the AS/400. If you specified *LIBL, all the libraries in your system library list and current library will be displayed.

Figure 22.4
SmartGuide

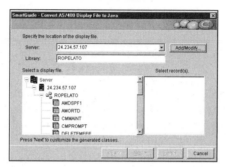

Figure 22.5 shows the screen record formats that are contained within the sample display file: SCREEN1 and SCREEN2. In this case, SCREEN1 is selected.

Figure 22.5
Display Record Selection

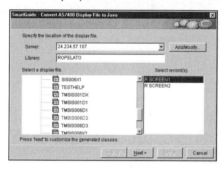

The next screen displayed by the SmartGuide lets you change screen colors and specify where the new class should be created (i.e., in which project and package). Figure 22.6 shows the specification of the background and foreground colors. If you don't remember where you want to store the newly created class, you can click **Browse** to locate your selection.

Figure 22.6
Look and Class Information

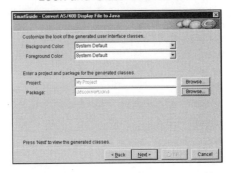

Next, the SmartGuide informs you which classes it is about to create. In our example, four different classes will be generated, as shown in Figure 22.7. The **main()** method will be generated in the **SCREEN1** class. There are also three helper classes: **SCREEN1EventMulticaster**, **SCREEN1Listener**, and **SCREEN1WindowListener**. In addition, another class, **DisplayFileIO**, will be generated to contain all the Visual Composition Editor components that are created. To generate the classes, you simply click **Finish** on this screen.

Figure 22.7
Generated Classes

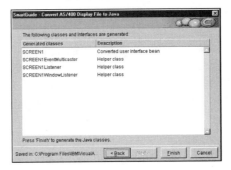

Figure 22.8 shows the finished Java class, **SCREEN1**, as it looks once the classes are generated. Notice the buttons in the figure. VisualAge for Java created these from the command key definitions in the DDS, not from the literals that appear on the AS/400 screen. Depending on the combination of DDS field attributes, some fields and literals may not be converted exactly as you would expect. In this example, the "Copy Mode" wasn't converted. (For more information, see the conversion rules discussed in the next section.)

Look closely at the components, or at what appear to be components. Before you can use the VCE to manipulate the screen components, you need to take a few steps in the VCE to complete the display file conversion:

1. On the menu bar, click **Bean**.
2. Click the **Construct Visuals from Source** menu item.
3. Click **Proceed** to replace the visual contents.

With these steps completed, you can access the components as you're accustomed to doing and begin setting up connections. Once the new components are present and accessible, you may want to delete some of the unnecessary ones.

Figure 22.8
Generated SCREEN1 Class

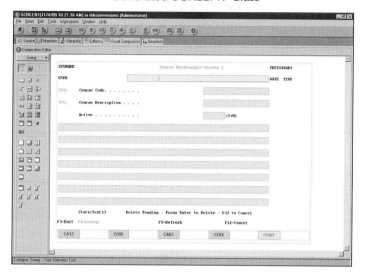

Java Generation Rules

VisualAge for Java creates quite a few methods as it generates the Java code for the converted screen. The following sections describe some of the rules and assumptions that are used during the Java generation process.

Display File Record Formats

Depending on the DDS record format type, different Java components are created. The following list identifies which component is generated for each display file record format type.

Record format type	Generated component
Standard record (R)	java.awt.Panel
Subfile (S)	java.awt.Panel
Window (W)	java.awt.Panel
Menu bar	java.awt.MenuBar

Display File Field Types

The following list identifies which component is generated for each display file field type.

Field type	Generated component
Text	java.awt.TextArea
Message constant	java.awt.Label
Check box	java.awt.Checkbox
Push button	java.awt.Button
Choice	java.awt.Checkbox.Group
Choice text	java.awt.Choice

Display File Keywords

The following list identifies the more common display file keywords and how the conversion to Java occurs.

Keyword	Conversion performed
CA, CF	A button is created and given a name identical to the command key keyword (e.g., CA12).
COLOR	The foreground color of the code is in comment only. If there are multiple COLOR keywords, only the last one specified is used.
DATE	A static text Abstract Window Toolkit (AWT) component is created.
DSPATR	If an HI (High Intensity) attribute is found, the foreground color is made brighter. If an ND (Non Display) attribute is found, the field is set to nonvisible. If a PR (Protect) attribute is found, the field is set to disabled. Any other display attributes are not converted.
EDITCODE	Attributes are created that coincide with the edit code.
EDITWORD	Attributes are created that coincide with the edit word.
HELP	A button is created with the label of HELP.
MENUBAR	A menu is created.
MENUBARCHC	A menu item is created.
PRINT	A button is created with the label of PRINT. No logic is created to perform a PRINT function.
RANGE	Range attributes are created that coincide with the RANGE keyword.
SYSNAME	A static text AWT component is created.
TIME	A static text AWT component is created.
USER	A static text AWT component is created.
VALUES	A drop-down component is created. The VALUES are used as the parts that make up the drop-down list.

Display File Functions

The following list identifies certain functions used in the display file that are associated with event methods that are generated.

Function	Generated method
Check box	ItemStateChanged()
Check box group	ItemStateChanged()
Push button	ActionPerformed()
Menu item	ActionPerformed()
Subfile	ItemStateChanged()

Summary

In this chapter you learned

- the basics of using the **Convert Display File** SmartGuide
- what the Java generation conversion rules are

The next chapter will introduce you to team development concepts.

Chapter 23

Team Development with VisualAge for Java

Chapter Objectives

- ☐ Understand the basics of team development in VisualAge for Java
- ☐ Learn how to change the owner of a program element
- ☐ Learn to add new users to groups
- ☐ Understand the Management Query tools
- ☐ Learn about repository cleanup

Chapter Project

- ☐ Three new team members will be created.
- ☐ Figure 23.1 shows the completed set of team members.

Figure 23.1
Chapter Project

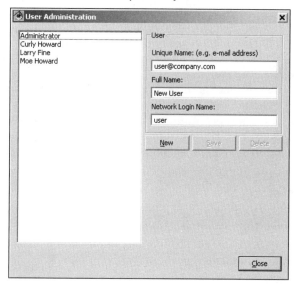

In Chapter 2, you learned a little bit about the VisualAge for Java repository. As you may remember, the repository is where all editions of all program elements are stored. You can load and unload editions from the repository into the workspace. The workspace you've been using throughout this book is where you created your object components or editions. In Chapter 21, you learned how to version a class, or create another edition of a class. In this chapter, you'll learn some of the basics about team development, which brings into play all these aspects of VisualAge for Java.

Team Development

Unlike VisualAge for Java's Professional Edition, the Enterprise Edition supports team development. An entire team of developers can share a repository installed on a server. This shared repository is accessed by a repository server program (EMSRV). Individual developers can each use their own individual repository, called a local repository. Team developers can use the team repository, also known as a remote repository.

Why would a team development approach be better than a single developer approach? Any time you have more than one developer building an application, you need to be able to effectively communicate changes, revisions, and new component creations to the team. The remote repository in the Enterprise Edition lets you accomplish this.

Ownership of Program Elements

If you're using a team development approach in VisualAge for Java, every program element (project, package, or class) has an owner assigned to it. Owners of classes are considered the "gatekeepers" that join, or merge, all the program elements on which various developers may be working. This merging of program elements is what allows the "public" release of the software to occur.

Roles and Responsibilities of Team Members

Each team member may have different assignments and responsibilities in the development cycle. Depending on the size of your team, you may have numerous levels of management and developer responsibilities within your team.

If your job function is defined as an Administrator role, your responsibilities might include setting up the team environment, managing the various team members, managing package and class group members, and maintaining program element owners.

If you job function is defined as a Developer, there are four different roles with which you might be associated:

- Project Owner — The project owner can open the project, version the project, create packages in the project, and delete packages in the project.
- Package Owner — The package owner can open the package, version the package, release the package, add users to the package group, delete users from the package group, and transfer ownership of the package.
- Class Owner — The class owner can open the class, edit the class, release the class, delete the class, and transfer ownership of the class.
- Class Developer — The class developer can open an edition of the existing class.

Creating the Team

In this section, you're going to create three new team members. As shown in Figure 23.2, you will call them Moe, Larry, and Curly.

Figure 23.2
New Team Members

Image courtesy of Sony Pictures Entertainment, Inc.

➢   If the workbench isn't started, start it now.
➢   On the menu bar, click **File**.
➢   Click the **Quick Start** menu item.

You should be looking at the **Quick Start** window (Figure 23.3).

➢   In the left column, click **Team Development**.
➢   In the right column, click **Administer Users**.
➢   Click **OK**.

Figure 23.3
Quick Start: Administer Users

Figure 23.4 shows the **User Administration** window. It indicates that the Administrator user is already present. This is the default user until other users are created. As you can see, three fields are required when creating a new user:

- Unique Name — This is the unique user name used to differentiate between users.
- Full Name — This is the name that appears in the workbench title.
- Network Login Name — If the team server requires passwords to connect to the remote repository, the network name is used as the log-on user ID.

➢   Click **Administrator**.

As shown in the figure, the Administrator's unique identifier is **Supervisor**.

Figure 23.4
Administrator

Create a new user.

➢   Click the **New** button.

Figure 23.5 shows the new user window. As shown in Figure 23.6, create the Larry@Stooges.com user name.

➢   In the **Unique Name** field, type **Larry@Stooges.com**.
➢   In the **Full Name** field, type **Larry Fine**.
➢   In the **Network Login Name** field, type **Larry**.
➢   Click **Save**.

You just created a new user named **Larry**.

Figure 23.5
New User Window

Figure 23.6

Larry@Stooges.com User Name

Now, create two new users named Curly and Moe.

> Click **New**.
> In the **Unique Name** field, type **Curly@Stooges.com**.
> In the **Full Name** field, type **Curly Howard**.
> In the **Network Login Name** field, type **Curly**.
> Click **Save**.
> Click **New** again.
> In the **Unique Name** field, type **Moe@Stooges.com**.
> In the **Full Name** field, type **Moe Howard**.
> In the **Network Login Name** field, type **Moe**.
> Click **Save**.

You should be looking at all the users as shown in Figure 23.7.

> Click **Close**.

Figure 23.7

All Users

Changing an Owner

Changing the owner of a program element is easy. There are a few differences between projects, packages, and classes that we'll discuss in this section.

To change a project owner:

➢ In the workbench, right-click the project **My Graphical Applications**.
➢ Click **Manage**.
➢ Click **Change Owner**.

Figure 23.8 shows the resulting window. Notice that all four users appear. Changing the project owner is as simple as double-clicking the new owner name.

➢ Click **Cancel**.

Figure 23.8
Change Project Owner

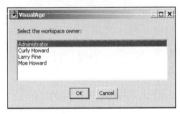

To change the owner of a package:

➢ In the workbench, right-click the package **buildingas400graphics**.
➢ Click **Manage**.
➢ Click **Change Owner**.

Figure 23.9 shows the resulting window. This time, notice that only the Administrator user appears. That's because when you're trying to change the owner of a package or class, the new owner must first be a group member.

➢ Click **Cancel**.

Figure 23.9
Change Package Owner

Creating a New Group Member

To be specified as the owner of a package or class, a user must first belong to the group associated with that package or class. A developer must also be a group member to be able to create, change, and delete types within a particular package.

To add a new group member:

➢ In the workbench, right-click the package **buildingas400graphics**.
➢ Click **Manage**.
➢ Click **Add User to Group**.

Figure 23.10 shows the **Add Users** window. This time, notice that only the three non-administrator users appear. That's because the Administrator user is already the owner of your package. Adding a new group member is as simple as double-clicking the new user name.

➤ Click **Cancel**.

Figure 23.10
Add User

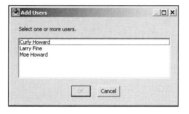

Management Query

When you're managing projects, it's often helpful to know what the various developers are working on, as well as the progress status of different classes. VisualAge for Java's Management Query feature facilitates searching through the repository to determine this information.

➤ On the menu bar, click **File**.
➤ Click **Quick Start**.
➤ In the left column, click **Team Development**.
➤ In the right column, click **Management Query**.
➤ Click **OK**.

Figure 23.11 shows the **Management Query** window. Notice that there are many options to select, depending on the type of query you want to execute.

Figure 23.11
Management Query

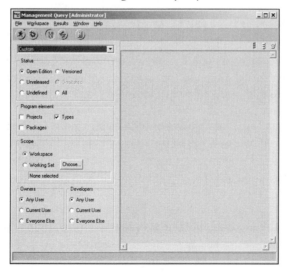

➤ Click to display the drop-down box as shown in Figure 23.12.

Notice that there are many predefined queries that make it much easier to set up your request. To start the query, you use just select the **Window** menu and then the **Start Query** menu item. Note that the query criteria you specify can affect the time it takes to perform the query.

Figure 23.12
Predefined Queries

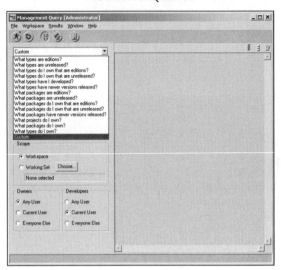

Tips and Tricks

You can use the resulting information from the Management Query in another form or document. To use this information, you select the *Results* menu and then select the *Copy to Clipboard* menu item to redirect your results to the Windows Clipboard. From there, you can copy the information into some other type of tracking or project management document.

Workspace and Repository Cleanup

There may be times when your workspace or repository needs a little housekeeping. This could happen for a number of reasons. It could be something as simple as having unwanted code or as complex as corruption problems with the repository. Whatever the reason, it's a good practice to periodically delete and purge program elements. A delete removes the program element from the workspace, but a copy is still available in the repository. A purge removes the final copy from the repository.

To delete a program element from the workspace, you display the shortcut menu and then select the **Delete** menu item. To purge a program element from the repository, you open the **Repository Explorer** from the **Window** menu, select **Names**, and then select **Purge**. You can also undo a purge with a **Restore** function.

Tips and Tricks

CAUTION: Make sure you know what you're doing before you try to clean up the workspace and repository. Read the VisualAge for Java documentation for the latest instructions on deletion and purging.

Tips and Tricks

There are times when it's helpful to know a few tidbits of information related to repositories, the workspace, and team development, such as the following:

- The name of the IDE program is ide.exe.
- A repository server administration utility is called emadmin.exe.
- Local repositories are stored in the \IBMVJava\IDE\repository directory under the name ivj.dat.
- Contents of the local workspace are stored in the \IBMVJava\IDE\program directory under the name ide.icx.

Summary

Team development can be a great benefit for building camaraderie as well as quickly getting large and complex applications out the door. In this chapter you learned

- how to create new users for a team development approach
- the basics of team development
- the responsibilities of different types of team development roles
- how to change owners
- the basics of Management Query

The next chapter — the last! — will show you how to deploy your VisualAge for Java applications.

Chapter 24

Deployment of Java Applications

 ## Chapter Objectives

- ☐ Understand the basics of Java application deployment
- ☐ Export to directories, JAR files, and the AS/400
- ☐ Understand ZIP and JAR files
- ☐ Set up CLASSPATH and PATH environment variables
- ☐ Understand runtime execution environments

 ## Chapter Project

- ☐ You will export the **PartsMaintenanceSubfileExample** class that you created in Chapter 20, as well as the **buildingas400graphics** package that contains it.
- ☐ Figure 24.1 shows what the sample class looks like.

Figure 24.1
Chapter Project

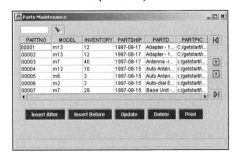

Welcome to the last chapter! This is one of those chapters that could be written as an entire book all by itself. In it, you'll learn about some of the basics of deployment — that is, exporting your Java code out of VisualAge for Java.

You may ask, why do I need to export Java code from VisualAge for Java? All code created in VisualAge for Java is stored in a repository. For users and other developers to use your Java code, you need to export it from the VisualAge for Java repository.

As you deploy a Java program, each operating system has its own runtime environment issues that are beyond the scope of this book. We'll take a cursory look at some of these issues. We'll cover the following topics in this chapter:

- exporting your Java code to a directory on a PC, what the necessary environment components are, and how to execute the Java program from a DOS command line
- exporting your Java code to a JAR file

- exporting, compiling, and running your Java code on an AS/400
- setting up the CLASSPATH and PATH environment variables and runtime execution issues

With the Enterprise Edition of VisualAge for Java, AS/400 programmers are probably interested in two areas related to exportation of Java code. First, the standard VisualAge for Java can export Java code within these file types and scenarios:

- Java bytecode (.class files)
- Java source code (.java files)
- Java archive files (.jar files)
- VisualAge for Java repository files (.dat files)

Second, the Enterprise Toolkit for AS/400 (ET/400) can do the following related to exporting Java code:

- export Java source code to the AS/400 (.java files)
- export Java bytecode to the AS/400 (.class files)
- compile Java bytecode into AS/400 optimized programs
- run AS/400 Java programs
- debug AS/400 Java programs

Exporting a Java Class to a Client Directory

When you're ready to export your applications from VisualAge for Java, you'll find that doing so is very easy. You can export your Java bytecode as .class files to the regular file system on your PC. You can export a single .class file, as well as a myriad of .class files, packages, projects, and interfaces. You can also export your Java source code — the .java files.

In Chapter 20, you created a class called **PartsMaintenanceSubfileExample**. As you may recall, it was part of the **buildingas400graphics** package. You are now going to export the **PartsMaintenanceSubfileExample** class and the **buildingas400graphics** package.

➢   If the workbench isn't started, start it now.
➢   Expand the project **My Graphical Applications** with a click.
➢   Expand the package **buildingas400graphics** with a click.
➢   Select the class **PartsMaintenanceSubfileExample** with a click.
➢   Right-click to display the shortcut menu, and select **Export**.

Figure 24.2 shows first window of the **Export** SmartGuide, which offers three export destinations from which to choose:

- **Directory** — This option exports to a directory in the file system.
- **Jar file** — This option builds a Java archive file (a JAR file) that contains all the necessary components for execution.
- **Repository** — This option lets you export to another VisualAge for Java repository.

One important distinction to keep in mind when performing an export is that .class and .java files come from the workspace, while a repository export comes from the repository.

This window also gives you the option of specifying a *manifest file*. If you do so, a file is created that identifies all the contents within the export function.

Continue with the export.

➢   Make sure the **Directory** option is selected.
➢   Click **Next**.

Figure 24.3 shows the next screen of the SmartGuide, the **Export to a directory** window. Here, you specify what is to be exported: .class files (bytecode), .java files (source code), and/or resource files. You're going to export the **buildingas400graphics** package definition, the **PartsMaintenanceSubfileExample** class, all the Java source code related to the class, and all the resources associated with both the package and the class.

What do the resources include? The resources at the package level include all the .gif files you used on the JButtons (e.g., the down button .gif file, the up button .gif file). Also included are the resources for any AS/400 utility JavaBeans — in our case, for the **ListManager** JavaBean.

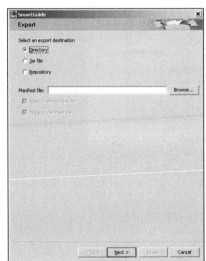

Figure 24.2
Export SmartGuide

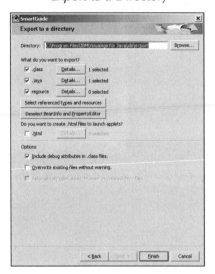

Figure 24.3
Export to a Directory

Class Export

➢ Next to the **.class** check box, click the **Details** button.

You should see a window similar to Figure 24.4, the **.class export** window. Notice that the **My Graphical Applications** project is already selected, as is the **PartsMaintenanceSubfileExample** class (type) within the **buildingas400graphics** package. That's exactly what you want.

➢ Click **OK**.

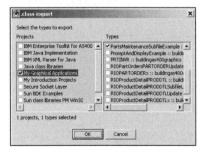

Figure 24.4
Class Export

Source Code Export

By default, the source code associated with the **PartsMaintenanceSubfileExample** class is also selected. Back in Figure 24.3, notice that only one .java file is noted as selected. That is the related source code. Typically, you wouldn't want to export the source code. The users don't care about it, and you wouldn't want just anyone to get his or her hands on your source code. But if you did move the source code over and wanted to compile it, would it be compiled correctly? Yes. That's the beauty of working with Java.

Resource File Export

Resource files typically will be image files, audio files, video files, properties files, or configuration files that the Java application needs to run correctly. Resource files aren't stored in the VisualAge for Java environment but in the normal file system on your PC. When VisualAge for Java creates a project, it automatically creates a folder with the same name as the project. It creates this new folder in the directory C:\Program Files\IBM\VisualAge for Java\IDE\Project_Resources. To use any external resources within the Java program, you must copy them to the resources directory. You may recall that you did this in Chapter 18 when you copied the four .gif files required for the JButtons.

Tips and Tricks

If you use any AS/400 Data File Utility (DFU) JavaBeans in your VisualAge for Java application, an additional .sos resource file is created as part of the project resources. You need this .sos file at run time for the application to be executed correctly.

Tips and Tricks

When you deploy your Java application, make sure all the Java program's resource files are distributed with the program. Deployed application resources are found at run time using the CLASSPATH variable.

Notice that Figure 24.3 says no resources are selected. For the application to run correctly outside the VisualAge for Java environment, you'll need all the resources associated with it. What would happen if you didn't select the resources? A couple of things are possible:

- If a .gif file used on a JButton is missing, the graphical button won't appear on the application screen. That will make things a little difficult for users working with the application.
- If the **ListManager** JavaBean is missing, you'll receive a Java runtime error.

Select the appropriate resource files.

➢   Next to the **.resource** check box, click the **Details** button.

The **Resource export** window, shown in Figure 24.5, is displayed. Notice that nothing is selected. You're going to change that.

➢   In the left pane of the window, select the **My Graphical Applications** check box.

As Figure 24.6 shows, you should immediately see, in the right pane, all the files, or resources, associated with the **My Graphical Applications** project. Notice that they are all selected. There are probably a few extra files here that you don't need for the **PartsMaintenanceSubfileExample** class, but that's okay. When you move the entire contents of a project, you normally want all the resources associated with that project. To deselect all the resources, you'd just clear the **My Graphical Applications** project check box. You can try it out if you like.

Figure 24.5
Resource Export

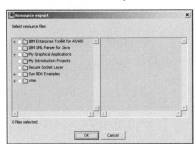

Figure 24.6
Resource Export with Selected Resources

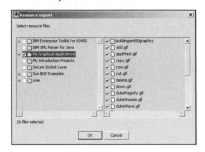

➢   In the left pane, expand the **My Graphical Applications** project.
➢   Clear the **buildingas400graphics** package check box, as shown in Figure 24.7.

Figure 24.7
buildingas400graphics Package

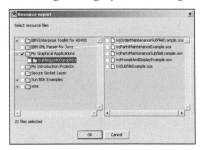

Notice that all the resources for the **buildingas400graphics** package appear on the right. None are selected.

➢   In the right pane, select the resource **ivjPartsMaintenanceSubfileExample.sos**, as shown in Figure 24.8. This .sos file is where the DFU **ListManager** JavaBean resource is kept.

Notice that the SmartGuide automatically selected the **buildingas400graphics** package when you made this choice. That was done to indicate that something within this package is now selected for export.

➢   Click **OK**.

Figure 24.8
Selected Resources

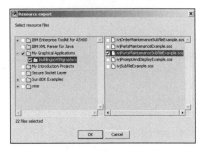

When you return to the **Export to a directory** window, 22 resources should be reported as selected, as shown in Figure 24.9.

Figure 24.9
Resource Details

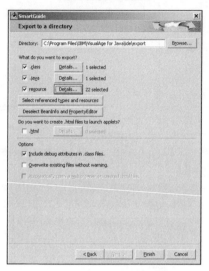

➤   Change the **Directory** entry at the top of the window to something meaningful on your PC. All the files from the export will be saved in this directory. Make sure the directory you specify exists. You can click **Browse** to make a selection. In Figure 24.10, the directory C:\Javacode\AS400 is selected.

➤   Click **Finish**.

Figure 24.10
Export Directory

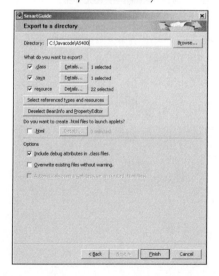

It may take a while for the export to occur. VisualAge for Java is creating the .class files, .java files, .sos files, and any additional resources required. Figure 24.11 shows the contents of the export directory once the export is completed. You can view this information using Windows Explorer or the DOS command prompt screen. Notice that directory C:\Javacode\AS400 contains the **buildingas400graphics** subdirectory as well as all the resources. As Figure 24.12 shows, if you drill down further to directory C:\Javacode\AS400\buildingas400graphics, you can see the .class files, .java files, and .sos files that were exported.

Figure 24.11

AS400 Directory

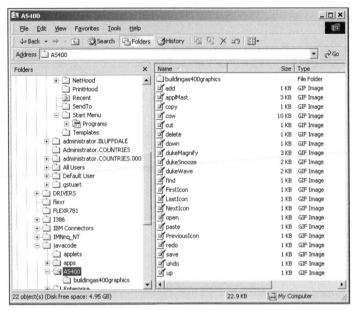

Figure 24.12

buildingas400graphics Directory

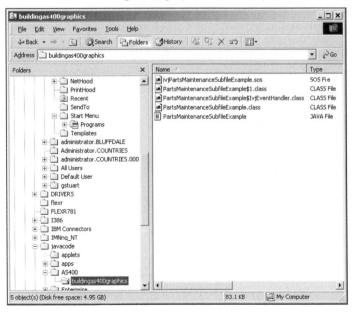

Client Environment Setup

Many options exist for setting up the client environment to run Java programs. You may want to review the IBM Java site for more information about this topic. Appendix C lists some good resources. With regard to the AS/400, there are many topics to discuss, including ZIP and JAR files, the CLASSPATH, the PATH, and execution of the Java application. We'll cover all these items in this section.

Tips and Tricks

You can use utility programs to facilitate deploying and updating applications on the client. Some of these programs use a push technology to push the applications out to the users, similar to an applet. They also can automatically download and install the latest version of an application. You can find one of these utility programs, Web Start, on Sun's Web site at *http://java.sun.com/products/javawebstart*.

ZIP and JAR Files

ZIP and JAR files are used to store Java classes. ZIP files have a .zip file-name extension and use an industry-standard compression technology. JAR files use a .jar file-name extension and use the Java archive file format. The Java Virtual Machine (JVM) can directly read both of these file types. The Java runtime environment can read classes and packages directly from .zip and .jar files.

Contained in the directory \IBM\VisualAge for Java\eab\runtime30 are .zip files and .jar files that can be used for Java applications that access AS/400-related classes. At run time, you'll probably need some of these files. The files include the following:

File	Contents
JT400.JAR	AS/400 Toolbox for Java
JT400MRI.ZIP	AS/400 Toolbox for Java translated text
AS400UT.JAR	ET/400 utility classes (com.ibm.ivj.et400.util and com.ibm.ibj.et400.util.awt)

Additional AS/400-related .zip and .jar files are available, including JT400ACCESS.ZIP, UTILITIES.ZIP, DATA400.JAR, JT400PROXY.JAR, JT400SERVLET.JAR, JUI400.JAR, UITOOLS.JAR, UTIL400.JAR, and X4J400.JAR.

CLASSPATH

The CLASSPATH is an environment variable used by the JVM to find Java classes at run time. Its function is similar to that of the AS/400 library list. Setting the CLASSPATH is like using the AS/400 EDTLIBL (Edit Library List) command. The JVM uses the CLASSPATH to locate or search for a particular ZIP or JAR file at run time.

You can store various classes, ZIP files, or JAR files on the local hard drive. They can also be mapped to a network drive or even stored in the AS/400 Integrated File System (IFS). Regardless of where the files and classes are stored, the JVM uses the CLASSPATH to find them at run time.

You're going to set up the CLASSPATH for a Windows 2000 environment. (Older Windows versions would use the DOS command SET CLASSPATH.)

➢ On the Windows desktop, double-click **My Computer**.
➢ Double-click the **Control Panel** icon.
➢ Double-click **Settings**.
➢ In the **System Settings** window, click the **Advanced** tab.
➢ On the **Advanced** tab, shown in Figure 24.13, click the **Environment Variables** button.

Figure 24.14 shows the resulting window, which lists various environment variables.

Figure 24.13
System Properties Advanced Tab

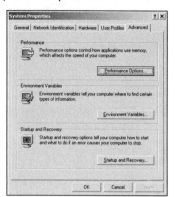

Figure 24.14
Environment Variables

➤ In the **System variables** list, double-click the **CLASSPATH** variable.

Figure 24.15 shows the actual CLASSPATH value, which specifies both a ZIP file (jt400.zip) and a JAR file (AS400UT.JAR) as part of the variable value. You may need to change your CLASSPATH for your application to run correctly. To change the CLASSPATH, you add an entry to the value field, separating the entry with a semicolon (;) from the rest of the field's contents. Then click **OK**. (You can also change or delete any part of the existing CLASSPATH value.)

➤ Close the CLASSPATH environment variable by clicking **OK**.

Figure 24.15
CLASSPATH Environment Variable

Tips and Tricks

If you're creating a CLASSPATH on the AS/400, you use the ADDENVVAR (Add Environment Variable) or WRKENVVAR (Work with Environment Variable) command to set the CLASSPATH. I like to set my CLASSPATH with my CL start-up program, so that the variable gets set correctly every time I log on to the AS/400. Remember to use a colon (:) as the separator character in this case, as opposed to the semicolon used in Windows environments.

How do you decide where to store your ZIP or JAR files — local hard drive, network drive, or AS/400 IFS? This isn't an easy question to answer. Several factors can impact the decision, including

- communications speeds between the client and the AS/400
- disk space concerns
- security issues related to application programs and components
- capabilities to download applications
- capabilities to manage different versions of applications

Before you set up your entire corporate-wide deployment procedures, do some experimenting to make sure you implement the correct solution for your environment.

PATH

To be able to run your Java application, you need access to the JVM. The PATH environment variable specifies the path to the directory that contains the JVM. You set this environment variable the same way you set the CLASSPATH. (Older Windows versions would use the DOS command SET PATH.)

Executing the Java Application

The operating system on which your application runs determines which options you have for initiating the application. In a Windows environment, for example, you can create a simple executable from a C program to call your Java application. In Unix, you can use a wrapper Korn-shell script to invoke the Java interpreter. These topics are beyond the scope of this book. From a programmer perspective, the simplest approach is to use the command line, although this usually isn't the best approach from a user perspective. For this chapter example, you will execute the application from the DOS command line.

➢   On the Windows **Start** menu, select **Programs**, then **Accessories**, and then **Command Prompt**.
➢   Change to the directory where you exported your package. In the example, the package was saved in directory C:\Javacode\AS400.
➢   Type the following command at the DOS prompt:

```
java buildingas400graphics/PartsMaintenanceSubfileExample
```

➢   When the application displays the AS/400 sign-on screen, enter your sign-on information.

Figure 24.16 shows the result. This is exactly the same program you saw in Chapter 20, but it's not running in the VisualAge for Java IDE. Congratulations! You've successfully exported your Java program and executed it outside the VisualAge for Java IDE.

Figure 24.16
Parts Maintenance Application

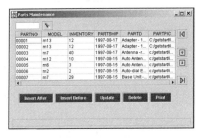

Exporting a Java Class to a JAR File

One of the best choices for deploying an application is by use of a JAR file. When you export your classes into a JAR file, your final Java bytecode and resource files are all compressed together for better performance and faster download times.

Exporting to a JAR file is nearly identical to exporting to a directory, as you did earlier in this chapter. When you're deploying a large application, it's usually a good idea to select deployment by use of a JAR file as opposed to a client directory. To export to a JAR file, you take the following steps.

1. On the **Export** SmartGuide, select **Jar file** as the export destination. Figure 24.17 shows this choice.
2. On the next window (Figure 24.18), enter the correct **Jar file** name.
3. As shown in the figure, you probably won't want to select the **.java** option. You normally wouldn't export your Java source code with the JAR file.
4. You can select whether to *seal* the JAR file. By sealing a JAR file, you guarantee to use the correct classes, as opposed to using a different referenced class based on the CLASSPATH. This approach is similar in concept to

using an AS/400 hard-coded library rather than a library in a library list. Sometimes when other software manufacturers use a class that you are using, their class may be at a different version level from what you are using. Sealing a JAR file helps prevent this conflict from occurring. You can also specify some packages to be sealed while others are not.

5. You can specify whether to compress the JAR file. Doing so is usually a good idea, especially when using a Java applet.

Figure 24.17	**Figure 24.18**
Exporting to a Jar File	*Jar File Export Options*

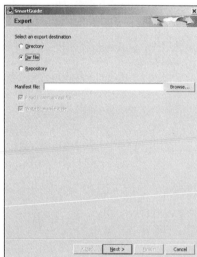
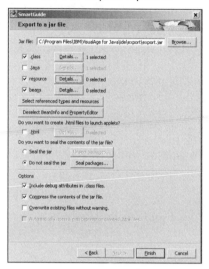

Tips and Tricks

Two tools let you perform updates to AS/400 Java Toolbox classes when program temporary fixes (PTFs) are installed on the AS/400. The *AS400ToolboxInstaller* class is used to update AS/400 classes on the client whenever the Java application is restarted. It must be included as part of the Java application when it is deployed. The *AS400ToolboxJarMaker* class lets you create smaller JAR files from a larger JAR file. It can remove any unused classes.

Exporting a Java Class to the AS/400 with ET/400

There may be times you export classes directly to the AS/400. Typically, you wouldn't execute a graphical Java application directly from the AS/400; this type of application normally would run on the client. But there are many cases in which you'd want Java classes moved to the AS/400 — for example, to execute a logic class on the AS/400, to use Remote Method Invocation (RMI) support, to execute server-based applications, or to deploy applications from the AS/400. There are two ways to accomplish the exportation of Java to the AS/400:

- Use one of the methods described earlier in this chapter to export the Java application from VisualAge for Java, and then move it to the AS/400 IFS.
- Use the export functions within the Enterprise Toolkit for AS/400.

This section will show you how to export Java applications using the second approach.

ET/400 lets you perform the following functions related to an AS/400 Java application:

Function	Description
Export	Lets you export a Java application, .class and .java files, to the AS/400 IFS.
Compile	Lets you compile a Java class into native AS/400 bytecode. (Before you can compile, you must have exported the class files to the AS/400 IFS.)
Run	Lets you run an AS/400 Java program from the VisualAge for Java workbench. (Before you can run the program, you must have exported the class files to the AS/400 IFS.)
Debug	Lets you debug an AS/400 Java program.
Start ET400 Daemon	Lets you avoid signing on to the AS/400 server more than once while using the SmartGuides.

Before you can execute an ET/400 export, compile, or run, you must set the associated properties for the function. Figure 24.19 shows the menu selections you make to set properties:

➤   From the workbench, right-click to display the shortcut menu.
➤   Select the **Tools** menu item.
➤   Select the **ET/400** menu item.
➤   Select the **Properties** menu item.

Figure 24.19
Enterprise Toolkit (ET/400) Menu

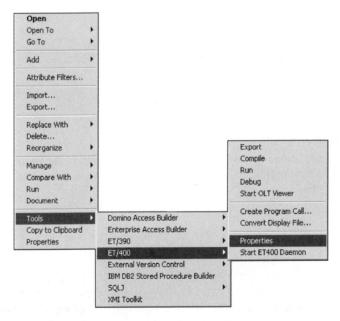

Figure 24.20 shows the ET/400 **Export Options** window. At a minimum, you must identify a server and the IFS directory for the export here.

Figure 24.20
ET/400 Export Options

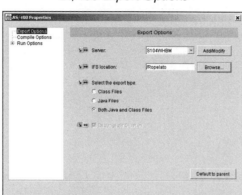

Figure 24.21 shows the ET/400 **Compile Options** window. You can accept the defaults here or change the settings. These settings are AS/400 compile settings.

Figure 24.22 shows the ET/400 **Run Options** window. You can use the first option, **Parameter values**, to specify one or more parameter values that are passed to the Java program.

Figure 24.21	**Figure 24.22**
ET/400 Compile Options	*ET/400 Run Options*

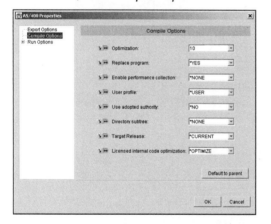 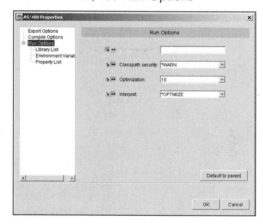

To set library list, environment variable, and property list options, expand the **Run Options** item in the left pane of the window. Figure 24.23 shows the ET/400 **Library List** window. If your Java application requires resources, use this window to specify the name of the library where the resources reside. Figure 24.24 shows the ET/400 **Environment Variables** window. If the variable is defined as a CLASSPATH, this path is used to find the classes.

Figure 24.23
ET/400 Run Library List Options

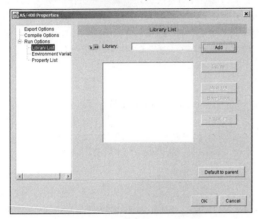

Figure 24.24
ET/400 Run Environment Variables Options

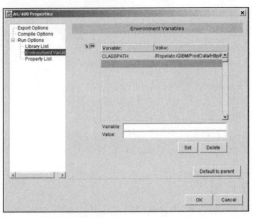

Figure 24.25 shows the ET/400 **Property List** window. This window specifies the Java property used in the Java program's class. If you plan to run a Java application using Java 2 on the AS/400 with V4R5 or V4R4, specify the property as follows:

```
java.version value: 1.2
```

Otherwise, the default JDK of 1.1.8 is used for V4R5 and 1.1.7 for V4R4.

Figure 24.25
ET/400 Run Property List Options

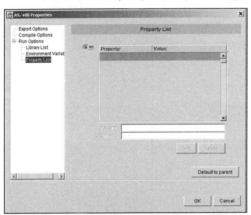

After you've set the properties, you can export, compile, run, or debug a Java application on the AS/400. To do this, you just select the package or class in the workbench, right-click to display the shortcut menu, select **Tools**, select **ET/400**, and then select the menu option you want to execute: **Export**, **Compile**, **Run**, or **Debug**. A progress bar will appear. When the function is completed, you'll see the completion information appear in the VisualAge for Java log window.

Summary

You can build a great Java application, but if the deployment of that application isn't done correctly, you can end up with some unhappy users. Experiment to find the best deployment solution for your organization. It will be worth taking the time to do so, and you'll end up with more-satisfied users of your Java applications. Giving users a new GUI won't keep them happy if you haven't addressed issues related to user response times.

In this chapter you learned

- the basics of Java application deployment
- how to export Java bytecode and source code to directories, JAR files, and the AS/400
- how ZIP files and JAR files are used
- how to set up the CLASSPATH and PATH environment variables in a Windows 2000 environment
- how to execute a Java application outside the VisualAge for Java development environment

Farewell

Congratulations! You've finished all the chapters. You should have learned enough throughout this book to now possess a solid foundation for developing applications in VisualAge for Java. You'll find there are many other topics and JavaBeans to explore that we didn't cover here. Following this chapter are three appendixes well worth taking your time to review.

Good luck in the future with all your new Java development projects!

Unit

6

Appendixes

Appendix A

AS/400 Java Toolbox

The AS/400 Toolbox for Java is a set of specially written Java classes that provide easy access to AS/400 data and resources. You can access AS/400 resources through a Java servlet running on the AS/400, a Java program running on the client workstation, or a Java applet running in a Java-enabled browser.

This appendix lists all the classes and JavaBeans associated with the AS/400 Toolbox for Java as of OS/400 Version 5 Release 1 (V5R1). The documentation can be found at *http://publib.boulder.ibm.com/html/as400/v5r1/ic2924/index.htm* (choose **Programming|Java|IBM Toolbox for Java**).

Access Classes

The access classes are used to access and manage resources and data on the AS/400. The access classes are contained in the package **com.ibm.as400.access**.

ActionCompletedEvent	AS400JDBCDatabaseMetaData	ConnectionEvent
AFPResource	AS400JDBCDataSource	ConnectionPool
AFPResourceList	AS400JDBCDriver	ConnectionPoolEvent
ArrayFieldDescription	AS400JDBCInputStream	ConvTableReader
AS400	AS400JDBCObjectFactory	ConvTableWriter
AS400Array	AS400JDBCPooledConnection	DataArea
AS400BidiTransform	AS400JDBCPreparedStatement	DataAreaEvent
AS400Bin2	AS400JDBCResultSet	DataQueue
AS400Bin4	AS400JDBCResultSetMetaData	DataQueueAttributes
AS400Bin8	AS400JDBCRowSet	DataQueueEntry
AS400ByteArray	AS400JDBCStatement	DataQueueEvent
AS400Certificate	AS400JDBCXAConnection	DateFieldDescription
AS400CertificateAttribute	AS400JDBCXADataSource	DatetimeConverter
AS400CertificateEvent	AS400JDBCXAResource	DBCSGraphicFieldDescription
AS400CertificateUtil	AS400JDBCXid	DBCSOnlyFieldDescription
AS400CertificateVldUtil	AS400JPing	DBCSOpenFieldDescription
AS400ConnectionPool	AS400Message	DecimalDataArea
AS400File	AS400PackedDecimal	DLOPermission
AS400FileRecordDescription	AS400Structure	DQAttsAuthorityEditor
AS400FileRecordDescriptionEvent	AS400Text	EnvironmentVariable
AS400Float4	AS400UnsignedBin2	EnvironmentVariableList
AS400Float8	AS400UnsignedBin4	EventLog
AS400FTP	AS400ZonedDecimal	FieldDescription
AS400JDBCBlob	BaseDataQueue	FileEvent
AS400JDBCBlobLocator	BinaryConverter	FloatFieldDescription
AS400JDBCCallableStatement	BinaryFieldDescription	FTP
AS400JDBCClob	CharacterDataArea	FTPEvent
AS400JDBCClobLocator	CharacterFieldDescription	HexFieldDescription
AS400JDBCConnection	CharConverter	IFSExistenceOptionEditor
AS400JDBCConnectionPool	CommandCall	IFSFile
AS400JDBCConnectionPoolDataSource	CommandLineArguments	IFSFileDescriptor

Access Classes continued...

IFSFileInputStream
IFSFileOutputStream
IFSJavaFile
IFSKey
IFSRandomAccessFile
IFSShareOptionEditor
IFSTextFileInputStream
IFSTextFileOutputStream
JavaApplicationCall
Job
JobList
JobLog
KeyedDataQueue
KeyedDataQueueEntry
KeyedFile
LineDataRecordWriter
LocalDataArea
LogicalDataArea
MessageFile
MessageQueue
NetServer
NetServerConnection
NetServerFileShare
NetServerPrintShare
NetServerSession
NetServerShare
ObjectEvent
OutputQueue
OutputQueueEvent

OutputQueueList
PackedDecimalFieldDescription
PasswordDialog
Permission
Printer
PrinterFile
PrinterFileList
PrinterList
PrintObject
PrintObjectInputStream
PrintObjectList
PrintObjectListEvent
PrintObjectPageInputStream
PrintObjectTransformedInputStream
PrintParameterList
ProductLicense
ProductLicenseEvent
ProgramCall
ProgramParameter
ProxyServer
QSYSObjectPathName
QSYSObjectTypeTable
QSYSPermission
QueuedMessage
Record
RecordDescriptionEvent
RecordFormat
RootPermission
SCS3812Writer

SCS5219Writer
SCS5224Writer
SCS5256Writer
SCS5553Writer
SecureAS400
SequentialFile
ServiceProgramCall
SpooledFile
SpooledFileList
SpooledFileOutputStream
SystemPool
SystemStatus
SystemValue
SystemValueEvent
SystemValueGroup
SystemValueList
TimeFieldDescription
TimestampFieldDescription
Trace
User
UserGroup
UserList
UserPermission
UserSpace
UserSpaceEvent
WriterJob
WriterJobList
ZonedDecimalFieldDescription

Data Classes

The data classes are used to simplify the calling of AS/400 programs from Java. The data classes are contained in the package **com.ibm.as400.data**.

PcmlMessageLog   ProgramCallDocument

Resource Classes

The resource classes use a generic list-based scheme to represent AS/400 resources. The resource classes are contained in the package **com.ibm.as400.resource**.

AbstractValueMap	ResourceAdapter	RJobList
ActiveStatusEvent	ResourceEvent	RJobLog
ArrayResourceList	ResourceLevel	RMessageQueue
BooleanValueMap	ResourceList	RPrinter
BufferedResourceList	ResourceListAdapter	RPrinterList
ChangeableResource	ResourceListEvent	RQueuedMessage
Presentation	ResourceMetaData	RSoftwareResource
PresentationLoader	ResourceMetaDataTable	RUser
ProgramAttributeGetter	RIFSFile	RUserList
ProgramAttributeSetter	RIFSFileList	SystemResourceList
ProgramMap	RJavaProgram	
Resource	RJob	

Security Classes

The security classes are used to provide user swapping using AS/400 token and authentication classes. The security classes are contained in the package **com.ibm.as400.security.auth**.

AS400Credential	AS400Principal	ProfileTokenCredential
AS400CredentialEvent	ProfileHandleCredential	UserProfilePrincipal

User Interface Framework Classes

The user interface framework classes represent the classes used for the Graphical Toolbox with the Panel Definition Markup Language (PDML). The user interface framework classes are contained in the package **com.ibm.as400.ui.framework.java**.

AbstractDescriptor	HandlerTask	PercentFormatter
ActionHandler	HelpEvent	PopupMenuButton
Capabilities	HelpViewer	PreChangeEvent
ChoiceDescriptor	InternetAddressFormatter	PropertySheetManager
ContextMenuManager	IntFormatter	ShortFormatter
DataFormatter	ItemDescriptor	SplitPaneManager
DateFormatter	JGroupingTableHeader	StringFormatter
DeckPaneManager	ListItemCellRenderer	TabbedPaneManager
DividerPanel	LongFormatter	TableHeaderUI
DoubleClickEvent	MenuManager	TableItemCellRenderer
DynamicPanelManager	MessageBoxDialog	TextDocument
EventHandler	MessageLog	TimeFormatter
FileChooserDialog	NodeDescriptor	UIFramework
FileClassLoader	PanelListModel	VerifyingTabbedPane
FloatFormatter	PanelManager	WizardManager
GroupingTableHeaderUI	PanelTableModel	

User Interface Utility Classes

The user interface utility classes are used for verification of different formatting options and displaying different types of command and message prompts. The user interface utility classes are contained in the package **com.ibm.as400.ui.util**.

AS400CharFormatter	AS400NameFormatter	ClMenuActionHandler
AS400CnameFormatter	AS400SnameIBMFormatter	CommandPrompter
AS400Formatter	AS400SQLNameColumnFormatter	MessageViewer
AS400MessageIdFormatter	AS400SQLNameFormatter	

User Interface HTML Classes

The user interface HTML classes help in defining forms and tables for Hypertext Markup Language (HTML) pages. An HTML tag is created for an element type that can be embedded into any HTML document. The HTML tags are compatible with the HTML 3.2 specification. The user interface HTML classes are contained in the package **com.ibm.as400.util.html**.

BidiOrdering	HTMLHyperlink	LayoutFormPanel
ButtonFormInput	HTMLList	LineLayoutFormPanel
CheckboxFormInput	HTMLListItem	OrderedList
DirFilter	HTMLMeta	OrderedListItem
ElementEvent	HTMLParameter	PasswordFormInput
FileFormInput	HTMLServlet	RadioFormInput
FileListElement	HTMLTable	RadioFormInputGroup
FileListRenderer	HTMLTableCaption	ResetFormInput
FileTreeElement	HTMLTableCell	SelectFormElement
FormInput	HTMLTableHeader	SelectOption
GridLayoutFormPanel	HTMLTableRow	SubmitFormInput
HiddenFormInput	HTMLTagAttributes	TextAreaFormElement
HTMLAlign	HTMLText	TextFormInput
HTMLApplet	HTMTransform	ToggleFormInput
HTMLFileFilter	HTMLTree	UnorderedList
HTMLForm	HTMLTreeElement	UnorderedListItem
HTMLHead	ImageFormInput	URLEncoder
HTMLHeading	LabelFormElement	URLParser

PCLWriter Classes

The PCLWriter classes define the methods necessary to render an area tree to a Printer Control Language (PCL) data stream. The PCLWriter classes are contained in the package **com.ibm.as400.util.reportwriter.pclwriter**.

PCLContext

PDFWriter Classes

The PDFWriter classes define the methods necessary to render an area tree to a Portable Document Format (PDF) data stream. The PDFWriter classes are contained in the package **com.ibm.as400.util.reportwriter.pdfwriter**.

PDFontext

Processor Classes

The processor classes are used to process Java Server Pages, report processors, and Extensible Stylesheet Language (XSL) report processors. The processor classes are contained in the package **com.ibm.as400.util.reportwriter. processor**.

JSPReportProcessor	ReportProcessor	XSLReportProcessor

Servlet Classes

The servlet classes work closely with the access classes. The servlet classes provide an interface between the AS/400 data, the Web server, and the client browser. The client browser connects to the Web server on which the Java servlet is running and working with the AS/400 data. The servlet classes are contained in the package **com.ibm.as400.util.servlet**.

AS400Servlet	RecordFormatMetaData	SectionCompletedEvent
AuthenticationServlet	RecordListRowData	ServletEventLog
HTMLFormConverter	ResourceListRowData	ServletHyperlink
HTMLTableConverter	RowData	SQLResultSetMetaData
ListMetaData	RowDataEvent	SQLResultSetRowData
ListRowData	RowMetaDataType	StringConverter

Graphical Classes

The graphical access classes are used to retrieve and manipulate data and to build the visual presentation interface to the user. These graphical classes use the Java Swing Foundation classes. The graphical classes are contained in the package **com.ibm.as400.vaccess**.

AS400DetailsModel	RecordListTableModel	VJobList
AS400DetailsPane	RecordListTablePane	VJobLogMessage
AS400ExplorerPane	ResourceListDetailsModel	VMessage
AS400JDBCDataSourcePane	ResourceListDetailsPane	VMessageList
AS400JDBCDataSourcePaneDataBean	ResourceListModel	VMessageQueue
AS400ListModel	ResourceListPane	VObjectEvent
AS400ListPane	ResourceProperties	VOutput
AS400TreeModel	SpooledFileViewer	VPrinter
AS400TreePane	SQLConnection	VPrinterOutput
CommandCallButton	SQLQuerybuilderPane	VPrinters
CommandCallMenuItem	SQLResultSetFormPane	VPropertiesAction
DataQueueDocument	SQLResultSetTableModel	VQueuedMessage
ErrorDialogAdapter	SQLResultSetTablePane	VSystemPool
ErrorEvent	SQLStatementButton	VSystemStatus
FileFilter	SQLStatementDocument	VSystemStatusPane
IFSFileDialog	SQLStatementMenuItem	VSystemValueList
IFSTextFileDocument	VActionAdapter	VUser
KeyedDataQueueDocument	VIFSDirectory	VUserAndGroup
ProgramCallButton	VIFSFile	VUserList
ProgramCallMenuItem	VJavaApplicationCall	WorkingCursorAdapter
RecordListFormPane	VJob	WorkingEvent

Utility Classes

The utility classes are used to assist in performing specific administrative tasks.

AS400ToolboxInstaller	JarMakerEvent	RunJavaApplication
AS400ToolboxJarMaker	JPing	VRunJavaApplication
JarMaker	KeyringDB	

Appendix B

VisualAge for Java Installation

This appendix contains some general instructions for installing the Enterprise Edition of VisualAge for Java. Before beginning your VisualAge for Java installation, you should read the instructions found in the IBM *Installation and Migration* guide that comes with your product CD. Also consult the README file and the Release Notes for more information about general product limitations and known problems.

Tips and Tricks

Don't be nervous about the installation! There's a fair amount of documentation, which can make installation an intimidating task. In reality, the process is fairly straightforward. And if you do make a mistake, you can always uninstall and then reinstall the software.

Hardware Requirements

Before you install the product, make sure you have the minimums mentioned below. IBM's minimum recommendations are

- Pentium II processor or better
- SVGA (800 × 600) display or better (1024 × 768 recommended)
- 96 MB of RAM (160 MB recommended)
- 750 MB of hard disk space

I strongly suggest you exceed the IBM requirements. I recommend a minimum of 256 MB of RAM. A much faster processor and a very fast hard drive will help immensely with performance. VisualAge for Java is a very resource-intensive application.

Software Requirements

IBM's requirements for software are

- Windows 98, Windows 2000, or Windows NT 4.0 with Service Pack 4 or later
- TCP/IP installed and configured
- frames-capable Web browser, such as Netscape Navigator 4.7 or later or Microsoft Internet Explorer 5.0 or later
- OS/400 Release V4R3M0 or later for development and V4R5M0 or later for runtime

Installation

➢ Insert the VisualAge for Java CD.

Figure B.1 shows the initial install screen.

Figure B.1
Install Screen

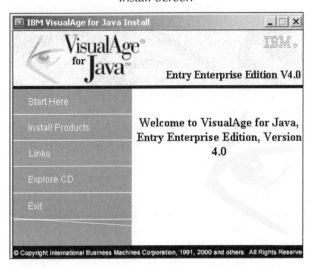

➤   Click the **Install Products** menu item to display the **Install Products** menu (Figure B.2).

Figure B.2
Install VisualAge for Java

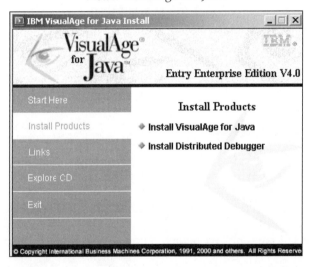

➤   Click **Install VisualAge for Java**.

Next, you'll see the language prompt screen, shown in Figure B.3.

➤   Select the appropriate language.
➤   Click **OK**.

Figure B.3
Language Selection

At this point, you may be prompted to reboot your computer.

➢   If you're prompted to reboot, click **Restart**.

Next, you'll see a screen informing you that an InstallShield Wizard will be created to walk you through the rest of the installation.

➢   Click **Next**.

You'll be prompted to accept the license agreement terms.

➢   Read the License Agreement.
➢   When you're ready to proceed, click **I accept terms in the License Agreement**.
➢   Click **Next**.

The next step will take a couple minutes to prepare. Eventually, you'll see the initial InstallShield Wizard screen, shown in Figure B.4. As you can see in the figure, you have three options from which to choose. The **Complete** and **Custom** setups produce a screen similar to Figure B.5. These options let you alter the features that will be installed. The **Custom by Scenario** setup produces a screen similar to Figure B.6. If you're developing for a particular environment and only that environment, you can choose this option and VisualAge for Java will determine which features you need.

Figure B.4
InstallShield Wizard

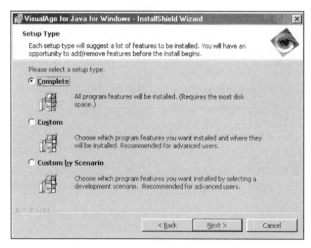

Figure B.5
Complete/Custom Installation Edit Features

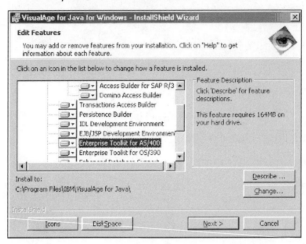

Figure B.6
Scenario Setup

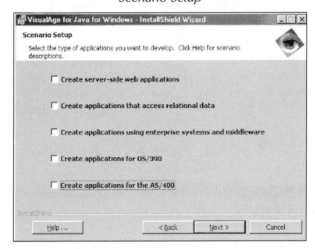

When I install VisualAge for Java, I normally select the **Complete** setup installation option. In this example, we'll select this option.

➤ Select **Complete**.
➤ Click **Next**.

You should be looking at the equivalent of Figure B.5. Here, you can remove one or more features by clicking the icon next the feature. If you need additional help on what to do, click the **Describe** button for more information.

➤ Accept the default of all features.
➤ Click **Next**.

Next, you must specify where the repository is to be located. The repository is where all your Java classes will be physically stored. If you want to store the repository on your local workstation, select **Local**. If you want to store it on your server, select **Server** and then enter the TCP/IP name of the server and the physical directory where you want the repository stored.

➢   As shown in Figure B.7, select **Local**.
➢   Click **Next**.

Figure B.7
Location of Repository

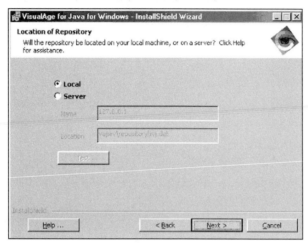

The next screen, shown in Figure B.8, is the final screen you see before the installation begins.

➢   If you're ready to install, click **Install**.

Figure B.8
Ready to Install Prompt

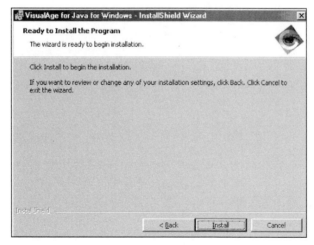

At this point, take a break. The installation will take anywhere from 10 minutes to an hour, depending on your hardware configuration and the install options you've chosen.

Tips and Tricks

The install can take quite a while. There may be times when you think it isn't working. Give it time; the installation will eventually be completed. I've seen installations take as long as an hour to finish, but the usual time required is about 10 to 15 minutes.

When the installation is completed, you'll see the VisualAge for Java splash screen appear. Congratulations, you've just completed the install. Now you can turn to Chapter 1 and begin working through the chapter projects. Good luck and enjoy.

Appendix C

Resources on VisualAge for Java

This appendix contains some useful resources to help you build up a good background concerning Java, VisualAge for Java, the AS/400 Toolbox, and the AS/400. The Web sites listed in this appendix were available at the time of printing. With the ever-changing world we live in, it's possible some of these links may not work by the time you read this.

Documentation

VisualAge for Java Documentation
> C:\Program Files\IBM\VisualAge for Java\ide\tools

AS/400 Toolbox Documentation — V5R1
> http://publib.boulder.ibm.com/html/as400/v5r1/ic2924/index.htm
> (Choose **Programming|Java|IBM Toolbox for Java**.)

Java 2 Platform, Standard Edition, v1.2.2 API Specification Documentation
> http://java.sun.com/products/jdk/1.2/docs/api/index.html

Books

AS/400 Java Books

Coulthard, Phil, and George Farr. *Java for RPG Programmers*, 2nd ed. MC Press: 2002. ISBN 1-931182-06-X.

Darnell, Daniel. *Java and the AS/400*. 29th Street Press: 1999. ISBN 1-58304-033-1.

Denoncourt, Don. *Java Application Strategies for iSeries and AS/400*, 2nd ed. MC Press: 2001.
> ISBN 1-58347-025-5.

IBM Redbooks

Building AS/400 Applications with Java. SG24-2163.

Building AS/400 Client/Server Applications with Java. SG24-2152.

Building Java Applications for the iSeries Server with VisualAge for Java 3.5. SG24-6245.

Java/VisualAge for Java Books

Asbury, Stephen, and Scott R. Weiner. *Developing Java Enterprise Applications*, 2nd ed. John Wiley & Sons: 2001.
> ISBN 0-471-40593-0.

Geary, David M. *Graphic Java 2, Volume 2 (Swing)*. Prentice Hall: 1999. ISBN 0-13-079-667-0.

Lemay, Laura, and Charles L. Perkins. *Teach Yourself Java in 21 Days*. Sams: 1996. ISBN 1-57521-030-4.

Monson-Haefel, Richard. *Enterprise JavaBeans*, 2nd ed. O'Reilly & Associates: 2000. ISBN 1-565-92-869-5.

Nilsson, Dale R., Peter M. Jakab, Bill Sarantakos, and Russell A. Stinehour. *Enterprise Development with VisualAge for Java, Version 3*. John Wiley & Sons: 2000. ISBN 0-471-38949-8.

Roman, Ed, Scott Ambler, and Tyler Jewell. *Mastering Enterprise JavaBeans*, 2nd ed. John Wiley & Sons: 1999.
> ISBN 0-471-41711-4.

Stanchfield, Scott, and Isabelle Mauny. *Effective VisualAge for Java, Version 3*. John Wiley & Sons: 2001. ISBN 0-471-31730-6.

Weber, Joseph L. *Using Java 2 Platform*. Que: 1999. ISBN 0-7897-2018-3.

Web Sites

IBM Web Sites

IBM Home Page
http://www.ibm.com

VisualAge for Java
http://www.software.ibm.com/ad/vajava

VisualAge Developer Domain
http://www7.software.ibm.com/vad.nsf

VisualAge Partner Catalog
http://www.software.ibm.com/ad/visage/rc

Web Application Servers
http://www.software.ibm.com/webservers

Java Technology Zone
http://www.ibm.com/developerworks/java

jCentral
http://www.jcentral.com

IBM iSeries Home Page
http://www.iseries.ibm.com

iSeries Information Center
http://publib.boulder.ibm.com/html/as400

IBM WebSphere Product Home Page
http://www.software.ibm.com/websphere

Non-IBM Web Sites

Java Technology Home Page
http://www.java.sun.com

Java Users Group
http://servlet.java.sun.com/jugs

Freeware Java
http://freewarejava.com

Java Tutorial
http://java.sun.com/docs/books/tutorial

Java Developer Connection Tutorial
http://developer.java.sun.com/developer/onlinetraining

VisualAge for Java Tips and Tricks
http://javadude.com/vaj

Java Magazines

Dr. Dobb's Journal
http://www.ddj.com/ddj

Focus on Java
http://java.miningco.com/computer/java

Java Developer's Journal
http://www.Javadevelopersjournal.com/java/index2.html

JavaPro
http://www.devx.com/javapro

Java Report Online
http://www.adtmag.com/java/index.asp

JavaWorld
http://www.javaworld.com

The Swing Connection
http://www.theswingconnection.com

Index

A

about box, 323–324
  changing, 324
  defined, 323
  displaying, 323
  illustrated, 323
Abstract Window Toolkit JavaBeans, 50
  controls, 51
  defined, 50
  listing, 50
  menu, 296
  Swing beans and, 51
  See also beans
access builders, 5
accessingas400databases package, 238
accessingas400objects package, 156, 170, 185, 198, 218
Add Package SmartGuide, 43
Add Project SmartGuide, 41–42
  defined, 42
  illustrated, 41
  starting, 41
  using, 42
addErrorListener() method, 223, 230–233, 251–253
  connections, 230–232, 252–253
  illustrated, 231
  parameter-from-property connection, 231–232, 252–253
  RecordLevelAccessExample JFrame with, 230
  SQLExample JFrame with, 251–252
addRecord() method, 342
ADTSLAB library, 221
  CUSTOMER file, 235, 257–258
  PARTORDER file, 388
  PRODDTL file, 263, 342, 349, 388
  PRODUCT file, 236, 258
  PRTINVR program, 444
Align option, 71
alignment, Layout Managers and, 85
All Problems view, 12
  defined, 18
  illustrated, 18
All Projects pane
  packages in, 43–44
  projects in, 42
  shortcut menu, 218
  See also workbench
Appearance options, 30–32
  illustrated, 31
  Lists, 31
  Source, 31–32
Applet Info window, 47–48
Applet Properties window, 45
Applet Viewer, 57
applets, 40
  building, visually, 54–59
  creating, 39–66, 44–48
  defined, 40, 69, 139
  life cycle, 40
  naming, 44
  running, 40, 57
  security restriction, 40
application class, creating, 139–141

Application deployment, 475–489
Application Details window, 297, 299
  illustrated, 297, 299
applications
  calling, 313
  creation types, 40
  defined, 139
  executing, 484
  look and feel, 312
  maintenance, 342–343, 387–409, 412–418
  modifying, 22–24
  multiple calls, 313
  multiple editions of, 25
  running, 22
AS400 bean, 141–143, 172, 202, 222–223, 330–331, 417–418
  defined, 141–142
  dropping, 202, 270
  FormManager1 bean connection, 350
  illustrated, 187, 202, 223
  ListManager1 bean connection, 393
  ListManager2 bean connection, 393
  properties, 143
  selecting, 142
  setRoot() method with, 189–190
  system property, 148
  systemName property, 331, 350, 391
  userID property, 331, 350, 391
AS400 context, 133–134
AS400DetailsPane, 186–187
  bean, 186–187
  table-type format, 186
AS400eList bean, 156
AS400ExplorerPane bean, 170
  adding, 172
  illustrated, 172
  loading contents of, 176–178
  location of, 172
  sizing, 172
  with VIFSDirectory bean, 186
AS400ToolboxInstaller class, 485
AS/400 commands, runtime execution, 147–152
AS/400 sign-on screen, 146
AS/400 Toolbox, 54
  current releases, 259
  illustrated, 142
AS/400 Toolbox beans, 51–54, 141–146, 147
  connecting, 144–146
  defined, 51
  event-to-method connections, 145–146
  list of, 52–54
  property-to-property connections, 144
  See also beans
Attributes Implementor window, 83, 84

B

background color, changing, 55, 128
bean categories, 48, 49–54
  AS/400 Toolbox, 54, 141–146
  AWT, 50
  Enterprise Toolkit for AS/400, 51–54
  Swing, 50–51
  switching between, 50
  types of, 49
  See also Visual Composition Editor (VCE)
Bean Information window, 100, 101
Bean menu
  Run option, 57, 63, 180, 193, 212, 233
  Save Bean option, 57, 80, 180, 193, 212, 233

BeanInfo page
  defined, 97
  Features pane, 99
  illustrated, 98, 103
beans
  AS400, 172, 187, 270, 330–331, 350, 417–418
  AS400DetailsPane, 187
  AS400eList, 156
  AS400ExplorerPane, 170, 172
  AS/400-related, 141–146
  AWT, 50
  Button, 54, 55
  CallPRTINVRProgram, 451
  CommandCall, 143–144, 148
  DFU, 262–263
  DriverManager, 241–242
  ErrorDialog Adapter, 223, 243
  ET400List, 156–165
  ET/400, 52–54
  FormManager, 219, 262–263
  IFS, 184–186
  IFSTextFileDocument, 184
  JButton, 88–92, 141, 147
  JCheckBoxMenuItem, 296
  JFormattedTable, 328
  JFormattedTextField, 78–80, 328
  JLabel, 73, 147, 200–201
  JMenu, 296
  JMenuBar, 296
  JMenuItem, 296
  JOptionPane, 379–385
  JPanel, 87–89
  JPopupMenu, 296, 318
  JRadioButtonMenuItem, 296
  JSeparator, 73–74, 296
  JTable, 328
  JTextArea, 200
  JTextField, 70–72, 147, 201
  JToolBar, 296
  JToolBarButton, 296
  JToolBarSeparator, 296
  label, 58, 59
  list, 330
  ListManager, 219, 262, 263
  LocalDataArea, 201–202
  lsObjectList, 159–161
  menu-related, 296–301
  morphing, 78–85
  nonvisual, 49
  PromptAndDisplayExample, 301
  RecordIOManager, 219, 262, 263, 419
  RecordListFormPane, 219, 222
  RecordListTablePane, 219
  saving, 57
  SQLConnection, 242
  SQLResultSetTablePane, 240–241
  Swing, 51, 157, 161, 296
  system value, 170–171
  SystemValue, 170
  TableColumn, 328, 336–339
  textField, 58
  VIFSDirectory, 184
  visually connecting, 61–65
  VSystemValueList, 170, 172
beans list, 70, 140–141
beginning-of-file message, 435
bookmark button, 35
bookmarks, 35–38
  defined, 35
  illustrated, 36
  moving, 37
  removing, 38
  selecting, 37
  setting, 35–36

Newest Books in the 29th Street Press® Library

GETTING STARTED WITH WEBSPHERE
The How-to Guide for Setting Up iSeries Web Application Servers
by Brian W. Kelly

This book is designed to be your practical companion for getting WebSphere Application Server up and running in an iSeries environment. The step-by-step approach and iSeries point of view — along with numerous hints and tips from one who's "been there" — will help ensure a smooth and successful installation. The book addresses all aspects of an iSeries WebSphere installation, including prerequisites, installation of WebSphere Application Server and its Administrative Console, and HTTP server configuration for use with WebSphere. 182 pages.

FORTRESS ROCHESTER
The Inside Story of the IBM iSeries
By Frank G. Soltis

Go behind the scenes and get the story on the design and development of IBM's new eServer iSeries. Dr. Frank Soltis, IBM chief scientist for the iSeries, examines the five sacred architectural principles of the system, hardware technologies, system structure, enabling technologies, and e-business. Special chapters cover iSeries security, Java, Domino, and Linux. 400 pages.

STARTER KIT FOR THE IBM ISERIES AND AS/400
By Gary Guthrie and Wayne Madden

Starter Kit for the IBM iSeries and AS/400 provides essential information to help you understand the basic concepts and nuances of iSeries and AS/400 systems. The book is arranged in logical order from basic system setup information through important areas you need to know about to operate, program, and manage your system. Comprehensive sections cover system setup, operations, file basics, basic CL programming, TCP/IP, and Operations Navigator. Whether you're a programmer, a system administrator, or an operator, this book will help you develop a basic working knowledge of many key concepts and functions and apply what you've learned to make your iSeries or AS/400 environment more secure, productive, and manageable. An accompanying CD contains all the utilities and sample code presented in the book. 578 pages.

IMPLEMENTING AS/400 SECURITY, FOURTH EDITION
By Carol Woodbury and Wayne Madden

For years, AS/400 professionals have depended on earlier editions of Implementing AS/400 Security to learn and implement essential AS/400 security concepts. This latest edition not only brings together in one place the fundamental AS/400 security tools and experience-based recommendations you need but also includes specifics on the security enhancements available in OS/400 V4R5. In addition, you'll find expanded coverage of network, communications, and Internet security — including thwarting hacker activities — as well as updated chapters covering security system values, user profiles, object authorization, database security, output-queue and spooled-file security, auditing, contingency planning, and more. 454 pages.

ILE BY EXAMPLE
A Hands-on Guide to the AS/400's Integrated Language Environment
By Mike Cravitz

Learn the fundamentals of the AS/400's Integrated Language Environment (ILE) by following working examples that illustrate the ins and outs of this powerful programming model. Major topics include ILE program structure, bind by copy, ILE RPG subprocedures, service programs, activation groups, ILE condition handling and cancel handling, and more. A CD contains all sample programs discussed in the book, as well as a sample ILE condition handler to address record locks and ILE RPG software to synchronize system clocks using the Internet SNTP protocol. 165 pages.

SQL/400 DEVELOPER'S GUIDE

By Paul Conte and Mike Cravitz

SQL/400 Developer's Guide provides start-to-finish coverage of SQL/400, IBM's strategic language for the AS/400's integrated database. This textbook covers database and SQL fundamentals, SQL/400 Data Definition Language (DDL) and Data Manipulation Language (DML), and database modeling and design. Throughout the book, coding suggestions reinforce the topics covered and provide practical advice on how to produce robust, well-functioning code. Hands-on exercises reinforce comprehension of the concepts covered. 508 pages.

MASTERING THE AS/400, THIRD EDITION
A Practical, Hands-On Guide

By Jerry Fottral

The latest edition of this best-selling introduction to AS/400 concepts and facilities takes a utilitarian approach that stresses student participation. The book emphasizes mastery of system/user interface, member-object-library relationship, use of CL commands, basic database concepts, and program development utilities. The text prepares students to move directly into programming languages, database management, and system operations courses. Each lesson includes a lab that focuses on the essential topics presented in the lesson. 553 pages.

DOMINO R5 AND THE AS/400

By Justine Middleton, Wilfried Blankertz, Rosana Choruzy, Linda Defreyne, Dwight Egerton,
*   Joanne Mindzora, Stephen Ryan, Juan van der Breggen, Felix Zalcmann, and Michelle Zolkos*

Domino R5 and the AS/400 provides comprehensive installation and setup instructions for those installing Domino R5 "from scratch," upgrading from a previous version, or migrating from a platform other than the AS/400. In addition, you get detailed explanations of SMTP in Domino for AS/400, dial-up connectivity, directory synchronization, Advanced Services for Domino for AS/400, and Domino administration strategies, including backup strategies. 512 pages.

PROGRAMMING IN RPG IV, SECOND EDITION

By Bryan Meyers and Judy Yaeger

This textbook provides a strong foundation in the essentials of business programming, featuring the newest version of the RPG language: RPG IV. Focusing on real-world problems and down-to-earth solutions using the latest techniques and features of RPG, this book provides everything you need to know to write a well-designed RPG IV program. The second edition includes new chapters on defining data with D-specs and modular programming concepts, as well as an RPG IV summary appendix and an RPG IV style guide. An instructor's kit is available. 408 pages.

E-BUSINESS
Thriving in the Electronic Marketplace

By Nahid Jilovec

E-Business: Thriving in the Electronic Marketplace identifies key issues organizations face when they implement e-business projects and answers fundamental questions about entering and navigating the changing world of e-business. A concise guide to moving your business into the exciting world of collaborative e-business, the book introduces the four e-business models that drive today's economy and gives a clear summary of e-business technologies. It focuses on practical business-to-business applications. 172 pages.

INTRODUCTION TO AS/400 SYSTEM OPERATIONS, SECOND EDITION

By Heidi Rothenbuehler and Patrice Gapen

Here's the second edition of the textbook that covers what you need to know to become a successful AS/400 system operator or administrator. *Introduction to AS/400 System Operations, Second Edition* teaches you the basics of system operations so that you can manage printed reports, perform regularly scheduled procedures, and resolve end-user problems. New material covers the Integrated File System (IFS), AS/400 InfoSeeker, Operations Navigator, and much more. 182 pages.

CREATING CL COMMANDS BY EXAMPLE

By Lynn Nelson

Learn from an expert how to create CL commands that have the same functionality and power as the IBM commands you use every day. You'll see how to create commands with all the function found in IBM's commands, including parameter editing, function keys, F4 prompt for values, expanding lists of values, and conditional prompting. Whether you're in operations or programming, *Creating CL Commands by Example* can help you tap the tremendous power and flexibility of CL commands to automate tasks and enhance applications. 134 pages.

Talk to Us!

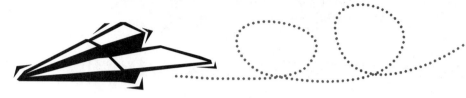

Complete this form to join our network of computer professionals

We'll gladly send you a *free* copy of

- ❏ *iSeries NEWS*
- ❏ *Business Finance*
- ❏ *Windows & .NET Magazine*
- ❏ *SQL Server Magazine*
- ❏ *e-Pro Magazine*

Providing help — not hype.

29th Street PRESS

Publisher of practical,
hands-on technical books
for iSeries
and computer
professionals.

Name _____

Title _____ Phone _____

Company _____

Address _____

City/State/Zip _____

Where did you purchase this book?

❏ Trade show ❏ Computer store ❏ Internet ❏ Card deck

❏ Bookstore ❏ Magazine ❏ Direct mail catalog or brochure

What new applications do you expect to use during the next year?

_____

_____

How many times this month will you visit one of our Web sites (29th Street Press®, iSeries Network, *Business Finance, Windows & .NET Magazine, SQL Server Magazine*, or *e-Pro Magazine*)? _____

Please share your reaction to *iSeries and AS/400 VisualAge for Java.*_____

_____

_____

_____

_____

❏ YES! You have my permission to quote my comments in your publications (initials)

_____

[BX001X1A]

Copy this page and mail to
29th Street Press • 221 East 29th Street • Loveland, CO 80538
OR **Fax to (970) 667-4007**
OR **Visit our Web site at www.iseriesnetworkstore.com**